BEHIND THE LAWRENCE LEGEND

Praise for Behind the Lawrence Legend

'This excellent account of those who underpinned the fighters in the Arab Revolt reminds us of the hardships and challenges of war in early twentieth-century Arabia. By looking behind the lines, Walker shows us the real scale of Lawrence's achievement and the achievements of those who supported him.'

Sir Mark Allen, ex-Foreign Service

'After another round of books on T. E. Lawrence 'of Arabia', published on the war's centennial, it seems scarcely credible that anything new can be said on the subject. But Philip Walker has discovered an astonishing wealth of new material in private collections. The *Forgotten Few* peers beneath the Lawrence legend to reveal the seamy underbelly of the Arab Revolt.'

Sean McMeekin, Professor of History, Bard College

BEHIND THE LAWRENCE LEGEND

THE FORGOTTEN FEW WHO SHAPED THE ARAB REVOLT

PHILIP WALKER

OXFORD

UNIVERSITY PRESS

OXFORD
UNIVERSITY PRESS

Great Clarendon Street, Oxford, OX2 6DP,
United Kingdom

Oxford University Press is a department of the University of Oxford.
It furthers the University's objective of excellence in research, scholarship,
and education by publishing worldwide. Oxford is a registered trade mark of
Oxford University Press in the UK and in certain other countries

First edition published in 2018

Impression: 1

Published in the United States of America by Oxford University Press
198 Madison Avenue, New York, NY 10016, United States of America

British Library Cataloguing in Publication Data
Data available

Library of Congress Control Number: 2017933788

ISBN 978–0–19–880227–3

Printed and bound by
CPI Group (UK) Ltd, Croydon, CR0 4YY

Acknowledgements

A large number of people over many years have helped me in the research and writing of this book, and I am very grateful to all of them. They include:

Michael Adam; Rosemary Adam; Scott Addington; Professor Ali Allawi; Patricia Aske, Pembroke College Library, Cambridge University; John Barnard; James Barr; Sarah Baxter, Society of Authors; Julian Beaumont OAM for information on Colonel John Bassett; John Bellucci; Shirley Bose; Frank Bowles, Cambridge University Library; Colin Boyes; Roger Bragger; Axel Bray; Howard Bray; Professor Carol Brayne; Mark Brayne; Sophie Bridges, Churchill Archives Centre, Churchill College, Cambridge; Jim Brown; Norman Brown; Gary Bryan; Peter Card; Michael V. Carey; Julie Carrington, Royal Geographical Society Library, for information on George Wyman Bury; Greville Cavendish; Piers Cavendish; Rebecca Child; Anthony Cochrane; Susanne Cochrane; James Cochrane; Lindon Cornwallis; George Cruddas;

Neil Dearberg; Brian Dobson; Barbara Duce; Mary Duffy; John Edmonds CMG, CVO; Sam Eedle; Charles Eilers; David Elliott; Wynne Evans; Rebecca Fellows; Sarah Felton; Dr Simon Fielding; Peter Finch; Ray Foster; Dennis Garrood; Gregory Gilbert; Tony Gilbert; Valerie Gilman; Jenny Glazebrook; Katherine Godfrey, Liddell Hart Centre for Military Archives, King's College, London; Adam Gotch; Francis Gotto, Sudan Archive, Durham University Library; Cynara de Goutiere; Tony de Goutiere; Howard Hamilton QC; Michael Hammerson; Fred Hancock; Jennifer Haynes; Richard Heywood; Dale Hjort; Jane Hogan, formerly of the Sudan Archive, Durham University Library; Raymond Holland; Professor Brian Holden Reid; Pauline Homeshaw; Keith Hopwood; Diane Horsfield; Michael Hughes, Bodleian Library, for information on the Marconi Archive;

Amanda Ingram, Pembroke College, Cambridge University; Kenneth Jacob; Professor Salah Jarar; Clifford Jones, Christ's Hospital School, for information on Lieutenant Leslie Bright; Christopher Kennington; Harriet

King; Hugh Kirkbride; Yvett Klein, Bonham's, Sydney, Australia, for information on Colonel John Bassett; Dennis Lalor; Vincent Landon; Zoe Lawson; Christophe Leclerc; Alice Lock; Andrew Lownie for information on Colonel John Bassett; Katharine Lumsden; Nicholas Lumsden; Nigel Lutt; Ian Mackenzie; Keith Mackenzie; Bridget McCrum; Catherine McIntyre; Henrietta McCausland; Christopher McKibbin; Stuart McKibbin; Alistair Massie, National Army Museum; Mohamed Mekabbaty; John Millensted; Polly Mohs; Claire Morgan-Jones; Michael Morrogh; Dr David Murphy; Peter Murphy; Dr Fiona Nash, Royal Geographical Society; Valerie Neill; John O'Brien, British Library; Simon Offord, Imperial War Museum; Dr Carol Palmer; Dr Suzanne Paul, Cambridge University Library; Helen Pearson; Mark Pearson; Ian Petrie; Richard Piggott; Rosamunde Pilcher; Robin Pilcher; Patricia Popkin; Gregory Pos; Michael Powell; Stephen Powell; John Price; Jean Proffitt;

Carole Qureshi; Jonathan Rashleigh; Ian Reid; Anthony Richards, Imperial War Museum; Richard Ridler; David E. Roberts; Martin Robertson; Eugene Rogan; David Sarsfield, Microform Academic Publishers; Sir Patrick Macdonnell Salt; Reg Saville; Alister Scott; Mark Scott; Desmond Seward; Fred Sharf; Jenny Shore; Mandy Stephens; Andrew Shepherdson; Sir Robert Sherston-Baker Bart; Lianne Smith, King's College London Archives; Paul Smith; Piers Smith-Creswell; Colonel Carron Snagge; Caroline Stone; John Storrs; Marietta Crichton Stuart; Ninian Crichton Stuart; Katharine Thomson, Churchill Archives Centre, Churchill College, Cambridge; Charles Tilbury; Michael Tilling; Debbie Usher, Middle East Centre Archive, St Antony's College, Oxford; Johnny Van Haeften; Simon Vickers; Professor David Walker; Laura Walker, British Library; Christine Walker-Kelley; Miriam Walton; Alixe Wallis; Alan Weeks; Hugo White; Vicki White; George Willey; Simon Wilson, Hull University Archives, Hull History Centre; Jeremy Wilson; John Winterburn; Patrick Wyman; Mohamed Zuber.

My particular thanks go to my outstanding agent Andrew Lownie, for his expertise, drive, and encouragement. He is truly the bee's knees, and it has been a pleasure to work with him and to learn from him. Anthea Gray was unfailingly helpful and hospitable in the face of all my requests and her often poor health. It is a matter of deep regret to me that she died while this book was in the production stage: she wanted so much to hold the book in her hands and to read of the wartime activities of her father, Lieutenant Lionel Gray. Joe Berton has been a constant source of information, advice, encouragement, and friendship. He, Sir Mark Allen, and James Stejskal read early drafts, and gave many useful comments for which I am very grateful.

My thanks are also due to Jacob Rosen and Professor Yigal Sheffy, who read parts of the typescript and also made helpful suggestions. Any mistakes are solely my responsibility.

For permission to quote from copyright published and unpublished records, and for advice on records not needing copyright clearance, I would like to thank: Professor Carol Brayne, for the Brayne Papers on loan at the British Library; British Online Archives provided by Microform Academic Publishers for the papers of Sir Mark Sykes; the National Archives; the Australian War Memorial; The Seven Pillars of Wisdom Trust for T. E. Lawrence; the British Library for India Office Records; the Syndics of Cambridge University Library for the Hardinge Papers and the Letters of Hugh Drummond Pearson; the Middle East Centre Archive, St Antony's College, Oxford for the collections of J. W. A. Young and Thomas Edward Lawrence; the Master and Fellows of Pembroke College, Cambridge for the Sir Ronald Storrs papers; the Churchill Archives Centre, Churchill College, Cambridge for the George Lloyd Papers; the provost and scholars of King's College, Cambridge and the Society of Authors as their representative, for the E. M. Forster quotation; the trustees of the Liddell Hart Centre for Military Archives for the Joyce Papers; Hull University Archives, Hull History Centre for the papers of Sir Mark Sykes; the Council of the National Army Museum for the papers of Captain Leslie Lionel Bright; the Imperial War Museum for the Private Papers of Major-General Sir Arthur Lynden-Bell; the Society of Authors, on behalf of the Bernard Shaw Estate.

Every effort has been made to contact copyright holders of material in the book, but the publishers will be pleased to make amends if anything has been inadvertently overlooked.

I am especially grateful to the staff at Oxford University Press, whose experience and diligence have helped to improve the shape and narrative flow of the book: Luciana O'Flaherty (publisher), Matthew Cotton (original Commissioning Editor), Kizzy Taylor-Richelieu (Assistant Commissioning Editor), and Terka Acton (editor). I am grateful too to Jen Moore who copy edited the book with such skill and insight, to Sally Evans-Darby, and to Vaishnavi Ananthasubramanyam who steered the book through the production phase.

I must also thank my wife, Janet, for her forbearance, advice, and support, while for more than seven years I told stories about Cyril, Lionel, Norman, and the others as if they were long-lost family members; and John Ette for his helpful comments.

Preface

The grave of Captain Thomas Goodchild at the British Protestant Cemetery at Alexandria, Egypt is derelict, the headstone missing. Like most people he has fallen through the cracks of the historical record. Not one of the more than one hundred books on T. E. Lawrence and the Arab Revolt of 1916–18 mentions the small part Goodchild played in those dramatic events during the First World War. This is hardly surprising: Goodchild was an affable veterinary officer who had no combat experience with Lawrence or his colleagues. While Lawrence used his powers of persuasion, his flair for guerrilla warfare, and his political nous to try to help some Arabs win independence from the Turks, Goodchild was worrying about how to prevent the spread of camel mange. Yet there was much more to Goodchild than met the eye.

We know about Goodchild's work because of a chance discovery at a garage sale. The fairly brief factual entries in his battered 1916 diary conceal a bizarre story. When I carried out detailed archival research, it became clear that Goodchild led a sensitive and totally forgotten mission to Jeddah in Arabia to buy baggage camels from the family of the region's leading camel breeder, who just happened to be the revolt's leader, Sherif Hussein of Mecca.

The overarching importance of Goodchild's mission was that it was part of a key British intelligence objective to deny baggage camels to the Turks and to improve the sometimes fragile relationship between the British and Hussein. Unlikely as it may seem, camels were a key strategic asset because they were so important for the mobile desert operations that the British were planning in Turkish-held Palestine.

The question then arose: what if there were other forgotten chapters of the Arab Revolt that, pieced together, might add something substantial to the narrative of this iconic campaign; perhaps even lead to a different perspective seen through a new lens? A counter-argument took shape almost immediately: given the bookshelves are groaning with an abundance of books on the subject, was there really anything new and important left to say about Lawrence and the Arab Revolt? Nevertheless, more in hope than expectation, I decided to hunt for other 'unknown unknowns' of the Arab Revolt. I spent seven years tracking down the descendants of twenty forgotten British officers, to ask whether diaries or memoirs, letters or photographs had been passed down to them. The hunt led to Panama, Jamaica, the USA, Canada, Australia, Denmark, Ireland, and all over the United Kingdom.

Perhaps surprisingly, thirteen families still had a wealth of Arab Revolt material that had stayed hidden for a century, and they were happy to let me examine it. One huge private collection in a suburban house was crammed into two large metal chests. There were hundreds of photographs taken in Arabia by a cipher officer in intelligence, Lieutenant Lionel Gray, together with hundreds of letters sent by him to his fiancée and family, as well as a captured Turkish pistol given to him by T. E. Lawrence and private confidences from Lawrence himself. There were also Arab robes and a headdress, secret cable message notebooks, and many more intelligence documents. I interviewed Gray's daughter and the descendants of many other men: their insights breathed personality and character into the mere names I had begun with. At Gray's daughter's ninetieth birthday lunch at a London hotel, I felt the eerie illusion of being within touching distance of the Arab Revolt.

★   ★   ★

The new evidence was intriguing but a key question had to be addressed. Was the evidence merely footnote material or was it likely to enlarge our understanding of the Arab Revolt and the British role in it? A pattern to the research soon emerged, which offered hope of an answer. A number of the forgotten or little-known men I had uncovered were based, like Gray, at the port of Jeddah. This town was strategically important for the delivery of supplies, weapons, and gold from the British to their ally, Sherif Hussein. Thousands of Muslims arrived by sea, many British Indians, who passed through on their way to Mecca for the annual Hajj or pilgrimage. The officers based at Jeddah worked for Colonel Cyril Edward Wilson, who was given the bland title of 'pilgrimage officer' by British intelligence, as a cover for his military and diplomatic duties helping Hussein's revolt.

Wilson was a rather stiff and correct figure, something of a Colonel Blimp—jingoistic, unimaginative, a stereotypically British officer. He was the antithesis of the brilliant and mercurial T. E. Lawrence. Wilson is portrayed as having a secondary role in the revolt and, like so many, came to be overshadowed by Lawrence's dazzling leadership and railway demolition skills—and by the Lawrence legend that turned the shy maverick with a touch of genius into an international icon after the war. Wilson stoically endured chronic dysentery and attacks from his own colleagues at General Headquarters in Cairo, who thought supporting the revolt was a waste of money, supplies, and effort, and that the real battle should be fought against the Turks in Palestine rather than in the backwater of the Hejaz, Hussein's province.

Yet there were tantalizing pointers to Wilson and his core team at Jeddah having made a key contribution to the Arab Revolt that has been overlooked. Wilson was given high praise by two senior officers who had wide experience of all the major players in the revolt. General Reginald Wingate, who as governor-general of the Sudan sent weapons and supplies across the Red Sea to Sherif Hussein, and then became British High Commissioner for Egypt, wrote to Wilson in 1936:

> I always feel that 'Little Lawrence', much as I valued and appreciated his wonderful qualities and powers of leadership, did not know or estimate at their true value, the marvellous work done by yourself...and other officers without whose knowledge, experience and self-sacrifice, the Revolt could never have succeeded and he could never have acquired the title of 'Lawrence of Arabia'!...he sailed in really to fame largely on the shoulders of men like yourself.[1]

This is rather hard, in one sense, on Lawrence, who did in fact acknowledge Wilson's role to Wilson privately, but the recognition of the pilgrimage officer's vital role could not be clearer.

The second endorsement of Wilson is from Captain William 'Ginger' Boyle, who commanded the Red Sea Patrol of the Royal Navy. The Red Sea Patrol played a crucial role in the Arab Revolt through its firepower, its supply ships, and its political role in boosting Hussein's morale. Boyle was at the heart of all these interventions and, after the revolt, as admiral of the fleet, wrote of Wilson: 'To the ability, tact, and energy of this self-effacing but able officer the ultimate success of the Arab rising was largely due.'[2] That a man as perceptive as Boyle should single out Wilson for such praise is significant. Boyle also referred to Wilson as 'the uncrowned King of Jeddah'.

Wingate's and Boyle's comments seem never to have been investigated in detail—perhaps they were seen as the rather overblown compliments of friends. Lawrence's famous book about his personal role in the campaign, *Seven Pillars of Wisdom*, made no mention of any key role for Wilson. This was not surprising since Lawrence also downplayed the role of other officers who are known to have made important contributions to the revolt. Yet the enigmatic Lawrence, so adept at smoke and mirrors, also lists, in his preface to *Seven Pillars of Wisdom*, the names of forty of his colleagues who, he states, 'could each tell a like tale' to his own.[3] Those names include Wilson and Gray. Lawrence could be perverse and loved toying and teasing: this seems to be false modesty and probably he did not really believe that so many officers could tell a story as well as he could, but that short preface gives a hint of hidden alternative narratives.

★   ★   ★

The search for other narratives was at the heart of my research. It became an investigation of what lay concealed in shadows—the shadows that were inevitably created around the limelight that has fallen on Lawrence for four generations. I began a lengthy trawl through the publicly available archives in London, Durham, Cambridge, Oxford, and Hull, and cross-referenced them to the fresh evidence in the private collections. The two classes of records complemented each other: the significance of each was enhanced through that association. The key findings were, first, that Wilson had a core team of four officers at Jeddah, the true hub of the revolt, who helped him stabilize the revolt on several occasions when it was at imminent risk of collapse—both before and during Lawrence's involvement in Arabia. The imperturbable Colonel John Bassett and the eccentric, half-deaf Major Hugh Pearson, both with a background in intelligence, were his able deputies. The highly strung Captain Norman Bray, a bloodhound on the trail of anti-British jihadists, was another intelligence officer. Lieutenant Lionel Gray was the fourth member of the team. There was also a colourful supporting cast based at or near Jeddah, including a resourceful Persian spy and a forgotten officer who lived with Bedouin tribes collecting important intelligence.

The second major factor was the extent to which the relationship between Wilson and Sherif Hussein underpinned the rickety edifice of the revolt, from before it broke out until its final weeks in September 1918. This relationship was crucial to the survival and, ultimately, to the hollow 'victory' of the revolt. Hussein ran a corrupt regime and was irascible, suspicious, and controlling, prone to fits of despair and suicide threats, yet for over three years Wilson kept the trust and respect—it was something akin to friendship—of the old ruler. Wilson managed this because of his honourable and principled behaviour, which was patently free from double-dealing. Wilson's undervalued influence over Hussein during critical phases of the revolt was at least as important as the well-known influence of Lawrence over Hussein's son, the Emir Feisal. Without the quiet diplomacy and intelligence work of the unlikely hero, Wilson, and his men, the revolt would have collapsed and the world would never have heard of 'Lawrence of Arabia'.

Gray's story is exceptional because it throws light on so many aspects of the revolt. This amiable and long-suffering cipher specialist, who was to be parted from his fiancée, Mabel, for about five years, was a junior officer who at first sight had less influence than his comrades at Jeddah. Yet he knew almost all the key British players in Arabia, where he served for over two and a half years. Furthermore, Gray helped Wilson by gaining the trust of Sherif Hussein himself and was even invited to Hussein's palace to take some stunning photographs of the old leader. He had intriguing discussions with Lawrence and, in his detailed commentary, Gray conjures up the sights, sounds, and smells of the strange world of Jeddah, rife with corruption, where spies jostled with jihadists bent on subverting the revolt and destabilizing British India with its seventy million Muslims. Mining the rich seam of Gray's remarkable images, letters, and other documents offers a unique insight into the twists and turns of the revolt. Gray's lost story holds a mirror to important overarching themes of the campaign, in particular the hidden world of intelligence and the role of the Royal Navy.

The story of Wilson and his men is interwoven with the bigger picture of the military campaign in the desert and with the familiar saga of T. E. Lawrence's role, but with new insights into Lawrence's deceptions and complex motivations, as well as into his achievements and writings. The narrative provides depth of field for the revolt by including the lost stories of other officers who were mostly at the large supply base at Aqaba: the link with Jeddah is provided by Gray who served at Aqaba too. This book offers a fresh interpretation of the Arab Revolt through a new lens and presents Colonel Cyril Wilson as a key figure of history.

Table of Contents

List of Illustrations

A Note on the Text

Transliterating Arabic words was difficult for the British involved in the Arab Revolt, and they spelt individuals' names, the names of tribes, and place names in a variety of ways. In quotations from archives and from T. E. Lawrence's and others' post-war writings, I have kept the actual spelling used—hence, for example, both 'Jeddah' and 'Jidda', 'Aqaba' and 'Akaba'. Elsewhere, to prevent unwieldiness for the general reader, I have employed Anglicized place names in the form most often used in contemporary British diplomatic and military sources. Examples are Mecca instead of Makka and Medina instead of Madina.

The terms 'Ottoman Empire' and 'Turkey' were used interchangeably by the Allied powers and often too, interestingly enough, by the nations they were fighting. I have followed this practice. Whenever I refer to a particular religious or ethnic group, to distinguish it from the Turkish majority, I mention, for example, 'Ottoman Arabs', 'Ottoman Armenians', or 'Arab prisoners of war from the Ottoman Army'.

List of Maps

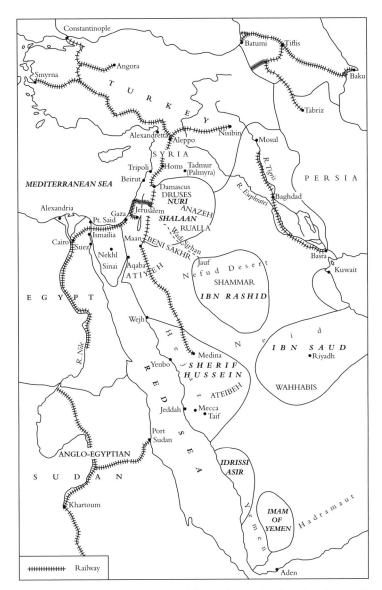

Map 1. The Middle East at the time of the Arab Revolt, showing the territories of Arab leaders and some of the main tribes.

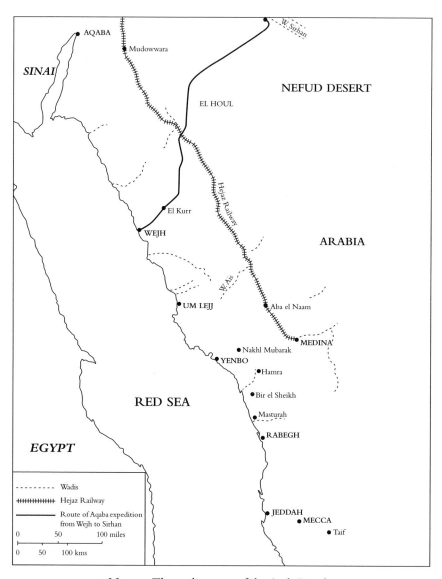

Map 2. The early stages of the Arab Revolt.

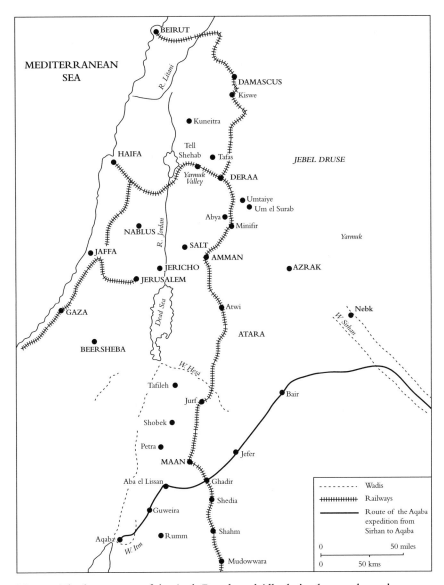

Map 3. The later stages of the Arab Revolt and Allenby's advance through Palestine.

I

'Anything could happen in such a place'

Suffering from chronic dysentery was bad enough. To be cooped up as well for over two weeks in the cramped quarters of a stationary Royal Navy warship, in the summer heat of the Red Sea, was barely endurable. But 43-year-old Colonel Cyril Wilson was made of stern stuff. Short and dapper, honest to the point of being abrupt, he had an unshakeable sense of duty. He knew that he was about to begin the most difficult and most dangerous mission of his life. He and two colleagues had had to stay on HMS *Fox*, anchored off Jeddah in Arabia, because conditions in the town had been too unstable for infidel Christians to go ashore. The unflappable William Cochrane was a shipping agent. John Young, aloof and hard to please, had been seconded from Egyptian Government service. The men had spent much of their time in shirt sleeves in the punishing damp heat, sending and deciphering secret coded telegrams.

It was 15 August 1916. The long agony of the Battle of the Somme on the Western Front was already six weeks old. Far from that mechanized slaughter, in a compelling sideshow of the First World War, the time had finally come for Wilson and his men to leave the safety of the ship and move to an alien land consumed by rebellion and intrigue. One of the strangest and most far-reaching campaigns of the war was about to begin.

Wilson should have been nowhere near Jeddah. Doctors had told him to retire three years earlier, because of his dysentery, but he had shrugged off all advice, leaving his wife, Beryl, behind at Erkowit, the hill station in British-administered Sudan that was the Wilsons' retreat from the fierce heat of summer. Perhaps his stubbornness had something to do with wanting to live up to the high standards set by his father, the distinguished soldier and diplomat, Major-General Sir Charles Wilson.

Wilson's father had been part of the heroic but vain effort to try to rescue General Charles Gordon at Khartoum in 1885. He had taken command of an advance rescue force in a desperate attempt by desert march and Nile steamer to reach Khartoum before the Sudanese rebels led by the Mahdi's forces (the relief expedition arrived two days too late). Gordon's death at the hands of the Mahdi made him one of the great imperial icons of Victorian Britain. The twelve-year-old Cyril would have been thrilled that the boys' books depicting the heroic 'Gordon of Khartoum' reflected his own father's adventures. Perhaps his imagination was stirred too by eye-witness tales from his father. Like all boys of his time and class, he would have been imbued with a belief in unquestioning duty to empire.[1]

Wilson was educated at Clifton College in Bristol (a well-known breeding ground for servants of empire) and Sandhurst. He was commissioned into the East Lancashire Regiment in 1893 and followed in his father's footsteps to the Sudan. Here he fought the Dervishes, followers of the Mahdi's successor, who were massacred at Omdurman near Khartoum in 1898.

Wilson subsequently served in the Boer War, and was then seconded to the Egyptian Army and Sudan Government, becoming governor and military commander of three Sudanese provinces. The Governor-General, General Reginald Wingate at Khartoum, saw Wilson as a reliable member of his inner circle.[2] Wilson's very conventional outlook, his granite sense of moral duty, brought an instinctive response: 'Play up! play up! and play the game!' Sir Henry Newbolt's poem described a man who was honourable, stoical, brave, loyal, courteous, and also plain-speaking, unintellectual, and not given to wit, irony, or an aesthetic sense. He could have been writing about Wilson.[3]

★   ★   ★

Wilson, Cochrane, and Young were assaulted by the brutal force of the Arabian sun as they stepped from HMS *Fox* on to a launch. Only small boats like this could navigate the narrow channels between the three dangerous sunken coral reefs that guarded the approach to Jeddah from the outer harbour. The walled town lay on a shallow lagoon. The white and grey houses, shimmering in the heat, were higher towards the centre and looked like a squat pyramid emerging from mist. Wilson had made the same journey on a reconnaissance trip in late June and was struck again by how the shallow water near the quays shone an eerily bright metallic green. He was greeted at the customs wharf by the familiar diminutive figure of a very experienced British spy wearing his trademark white linen suit. Forty-one-year-old Hussein Ruhi was a Persian of the Baha'i faith. He was resourceful and somewhat louche (Wilson called him 'weird').[4] Ruhi had first-hand knowledge of the Hejaz, the western coastal part of Arabia between the Red Sea and a viciously serrated mountain range. For a British officer it was the back of beyond and it was now to be Wilson's home.

The men passed the mosque near the newly built Customs House, its minaret reflecting the sun fiercely from the local white coral stone. They went through the arched entrance to the souk or market place, almost invisible in the intensely dark shadows. The air was foetid with decay and fed by a remorseless sun. Waves of an overpowering miasma enveloped the men, a malign stench of rotting meat and fish, fruit, and dung. The elusive aroma of tamarisk wood registered all too briefly. The men followed an alley through the food market and absorbed the languor and long-standing decay that seemed to permeate the town. Wilson felt again the sense of foreboding that was as palpable as London fog.

The men soon reached the British Consulate, a ramshackle but picturesque structure of four stories in the ubiquitous coral stone. Wilson showed Young and Cochrane their rooms and the spacious mess room on the first floor. Young was fastidious and self-righteous and liked order, and so found the bats zooming from one floor to another in the dusty building annoying and above all disorderly. The imperturbable Cochrane, however, could take them in his stride. The two men were to carry out intelligence and consular work. Cochrane, who had worked in Jeddah before the war, saw from the mess room balcony the familiar long, low former barracks building of the Turkish Army, beyond the Medina gate and the crumbling town wall. But there was a ripple of change too: distorted in the heat haze, Egyptian Army artillerymen moved like ghosts and large chunks of the barracks' coral stone lay pulverized in the sand.[5]

The barracks had been one of the flashpoints of an uprising against an imperial power. That power was the Ottoman Empire, which controlled large swathes of the Middle East comprising Sinai, Greater Syria (Syria, the Lebanon, and Palestine), the Yemen, and parts of what later became Jordan and Iraq as well as the Hejaz. The Turks of the sprawling Ottoman Empire regarded the Hejaz, which they had run for four centuries, as a backward and corrupt part of their sprawling territories, which had little economic significance. They tended to leave Hussein to his own devices. But they were very much aware of two things. First, Sherif Hussein, as leader of the

Hashemite dynasty, was a direct descendant of the Prophet Mohammed and was 'Protector of the Two Holy Cities', Mecca and Medina, the epicentre of the Muslim world. After the Ottoman sultan, who was also caliph or spiritual head of all Sunni Muslims, Hussein was the second highest religious authority. Much of the prestige of the Ottoman Empire was bound up with control of Mecca and Medina and with the smooth running of the annual Hajj pilgrimage to Mecca. Second, Hussein had been intriguing for ten years to win independence for the Hejaz, and he also wanted freedom for the Arabs of Greater Syria and beyond. Now Hussein had thrown in his hand: the revolt had begun unofficially on 5 June 1916 and five days later the 63-year-old leader had dramatically signalled to his supporters, according to one story, that the revolt was official by firing an old rifle from a high tower in his palace at Mecca. The city was fully in Hussein's hands by 9 July.

Hussein's sons had led sporadic attacks by Bedouin tribesmen on a number of Turkish fortifications. The complexity of tribal alliances and rivalries meant that by no means all the Bedouin supported Hussein. Some tribes sat on the fence or took Turkish gold to keep out of the revolt. Hussein dispensed British gold sovereigns, sent over from Suez or Port Sudan, to buy the loyalty of other tribes. Hussein's political influence varied: in Medina it had always been tenuous. The Ottoman Army, anticipating trouble in the Hejaz, had moved its Twelfth Corps of at least ten thousand men to Medina in late May. Hussein's Bedouin allies were poorly armed and the holy city easily withstood ineffectual attacks by poorly armed tribesmen under Feisal, Hussein's third son. The Ottoman troops were supplied by the strategically important Hejaz Railway, which ran from Damascus to Medina: the trains also carried pilgrims to the holy city on the annual Hajj. After the setback at Medina, Feisal and his brother, Ali, had then limited themselves to attacking the railway line to the north: the track had to be torn up by hand, because at the time they had no explosives, and it was easy for the Turks to repair it.

★ ★ ★

Wilson was greatly relieved that the rebels had fared better at Jeddah. The barracks and the defensive trenches near them had been bombarded intermittently for five days by ships of Captain 'Ginger' Boyle's Red Sea Patrol. Bombing raids by seaplanes from the carrier *Ben-my-Chree* had brought Ottoman resistance to an end on 17 June. Hussein Ruhi was an eyewitness to this dramatic intervention. He had seen how the Royal Navy had been a crucial factor in stiffening the resolve of Sherif Mohsen and his Bedouin warriors to seize Jeddah.[6] The small ports of Rabegh and Yenbo soon fell to British sea power.

Britain had by then been at war with the Ottoman Empire for some nineteen months. Turkey's decision in November 1914 to side with Germany and declare war on the Allies (principally Britain, France, and Russia) was unexpected by many. Britain had hoped that Turkey might stay neutral or even join the Allies, but Germany had been patiently courting Turkey, training its army and building the Berlin to Baghdad Railway to cement trading, diplomatic, and military links. In 1915 Winston Churchill, as First Lord of the Admiralty, had tried to knock Turkey out of the war by seizing Constantinople through a daring naval and military attack at Gallipoli. The attempt was a disastrous failure through bad planning and leadership, coupled with an underestimation of tenacious Turkish troops who were well dug in and determined to defend their motherland at all costs.

Another way to beat the Turks would have to be found. In the meantime, the British had to respond to the declaration of jihad or holy war that had been made against the Allies, on 14 November 1914, by the Ottoman sultan and caliph. The idea of holy war was encouraged by German intelligence, and the Ottomans expected all Arabs and Turks throughout the empire to answer the call. The awkward matter of some non-Muslims—the Germans and Austrians—being allies of the Ottomans and so beyond the reach of holy war was swept under the Turkish carpet. The British were anxious about the threat from jihad: there were about seventy million Muslims in British India, a fifth of its entire population, and anti-British plotters had been active amongst them for many years. The British nightmare was that this small minority could be swelled by a huge number of newly fired-up Muslim jihadists.

The British therefore tried to neutralize the Turkish call for holy war.[7] In the course of an eight-month exchange of letters, known as the Hussein-McMahon Correspondence (named after the British High Commissioner in Egypt), the British had made vague promises of support for a fairly large Arab empire for Hussein after the war, if he would rebel against the Turks. The British never expected to have to honour these ill-defined undertakings—they were well aware that the French would never give up what they saw as their historic right to exercise control in Syria and Lebanon.[8] The British hope was that, given their support for the revered Sherif Hussein, their own Muslim citizens in India would find it difficult to rise up against them.

Wilson had played no part in this high-level diplomacy, but he had a covert role behind the scenes. While governor of the Red Sea Province at Port Sudan, he had been secretly involved in sending weapons, ammunition, food supplies, and gold across the Red Sea to Hussein in the months leading up to the revolt. Wilson was working closely with the tireless Captain Boyle and his Red Sea Patrol ships. The two men also kept in touch with Sherif Hussein through secret messengers who were landed at remote spots on the Hejaz coast and later picked up for return to the Sudan. One of these agents, Sheikh Oreifan of the Harb tribe (given the unimaginative code-name 'O'), met Sherif Hussein in Mecca. Back in Port Sudan, Wilson had Ruhi beside him when necessary to translate Hussein's messages. Ruhi also crossed the Red Sea at times and disappeared into the souks of Jeddah to ferret out intelligence and boost the morale of the agents he had in place there. He was skilled at reassuring and flattering them as they went about their dangerous work.

Ruhi was on HMS *Hardinge* off Jeddah before and during the early days of the revolt. His diary for the crucial period 8 May to 14 June 1916 offers a unique insight, by a well-informed eyewitness, into British strategy and operations. The entries include requests by Hussein and his family for British gold, weapons, food, and other supplies; copies of correspondence between Captain 'Ginger' Boyle and the Hashemites; and intelligence from agents on Turkish and German positions and movements. Ruhi gives meticulous accounts of the naval bombardment, describing the echoes of the shelling as like a thunderstorm (9 June, the first day of the attack). One of Ruhi's agents reported that the Turkish trenches near the barracks ran down to the north wall of the town, on which the Turks had placed artillery and fifteen soldiers: Ruhi concluded that the Turks were prepared to defend the town for a long time.[9] This entry helps explain why more accurate bombing from British sea planes was needed a few days later to finish the job.

Ruhi vividly describes how he accompanied Commander Linberry of HMS *Hardinge* and two of his officers on an intelligence mission to the town—they climbed to the flat roof of a house and drew up a sketch plan of the Turkish fortifications.[10] In a letter to Storrs detailing the British offensive, Ruhi added a note which perhaps suggests an agent he had recruited among the Turks: 'Jeddah is going to surrender today at 5 p.m. 16/6/1916.'[11]

★   ★   ★

For now, as Wilson sat in his dusty Consulate office, watching lizards trek languidly across the ceiling, he might have reflected wryly that he had talked

himself into his daunting job. He had first visited Jeddah with Cochrane on
HMS *Anne* on 28 June, just eleven days after the fall of the town to the
rebels.[12] His task had been to set up two artillery batteries of the Egyptian
Army, which was under the control of the British, in the old Turkish barracks. It was hoped that Egyptian soldiers, as Muslims, would be more
acceptable to the fiercely independent-minded Bedouin than Western
soldiers. After his mission Wilson had reported to General Wingate in
Khartoum, who was initially in charge of equipping and funding Hussein,
that if the revolt failed then the Sherif might well blame the British for not
giving him enough supplies when he needed them. This would have dealt
a crippling blow to British prestige. So Wilson argued for a permanent
British officer based at Jeddah, to ensure better diplomatic and military
liaison with Hussein. Wingate trusted Wilson and told him he was the man
for the job.

After its rapid initial successes, the revolt now seemed to be moving at
the pace of the lizards on Wilson's ceiling. The doughty officer's job was to
liaise with Hussein on diplomatic and military matters, supply him with
what he needed, discreetly persuade him to do what was in British interests,
and maximize the impact of the revolt on the Turks. This was a tricky business: Hussein was devout, dignified, and respected by many Bedouin tribes,
but he was also blinded by ambition and ran a cruel government that had
alienated both the merchants in the towns and several tribal leaders. He was
controlling, expected to be consulted on every detail, and was suspicious of
even his own four sons. To Wilson's frustration, Hussein was just as likely to
telephone him on a trivial matter as on an important one.[13]

A bluff and undiplomatic character, Wilson was an odd choice for a diplomat in a hot spot. His official job title was the harmless-sounding pilgrimage
officer, but this was a fiction to allay Arab sensitivity to British soldiers based
near the holy places of Mecca and Medina. Wilson was supposed to be
solely in charge of the smooth passage of British Muslim pilgrims, who
came mainly from India, after they disembarked at Jeddah and went on the
yearly Hajj to Mecca. His sense of humour sometimes broke through his
Colonel Blimp stiffness: he brought a flavour of the Home Counties to the
consulate by playfully calling it 'Pilgrims' Rest'.[14]

But Wilson knew that a disrupted pilgrimage could deal a fatal blow to
the revolt. It would hand a propaganda coup to the Turks and to the jihadists, who would shout from the rooftops that the British could never be
trusted with the pilgrimage and were not true friends of Muslims. The next

pilgrimage was due in six weeks or so, and the British were determined that it should be well run and reflect their prestige and that of Hussein. Wilson would soon discover that there were forces at work that aimed to undermine both. And there was a more immediate problem. The Turks wanted to break out of Medina and recapture Mecca and Jeddah before the pilgrimage, at a stroke crushing the revolt and presenting 'business as usual'. Disaster lurked around the corner and the stakes could not have been higher.

★   ★   ★

The Arab Bureau was well aware of these dangerous undercurrents. Set up in early 1916, it was a think-tank of bright and often eccentric characters, both military and civilian. Its role was to coordinate intelligence and influence policy on the whole Muslim world. Its members included an adventurous half-blind Member of Parliament (a master of disguise who was the model for Sandy Arbuthnot in John Buchan's *Greenmantle*) and a pioneer psychical researcher who had exposed fraudulent mediums.[15] The Arab Bureau was detested by the British Indian Government, which regarded the Persian Gulf and the Arabian peninsula as its own backyard. The bureau was also greatly disliked by General Headquarters (GHQ) of the Egyptian Expeditionary Force (EEF), which thought that supporting an Arab rebellion in a place few had heard of was a dangerous and expensive distraction from the real business of fighting the Turks in Sinai and Palestine. GHQ fulminated about 'an infernal thing called the Arab Bureau. It is run by civilians and is totally unbusinesslike [sic] and un-military'.[16]

From July onwards the Arab Bureau organized all the weapons and supplies that went to the Hejaz. General Gilbert Clayton, its chief, also funded the Jeddah mission from his 'special account': 'The item of £100 per month for intelligence agents and sundries is not likely to be fully spent, but Colonel Wilson is most anxious to form an efficient Intelligence system and has therefore purposely put the figure somewhat high'.[17] The problem was that Wilson's unswerving moral compass made him hate the idea of spying and this tension within him was to play its part later in a near breakdown.

★   ★   ★

Someone who had no qualms at all about spying was the irrepressible Ruhi, who briefed Wilson with his usual mix of hard intelligence and scurrilous gossip. Wilson wrote of his unconventional assistant: 'Ruhi is of course a treasure and works like a brick.'[18] He was later described as 'Ruhi the degenerate who brought us all those stories of unnatural vice. Ruhi had tastes that way'.[19]

John Young, by contrast, came from a prosperous family of Anglo-Irish merchants in Ballymena. Rangy and thin and rather self-satisfied, he joined the Egyptian Survey Department in 1907 and travelled widely throughout the Ottoman Empire, including Sinai (so important as a buffer zone to the British-run Suez Canal in the event of war). He did survey work in Turkey and would have been a valuable source for British intelligence. His spying continued after the outbreak of war: he was sent to the remote Egyptian port of Sollum, near Libya, to watch for arms smuggling to the Senussi warriors, who were allies of the Turks. At Jeddah, Young was on what he called semi-military and diplomatic duty.

Wilson's other member of staff, William Cochrane, had already experienced the unsettling character of life in Jeddah. 'Cocky', as he was known, shared Young's Anglo-Irish ancestry and like him was tall and slim, but the personality of the two men was very different. Outgoing and genial, Cochrane was a shrewd judge of character and exuded calm, good sense. Before the war he had been seconded from the shipping agents Gellatly Hankey in Port Sudan to their Arabian office, a short stroll from the Consulate. He had helped organize the pilgrimage to Mecca from Port Sudan and would have assisted at Jeddah too. So he was the ideal man to help Wilson with the pilgrimage under war conditions, where one false move could have meant disaster for the British and for the prospects of the revolt.

Jeddah was a town of creepy strangeness where Greeks let down alcohol from high windows for surreptitious sale in the alleys below, and where both alcohol and hashish were openly sold outside the walls.[20] Ruhi seemed to thrive on the town's atmosphere of insidious menace, but Wilson, Young, and Cochrane all felt oppressed by it. Young caught the spirit of the place well. He wrote:

> There was an unhealthy atmosphere about the people of Jeddah that was difficult to describe. Walking through its streets one felt that anything could happen in such a place; the promotion of a thief to Head of Police: a Takruri boy kidnapped for a slave: a merchant called to Mecca and never seen again. No one was free from the depredations of Sherif Muhsen's Bisha police and no-one was safe in Jeddah or Mecca from the caprice of King Hussein [as he became] or his intimate advisers. Ancient Rome must have been something like it under Nero or Commodus: Constantinople under its worst Sultans.[21]

The townsfolk in cosmopolitan Jeddah and Mecca mistrusted Hussein and his revolt and simply wanted to get on with trade (they were mostly Hindus, Sudanese, Javanese, Persians, and other non-Arabs). Hussein's men tried to milk them for their wealth, and the townspeople in return loathed Hussein for the corruption and incompetence of his administration, which mirrored that of the Ottoman Turks from which, ironically, the old leader longed to be free.

★   ★   ★

Just eight days after taking up residence in his second-floor office, Wilson channelled the tensions of his post through a minor gripe: 'Cochrane and I do all the filing and I really could not go the present pace much longer.' Another of his concerns was his uniform: he knew the Arabs might accept him more readily if he wore at least their head covering, but he could not bring himself to abandon his helmet, that symbol of his identity. He spluttered indignantly: 'The Sherif is sending me down a silk scarf and the Bedouin rope thing which I will wear over my helmet. I absolutely refuse to disguise myself as an Arab, if I'm scuppered I propose to be scuppered in my own uniform.'

Wilson was about to set off for Yenbo to meet Emir Feisal. Ever the realist, he thought the Turks at Wejh further up the coast would hear of his departure from Jeddah (he knew there were spies in the town) and 'might have a shot at intercepting me on my way back'. He asked for his wife to be given a good pension settlement. His innate sense of honour shone through. Wilson had sat on a letter from the High Commissioner in Cairo, who had said he would pay Hussein for only four months. Wilson knew the revolt could not be won on this timescale, but the Foreign Office relented: 'If the FO had stuck to the 4 months I should have resigned.'[22] This was not to be the only time that Wilson threatened to resign on a matter of principle.

Wilson arrived at the run-down port of Yenbo and met Feisal (he was the first British representative to do so) on 27 August. Wilson was impressed by the Arab leader—a tall, thin man in his early thirties who was personable and dignified. Feisal was a sophisticated political operator (he had been a member of the Ottoman parliament in Constantinople) but he was troubled and felt he was losing face because he needed more men and money, and also explosives, to help his men destroy the railway. He blamed the British for delays. Wilson, frank as ever, said he should blame his father: 'sixty-odd boxes of bombs had been on board a warship for weeks as the Sherif said he did not want them landed'. Egyptian Army men trained in explosives to blow up the railway had also been stopped by Hussein from coming over to Jeddah, because he feared the Bedouin tribes would not stand for it (they hated the Egyptians, even though they were fellow Muslims).[23]

Wilson did some important work at Yenbo. He persuaded the head Sheikh of the Geheina tribe, Saad ibn Ghonein, to meet Feisal. Wilson then bought Saad's allegiance (for £40—'cheap at the price').[24] As a result more than two thousand Geheina tribesmen came to the town and swore an oath of loyalty to Feisal. Wilson also interrogated a captured Turkish officer, the former governor of the port of Wejh, and learned about Turkish fortified posts between the port and the railway, and the number of troops in that area.[25] But he was well aware of the threat from the Turks. He knew they were buying loyalty just like the British.[26] He wrote from Yenbo: 'The situation *is* serious ... We may see the Turks on the coast.'[27] Wilson knew that a crisis was looming. The Turks had already put forward a puppet Emir of Mecca, Sherif Haidar, who had condemned his old rival Hussein for his involvement with the infidel British.

As if all this were not bad enough, Wilson was also suffering from a vindictive campaign by GHQ near Cairo. General Lynden-Bell, the Chief of Staff, thought support for the Arab Revolt was a waste of time, money, and effort. He also resented the fact that the Arab Bureau was running a campaign on his own patch. He complained about what he called the stupendous demands made by the Sherif.[28] Lynden-Bell made a direct personal attack on 'a wild man called Wilson'[29] who 'seems to be an extraordinary fellow without any military instincts of any sort or kind. His sole qualification for his present position appears to be a knowledge of Arabic. He is at the present moment living entirely alone in a house at Jeddah, and is liable to have his throat cut at any minute.' Lynden-Bell dismissed the Arabian venture as a 'comic opera performance'.[30] Factual errors aside, his single-minded focus on defeating the Turks in Sinai and Palestine meant he was unwilling to recognize the point of supporting the revolt, the diplomatic and intelligence advantages of having a reliable man at Jeddah, the huge difficulties of dealing with the autocratic Hussein, or Wilson's success against the odds in doing so.

By contrast, Wingate fully appreciated Wilson's vitally important work. He acknowledged Wilson's uphill task and his 'firmness and the perfectly frank and candid way' in which he dealt with Hussein, 'and I am convinced that if anyone can succeed in creating order out of chaos it will be yourself'.[31]

Wilson knew, however, that ringing endorsements would not impress the senior staff at GHQ. He was summoned to a conference at their Ismailia base on 12 September, to discuss the vexed question of sending a brigade of

British troops to the port of Rabegh. It was thought that when the Turks headed for Jeddah and Mecca they would need to travel past Rabegh, and that Hussein's army would be brushed aside. General Lynden-Bell and his boss, General Murray (Chief of the EEF), had another agenda too. As Wilson put it, 'I had no idea that I had been brought to the conference to have a very considerable lot of mud slung at me . . . . Murray criticised my telegrams, reports, requests, in fact every blessed thing I have done.' Murray's 'damned caddish manner' was a cynical ploy: GHQ was attacking its real target, Sir Henry McMahon (the High Commissioner in Cairo) and his Arab Bureau, through Wilson. Wilson, decent and dutiful, was the fall guy. He argued for troops to be sent, but the War Office later agreed with Murray's line that the Arabian sideshow should not absorb his forces.

On his way back to Arabia, Wilson collected some Beni Ali tribesmen after their explosives training at Suez. Wilson was pressing for demolition work on the Hejaz Railway five months before T. E. Lawrence ('Lawrence of Arabia') blew up his first length of track. Wilson spent some time at the ports of Yenbo and Rabegh to persuade Feisal and his brothers, Ali and Zeid, to work out a coordinated plan of operations.[32] But Hussein was unfathomable at times. Every month he had been amassing British gold sovereigns, pleading their vital importance to keep the revolt going. But what had he been doing with them? Wilson had told the intelligence chief, Clayton, the exasperating truth:

> The Sherif has been very remiss . . . in distributing money to buy over the tribes around Medina. He confessed to Wilson that he had saved about £200,000 out of the first two consignments of £125,000 sent to him . . . The Turks have been paying the tribes, but the Sherif could have outbid them easily as we have information that they are not paying heavily by any means, and £100,000 [in] golden sovereigns sent to Feisal and Ali a couple of months ago would have done wonders. Wilson has spoken very seriously to the Sherif [to] warn him that he is jeopardising his success seriously by his parsimony.[33]

Wilson showed dogged perseverance and transparent good faith, in the face of nearly insuperable hurdles and chronic ill health. His great gift was to inspire such confidence when dealing with the suspicious Hussein. Wilson might have lacked imagination at times, but his openly honourable nature and his lack of diplomatic tricks or hypocrisy struck a chord with Hussein (who, however, was not averse to hoodwinking Wilson over money).

It is hard to say whether Wilson realized that Hussein's mantra to his sons about always trusting the British implicitly was disingenuous—Hussein had political acumen and was too shrewd really to believe this. He probably reminded Wilson about his faith in the word of the British as a way of putting subtle pressure on a man whom he knew had a strong moral compass. It is true that Wilson's colleagues at times thought he was gullible over Hussein. Kinahan Cornwallis of the Arab Bureau was one, yet he later commented perceptively to Clayton that Hussein 'evidently likes Wilson very much and trusts him'. Wilson's 'transparent honesty and shall we whisper stupidity avail where another man's cleverness would fail'.[34] The astute Clayton regarded Wilson highly. Stupidity was not a charge that would stick, but Cornwallis had glimpsed the essence of Wilson's rapport with Hussein.

Clayton, a far-sighted intelligence officer with cool insight, knew exactly what the young revolt owed to the long-suffering 'pilgrimage officer': 'I only hope Wilson's health will hold out. He is invaluable and doing wonders but, when this crisis is over, he will have to come here for a rest.'[35] These words were prophetic. With the make-or-break Muslim pilgrimage fast approaching, and intrigue and subversion casting a deep shadow, Wilson would somehow need to find fresh reserves of strength to support him through the pivotal weeks ahead.

2

'A town that hung heavy
on the soul'

Wilson returned to Jeddah on the evening of 24 September, hoping to recharge his batteries after the mauling he had received from the generals in Cairo. Walking past the guard of tall Sudanese policemen on the steps of the Consulate,[1] he was surprised and irritated to be met inside by the bear-like figure of Colonel Edouard Brémond and two officers from his French Military Mission. They had arrived in Jeddah three days earlier. Wilson had known they would be coming over from their camp at Suez, but had not thought they would be waiting for him in his own building. He respected Brémond, a tough career soldier who had fought with distinction in the French North African colonies and at the Somme. Tall, stooping, and heavily built, with a bushy black beard and rimless spectacles, Brémond had undoubted presence—but Wilson wished it were elsewhere.

Wilson had a sense of foreboding about the French Mission, most of whose personnel were based at Mecca so as to have the ear of Sherif Hussein. The Mission had grown from an original armed escort for pilgrims from French North Africa. Wilson thought it would weaken Britain's position as chief supporters and funders of the revolt. He had been warned in Egypt about two of the Muslim diplomatic contingent from French North Africa, one of whom was 'one of the biggest intriguers in the Near East'.[2] This man, Mamar Benazzouz, had been an interpreter at the Jeddah Consulate and was now appointed vice-consul in Mecca.[3] As a diplomat representing France to Sherif Hussein, he and Brémond soon attempted to undermine Wilson's position. One of the ways they did this was Brémond's attempt to have French North African troops sent over to the Hejaz to bolster Hussein's not very effective forces: this idea went down well with the old sherif. Brémond thought this could trump British influence over Hussein, since he knew the British were nervous about sending troops as they feared upsetting the Bedouin tribes so near the Muslim holy places of Mecca and Medina. Brémond also used disinformation in an attempt to drive a wedge between the British and Hussein.

Why this problem with the French, who were after all Britain's allies? At heart they wanted to steer the revolt to suit their imperialist interests, which was also the British approach. Both nations had wider geopolitical interests and were taking a long-term view, anticipating the effects of their policies as the war developed and also after its end. The French wanted to be seen to be helping Hussein, to stop their North African colonies from being disaffected and arguing that the French were not the real friends of Muslims. Then there was the matter of a secret agreement between Britain, France, and Russia—known as the Sykes-Picot Agreement after two of the diplomats involved—that would have staggered both Brémond and Wilson if they had known about it. But they had been kept out of the loop. The agreement had been signed earlier in 1916 and anticipated the carving up of the Ottoman Empire between the imperial rivals as victors in the war. France would get much of Syria and Lebanon, while the British would get most of Mesopotamia (present-day Iraq). In addition, a zone of French influence would cover the rest of Syria, while British influence would extend to what is now Jordan. Palestine would be under international control.[4]

Knowing nothing of this, Brémond's instinct was to contain the Arab Revolt within the Hejaz and stop it spreading to Syria, where he thought it would harm French commercial and cultural interests. But his own government thought that if the Bedouin tribes rose up in Syria the dismemberment of the Ottoman Empire would be hastened, and the Sykes-Picot Agreement could be implemented. So the hapless Brémond was on a collision course with his own government and there could only be one winner as events unfolded.

★   ★   ★

For the present, Brémond had mixed memories of two rather unusual meals, on successive evenings, which had been laid on to welcome him and his team. The first meal was provided by a merchant and Young, who was a guest with Cochrane, said in his usual carping tone, 'the dinner was depressing in the extreme, interminably drawn out and badly served. The room was lit by candles in large chandeliers hanging from the ceiling, covered with flies which from time to time flew drowsily round the guests and fell into the food.' An overawed soldier from the French colony of Senegal, 'overcome by shyness, remained silent, swallowing food and flies together'.[5]

Twenty-four hours later, the same party of eighty gathered for a similarly drawn-out meal complete with flies. This time the reception was at the expense of the leader of the town council, Suleiman Qabil, and was held at the municipality building. The party ate in the open air on the roof of the building, and some hastily borrowed carpets and decorations of French, British, and Sherifian flags gave a pleasing *ambience*. True, Sherif Mohsen refused to eat anything for fear of being poisoned, but that was his default position when eating out. And the large block of ice placed on a table in the middle of the room was dripping on to the fine carpets below, though at least it gave the impression of coolness. Young noticed that Suleiman Qabil appeared radiantly happy, thinking his political future had been secured. Then, just as the meal came to an end, the French guests were jolted out of their stupor as the block of ice crashed on to the floor. Suleiman Qabil must have thought his prospects had gone in the same direction.

Wilson would have been delighted to have been away from Jeddah during these awkward meals. He now had to try to outwit Brémond's wiles, while at the same time try to outmanoeuvre the French vice-consul in Mecca and the factions in Jeddah and Mecca that were actively working against Hussein—not to mention the need to inject more momentum into the stalling revolt. The pressures on him were relentless. Had he known at that time of the Sykes-Picot Agreement, which cynically undercut the earlier vague British promises of an independent Syria and other lands for Hussein if he were to rebel, Wilson would probably have resigned. With stiff-lipped understatement he restricted himself to commenting that 'there is a deuce of a lot to be done'.

In practical terms this meant working punishingly long hours, in a climate that would have taxed a man half Wilson's age who was not suffering from his chronic dysentery. Wilson complained: 'I am at my table from 6.30 am to 8 pm with half an hour only after lunch off and yet I cannot get through the work. I have begged for someone to be sent from Egypt merely to do cypher work and I could do with a British officer for Intelligence work.' Young and Cochrane, he said, were working similar hours on ciphering secret cables. 'In *absolute* confidence please I may tell you I have discovered the secret cyphers used by Ali, Feisal and Sherif when wiring to each other, it is sometimes useful but I do not want it talked about as you can well understand.'[6] Wilson was almost certainly brought this information by Ruhi.

But once again he was out of the loop: Wilson had no idea that the Arab Bureau had broken Sherif Hussein's codes months before.[7] It did not think Wilson had a need to know. Perhaps the Bureau wanted to check what Hussein told Wilson against what the old leader told his own sons.

The long-suffering 'pilgrimage officer' needed a break but he was to get no respite. While Wilson battled on, his colleagues supported him as best they could. John Young, when he was not toiling over the endless waves of secret cables that needed to be encrypted and decrypted, was patiently filling two large exercise books in his neat hand with detailed and pithy comments on the leading personalities in Jeddah and Mecca. He did not pull his punches. His shrewd and astringent character sketches—character assassinations in many cases—were just what the Arab Bureau had ordered. It planned a second edition of the *Hejaz Handbook*, an intelligence manual, and Young's work, aided by Hussein Ruhi's ferreting, would form an important contribution. Young was critical of Ruhi at times, referring to what he called inaccurate gossip, but appreciated his excellent contacts and the intelligence nuggets that he unearthed.

Government in the Hejaz was corrupt, incompetent, and dysfunctional and Young was very disparaging on the subject. He wrote from the usual racist perspective of his time: the patrician representative of imperial power dismissing the 'natives' who knew no better. He lists his subjects alphabetically and gives their physical descriptions, biographies, and political loyalties, with generous lashings of corruption and scandal. He describes ministers, court officials, foreign residents, merchants, and suspected spies. The selection of the former leader of the Jeddah Chamber of Commerce was 'apparently a joke—as he is quite ignorant of the world and of all recognised business methods'.

Young described Sherif Mohsen, who was Hussein's relative as well as governor of Jeddah, as 'an unscrupulous ignorant tyrant'.[8] Mohsen had a fearsome reputation for casual as well as considered cruelty. The British generally turned a blind eye to this behaviour since they saw him as a reliable ally. Wilson, though, had argued with Mohsen about the morality of slavery, with which he was heavily involved. Young mentioned how Mohsen treated criminals, slashing them about the head with a sword and sometimes cutting off hands. '"When we think of Sherif Muhsen [sic] our loins tremble" was a common saying in Jeddah.'[9] When the Ottoman soldiers surrendered Jeddah to the Arabs, Mohsen took advantage of the confusion to plunder the town's Treasury with his cronies. His excesses made for enemies: his paranoia meant that he often refused to eat outside his own house for fear of being poisoned.

Young chronicled the intrigue that was endemic to Jeddah and that caused so much vexation to Wilson. He described Sheikh Moatig as the chief burglar of Jeddah. Ahmed Hegazi was formerly a highway robber and reputed to be responsible for many useful murders.[10] Sheikh Hussein El Zeidi was suspected by Sherif Hussein, rightly or wrongly, as being pro-Turk: he was reduced to selling beans and bread in the Jeddah souk or market. Another figure was a Muslim slave dealer who kidnapped the children of poor pilgrims from Africa and who plied his trade in the murky underworld of Jeddah. Ruhi had a knack for winkling out this sort of information or rumour. Sherif Taha, Hussein's controller of the Pilgrimage Committee, was 'ignorant, immoral, coarse in appearance, resembling . . . a bottle-nosed bandit'. In his previous job, receiving payments for the use of Jeddah's water condenser, he had felt that keeping financial records was tiresome and had simply embezzled much of the income.

The bizarre cast of characters monitored by Young and Ruhi included Hussein's 'Admiral of the Red Sea' (actually the Jeddah harbour master), who moonlighted as a smuggler and slave dealer. The Minister of Justice was so ignorant that he could barely express his judgments, 'and the court frequently burst into laughter on hearing them'. He had apparently been heard to say that he hoped the revolt against the Turks would never end, as then the liberal showers of gold sovereigns paid as the British subsidy to Hussein would end too. The young director-general of security, a Syrian, 'timid, effeminate, a master of intrigue', paid too many visits to the Consulate for Young's liking.

Hussein's household at Mecca was also riddled with intrigue. The sherif had a Turkish-born private attendant who controlled his finances and dispensed favours at a price. A freed Abyssinian slave had huge powers and a lucrative blackmail business, imprisoning people at will in remote towns to the despair of their families who often never saw them again. Most feared of all was Hussein's private prison, the Qobu, which lay under his palace. Young knew of a Jeddah merchant who for some reason had displeased Hussein and was summoned to Mecca: he was languishing in the Qobu the very next day. Any prisoner who was not given food by friends outside was likely to die.[11]

★ ★ ★

What the upright Wilson made of the murky shenanigans in Jeddah and Mecca can only be imagined. He would have found many of Young's waspish assessments distasteful, but would have appreciated his officer's detailed report on the fall of the Turkish garrison at Taif, a walled town in the hills about seventy-five miles south-east of Mecca. Taif was much cooler than Mecca and a welcome retreat for wealthy residents of the Holy City in the debilitating heat of summer. The town had quickly been captured by the forces of Abdullah, Hussein's second son, soon after the outbreak of the revolt in June, but the Turkish soldiers in their fort were in no mood to surrender. Turks were resolute fighters in defensive positions, as British and colonial troops had found at Gallipoli and were to discover to their cost in the Arabian and Palestine campaigns. Bedouin Arabs were skilled in fast raids against enemy tribes in the desert, after which they would disappear just as quickly with their loot. They had no aptitude for sustained offensive operations against well-entrenched opponents. So while Taif's delicious apricots, pomegranates, pears, and vegetables continued to be brought to the Jeddah Consulate for Wilson and his men, the fort was besieged by the field guns of a small Egyptian Army detachment under Said Ali. The campaign was to last more than three months. Hussein opportunistically got the gunners to shell the town houses of some of his opponents too, presumably on the pretext that they were dangerous plotters.

Young had accurately reported to the Arab Bureau on 9 September that the Taif garrison could not last more than fourteen days.[12] He got this information from two Egyptian Army officers who arrived at Jeddah with a few field guns destined for the army of Hussein's third son, Feisal, who was up the Red Sea coast at the port of Yenbo. Young heard that the garrison would have surrendered much earlier if the Bedouin forces could have been persuaded to attack. Instead, every day the Egyptian gunners fired on the fort and inflicted heavy damage, but the Arabs failed to follow it up and expected the Egyptians to do all the work. The damage was then repaired and the process began again. Young dismissed the Arabs with his usual disdain, calling them undisciplined, lazy, and unreliable. The Egyptian troops

> were in great danger at night from their random firing into the air to pass away the time. The Arabs collected in great numbers round Taif on pay days. After getting their pay they then drifted off to their families and often did not return until the next pay day. Some of them had been known to rob Egyptian officers and all of them boasted of their high hopes of seizing the wives of the Turkish garrison.

The garrison finally surrendered on 23 September. This was welcome news for Wilson when he returned to Jeddah the following day from his mortifying grilling at Cairo. The Egyptian officers claimed that their men prevented a massacre by the Arabs at Taif, though Abdullah, Hussein's second son, should be given credit too. He ensured that eighty-three officers, nearly two thousand men, and seventy-two civilian officials and wives were conveyed safely to Mecca.

The story of the siege of Taif illustrates some wider points and shows just how difficult a task the British had in the Hejaz. Egypt had been annexed as a British Protectorate in November 1914 (its High Commissioner was in charge of the Arab Bureau). So they sent over Egyptian artillerymen to help the Arabs, because as fellow Muslims there was a better chance they would be tolerated in close contact with the Bedouin than the infidel British would be. But there was a problem: Arabs and Egyptians each looked down on the other and this mutual dislike had been going on for centuries. Fights would later break out in Jeddah. Putting the Egyptians cheek by jowl with the Bedouin outside Taif was always likely to end the way it did.

At this time, too, three months into the revolt, the British in general failed to appreciate the need for the Arabs to play to their strengths—primarily guerrilla warfare, hitting and running, striking across the desert like ships in a huge ocean, and then being swallowed up again by an environment they understood so well. Wilson, however, had grasped this point and had argued, as we have seen, for Arab guerrilla attacks on the Hejaz railway. In a few weeks' time a shy young junior intelligence officer with uncanny empathy, temporary Captain Thomas Edward Lawrence, would arrive in Jeddah and look on the Arabs' capabilities and potential in a very different way from Young and from most in the Egyptian Expeditionary Force.[13]

★   ★   ★

For now, Wilson had a more pressing concern. The annual Muslim pilgrimage or Hajj was fast approaching. One of the reasons for the detailed intelligence assessments drawn up by Young and Hussein Ruhi was Wilson's concern—shared by the Arab Bureau—about pan-Islamic jihadist agitators. They had proof that some were amongst the at least three hundred British Indian Muslims who lived in the town (the unofficial number was probably considerably higher). These men were organized in underground societies and were scheming against Hussein for daring to throw in his lot with the infidels. They were likely to be joined by sympathizers amongst the more than two thousand British Indian Muslim pilgrims who would soon be pouring through the port of Jeddah on their way to Mecca. They wanted to disrupt the pilgrimage, discredit the British in Arabia, and spread anti-British subversion back in India. The stakes were high because, if the pilgrimage was not a success, Sherif Hussein would also lose face and the revolt itself would be put in jeopardy.

The unflappable 'Cocky' Cochrane helped Wilson with arrangements for the pilgrimage. He was familiar with them from before the war, through his work with the shipping agents Gellatly Hankey at Port Sudan across the Red Sea and at their Jeddah office. As pilgrimage officer, Wilson had set up a Pilgrimage Committee, which reduced by half the previously punitive tax imposed on pilgrims entering the country, and also made a considerable cut in the boat hire for landing pilgrims. It was still difficult to stop the over-charging by metowifs (guides), brokers, and other intermediaries in the Hejaz, who for generations had 'made a life study of the art of exploiting pilgrims'.[14] This racket extended to hiring camels to get the pilgrims from Jeddah to Mecca. Hussein had a strong financial interest: he set the price for camel hire for both pilgrims and merchant caravans, and received a large income from taxing these transactions (some of the money went to the Bedouin tribes for permission to cross their grazing lands).

Cochrane was well aware of the pilgrimage scams. He discovered that three hundred single tickets had been bought at three pounds each by a pilgrim sheikh in Jeddah from the Indian agents of a Bombay shipping line. The sheikh promptly sold them on to pilgrims at a much higher price via the ever-eager brokers and guides. Cochrane had to intervene to prevent a large number of pilgrims from being stranded in Jeddah. They had return tickets to India, but shipping agents in Jeddah were unscrupulous about fill-ing the ship with pilgrims who could pay on the spot, and had no qualms about overlooking the prior claims of those who already had their return tickets. Cochrane worked tirelessly and made sure the pilgrims got home to India. His phlegmatic outlook made him perfectly suited for the post. Young called him 'invaluable...a rock of sound common sense and a bastion of defence' against Ruhi's gossip. Cochrane could escape from Jeddah's blan-keting intrigue, if only briefly, by relaxing with Young and Ruhi in the Consulate's large mess room. He enjoyed listening to records played on the gramophone he had brought with him from Port Sudan—the soprano Carrie Tubb singing 'Valley of Laughter' was a particular favourite.[15]

Wilson was fortunate to have the Cochrane and Young double act to support him. Cochrane helped him with more than the pilgrimage: he also had a wise head for political correspondence and consular questions, and took charge of the £125,000 in gold sovereigns that was brought to Jeddah each month by the Red Sea Patrol of the Royal Navy. This was the British subsidy to Hussein and Cochrane ensured that it went to him. Cochrane had earlier helped in the landing of supplies and military equipment for the Egyptian Army gunners. Cochrane and Young were different in character but they were a good team. More than that, Young was to call him 'a very great friend'.[16] Hussein was to go further, in his typically flowery and convoluted style: he called Cochrane 'the equivalent of an anvil jewel, the splendour of which is amplified as it remains pristine' (perhaps something has been lost in translation). Hussein valued Cochrane's 'striking loyalty' and was to present him with the Nahda medal, a signed photograph, and a beautiful jewel-encrusted ceremonial sword.[17]

For the present, Wilson was thankful that Cochrane and Young's conscientious work was being underpinned by a sensitive secret mission. This had been underway in Jeddah and Mecca for about two weeks before his return to pick up the reins in the Consulate, and was an expression of British concerns about the pilgrimage, the present state of the Arab Revolt, and the possible threat to the British Raj in India.

3

'A vast pan-Islamic conspiracy'

Wilson had told the director of the Arab Bureau in August 1916 that he needed help to combat underground Indian groups which were bent on sedition:

> In view of coming pilgrimage and the existence of secret Indian Societies in Jeddah I suggest that it would be an excellent move if a really trustworthy Indian could be sent here, ostentiously [sic] to assist me with Indian pilgrims but his duties would primarily be to get into [sic] touch with and keep an eye on Indian Sedition Mongers here...Jeddah is a hotbed of intrigue and spying.[1]

Enter Captain Norman Napier Evelyn Bray, a singular man on a singular mission. A slightly built 31-year-old, an Indian Army officer with the 18th Bengal Lancers, he arrived in Jeddah on 10 September straight from the trenches of the Western Front.[2] He brought with him two hand-picked Indian officers and a small band of soldiers. Bray was well acquainted with espionage and subversion, and was the perfect officer for a special mission to target what he later called 'a vast pan-Islamic conspiracy'. He saw anti-British jihadists as a dagger aimed at the heart of India, and was driven by the conviction that Indian Muslim plotters had to be neutralized.

Bray reacted like the others in Wilson's Jeddah circle to 'a climate which at times tears the vitals out of you'. He noticed that 'Everything is crooked; the walls of the houses lean over at queer angles, the balconies sag dangerously.' Bray was struck by 'the sensation of walking on the earth of the narrow streets, earth beaten down by the bare feet of countless generations of pilgrims, so that it had the resilience and silence of india-rubber from which our footsteps gave back no echo'.

The Consulate seemed to transport Bray back to his own world, with 'the bustle, the click of typewriters, the sound of boots upon stone floors'.

If Colonel Wilson knew that Bray's uncle-in-law was General Arthur Lynden-Bell, his tormentor at the recent Cairo conference, he seems to have said nothing about it. Bray found Wilson on his return 'a dapper, soldierly little figure...[who] looked tired, like a man grappling ceaselessly with insoluble problems.' Most of Wilson's time was taken up with

> lengthy arguments, on paper and by telephone, with the Sherif, regarding the extent of the new Arab kingdom...The Sherif wished to decide every question which arose, whether with regard to policy or military action. He trusted no-one, not even his own sons, of whom he was as suspicious as of all with whom he had to deal. Every petty detail of supply, finance or administration was dealt with by him personally. He reached no decision till after long argument and then gave his consent grudgingly...I was sometimes amazed at Wilson's patience and forbearance...[and was] heartily glad that I was not in his shoes.[3]

Bray had had an adventurous past. He had travelled all over India as assistant to General Sir Percy Lake (almost certainly as an intelligence officer), and was deeply disturbed by the activities of revolutionary organizations in Bengal and elsewhere in the years before the First World War. The head of the Indian Secret Police had told him that subversion was being orchestrated from outside India. On leave, he travelled in 1913 at his own expense to Syria, learned Arabic, and got in touch with anti-Turkish Arab nationalists. Not surprisingly, he was harassed by Turkish and German intelligence and tried to escape these attentions by crossing into Lebanon.[4]

Bray went back to Syria in May 1914. In Damascus he met a suspiciously friendly Major von Hochwaechter of the German Army. The Germans had been reorganizing and training the Turkish armed forces for some years, and had a vital strategic interest in the region in the shape of the Berlin to Baghdad railway, which was being built by the Germans and which they hoped would help destroy the British Empire. The railway was one strand of an ambitious German scheme to turn the Muslim world against Britain and rain down jihad or holy war against their imperial rivals. German spies, archaeologists, and soldiers were intriguing from Libya to Afghanistan, encouraging jihad and providing gold and guns. Bray took the measure of Major von Hochwaechter and discovered that he was about to visit India on an intelligence mission. Bray was later able to ensure that negatives of photographs of sensitive sites taken by the Major in India were mysteriously exposed to the light.

While talking to von Hochwaechter in Damascus, Bray found the German was trying to get him drunk on champagne to winkle military secrets out of him. This plan backfired when von Hochwaechter himself slid under the table. Bray was able to read a secret despatch addressed by the German to his personal friend, Kaiser Wilhelm, which seemed to state that Germany intended to make war in August 1914. In what could be a passage from Buchan's *Greenmantle* or *The Thirty-Nine Steps*, Bray said he rushed to England immediately, telegraphing his well-connected father-in-law to get him to line up an interview with the Foreign Secretary, Sir Edward Grey. A meeting was not feasible, so Bray returned to India before his leave ran out, where he was frustrated to find that his boss did not give much credence to the German despatch.[5]

★   ★   ★

Bray's preoccupation with jihadism was intense. With hindsight, it seems that Germany and the Ottomans overrated the power of pan-Islam, just as Britain 'over-rated the appeal of Arab nationalism to gain the support of Ottoman Arabs for Britain's ends'.[6] But Bray knew that subversives in the Hejaz and elsewhere, and their Turkish and German choreographers, could still do real damage. His role was not just to give intelligence support to Wilson, but also to act for the Government of India. In this respect Bray brought into focus a strange dislocation in British foreign policy. India had its own foreign policy concerns in its sphere of interest, which included the Arabian Peninsula, the Persian Gulf, and Mesopotamia (modern Iraq). These interests were separate from those of the Foreign Office in London, which ran the Arab Bureau in Cairo. The Government of India thought British support for the Arab Revolt was misguided and wanted its ally in the Nejd of Central Arabia, the powerful warlord Ibn Saud, to be the chief British ally in Arabia rather than Sherif Hussein. Bray had the same view, but he also thought Hussein's revolt should be encouraged as a way of blocking the manipulation of the pan-Islamic movement by Turkish and Egyptian extremists.

Thanks to his wife's well-connected family, Bray had been given the chance, while on leave in London in July 1916, to discuss his concerns with the effervescent diplomat Sir Mark Sykes. Sykes claimed that he saw in Bray's idea of a mission of Indian officers to the Hejaz an opportunity to harmonize the Indian and Foreign Office policies. The mercurial Sykes, who could devise and then contradict policies in the blink of an eye, had a good line in undiplomatic language only two months later: 'Co-operation with the Government of India is impossible, it understands nothing—it does not see beyond its crabbed parsimonious finance…and its immense under-staffed feeble self—the Government of India is an anaemic giant with a head like a pea'.[7]

One of Wilson's many headaches was an anti-British Indian agitator called Mahmud Hassan. The head of a fundamentalist Muslim theological college at Deoband in northern India, he had been in the Hejaz for some months and Wilson's job was to find him and neutralize him.[8] This was where Bray's special expertise came in. In August he had helped the Indian authorities uncover the 'Silk Letters' conspiracy, a plot led by the 'Army of God' to unite Islamic countries against Britain. The letters had been written to Hassan in July by one of the plot's ringleaders in the Afghan capital, Kabul. The courier of the letters was interrogated and confirmed that Mahmud had been intriguing in Medina, and was currently living in Mecca where he was trying to stir up feelings of Indians and other Muslims against Hussein. Many resented Hussein's rebellion because they saw the Ottoman sultan and caliph as the bedrock and heart of their religion.

With the pilgrimage imminent, Bray wasted no time in getting his mission underway. The day after his arrival, he sent his two Indian officers on the 60-kilometre journey to Mecca. Bray had hand-picked the 14-stone Gulmawaz Khan and his colleague Hassan Shah. Gulmawaz's mule protested as he lowered his considerable bulk on to it, then the officers and a few men set off on their eight-hour journey. The officers took with them a deal box containing silver gifts for Hussein. Their task was in part to convince Hussein that his revolt was at risk from Indian pan-Islamic subversives, and to exploit divisions between the Indian Muslims and the Turks.

★ ★ ★

The Arabic-speaking Hussein Ruhi was in a perfect position to help Bray. He had been a schoolteacher in Cairo before the war, having obtained a qualification as an English teacher in the USA.[9] At the outbreak of the First World War, Ruhi was living in Cairo with his second wife, Nagiba, and their children.[10] As we have seen, Ruhi had been visiting the Hejaz on clandestine missions for Wilson in the run-up to the revolt, and had been based at Jeddah prior to Wilson's arrival there. He had earlier exposed the unreliability of the former Ottoman Army officer and Arab nationalist, Sherif Mohammed al-Faruqi. Ruhi was run as an agent by Ronald Storrs, the urbane and brilliant Oriental Secretary to the British High Commissioner,

Sir Henry McMahon, in Cairo. Storrs was also part of the Arab Bureau. He gave Ruhi the not very obscure code name 'Persian Mystic' and also ran Ruhi's father-in-law, Ali Asgar, whom he called 'agent X' (and who was a go-between when Abdullah, Hussein's son, visited the then High Commissioner, Lord Kitchener, and Storrs back in 1914 to discuss possible cooperation between the Hashemites and Britain).

In early 1915 Ruhi was sent to the Suez Canal area on a dangerous mission to thwart desertions by wavering Muslim Indian soldiers, who were defending the canal. The Turks were attacking the strategically vital water-way and the stakes were high. They had agents in place who were trying to influence the Indians and also turn ordinary Egyptians against the British. Ruhi was imprisoned a number of times, perhaps by officers of the Indian Army who were unaware of his confidential mission. If he had been detained by the Turks on the Sinai side of the canal, his escape or release both seem implausible—though Ruhi's gift of the gab should not be underestimated.[11]

Ruhi had acted as Arabic translator for McMahon and Storrs in the course of the McMahon–Hussein correspondence, which broadly declared that Hussein would revolt against the Turks with British support, in return for which Britain would recognize Arab independence in an ill-defined area. Storrs was rather disparaging, in his patrician way, about an important detail of Ruhi's translation (which unfortunately led to either a misunderstanding or to self-deception on the part of Hussein), but he valued his Persian spy and admired his bravery.

A few weeks after the capture of Jeddah, Ruhi had been installed at the British Consulate with a cover job as Wilson's Arabic secretary.[12] Like many agents he was not slow to bolster his reputation. He wrote to Storrs: 'I am known here as an Alem or Mohammedan theologian as I went into Mosques and delivered lectures...All the great people here are my friends. I picked some of them who I found really pro-English and they may be a great help to our work' (a reference to possible agent-running). It has to be said that a vision of Ruhi as a Muslim theologian is stretching credulity—but no doubt it suited his intelligence work if some had this perception of him.

Ruhi's showmanship and panache were as different from Wilson's style as could be. He respected and liked Wilson, telling Storrs in the same letter: 'Nothing pleased me in the world as having [sic] Colonel Wilson as the agent to the High Commissioner. Here all the people like him and speak well of him.'[13] The strait-laced Wilson, though, seems to have been rather ambivalent about Ruhi (we have seen how he called Ruhi 'weird'). T. E. Lawrence was to call him, 'Ruhi the ingenious, more like a mandrake than a man'.[14]

For all that, Ruhi played a starring role in Bray's intelligence mission. Bray conferred with him at once to make best use of the Persian's expertise in the town's seething underworld. Ruhi, who had an inefficient Baha'i assistant, had a network of contacts and possible agents including Mohammed Ali Lari, the Persian consul, who was a Baha'i like him, and a Persian shipping agent and merchant.[15] Ruhi put his life at risk through contact with two underground pan-Islamic secret societies, the Anjuman-Khudam-I-Kaaba and Al Janud Al Rabbania, in Jeddah. He both recruited and, unusually, ran agents from these organizations (his dual role added to the risk he was running) and was able to pass useful information on their members, structure, influence, and intentions to Captain Bray.

In this connection Ruhi made a dangerous trip—not his first—to Mecca. To be exposed as a Baha'i in the Holy City would have meant certain death. The danger came not just from the presence of Turkish and German intelligence agents, but from the fact that the population was almost all pro-Turk.[16] Ruhi drew two accurate maps of Mecca, identifying the town's thirteen districts with the name of their sheikhs. He commented, 'Morality seems to be at a very low ebb, very many of the men having unnatural taste... Corruption is practised everywhere, even in the Sherif's house.' He noted that Sudanese and Abyssinian slaves were sold at several inns.

Ruhi noted the names of two Indians who were sticking anti-Hussein notices on the walls of the Sherif's house, and intercepted two letters to Hussein, one from his great rival Ibn Saud. He even found the time, as a former teacher, to visit all of Mecca's schools, which did not take long as there were only three. His report on them (poor educational methods and 'indifferent management') reads like that of a government inspector. Ruhi reported that of Mecca's population of one hundred and fifty thousand, barely five thousand were pro-sherif, of whom only five hundred were influential. Plotting against Hussein was rife. The Shanabrah branch of Ashraf (the plural of Sherif) were nearly all against him, a symptom of the age-old, Machiavellian intrigue that bedevilled the Hejaz. Ruhi noted that some plotters were 'trying to get hold of the Grand Sherif [i.e. Hussein] and hand him over to the Turks'.

Bray soon discovered, through Ruhi's undercover visit and intelligence from the Persian spy's well-placed agents, that his number one target, Mahmud Hassan, planned to return to India after his campaign of subversion and disinformation in the Hejaz. Back in India, by vilifying and discrediting Hussein in the eyes of Muslims, he would try to spread discontent and even mutiny among the men of the Indian Army.[17] While at Mecca, Mahmud had been in secret communication with Fakhri Pasha, the Turkish Commandant in Medina. Bray took swift action, advising Colonel Wilson to ask Hussein to arrest Mahmud and have him sent to Jeddah for interrogation. Hussein as usual dug in his heels, called the man saintly and said he should not be treated in this way, but soon changed his mind when it was pointed out to him that Mahmud was agitating for Hussein's throat to be slit. When Bray saw Mahmud the next day, he was surprised to find that his adversary, who 'had been concocting plans to have officers murdered in their beds and women and children murdered in cold blood', was 'an old man of benevolent aspect, with a flowing, snow-white beard and kindly eyes'. If Mahmud looked like Father Christmas, his younger disciple fitted the stereotype of conspirator: he had a snakelike appearance and his furtive eyes 'flashed a look of bitter hatred'. Bray had precise intelligence from Ruhi on Mahmud's whereabouts when he was practising sedition. Mahmud did not deny this and soon found himself with his disciple at an internment camp in Malta, where they spent the rest of the war.

Bray was concerned enough about Mahmud's campaign to discredit Hussein, both in the Hejaz and in India, to get Colonel Wilson to ask the sherif to come to Jeddah for a meeting. An anxious Hussein came that same day, and Wilson and Bray set off from the Consulate for a midnight meeting at the sherif's palace. They found Hussein alone in an empty chamber upstairs, where he was pacing back and forth 'with short, agitated steps . . . like a caged animal'. He recovered his dignity at once as soon as he sensed the presence of the British officers, but Bray was to remember 'a soul laid bare, a frail, frightened old man'. He wanted Hussein to be less arrogant towards Indian opinion, and to realize the importance of gaining the sympathy and support of Muslims from India rather than alienating himself from them. But Hussein was contemptuous and said he needed no help in dealing with the Indians and their plot against him in Mecca. Hussein was wily and shrewd but was hamstrung by his capacity for hubris and self-deception. Bray feared the worst for Hussein's prospects as an Arab leader with the power to unite.

★ ★ ★

It was Ruhi's excellent work that had brought matters to this point. His report on his visit to Mecca was considered so important that Sir Henry McMahon, the High Commissioner in Egypt, sent it on 3 November not only to Lord Grey, the Foreign Secretary, but also to the highest level of the Indian Government.[18] But Ruhi's work was already well known in the subcontinent: it can now be revealed for the first time that he was a clandestine agent for both the Arab Bureau and for the organization that detested the Bureau for its involvement in the Arabian peninsula—the Government of India. Bray argued that Ruhi's services deserved special recognition by the Government of India because he had 'devoted a great deal of his time and energies on work in [its] interests...I cannot speak too highly of his work in this respect, and I personally feel I owe him the deepest debt of gratitude for the earnestness of his work and the useful results obtained.' Bray went further: Ruhi had 'been employed for a very considerable time, *in addition to his normal work*, on work on behalf of the Indian Government' (author's emphasis). The following year India reluctantly decided not to award Ruhi a title, because the grant of an Indian decoration would mark him out as a protégé of the Government of India and would debar him from useful intelligence work amongst Indians.[19]

Wilson was well aware that Ruhi's undercover work in the Hejaz was of great value to India, and endorsed Bray's praise. But it is most unlikely that Wilson knew that Ruhi was actually working for the Government of India too. As for Ronald Storrs, who was possessive of 'my most trustworthy Persian emissary', there has to be doubt as to whether he really knew what his spy was up to. 'Ruhi the ingenious' was also Ruhi the ambiguous, harnessed to the claims of both Ibn Saud, protégé of the India Office which paid him in gold, and of Sherif Hussein, bankrolled by the Arab Bureau. Ruhi was awarded £100 by the Indian Government in recognition of his singular services.

★ ★ ★

The action taken by Bray and Ruhi had helped safeguard both the Arab Revolt and the Raj, though the threat to both should not be overestimated, as it is not clear what Mahmud Hassan and other plotters might have been capable of achieving. But there was another, more pressing threat to the revolt. Bad news had come from Rabegh, the small port up the coast, which was on the road between Medina and Mecca. Emir Feisal's forces had had a setback near Medina, and the Turks threatened to rush down to Rabegh, deal with his brother Ali's Bedouin there and press on to Mecca. Wilson had in fact decided to head straight for the port following his mauling at the Cairo meeting, and was reunited there with Bray and his two Indian officers, who had returned from their mission to Mecca. Wilson appreciated Bray's skills, telling Wingate: 'I am leaving him here as he knows Arabic, full of tact and an excellent fellow and he can act as liaison officer between the RFC [Royal Flying Corps] and ships and Ali Bey etc. as well as being my representative.'[20] Bray was relieved to have left Jeddah, 'where everything seemed unreal, hampered'. With other officers, Wilson and Bray were taken to Emir Ali's camp. The signs were not good. Rabegh's sheikh was pro-Turk, and propaganda was rife that the British intended to occupy the country in the guise of helping the Arabs. Ali was swayed by these stories for a time and Wilson was concerned about the effectiveness of his few thousand men. Bray was given permission to carry out a survey to map the land around Rabegh, to assess defensive positions, and he also gathered intelligence. The loss of Rabegh was seen as a death knell for the revolt, but the British Army and Government at the highest levels continued to anguish over the sending of British troops and aeroplanes, which would be seen as a provocative act so near the holy places. So while the Turks were cautious about pressing far from Medina, owing to raids by Feisal's men, Wilson encouraged Ali to

Figure 1. General Fatmi Pasha (centre foreground) on HMS *Hardinge*, which brought the Holy Carpet from Suez to Jeddah for the 1917 Hajj pilgrimage. Colonel Cyril Wilson is in darker army uniform to right of centre.

Figure 2. Arrival of the Holy Carpet under the Mahmal (tented covering) at Jeddah, 1917. Escort of Egyptian soldiers in white pilgrim clothing.

recruit 5,000 men to form a force of Arab regular soldiers. They were trained by two former Ottoman Army officers, Aziz Ali al Masri and Nuri as-Said, who were also Arab nationalists. The British crossed their fingers and hoped these Arabs, with Royal Navy support, would hold the line if the Turks came calling.

★ ★ ★

Meanwhile Wilson's team still had to negotiate a successful pilgrimage. Cochrane's careful preparations and the neutralizing of dangerous plotters gave the great event a favourable wind. On 27 September 1916, the Royal Navy warship, HMS *Hardinge*, escorted by Vice-Admiral Rosslyn Wemyss in his flagship, HMS *Euryalus*, brought the Holy Carpet to Jeddah. This embroidered black tapestry was made each year in Cairo for the pilgrimage, and was sent with a guard of honour under the Egyptian General Fatmi Pasha, the Emir el-Hajj (prince of the Hajj). He was a huge, fierce-looking man dressed in the white robes of a pilgrim, the ensemble completed by sandals, Sam Browne officer's belt, and pistol in a holster. Wilson, Young, and Cochrane watched from the roof of the municipality building as a dhow brought the carpet and its entourage to the harbour.

Figure 3. Presentation photograph signed in person at the bottom by Sherif Hussein, accompanying the Hejazi Order of Al Nadha (Renaissance) awarded to Captain William Cochrane in 1920.

Wilson was delighted to see the morale-boosting effect of the Admiral's visit on Sherif Hussein, Sherif Mohsen, and other leading Arabs. Wemyss was well aware of the huge political importance of a successful Muslim pilgrimage, and marked the ceremonial of the Holy Carpet by dressing his flagship with dozens of brightly coloured signal flags. Sherif Mohsen, impressed, formally welcomed him to the town with two guards of honour and a salute fired from his shore battery. Wemyss was conscious that his visit marked 'the first time that a Christian has been officially welcomed in the Hejaz and on the holy ground of Islam'.[21] Mohsen was that afternoon given

Figure 4. From left: unknown officer, Fatmi Pasha (Emir el Hajj), and Colonel Cyril Wilson.

a tour of the huge four-funnelled *Euryalus*, and was astonished at the size of the 9.2-inch guns, the wireless operators' room, and the searchlights.

Wilson was very grateful for the Rear-Admiral's deft political footwork, and recorded 'the excellent effect of His Excellency's visit which has made a very great impression and will be of immense assistance to me, especially after the reception accorded the French Mission, the effect of which has now been entirely eclipsed'.[22]

Ronald Storrs, who had voyaged on the *Euryalus* with Wemyss, was also feeling positive and was pleased to see once again 'my ubiquitous and ineffable Ruhi'.[23] He went with Ruhi to see 'the leading Persian of Jeddah, a Baha'i, who has rendered us considerable service in providing information himself, and also protecting some of our secret agents'.[24] Storrs also had lunch with Young and Cochrane and found them overworked.[25]

The climax of the Hajj was now close. A Mahmal or tented covering protected the Holy Carpet and was hoisted on to a camel the day after its arrival, for the procession to Mecca. Here the carpet would cover the huge black rock or Kaaba. Nine hundred pilgrims and five hundred Egyptian troops were part of the convoy. Cochrane and Young 'saw from the verandah of the Consulate the stately Mahmal rising and falling like a ship in a swelling sea, and the long line of dust-covered camels which followed it into the pearly desert in the half light of the dawn'.[26]

The official pilgrimage date was 8 October, and about twenty-seven thousand pilgrims found their way to Mecca. Nearly seven thousand of them passed through Jeddah. This was the first time the Hajj had taken place without Turkish involvement since 1833, and it passed off without a hitch.

Colonel Wilson, the 'pilgrimage officer', could breathe a huge sigh of relief, but it could only be temporary. The familiar circular pattern of simmering underlying problems, crisis, then short-term solution seemed likely to continue. At this pivotal period of the revolt, when a strange kind of suspended animation hung over the Hejaz, the injection of a game-changer was near. Wilson's main concern at the Consulate was the imminent arrival of a specialist cipher officer to take some of the huge pressure off Young, Cochrane, and himself. But it would be another little-known junior intelligence officer, arriving at the same time, who would in due course exert his strange influence well beyond Jeddah.

4

Sharing a Cabin with Lawrence

On 12 October 1916 two junior officers from the British Army Intelligence Department in Egypt met at a hotel in Suez. The drab surroundings contrasted with the salubrious Savoy Hotel in Cairo, which had been partly converted into offices for their desk jobs. Their missions were different and both were extremely sensitive. Lieutenant William Lionel Gray (he preferred to be called Lionel) was 33 years old and was the urgently needed cipher officer heading for Wilson's expanding Jeddah team. Five feet nine inches tall with blue eyes and curly brown hair, Gray was London-born and the son of a civil engineer of Irish extraction. An expert in codes before the First World War, he had been hand-picked earlier in the year for a commission in intelligence, after combat service in the Gallipoli and the Western Desert of Egypt. His orders were to meet a 28-year-old captain who had been making his unofficial mark in the shadowy Arab Bureau for rather longer than the older man.

The personalities of the two officers were strikingly different. Gray was outgoing and gregarious. By contrast, Thomas Edward Lawrence, the illegitimate son of an Anglo-Irish baronet, was a noticeably shy man, prone to high-pitched giggling when he felt ill at ease in company. Just 5 feet 5 inches tall with a disproportionately large head, he had piercing pale blue eyes, a penetrating intelligence, and an unmilitary bearing. The eyes were what most people noticed first. Lawrence wore his uniform sloppily and his hair was rather longer than the usual officer cut. Gray, immaculately dressed, had been told to take Lawrence to a steamship that was to carry them down the Red Sea to Jeddah.[1] For both men this was to be their first visit to Arabia. They had no idea that the ripples from that voyage would spread far beyond their own lives.

The forgotten meeting in the Suez hotel is also a marker of a forgotten episode of the Arab Revolt. Lawrence's role included the delivery to Jeddah

of a specially devised secure cipher for sending and receiving secret tele-
grams. The day after the meeting, the Arab Bureau informed Wilson and
Wingate that they had sent a special cipher: 'Lawrence who sailed today on
HMS *Laura* [a misspelling for *Lama*] has copies for Wilson, Boyle and
Parker.'[2]

Lawrence had acted as a cipher courier before: in November 1915 he had
taken a code he had compiled himself to the little port of Sollum, near the
Western Desert of Egypt, when the British forces there realized that the Turks
had broken the one then in use.[3] We have no proof, but on this occasion the
hotel meeting suggests that Gray had compiled the special cipher for Arabia,
and that his orders were to hand it over to Lawrence and brief him on it.

HMS *Lama* had been hurriedly prepared. A small liner converted for use
as an armed boarding steamer with the Red Sea Patrol of the Royal Navy,
she was a late substitute for SS *Maltby*, which had been delayed.[4] A group
of Egyptian dock workers at Port Tewfik, the working heart of Suez, had
toiled in the piercing autumn sun for nearly eight hours to load the ship
with a huge cargo of weapons, ammunition, wheat flour, barley, and medical
supplies.[5] There were nineteen heavy wooden cases, at least two of which
were iron-bound and had been brought to Suez on a special armoured train
under military escort. The dockers had no inkling that these cases contained
£10,000 in gold and £4,000 in silver coins (worth about £1 million now),[6]
to be used on a secret mission in the desert wastes of Arabia.

★　★　★

On their early evening stroll down to the docks, the amiable Gray was
enjoying talking to the oddball Lawrence. The two had not had many dealings in Cairo. Gray, one of a team of cipherers at General Headquarters,
Ismailia, had been locked into a high-pressure world of deadlines and painstaking attention to detail.[7] He was given a break in August when his boss,
Colonel Holdich, sent him to British Headquarters at Salonica in northern
Greece to deliver secret documents, which almost certainly included a new
cipher that he had compiled himself. He travelled there by sea as king's
messenger, in other words as an official government courier.[8] By contrast,
Lawrence had a broader and deeper grasp of the secret world. An expert in
the map room in intelligence, he knew better than anyone else the location
of Turkish military units in Arabia and Greater Syria, which included
Lebanon and Palestine. Part of this knowledge had come from his interrogation of Turkish prisoners, many of whom were Arabs from Ottoman Syria

and Mesopotamia. His knowledge of Arabic, picked up before the war in Syria where he had worked as an archaeologist, was of considerable help. He had been punching above his weight and his strategic thinking was highly regarded by General Gilbert Clayton, for whom he had been moonlighting at the Arab Bureau. Lawrence had also edited and written for the Bureau's *The Arab Bulletin*, a top secret intelligence publication with a very restricted circulation list.

Lawrence told Gray that he was notionally on ten days' leave, but this was just a convenient mechanism for Clayton to prise him from General Headquarters intelligence and get him over to Jeddah on a crucial mission as the diplomat Ronald Storrs' assistant. Clayton, far-sighted and subtle, was delighted to have this unusual officer's involvement, as he valued Lawrence's breadth of vision and acute powers of analysis. Most of the rest of the top brass, as Gray was well aware, thought Lawrence was an insufferable pain in the neck. He seemed to treat the conventions of military life as a joke, and drove senior officers to distraction by his irreverence, untidy uniform, and sarcastic remarks. Captain Lewen Weldon, a fellow intelligence officer in Cairo for a time from December 1914, wrote:

> Lawrence in those days was a weird person…One day I was walking down the street with him when we passed a General. I saluted: Lawrence did nothing. 'Why didn't you salute?' I asked him as soon as we had got clear of the military personage. 'Because I don't know how to', Lawrence said simply…He had two stars on one of his shoulder straps and three on the other.[9]

Lawrence had an exit strategy and wrote: 'I took every opportunity to rub into them their comparative ignorance and inefficiency (not difficult!) and irritated them yet further by literary airs, correcting split infinitives and tautologies in their reports.'[10] Lawrence had had enough of the poisonous atmosphere in Cairo between Military Intelligence and the Arab Bureau, whom the General Staff regarded as intrusive meddlers on their own patch. He was bored and also restless, partly because of the death of two younger brothers, first Frank and then Will, on the Western Front in 1915. He felt he ought to get out into the field, as they had done, rather than stick behind a desk. As he put it later of this period: 'I was all claws and teeth, and had a devil.'[11]

Gray sensed that Lawrence envied his experience of front-line fighting. As a sergeant in the machine-gun section of the Westminster Dragoons, the 2nd County of London Yeomanry Regiment, Gray had taken command after his officer had been killed by a sniper at Suvla Bay, Gallipoli. He had been highly recommended for a commission in intelligence by his fiancée's uncle, Ernest Bentley, who had a key role in the secret war back home. Bentley had friends in government circles, and because of the expertise of his ciphers company he had been given a highly sensitive role researching and developing new codes for the war effort.[12] In a telegram Bentley told Gray he was wanted for 'special work similar [to] mine'.[13] Gray had proved of great help devising codes in Bentley's London office before the war, and the businessman's recommendation meant that Gray was soon plucked from the sandstorms of the Western Desert and dropped into a comfortable intelligence office in the Savoy Hotel. He was determined to make the best of this unlooked-for opportunity.

Gray sensed the potential danger of his exotic new posting. On the day he met Lawrence he wrote to his sister, Cecelia (known as 'Cecil'), in the breathless style of the Victorian *Boy's Own Paper*: 'I have got a good revolver & ammo. & also my faithful servant with a rifle & ammo. Everyone thinks I am a jolly lucky chap & so do I. I might get a small decoration but only might.'[14]

It was still hot at six o'clock that evening as Gray and Lawrence boarded the *Lama* with a motley collection of officers, their servants, and civilians. The key man was Ronald Storrs, Oriental Secretary to the British High Commissioner in Cairo and, as we have seen, one of the architects of British involvement in the Arab Revolt. Captain Thomas Goodchild was on a bizarre secret mission accompanied by a disaffected Australian Major, Harold Suttor, and six Bedouin camel men, who looked distinctly uncomfortable as they left dry land behind them. Also walking up the gangplank were a police chief for Jeddah, two Arab interpreters for a British spymaster in the Hejaz, and an Arab secret agent called Hajj Abbas who was on a dangerous operation for the British.[15]

These men had been thrown together at a time of crisis, their various missions aimed at regaining the military and political advantage, as the Turks threatened to march out of Medina and recapture Jeddah and Mecca. The most important mission was that of Storrs and Lawrence. They were to assess the present state of the revolt, which was stalling and risked collapse. Lawrence was also to assess the four sons of Sherif Hussein for their leadership potential. Clayton trusted Lawrence but had other, devious motives for sending him: he knew that Lawrence, like himself, was opposed to sending British troops to the Hejaz, and that his report was bound to support the argument against this course of action. He also wanted Lawrence to wrongfoot Colonel Brémond's French Military Mission. Lawrence would have no qualms about this: he mistrusted French imperial motives in the Middle East and thought they had no right to Syria.

Clayton knew that Storrs and Lawrence were well matched and got on well.[16] The two men had met in July that year, when Storrs sought Lawrence's help to design some postage stamps for the Hejaz to proclaim its new independence to the world, in time for the Muslim pilgrimage. This scheme was typical of the politically savvy Storrs, who recognized the propaganda value of stamps on pilgrims' letters home. Storrs was on his third visit to the Hejaz: his last trip had been barely a month before, for the arrival of the Holy Carpet, and he was now on his way back at the urgent request of Abdullah.

By contrast, the forgotten mission of the amiable Goodchild was far narrower in scope. Thirty-seven years old and a veterinary officer in the Remounts Department, which procured, trained, and cared for all the animals needed by the Army, he was the man in charge of the £14,000 in gold and silver coins in those heavy iron-bound crates. He was on an extraordinary and politically sensitive secret operation to buy baggage camels for the British army in Egypt from the most important family of camel breeders in the Hejaz, which just happened to be that of Sherif Hussein himself.

Storrs makes an intriguing reference to Goodchild and Suttor in his diary, saying that on the *Lama* were 'two young vets. going to Jeddah to buy, as a first consignment, £10,000 worth of camels. Lawrence shared a cabin with one of the vets.'[17] Goodchild must have been the man.[18] He kept a diary in which he jotted down snapshots of shipboard life: the gold and silver coins were kept in a specially secure cabin; the six camel men had their own quarters at the stern or rear of the ship; SOS signals were picked up during the first night from a ship in the Mediterranean.

The voyage had begun the day after the men boarded the *Lama*, and it had not got off to a good start. As Storrs put it, 'ten minutes after the Commander had remarked upon the ill omen of a departure on Friday 13th, the bursting of two boiler tubes...was broken to us by the Chief Engineer'.[19] The ship was also loaded two feet above the safety line. The *Lama* limped steadily on in the appalling heat and Storrs was becoming more and more disgruntled. He was tired of the long trips down the Red Sea and became fractious because, apart from Lawrence, the company and conversation were not up to what he considered his own high standards. As Lawrence put it, 'Storrs' intolerant brain seldom stooped to company.' He walked around the decks and 'sniffed, "No one worth talking to" and sat down'.[20]

Storrs was also fed up with the noise caused by some of the passengers blasting away on deck with their revolvers. He grumpily noted that, 'Revolver practice on deck at bottles after lunch, in which I was too sleepy to take part, tore my ears and effectively ruined my siesta.'[21] Gray was one of those happy to join in with this novel way of coping with the tedium of the voyage: 'Have been having lots of fun firing at bottles chucked into the water with our revolvers...We tied a bottle to a boom & fired from about 15 yards or so'.[22] Lawrence probably thought up the target practice stunt. He had been an expert shot since his Officers' Training Corps days at Oxford University, and his long and sometimes dangerous walks through Syria and Lebanon before the war. He had an impish sense of humour and would probably have enjoyed annoying Commander Charles Scott and his naval officers with the noise. The officers would have been all the more aggrieved since they had given up their cabins for this unusual bunch of passengers.

Later Gray watched Lawrence stroll around the deck with the fastidious Storrs, who was immaculately clad in a white tropical suit. Gray had been able, like Storrs, to see beyond Lawrence's natural shyness, to other aspects of his complicated make-up—flashes of insight, empathy, the intuitive ability to get inside other people's heads. A provocative and brilliant talker when in the mood, Lawrence also had a great gift for silence and was a good listener—an important attribute for an intelligence officer. His reticence could readily morph into that mischievous sense of humour, which brought out his acting ability and helped hide the shyness.[23]

Lawrence's sense of humour even ran to teaching Storrs about ciphers on the voyage—perhaps even about the very cipher that Gray seems to have delivered into his care. Lawrence thought the normal rules for a cipher officer—in fact for any army officer—were tiresome.[24] Gray makes no mention of these discussions in his letters home.

Gray wrote to his sister, Cecil, again on 15 October, two days into the three-day journey to Jeddah. He was moved by the brilliance of the reflected night sky: 'You could, if you were here, see the stars come up right out of the water & would think they were ships' lights. They have often been reported as such.' The SOS signals picked up the previous night (mentioned in Goodchild's diary) had at first excited the ship's crew who thought they came from close at hand. In fact they had come from the Mediterranean near Malta. Gray thought the SOS call probably resulted from a German submarine attack. Submarines had done huge damage, and even on the other side of the well-protected Suez Canal, they caused anxiety to the Red Sea Patrol of the Royal Navy. Gray describes the fog of war and a jittery gun crew:

> Recently a Dutch submarine was on its way through this way to Dutch East Indies under escort of a tug. The *Mongolia* fired 5 shots at her by mistake. Last night they were saying here she was a German sub in disguise & she should have been sunk & not allowed through the Canal. Of course that was all nonsense as the Admiralty had issued instructions about her.

★   ★   ★

Gray was relieved that the voyage of the *Lama* was nearly over. Dropping off the two Arab interpreters/spies at Rabegh provided a welcome break and a brief change of scene: the men had been sent to work for Colonel Alfred Parker, senior intelligence officer in the Hejaz who was based at the port. At seven o'clock in the morning of the third day, 16 October, the ship put down her anchor in Jeddah's outer harbour, about a mile from the walled town. The three parallel and dangerous coral reefs could be negotiated only by a small boat. Shortly before nine o'clock, Gray's spirits were lifted at the sight of the Union Flag at the bow of Colonel Wilson's launch as it steadily approached the *Lama*. John Young was on board to welcome the men and collect the first batch of passengers. The second batch was picked up an hour later. Thirty-six Arabs from the town were needed to transport the massive cargo to the quayside in their triangular-sailed dhows.[25] Lawrence memorably described arriving at Jeddah: 'then the heat of Arabia came out like a drawn sword and struck us speechless'.[26]

 The men were greeted at the customs wharf by a cobbled-together guard of honour and by Storrs's 'Persian Mystic', Ruhi. They traced the route past the customs house and through the fly-ridden market that Colonel Wilson had taken three months earlier. At the Consulate they dispersed, Goodchild and Suttor heading for quarters at the nearby office of the shipping agents Gellatly Hankey. Gray was shown to his spacious room on the second floor of the Consulate, next to Cochrane's at the back of the building. The view from Gray's shuttered windows with their cotton awnings was of a deserted open area with, to the left, the adjoining Austrian Consulate, which the British had been quick to commandeer for extra accommodation.[27] The new arrival warmed to Wilson who treated him well.[28] The hard-to-please Storrs was not inclined to be charitable: 'Found Wilson in a rather defiant mood: uncertain whom he represented and from whom he was to take orders.'[29] But Storrs was probably not fully aware of the huge pressure that Wilson had been under for the past four months.[30]

While Gray explored the mess rooms and the main office, then threw himself into a huge workload, Wilson and Storrs rode out through the Medina Gate for a brief courtesy call on Sherif Abdullah, Hussein's second son. Concerned about fever in Jeddah, Abdullah and his bodyguard were camping about four miles outside the walls. But the real business of the day would follow that afternoon, when Abdullah came to the Consulate. There he was hit by a triple blow. First, Storrs had to tell him that he had not come with the £10,000 that Abdullah had requested in a personal appeal (the British line was that Hussein's subsidy of £125,000 per month was quite enough). Then came the news that the hapless Wilson had only just heard about. The British had finally decided, after much shilly-shallying, to overturn their previous line and abandon the possibility of sending troops to Rabegh to support Hussein. The risk of upsetting the sensibilities of Muslim tribesmen, and in particular of tipping India into rebellion, was held to be just too great. The British and Abdullah were well aware of the likelihood that the revolt would collapse if the Turks broke out of Medina, via Rabegh, to re-take Jeddah and Mecca. The news got even worse for Abdullah: the British were withdrawing a flight of aeroplanes that had been promised and even despatched in 'flat pack' crates to Rabegh.

The following day, 17 October, Abdullah visited the Consulate again. He was appalled to hear from his younger brother Feisal, who was closer to Medina, that his forces were being bombed by Turkish aircraft, just as the British ones were being withdrawn. As Wilson put it, Abdullah 'had us on toast...and personally I felt a worm at times because we have changed our minds such a lot'.[31] Abdullah made dignified but fruitless attempts to get the British to change their mind again. Sherif Hussein badgered Storrs that afternoon by telephoning time after time on the same subject. Gray took a superb photograph of Abdullah, lost in his thoughts, seated on the verandah in front of Wilson, Ruhi, Said Ali (Hussein's Minister of War), and Aziz Ali al Masri, Chief of Staff of the Arab regular army. Gray wrote: 'Great dinner party last night with captured Turkish band which played Turk music. Fearful row and we had to tell them to shut up. Abdullah was chief guest.' Gray and Lawrence sat opposite each other, at the less important ends of the table.[32]

★   ★   ★

Lawrence had been listening carefully to everything he heard. He sent a perceptive telegram to Clayton on 18 October reporting on the discussions with Abdullah and saying that nobody really knew what was going on at

Rabegh.[33] Young remarked on Lawrence's quiet self-sufficiency: he would glide into a room like a cat and,

> always modest and unassuming, could easily dissociate himself from his sur-roundings. When he wrote his reports in our mess room he was unperturbed by the talk going on around him and would even, when so occupied, join in the conversation, and again take his pen to pick up the even thread of his elaborate and well-turned sentences.[34]

Lawrence went with Storrs and al Masri by sea to Rabegh the next day, and met Sherif Ali, the eldest of Hussein's four sons, and the youngest son, Zeid. Lawrence was not impressed by the potential of either for military leader-ship. Fortunately the far-seeing officer had Abdullah's written permission, with Hussein's sanction, to visit the 31-year-old third son, Feisal, inland. Lawrence then went by camel on a dangerous 100-mile journey, across land controlled by pro-Turkish or neutral tribes, to meet Feisal on 23 October at Wadi Safra. Feisal was exhausted and his spirits were low after a series of setbacks against the Turks. Lawrence found him looking 'very tall and

Figure 5. Emir Abdullah, Sherif Hussein's second son, seated at the British Consulate, Jeddah, on 17 October 1916. Standing from left: Hussein Ruhi, Said Ali (Egyptian Army artillery officer), Colonel Cyril Wilson, Aziz Ali al-Masri (former officer in Ottoman Army and Arab nationalist).

Figure 6. British Consulate, Jeddah. Meetings were held on the large projecting balcony on the third floor (side elevation, to the left). The commandeered Austrian Consulate is to the right.

pillar-like, very slender, in his long white silk robes and his brown head-cloth bound with a brilliant scarlet and gold cord...His hands were crossed in front of him on his dagger.' The meeting got off to a difficult start, but the next morning, hearing the passion in Feisal's speech and seeing how he had managed to unite a number of fractious tribes behind him, Lawrence felt that here was a leader he could have confidence in. He later wrote, 'I felt at first glance that this was the man I had come to Arabia to seek—the leader who would bring the Arab Revolt to full glory.'[35] These dramatic words are perhaps rather disingenuous as well as astonishingly arrogant. Lawrence had been immersed in raw intelligence and its analysis for two years before his first visit to Arabia. It would be surprising if he did not already have a shrewd idea, having decided that Abdullah was too ambitious and not pliable enough, that the British should pin their hopes on Feisal, who had been taking the lead in military operations.

And Lawrence's grandiose rhetoric masked a truth he wished to conceal. He made no mention of Bray's astute intelligence report of 18 October 1916, written after his earlier mission to Rabegh with Wilson. This report had already highlighted Feisal's potential as a leader and recommended that a British liaison officer should be sent to help him cut the Hejaz railway. Bray's paper was completed five days before Lawrence met Feisal for the first time.[36] Lawrence later fell out with Bray, and it is not surprising that the Indian Army officer's name is not one of the forty who Lawrence said in the Preface to *Seven Pillars of Wisdom* 'could each tell a like tale' to his own. Bray's role has been all but forgotten, lost in the darkness beside the limelight that was to shine on Lawrence. Those same deep shadows cloaked the often vital efforts of Wilson and the rest of his Jeddah circle. Without their crucial work, the Arab Revolt could already have been blown off course or sunk, through Hussein's indecisiveness and intransigence, and the plotting of jihadists and other dangerous foes. But treacherous waters still had to be navigated: the game was afoot and Wilson had every intention of carrying on playing it.

5

'Just go on sticking it'

Wilson and Lawrence both had a strong moral compass, but their personalities were markedly different. Storrs had almost certainly given Lawrence his opinion of Wilson during their talks in Cairo and on HMS *Lama*'s long, slow voyage. On the day they arrived at Jeddah, Storrs had written: 'Wilson impresses Lawrence also as being irritable and aggressive, & totally unsuited for anything beyond Provincial Administration, which he does exceedingly well.'[1] But Storrs was careful to confine these snide comments to his diary and kept them out of his official reports. This was because he had been afraid, from the very beginning of the revolt, of being given the poisoned chalice of Wilson's job. Storrs' put-down should also be seen in context: Wilson had been doing an exceedingly difficult job, almost alone and suffering from ill health, for four months. He had told Hussein many times that troops were being held on stand-by and that aircraft were about to arrive, only to be mortified when told by Wingate the day before the meeting with Abdullah that the plug had been pulled on them. And to cap it all, Wilson was told about the political football of the Rabegh affair by an annoyingly flippant junior officer, new to Arabia, who wouldn't even wear his uniform properly. So of course Wilson was irritable.

Wilson had been kept in the dark again, and his sterling efforts to keep the Arab Revolt from foundering deserved better than this shabby treatment. Wilson was soon to take out his annoyance on an easier target, the young upstart, telling Clayton: 'Lawrence wants kicking and kicking *hard* at that then he would improve.' He added that Lawrence was 'a bumptious young ass who spoils his undoubted knowledge of Syrian Arabs etc by making himself out to be the only authority on war, engineering, running HM's ships and everything else. He puts every single person's back up I've met, from the Admiral down to the most junior fellow.'[2] The irony of this situation is that the long-suffering Wilson almost certainly had only a hazy idea of Lawrence's own backstage role in the revolt.

What Wilson would have known, however, was something that Lawrence never acknowledged in writing, and almost certainly never spoke about either: the young officer had relied heavily on Hussein Ruhi for much advice and guidance. Storrs sent Ruhi to Lawrence's Cairo office, before the *Lama* voyage, 'to pass on all he had discovered about the Hejaz, the tribes, routes, wells, and distances...Ruhi, whom I had instructed to watch over him in the beginning, told me that Lawrence came to him in Jeddah for further information about the customs and habits of the Hejaz Arabs.' Ruhi compiled a vocabulary of local vernacular Arabic expressions for Lawrence, and commented that Lawrence spoke Arabic with a 'horrible mispronunciation'. And it was Ruhi who first suggested that it would be wise for Lawrence to wear Arab robes, so as to blend in to his surroundings to some extent.[3]

★   ★   ★

While tensions and hypocrisy eddied around the Consulate and plans for injecting new life into the revolt were discussed, Gray had other things on his mind. As he told his mother,

> Everyone in the world has heard that we now have a cipher officer & they are increasing the cabling accordingly. I cannot say very much about what I am doing at present...I have been working very hard today & can hardly keep my eyes open just to write this.[4]

As Gray explained to his younger sister, Cecil, he had to encipher 'all the secret & official messages...and translate the sheets of figures, which arrive from all parts, into intelligent messages'.[5] The figures were sometimes mutilated in transmission or mistakes were made enciphering at the other end: this could mean that much time was needed to get the message straight.

The context for this punishing regime was that intelligence-related work was arguably more important in the Arab Revolt than in any other theatre of the First World War, and encrypted cables were a key aspect.[6] Late 1916 saw a surge in such work and on one day Gray had to deal with fifty-seven cables.[7] Significantly, the British were intercepting Turkish wireless communications.[8]

In addition, the anguished debate about the high risks of landing infidel British troops at Rabegh, so near the Holy Places of Islam, had surfaced again and generated much extra cable traffic. And when Sherif Hussein assumed the title 'King of the Arab Nation' on 29 October, without any warning, it caused diplomatic convulsions for the Foreign Office and Britain's allies and imperial rivals, the French, resulting in a huge number of cables. As we have seen, the two countries and Russia had signed the secret Sykes-Picot Agreement in May 1916, which made arrangements for splitting the Ottoman Empire between them at the end of the war. This would keep Hussein from Syria and many other regions, contrary to what the British had already promised him.[9] Finally, Gray had to cope with secret messages from a number of other sources, including Lawrence, whose reports were, at least initially, sent via Jeddah. A prodigious number of telegrams and letters streamed in from Wingate in Khartoum as well as from General Headquarters in Cairo. These messages all had to be decrypted and then the cipher officer had to encrypt the replies, while all the time Wilson was generating additional work through his frequently wordy reports and telegrams.

When it all got too much, Gray dragged himself out briefly one afternoon to see the captured Turkish trenches outside the Medina gate. There was brief respite on 3 November for the official coronation of King Hussein: 'This is Coronation day and the town crier was round this morning ordering everyone to celebrate it...whether they want to or not, for fear of having their houses raided and any articles of value they have, seized'.[10] In occasional breaks he took more stunning photographs, hundreds of which survive.[11] Gray was thrilled to have been in 'lots of places where no white man has ever been' (probably an exaggeration), and was proud at having entertained Sherif Hussein's Minister of War, the Egyptian-born Kaisuni—'as big as Kitchener, or bigger'—at another dinner for Sherif Abdullah.[12] But these were fleeting escapes as inevitably a huge amount of work accumulated. Gray started at 6.30 some mornings and went on until dinner, often without a break. Soon after dinner was over at 9.15 pm, exhausted, he would often startle himself from sleep at the dining table when his pipe dropped from his mouth and clattered on to the wooden floor. Even then he sometimes had to force himself back to his office for particularly urgent work.[13]

The surreal quality of Gray's life at Jeddah kept breaking through. While the fate of the revolt hung precariously in the balance, he found himself troubled by stamp collectors. Some of his former colleagues were badgering him for the first issue postage stamps of an 'independent' Hejaz—the stamps that had been designed by Lawrence and Storrs. They had become valuable and so were hot property.[14]

For all these diversions, the pressure on Gray was close to unbearable. Colonel Wilson saw the strain that his cipher officer was under and the risks to his health in Jeddah's harsh climate. Gray was waging a vain fight against an unspecified ailment known as 'Jeddah fever', to which Europeans were particularly vulnerable. In his stoical way he tried to make light of his trials, writing: 'This is a show for work but the Colonel is a champion. He insists that my health is more important than my work in a way. If I am sick...he sends for his horse and I am compelled to go out on it'.[15]

Wilson followed the chivalric, paternal code of the army officer, and this sense of a duty of care extended to his junior staff. But his solicitude was to have a very unfortunate result. On 11 November Gray joyfully galloped into the desert with Major A. J. Ross, Commander of 'C' Flight, 14 Squadron Royal Flying Corps, which had four aeroplanes at Rabegh.[16] Gray had been asked to guide Ross to potential emergency landing grounds near Jeddah, in case Rabegh had to be evacuated. Gray was an expert horseman and was enjoying the freedom of the moment, but this did not save him from being thrown from Wilson's Arab pony and he hit his head on the hard sand, suffering severe concussion. His fever, which may have been malaria, probably played a part in the accident. The pony 'came down with me while galloping...the Col. was awfully decent & made me stay in bed for 3 days...I slept most of the time...He had two doctors to examine me, one from the navy.'[17]

During Gray's illness, Wilson pressed at once for an assistant, saying that Gray had more work at Jeddah than he and three others had in Egypt at General Headquarters Ismailia. For the time being, Wilson's dependable John Young and William Cochrane did their best to help, as did the camel-buying Captain Thomas Goodchild and Major Harold Suttor. But these four had no expertise in ciphering.[18] Ciphering help arrived before too long: Major Weldon, a 'dug-out' brought back from retirement, arrived from the Sudan in late November,[19] followed in mid-December by Lieutenant Arnold from the Essex Regiment in Cairo as a second assistant cipherer.[20] Two non-commissioned officers also arrived at Jeddah in mid-December to help Wilson with administrative work.[21]

★ ★ ★

Just two weeks before Wilson was confronted by the new crisis of Gray's concussion, Lawrence had ridden from Feisal's camp at Wadi Safra to the little port of Yenbo, to the north of Rabegh and lying 320 km north of Jeddah. A British ship was due to arrive there on or about that day, 26 October. Lawrence was keen to get back to Cairo to deliver his report. When the ship was delayed—for a full five days, as it happened—Lawrence used the opportunity to write an astonishingly precise and eloquent paper of some seventeen thousand words which, unlikely though it would have seemed, was to provide a springboard for the future course of the revolt. Living in a small house on the waterfront, this junior officer who had no military training or battlefield experience used his analytical skills to draw out two conclusions that ran counter to the views most British officers had been promoting. First, Lawrence thought there should be no large force of British troops in the Hejaz, just a small mission to advise and train the Arabs on the coast. He knew the Turks would use any large landing as propaganda against infidel Christians near the Holy Places, and that many tribes could turn against Hussein as a result. While this was just the recommendation that Clayton wanted and expected Lawrence to make, General Wingate, Colonel Wilson, Colonel Parker, and other senior officers were all pressing for troops to be sent in.

Lawrence's other main conclusion was also contentious. Storrs and other British officials thought Abdullah would be a more dynamic leader of the Arab forces in the field. Lawrence, following in Bray's wake, put forward Feisal as a leader and as what he called the 'prophet' of the revolt. He described Feisal as 'almost regal in appearance...hot tempered, proud and impatient', but 'full of dreams, and the capacity to realise them'.[22]

That Lawrence's views were not only carefully studied but also acted upon is extraordinary testimony to his broad knowledge, his presentation skills, and his surefootedness in bureaucratic infighting. Bray, whose report advocating Feisal was also considered by Clayton in his big decisions, was airbrushed out of the narrative by Lawrence. It is true that Lawrence knew all the major players in Cairo and was adept at wrong-footing those whose views he disagreed with. He also succeeded in outmanoeuvring Colonel Brémond, following the arrival at last of Captain 'Ginger' Boyle on HMS *Suva*. Boyle was startled by the 'small, untidily dressed and most unmilitary figure...hands in pockets and so without a salute'.[23] Lawrence was needed in Khartoum to brief General Wingate directly. The *Suva* took him down to Jeddah where he found Vice-Admiral Rosslyn Wemyss and HMS *Euryalus*, the flagship of the Red Sea Patrol. Wemyss wanted to hear all about Lawrence's mission. So did the scheming Colonel Brémond, who invited Wemyss and Lawrence to dinner. Lawrence knew that the French Colonel wanted a large number of Allied troops in the Hejaz to help control events and prevent the revolt from spreading to Syria. Lawrence stunned him by saying that a large force was unnecessary because all the Arabs had to do was command the higher ground, with its almost impassable defiles, between

Medina and the coast. So Rabegh would be safe and why all the fuss? Brémond was wrong-footed a second time when Lawrence promoted Feisal as leader: he was known not to trust the French and Brémond had never met him.

Lawrence arrived at Khartoum with Wemyss on 7 November and impressed Wingate with his clear thinking. Around this time the Red Sea Patrol had to make a show of cooperation with the French navy, whose warships *Pothuau* and *d'Entrecasteaux* joined HMS *Hardinge* in bringing reinforcements of Arab Army men and artillery to Rabegh on 8 and 10 November.[24] Nevertheless, the British were always keen, using the political prestige of the Red Sea Patrol, to score points against the French whenever the opportunity arose. On 16 November, Sherif Feisal arrived at Rabegh from Yenbo on the armed boarding steamer HMS *Scotia*. With him were twenty-eight sheikhs from the Juheina tribe, who were shown all the guns and given a demonstration of their firepower. This charm offensive was dampened somewhat when Feisal's brother, Ali, was invited on board, and the emirs promptly launched into a heated row which tested Colonel Alfred Parker's considerable diplomatic skills.[25]

Figure 7. Colonel Edouard Brémond (centre, looking at camera), head of French Military Mission, Jeddah. Captain Norman Bray to right.

Figure 8. House of Sherif Mohsen, Hussein's representative at Jeddah. Mohsen is on the horse to the left; General Bailloud, chief of French forces in the Middle East, is on his horse to the right.

Meanwhile Lawrence had travelled on to Cairo and met Gilbert Clayton, head of the Arab Bureau, on 16 November. Lawrence moved swiftly to stymie the pro-intervention lobby, which was still strong. In his dealings with Wingate and other senior officers he had no qualms about using stratagems and subterfuge, so determined was he to push through the policy he was convinced was right. He wrote a concise four-page memorandum for Clayton whose non-intervention argument was seized upon by General Murray, Wilson's nemesis at the Cairo meeting. This report was perfectly in line with Murray's wish to keep troops back for the Palestine push and not waste them in an Arabian adventure. Lawrence's argument won the day and his paper was sent to London for a decision.

Clayton wanted to keep Lawrence in Cairo to run the Arab Bureau's new propaganda department. Wingate, however, wanted Lawrence to be a temporary unofficial liaison officer to Feisal based at Yenbo—the post that Bray had been the first to propose. So Lawrence returned to Yenbo in late November and was pitched immediately into a crisis. On 1 December, General Fakhri Pasha, the Turkish commander at Medina, left the town with two brigades, intending to recapture Yenbo. Feisal had been camped outside the port with about nine thousand men, but many had melted into the desert after military setbacks. By 9 December, the poor judgement of Feisal's brothers, Ali and Zeid, meant that Arab forces were under great pressure: they hastily retreated from the Turks and the route to Yenbo lay open. Lawrence, sleepless after forty-eight hours' hectic activity, was in despair and cabled Wilson that Feisal now felt that without British troops in Rabegh, the whole revolt could collapse in three weeks. Lawrence had been using pigeons, sent to him by the Arab Bureau, to carry messages between him and Feisal's camp.[26] Lawrence now saw his strategy and his dreams disappearing into the sand like desert rain.

Ironically, Lawrence was for a time in agreement with Captain Norman Bray, who now reappears in our story. Bray had gone to London following his successful anti-jihadist campaign in the Hejaz and his involvement at Rabegh with Wilson. He had taken a diametrically opposite line to Lawrence, arguing like Wilson that a British brigade was vitally needed at Rabegh, and he was now fighting his corner in the imperial capital. Here he had another long talk with Sir Mark Sykes, was seen by the head of Military Intelligence, and, to cap it all, had a private audience for one hour with King George V. But Sir William Robertson, Chief of the Imperial General Staff, disagreed strongly with Bray's line. He had endorsed General Murray's support for Lawrence's paper arguing against a British brigade, and this view carried the day.

Fortunately for Lawrence, his despair about the unravelling of the Arab forces in front of Yenbo was short-lived, and he could soon go back to Plan A. Five ships of the Royal Navy's Red Sea Patrol made a crucial intervention to stop Yenbo falling again to the Turks. Naval firepower and seaplane attacks deterred them, and the enemy troops were also unnerved by the ships' powerful searchlights as they swept the plain behind the port. Fakhri had camel transport and other logistical problems too, and failed to sustain his attack during the night of 11/12 December. This in effect ended Turkish hopes of retaking Yenbo.

Lawrence, the young officer with no combat experience, could say that he was right all along about keeping British troops away from Rabegh. He was soon given a permanent appointment as liaison officer with Feisal. Lieutenant-Colonel Stewart Newcombe, originally destined for the role, was to lead a very small British military mission to the Hejaz to give advice and other support to the Arabs. Lawrence had seamlessly morphed from being Storrs' intelligence aide to being a key delegate on the ground at the heart of the revolt. It was knowledge of his trickery, though, that had led to Wilson's outburst against the 'bumptious young ass'—he knew that Lawrence had at times bypassed him to send a cable direct to Clayton or Wingate (Wilson was his boss and everything should have gone through him). At other times, Lawrence brazenly claimed that he could not understand cabled instructions with which he disagreed because they had become garbled when encrypted. As a result of all this, Wilson was opposed to Lawrence's return but his wishes were overruled.

★   ★   ★

Following the re-emergence of Bray, Gray now also returned to the stage. He had recovered from the concussion suffered in his riding accident, but was back to his default position of working under considerable strain and was suffering from the usual Jeddah ill health. Captain George Lloyd from the Arab Bureau, who had come to Jeddah partly to thwart French moves to take over the Ottoman Bank there,[27] reported: 'The whole of this office is down with fever just at the busiest moment and yesterday we finished up at 3 a.m. There is enough telegraph work to keep six people ciphering and deciphering all day. Indeed six were so doing yesterday.'[28] Gray thought his Jeddah fever could be malaria, and he was being given injections of quinine to counter his delirious ramblings. He was sometimes working 18 hours a day, but knew he had 'to stick to it though until we win through or get kicked out . . . The installation of W/T [wireless telegraphy] here just about doubled my work recently but it proved a valuable asset just in time.'[29] The last three words are intriguing and must relate to vital signals intelligence regarding Turkish intentions. Writing of Jeddah, Gray told his mother, 'we are likely to be pressed here & may have to resort to our Navy for refuge soon'.[30] He, Young, and Cochrane were all acutely aware that the Turks still posed a real threat to Rabegh too if not to Yenbo.

Gray was soon to find himself at Rabegh, the dusty little port in the back of beyond that had been the focus of so many thoughts, fears, reports, and heated discussions, from junior officers on the ground to the War Committee and Cabinet Office in London. After he turned away from Yenbo, Fakhri Pasha and his troops had headed south and had got to within 50 kilometres of Rabegh. British alarm bells were now ringing once again. Gray's ciphering skills were needed at the current hot-spot of the revolt, and perhaps he had been called upon for other work too. He wrote to his old boss, the code expert Ernest Bentley: 'now on board H.M.S. "Scotia" off Rabegh where I have come with Colonel Wilson on a special mission'.[31] He gives a valuable eye-witness account of the bustling activity at the port, whose harbour offered a fine deep-water anchorage for large vessels. 'There has been a little excitement here recently, & it is not quite over yet... Aeroplanes are busy this morning. I have watched two arrive back from reconnaissance. They have been doing very useful work & report that Turks are retiring.' Gray counted three French ships and five British ones at Rabegh. Major Herbert Garland, who was ill and about to leave for Suez on a French warship, said he would post the letter to Bentley. Garland was a demolition expert who had begun to teach Lawrence and the Arabs at Yenbo about explosive charges.

Wilson was at Rabegh partly because General Wingate insisted that he had a change of air. Wilson was running on empty. He had spoken of sleep-lessness and of an addled brain. The day before Lawrence had written to him in despair, fearing that without British troops at Rabegh the entire revolt might collapse. Wilson himself had been the subject of anxious debate about his state of mind. Wingate had written to Clayton:

> I am getting very nervous about Wilson's health and feel that he may break down at any moment—he is altogether overworked... I doubt anyone stand-ing the extraordinary strain which the present situation must cause to those situated as he is in the midst of that network of intrigue and inefficiency.[32]

Wilson's approach had for months been: 'Just go on sticking it... it's the only thing a decent man can do'.[33] But Wingate had to intervene. Citing a med-ical necessity, he told Wilson that he would be replaced at Jeddah for the time being by another of his old Sudan hands, Major Hugh Pearson.

★ ★ ★

Wilson had escaped the enervating grip of Jeddah but he remained in the thick of things. By 24 December, he and Gray were on dry land at Rabegh where they met the British advisers Major Joyce, Major Davenport, Major Dobson, Captain Goslett, and Major Macintosh.[34] Gray gave a dramatic first-hand account of the retreat of Ali, King Hussein's eldest son. From his Rabegh base he had pushed north towards Wadi Safra, in a joint attempt with Feisal's forces to frustrate the Turks' advance. Ali's retreat had apparently been based on a false rumour.[35] Gray recorded that he arrived back at Rabegh,

> post-haste... I believe he had to run like the devil. He was going on so merrily when a tribe supposed to be friendly he found had joined the Turks & were

coming for him...I met him when he arrived with Aziz al Masri (Minister of War) and Said Ali Pasha (C. in. C. Egyptian forces) also Cadi [of the French Military Mission]. I shook hands with all of them and gave them a welcome. They say this place will fall in 3 days. Of course it won't.

Gray's confidence came from the navy's awesome firepower. The British officers had a 'nice little camp here on sea-shore & I am sharing a big square tent 8 yards by 7 with Capt. Goslett of A.S.C. [Army Service Corps] who is here to look after stores to be handed over to the Sherif's army'.[36]

A familiar face appeared on Christmas Day. Captain Norman Bray had been sent back to the Hejaz by Sir Mark Sykes and General Clayton. Reunited with Wilson, he was to act as his intelligence officer again. But fast-moving military events could not be allowed to stop a traditional British Christmas dinner, or as close as could be managed to one. A turkey and a ham were to be cooked on board one of the three remaining Royal Navy ships at Rabegh, HMS *Minerva*, a cruiser, the *Scotia*, and the *El Kahira*. The officers would also enjoy their unusual 'Rabegh special': two or three raw prunes pickled in brandy and port, which they ate every day after dinner, followed by several whiskies. Gray was less impressed with the normal run of food. The soup the previous night tasted like 'brass spoons'; the mutton was tough and virtually cold; half a tiny carrot was accompanied by one slice of 'the root of some other abominable weed'. At least the bread was good (it was sent ashore by the navy). Gray stoically wrote of the meal that he had eaten worse.

Gray ate much better (including exotic beef and apples) on HMS *Hardinge* off Yenbo on 27 December, where he was present for Wilson's meeting with Feisal to discuss military tactics. Bray and Lawrence were also present. Gray took a stock of the ship's headed notepaper back with him, which served him for a few months. Wilson seemed to have been given a new lease of life in the bracing cold air of Rabegh. By 31 December he was feeling fitter than he had for months,[37] but within a couple of days the Hejaz gremlins were nipping at his heels again: 'This place is a damned place for intrigue like Jeddah.' The Baghdadi and Syrian officers in Feisal's regular Arab Army were rowing with each other and had even come to blows, and 'one can't trust any one of the blighters in this place'.[38]

Wilson's character, however, put him in a unique position to act as go-between and win trust. Captain George Lloyd, a shrewd observer, mentioned

Wilson's gift of dealing with men which matters here. It is curious how well
Wilson has got on with the people who both fear him and like him, much as

the people feared the Delphic oracle although it often spoke in language quite uncomprehended by the people. Just so Wilson whose Arabic no-one except a Soudanese servant could understand impresses the Arab here. It is just a gift.[39]

Wilson would need this gift more than ever, as the Rabegh wind ushered in a new year with all its uncertainties and all its hope.

6

Camels and Secrets

While Wilson and Gray were enjoying their unusual Christmas dinner on the beach at Rabegh, Colonel Hugh Pearson, temporarily in charge at Jeddah, and six other officers demolished a large turkey followed by Wilson's plum pudding, which was considered fair game. Cochrane got out his well-travelled gramophone and while the whisky and gin flowed the men 'played the fool a bit'. The end-of-term atmosphere was accompanied by the thrumming of torrential rain, which stove in the roof of the wireless station on top of the Consulate and tossed aside the aerial: 'for the last two days our wireless communication has been altogether cut'.[1]

One of the officers particularly happy to let his hair down had just come to the end of a bizarre clandestine mission that has been unknown for a century. Captain Thomas Goodchild, the diary-writing veterinary officer who had shared a cabin with Lawrence on HMS *Lama*, had come face to face with the intrigue endemic to Jeddah as he struggled to buy sufficient baggage camels to be shipped back to the Egyptian Expeditionary Force (EEF).

Goodchild, stocky and square-jawed with a broad and fleshy face, was 37 years old and an amiable and popular officer. He was born to a life of privilege at Rotherby Manor House in Leicestershire, where his father was Lord of the Manor and a pillar of society.[2] But when he was barely into his teens, Goodchild's world came crashing down: the house had to be sold and he was withdrawn from his private school after just one term, following the spectacular bankruptcy of his father.[3] After agricultural college, Goodchild escaped the family shame by moving to Egypt. He became an agricultural inspector at Cairo and married there in 1910.[4]

Shortly before the Jeddah mission, Goodchild had been in Cyprus as a Remounts officer, assessing and buying donkeys and mules for the Salonica campaign, which was being fought in Macedonia and Serbia.[5] He was brought back to Egypt at short notice because of the army's urgent need for

thousands of baggage camels. He was given detailed briefing on his forthcoming operation, which would be like no other Remounts mission before
or since. Goodchild was well aware of the huge importance of camel buying
for the British in 1916. The EEF needed the animals to supply large detachments, sometimes more than twelve thousand at a time, of fast-moving
mounted soldiers. Camels were also needed for the expanding Imperial
Camel Corps. General Murray in Egypt was planning a major advance
against the Turks through the Sinai desert to Gaza and on through Palestine,
towards Jerusalem and Damascus. Water, food, ammunition and weapons,
tents, and supplies of all kinds would have to be transported along very
lengthy lines of communication, in frequently sandy surroundings unsuitable
for vehicles. Even though a railway and a water pipeline were being con-
structed in late 1916 from Kantara, near the Suez Canal, to El Arish on the
Sinai coast, huge camel convoys were still needed to distribute supplies to
the troops from the railhead. As Brigadier General Guy Dawnay put it to his
wife on Christmas Day, 1916:

> It necessitated the fitting out of much the biggest desert column that there has
> ever been, with actually *tens* of thousands of camels. No wheels practically:
> camels, camels AND camels! Then we have had to lay a railway 100 miles long
> over a howling wilderness for the supply of the troops, the camels being used
> to carry on the supplies etc. in front of railhead.[6]

In all, the EEF needed more than seventy-two thousand camels, the largest
camel force ever assembled on earth. Camel buying was booming all over
Egypt, the Sudan, Somaliland, Algeria, Tunisia, and India.[7] The objective by
the end of 1916 was fourteen companies of the Camel Transport Corps
(each with 2,030 camels), three battalions of the Imperial Camel Corps, and
two camel Remount depots.[8] A cavalry officer described the vital importance of camels to the Palestine campaign: 'In no other theatre were the
fighting troops so utterly dependent for their supplies upon four-legged
beasts, and without the services of the Egyptian Camel Transport Corps
neither Murray's nor, later, Allenby's men could have carried on the struggle.'[9] In other words, there would have been no prospect of seizing Jerusalem
and Damascus from the Turks without the vital work of camel buyers like
Goodchild and of the Camel Transport Corps.

★ ★ ★

It had all seemed fairly straightforward when Goodchild, the Australian
Major Harold Suttor, and six seasick Bedouin camel men were assailed by

the violent heat of Jeddah on 16 October. The objective was to buy as many camels as possible from Sherif Hussein's family, which controlled camel supplies in the Hejaz. Wilson had played a key role in setting up the mission and would have had high hopes that it would reinforce his already good relationship with Hussein. The wheels of the operation had been well oiled. And the day after arriving at Jeddah, Ronald Storrs had put in a word to Hussein's son, Abdullah, to try to help Goodchild's mission.[10] So from Goodchild's perspective, what could possibly go wrong?

But there were disturbing signs. Sherif Hussein seemed oddly disengaged from the mission before it arrived, prevaricating over how many camels could be obtained, and then saying they would have to be bought in bulk, based on a choice of one of three specimen types sent to Goodchild, but not subject to veterinary inspection.[11] This was clearly unsatisfactory, but Wilson decided he had to make the best of it for the time being. He probably hoped he could nudge Hussein into a less contrary attitude. Goodchild recorded in his diary that the specimen camels turned up quickly, on 18 October. A choice was made, and Wilson arranged with Hussein for 1,000 camels to be delivered in ten days.

Major Harold Suttor must have wondered what he had got himself into. He outranked Goodchild, but because of his Remounts experience Goodchild was entrusted with the £14,000 in gold and silver coins, and with the running of the mission. A 36-year-old Boer War veteran and a wool broker from New South Wales, Suttor was nearly 6 foot tall, wiry, and fit. He and his wife Emily, an army nurse, had met Lawrence in Cairo. Suttor had fought with distinction with the Australian 7th Light Horse Regiment at Gallipoli and in the Sinai campaign in the summer of 1916. So what on earth was he doing buying camels in the back of beyond? At the battle of Romani, in August, he had taken over from his commanding officer who had been wounded. But the two did not get on and his commanding officer insisted that command of the regiment should be given to a less experienced officer. Furious and frustrated, Suttor asked for a transfer to a training regiment and was then moved to the Remount Service.[12]

★ ★ ★

Goodchild's strange mission was just one aspect of the British High Command's wide-ranging strategy. But its location meant that the Hejaz operation had a uniquely political and highly sensitive character, beyond a purely military purpose. British intelligence was inevitably involved, though Goodchild probably had at best no more than a hazy and incomplete vision of the background. The Arab Bureau, on the other hand, would not have been surprised by the games Hussein was playing. It was well aware of the strategic importance of camels as a vital resource in both the Arab Revolt and the Palestine campaign. The bureau was waging a hidden war with Turkish and German intelligence, each side trying to outwit the other by encouraging the purchase of available camel stocks or denying them to the enemy. The Turks were intriguing with tribes they wanted to turn against Hussein and were offering large sums of money for their camels.

Ronald Storrs captured the importance of Hussein in this sub-plot of the revolt:

> We were aware that camels were the indispensable and only effective transport for invaders, and that the Arabs of the Hejaz could marshall them by fleets of myriads, and so were in a position either to speed the Turkish attack, to weaken it by abstention, or seriously to threaten its left flank.[13]

Perhaps Storrs's subtle deviousness made him suggest a camel-buying mission in the Hejaz. A plausible scenario would be that the Arab Bureau suggested to the director of Remounts that Arabia could be a further useful source of camels given the hugely increased demand for them. If the Arab Revolt failed, as was a distinct possibility, then the British would have bought up perhaps much of the major asset the Turks would have needed in any further attack against the Suez Canal. And more money for Sherif Hussein would have demonstrated British good faith at this critical time when otherwise it seemed to be lacking, during the shilly-shallying over British troops for Rabegh. Perhaps Storrs discussed this strategy with his friend Lawrence, who knew a lot about the camel trade of Greater Syria.

Whatever really went on in the run-up to the mission, there are tantalizing suggestions of Arab Bureau involvement. After giving Goodchild his £14,000 on 9 October, the EEF's command paymaster had spoken to Bertie Clayton, head of the Arab Bureau, within forty-eight hours about withdrawals of gold.[14] And Goodchild's boss, the director of Remounts, includes no details of the Jeddah mission in his official war diary—a glaring omission given his copious references to other animal-buying operations, including Goodchild's earlier one in Cyprus.[15] The only reasonable explanation is the apparent channelling of the camel purchase money through the Arab Bureau, and the sensitivity of the mission.

Goodchild and Suttor were inadvertently caught up in a covert camel war, in which the control of camel supplies was a major intelligence and diplomatic objective for the British at the highest levels. Hussein tried to win over Ibn Rashid, the pro-Turk leader of the Shammar federation of tribes of north-central Arabia. The Arab Bureau had told Wilson that 'the Sherif has...been in correspondence with him and if he can win him over the Turks will lose one of their chief camel markets and have a troublesome enemy on their flank'.[16] But Hussein had no success with Ibn Rashid. The British themselves had written to the other member of the triumvirate of powerful leaders in Arabia, Hussein's great rival Ibn Saud, ruler of Nejd in central Arabia, 'asking you to co-operate in the matter of the purchase of camels'.[17] But Ibn Saud was an astute leader who played a long-term game, content to wait and see whether the Sherifian revolt with British help would come out on top, or whether the Turks and Germans would prevail.

The Arab Bureau was acutely aware that the stakes were very high. It had told Wilson: 'Information has been received [this was code for intelligence from intercepted Turkish wireless messages] that on 21st. Turks Medina had spent or proposed to spend about 50,000 pounds on camels.'[18]

★ ★ ★

Goodchild had to stay focused on the logistics of his mission, while a stream of secret camel-related cables pinged in and out of Jeddah like tennis balls over a net, most of them being received and batted back by Gray. Three days after arriving, Goodchild met Suleiman Qabil, the head of the town council, whom Young called 'a cheery if somewhat unscrupulous character'.[19] Qabil told Goodchild that he had to have an armed guard when leaving the walls of Jeddah to choose a site for a camel depot. A site was quickly found and then Goodchild had to do some hard bargaining over the extortionate cost of a new well with a drinking trough. He signed an agreement on watering the camels with Sheikh Ahmed Talat, Sherif Mohsen's secretary and trusty fixer. Goodchild's frustration returned when he could get no news from Mecca on camel deliveries, in spite of telephoning Sherif Hussein three times. He may have spoken to the suspicious Hussein himself, who was reluctant to delegate to his secretary and needed to stay in control of the smallest details. Meanwhile Goodchild and Suttor marked out the picket lines for the camels, and arranged for the tethering ropes and hundreds of bales of tibben (chopped barley straw) and dhurra (sorghum or corn) to be transported in a fleet of carts from the Customs House, where they had been landed from HMS *Dufferin*.

The camels remained elusive, however, and Goodchild was beginning to lose patience. There were occasional compensations. He was delighted to be given a Turkish sword by Wilson, very possibly the one belonging to an officer captured by the Arabs at Taif in September. This officer had been embarked on HMS *Dufferin* for a prisoner-of-war camp in Egypt on 15 November, just two days before Goodchild's diary entry.[20] The camel buyer also had lunch at the French Military Mission, and dinner at Sherif Mohsen's house in honour of the new Italian Consul, Colonel Barnabi.[21] Wilson was wary of Italian claims over some Red Sea islands, and testily described Barnabi as a 'fellow who looks (and probably is) a blighter'.[22] But Goodchild was ambivalent about the meals he enjoyed with Jeddah notables, as some of them were the very people who were frustrating the camel buying. Sherif Mohsen showed his ruthlessness following an ugly brawl recorded by Goodchild, in which some Egyptian soldiers were wounded by local Arabs. Wilson intervened: 'I kicked up the devil's own row and Mohsen wanted to cut the Arabs' right hands off but was prevented by Said Pasha and other officers but Mohsen cut their heads open with his sword.'[23]

On 25 October Goodchild saw six hundred or more Turkish prisoners, but what he really wanted to see was the same number of healthy camels. A few arrived the next day, but they were in poor condition and suffering from mange, a virulent disease that could only be beaten by clipping the camels' coats and dressing them with tar.[24] Sheikh Ahmed was still dragging his heels, so Goodchild asked Wilson to help speed up the camel delivery. While the camels were dribbling in, Wilson assigned Goodchild to ciphering duties to support the beleaguered Gray. Goodchild's diary makes nineteen references to ciphering and decoding, and on six days he was doing this work for virtually the whole day.

By 18 November the EEF was getting fed up. Its chief asked Wingate: 'Can you use your personal influence with Sherif to expedite delivery of camels at Jeddah. Our commission has been there five weeks & has only obtained 71 camels. We are helping Sheriff in every possible way think he should reciprocate.'[25] At last some light is shed on the shenanigans: Sheikh Ahmed kept offering Goodchild unsuitable animals with bad backs. As Wilson explained:

> Majority of camels Mecca and here have wounded backs therefore no use and camels have to be brought into Mecca from varying distances. Sherif has been doing all he can and perhaps is too particular. Average price very cheap about 7 pounds. Suggested to Sherif to raise price but he wishes to get them as cheap

as possible. 72 camels with sores or in dangerous condition requiring say 6 weeks treatment were accepted and more could be got.[26]

In spite of Ahmed's dubious dealing there were 190 camels at the depot by 24 November. But on that day, Hussein astonished Goodchild with a startling volte-face. Wilson wrote: 'Sherif informs me he does not propose to accept any payment for them. He wishes camels to be regarded as a present from him to HM's Government.'[27] Goodchild had mentioned this bizarre change of mind in his diary the previous day, in relation to forty-seven camels that had just arrived from Mecca. In a further twist, Wilson went on to say: 'I understand privately that from beginning he never meant to accept money.'[28] This just does not ring true, as, only four days before, Hussein was still expecting to be paid and Goodchild had been giving a steady stream of gold sovereigns to Sheikh Ahmed, Sherif Mohsen's right-hand man, over the past few weeks. Was Hussein perhaps embarrassed, aware that sub-prime camels had been sold to Goodchild and not wanting his family to lose face?

But the waters in 'this land of intrigue', as Wilson put it, seem to have been even muddier. Young and the Arab Bureau regarded Sheikh Ahmed as 'trustworthy and pro-British',[29] but it seems that Ahmed may have been engaged in some shady private enterprise of his own. Pearson had said that Mohsen and Ahmed were 'working on their own account I believe to line their own pockets'.[30] It seems quite possible that Ahmed was offloading on to Goodchild injured and sick camels that Bedouin raiders had captured from the Turks, who were known to have a shockingly low quality of veterinary care. Perhaps also Ahmed was supplying overworked camels that had been hired out for the recent pilgrimage, or ones which had not been fit enough to transport pilgrims. However sincere were Hussein's protestations about not wishing to be paid, Goodchild was still occasionally buying camels up to 18 December.

A further source of frustration to Goodchild was tersely expressed by General Headquarters: 'Understand that Arabs unwilling to part with their camels as they are obtaining so much money from other sources.'[31] This would have been a killer blow to the camel buyers, who must have felt they were wading through treacle. 'Other sources' probably indicated Turkish bribes. The Turks had also been buying camels: Colonel Alfred Parker, the intelligence chief based at Rabegh, had reported back in October, a week after Goodchild's arrival, that the Turks were well supplied with camels.[32] And there was a yet further complication. We know from Parker's diary that

Goodchild was, bizarrely enough, in competition over camel purchase by 4 November with a British ally, the former Ottoman officer Aziz Ali al Masri, who was in command of Sherifian troops: 'Aziz al Masri, having experienced great difficulty in the purchase of camels, suggested formation of a purchasing board. To this Ali agreed.'[33] Aziz al Masri was working closely with Hussein's son, Ali.

The dice seem to have been loaded against Goodchild from the start. The Bedouin tribesmen were not getting a huge amount of British gold from Hussein, who, as we have seen, had confessed to Wilson that he had *saved* about £200,000 of his first two monthly subsidies totalling £250,000. Clayton complained: 'The Turks have been paying the tribes, but the Sherif could have outbid them easily.'[34] The Turks were buying camels as well as the loyalty of the tribes. The Arab Bureau was monitoring, and trying to frustrate, their attempts. In mid-December it told Wilson: 'Information has been received that mission for buying camels has gone from Medina to Hail.'[35] Hail, in north-central Arabia, was the power base of the pro-Turk Ibn Rashid—the subject of Hussein's unsuccessful charm offensive.

Perhaps Hussein was aware, too, that his loyal fighters wanted to keep their best camels for themselves and their families. It is hard to avoid the conclusion that Hussein had deliberately misled Wilson as well as Goodchild on the prospects for a successful camel-buying mission. Wilson's hopes that camel diplomacy would lead to a strengthened relationship with the Arab leader were dashed. The dead hand of Jeddah intrigue touched all.

The Arab Bureau, too, was no stranger to intrigue. Wilson urgently needed more money for intelligence and other purposes. The bureau recommended that he should be given an extra £500 in gold.[36] The High Commissioner agreed, and just four days later, on 3 November, Goodchild's diary recorded that Wilson took £500 from the consulate safe. This sum could only have come from the camel purchase money. The withdrawal happened *three weeks before* Hussein told Goodchild that he did not want to be paid for the camels. The question has to be asked: did the Arab Bureau already know that most of Goodchild's money would not need to be spent? Did the bureau even intend from the outset to try to shift all or most of the money to its own projects in the Hejaz? It had to fight hard for its resources and would have been very happy to see this sort of sum diverted to intelligence-related work at the Jeddah Agency.

However, the Arab Bureau did not always get all its own way. Goodchild had spent only £2,000 in buying 310 camels, less than a third of the initial target figure of one thousand animals. He had returned the £4,000 in silver coins to Egypt within three weeks of arriving, because of a very unfavourable exchange rate.[37] That left £8,000 in gold unspent. It was the Arab Bureau, whose fingerprints were all over Goodchild's mission, that reported on the underspend. It also made an opportunistic bid to grab it by approaching the command paymaster in Cairo, bypassing the director of Remounts. This is more evidence for the camel-buying funds being channelled through the bureau. But Remounts fought back, saying the underspend was needed for camel purchasing elsewhere. They came out on top in this power struggle, but the bureau did at least prise away an extra £500 for Wilson.[38]

★ ★ ★

While Goodchild was doing his best to cope with the double-dealing and trickery that seemed to be inescapable in Jeddah, he also had to keep a sharp eye open for the sly stratagems of the camels themselves. He would have warned Suttor of the dangers of working with them. The male camels used for transport were cooped up together during the mating season (usually from March to December), when they foamed at the mouth and tended to go mad with lust. They would then attack anyone near them and the results could be deadly. There are military reports of the arms of Egyptian camel attendants being bitten off whole, and in one case of a man's head being bitten off. Camels were grimly methodical in their assaults and were not content with just grievous bodily harm: 'When a camel attacks a man he uses his teeth first, and then attempts to crush the life out of him by kneeling on him and pounding him with his hard horny knees.'[39]

Wilson made full use of Goodchild when the need arose. Not content with drafting him in as an emergency ciphering officer, he asked the camel buyer to escort a Royal Flying Corps officer, 2nd Lieutenant J. N. Wilkinson, 'to view landing place near camels for aeroplanes.' Wilkinson was on the staff of Major A. J. Ross, Commander of 'C' Flight, 14 Squadron Royal Flying Corps (RFC), and the ride out of Jeddah happened on 14 December. The landing ground had already been marked out by Ross, when Gray had taken him to assess possible sites on his ill-fated gallop into the desert the previous month. Here was another symptom of the continuing crisis over Rabegh: the RFC wanted an emergency evacuation landing ground at Jeddah in case they had to get out of Rabegh in a hurry.[40]

Goodchild himself was by now anxious to take his leave of Jeddah as soon as possible. Around Christmas time he had a scare after he and Major

Suttor had noticed items that had been disturbed in their rooms at the ship-ping merchants Gellatly Hankey. This had happened over two days and the following night Goodchild woke up to find an intruder in his room. He challenged the man, who escaped while Goodchild was struggling to get out from under his mosquito net. The story was later told that the man had been outwitted by Goodchild in a camel deal and had come back with a knife to exact revenge; or alternatively that he was a thief looking for that king's ransom in gold sovereigns.[41]

Goodchild's strange experiences as one of Wilson's Jeddah circle had run their course. A camel transport ship, SS *Queensland*, arrived from Port Sudan in late December and 348 bitterly complaining camels were cajoled and prodded on board. As we have seen, Goodchild recorded buying 310 of them, so some at least seem to have been gifts from Hussein. The camels, accompanied by their buyers, arrived at Suez on 4 January 1917. The animals were considered 'mostly in good condition and of a suitable type for ser-vice'.[42] After experiencing all that Jeddah could throw at them, Goodchild and Suttor might have been relieved to settle for a similar report on themselves.

Meanwhile Wilson had tried to be positive over the disappointments of the camel-buying venture. Contrasting with what Colonel Parker had reported in October, he wrote at the end of December: 'All of the informa-tion I have received shows that the Turks have great difficulty in finding camels and the Arabs frequently capture convoys.'[43] Perhaps this reflected covert intelligence work more than Goodchild's mission, but the camel buyer's work undoubtedly contributed to a wide-ranging Arab Bureau strategy. Wilson had benefited from his change of sea air up at Rabegh and Yenbo, but as ever he had been working extremely hard. He set off for Cairo and a few days of well-earned leave. When he returned to take up the reins again in Jeddah, he would take a brave and decisive stance that would help resolve for good the anguished debate over British troops for Rabegh.

7

Combat and Confusion

Wilson was given a shock when he arrived back in Jeddah on 6 January 1917. He discovered that General Wingate had seized on a telegram from Hussein's secretary, Fuad el Khatib, which seemed to accept a landing by Allied troops. Wingate and Brémond swiftly arranged for a joint force to embark from Suez on 9 January. Wilson had apparently called in at Yenbo and spoken to Lawrence there, while returning to Jeddah. He had the courage to change his mind on the issue of British troops for Rabegh, and now agreed with Lawrence's view. He bravely told Wingate that he thought the telegram from Mecca was ambiguous and asked for clarification, but none was forthcoming. When the War Cabinet in London heard of this it decided that a British force would not be sent unless Hussein expressly asked for it. Wilson diplomatically pressed Hussein, who finally stated on 11 January that he did not need Allied troops. This drew a permanent line under the vexed Rabegh question.

Not for the first time, Wilson had risked putting his head on the block on a matter of principle. He gave his advice in clear language knowing full well that Wingate was itching to send troops to the Hejaz, and that he would not take kindly to his old Sudan colleague changing his mind and swinging round to the views of Lawrence—the young officer Wilson had described as an annoying whippersnapper not many weeks earlier. But for Wilson, duty and doing the right thing always came before pride or personal advancement. He also had the decency not to put all the blame on Hussein for his prevarication.[1] If Wilson had not spoken up against Wingate's plan, British troops would have been on the ground within three days, with probable disastrous results for the revolt and the prestige of the British, and perhaps too for the safeguarding of India.

In mid-December Wilson had pressed for the occupation of Aqaba at the northern end of the Red Sea and demolition raids on the Hejaz Railway.

Figure 9. Sherifian soldiers disembarking from a British ship at Rabegh, early 1917.

He was now asking Feisal and Abdullah to let Lieutenant-Colonel Newcombe, Lawrence's boss and in charge of the small British Military Mission, go inland on railway raids. But he thought Newcombe had 'really rather weird ideas, he was under the impression that he was to be actually Commander-in-Chief of the Arab Armies, should order Feisal etc. & tribes about as he liked'. A warning bell rang and Wilson took swift action, spending over a day talking to Newcombe and steering him in the right direction. One of Newcombe's ideas, hit firmly into the long grass by Wilson, was that Cox, an artillery officer, 'should go to Rabegh and live with Zeid in his house to collect information. To anyone knowing the situation it is absurd and just the way *not* to get information.'[2] Wilson's instinctive understanding of Arab sensibilities was curiously similar in some ways to Lawrence's empathy and to his intuitive approach to influencing people. Wilson often found his job irritating and disheartening, but 'thank God I have never lost hope & still believe the Arabs will win through on their own, if they do I shall die happy'. As so often, Wilson's intervention was timely, discreet, and vitally important.

Wilson had helped to scupper Brémond's move to send troops over to Rabegh, but the French officer remained a bugbear: Wilson complained that Brémond went behind his back and spread disinformation with the help of his 'minions in Mecca'.[3] Yet Wilson was very angry that Bray and Newcombe had reported friction between himself and Brémond. He could not help but like his opposite number, who would come round to the Consulate three or four times a week to drink whisky and talk for one or two hours. Wilson was affronted by any perception that he had used underhand methods that may have annoyed Brémond: 'I do no spying & intriguing, never have done & don't propose to begin now.' His sometimes priggish moral code drew a line between deceiving an officer and a gentleman and deceiving anybody else. The reality, however, was more complex. Wilson had discovered (no doubt through Ruhi) the secret codes used by Hussein and his sons, and he somewhat reluctantly made use of the information. And Ruhi had been spying on the French for some time. So there were contradictions, but Wilson's stance over Brémond, seemingly naive and self-defeating at first sight, flags up how principled behaviour can complement the darker arts of espionage and diplomacy. Wilson was an accidental spy, perhaps learning as much from two hours of drinking whisky with Brémond as Ruhi gleaned from piles of reports from his agents in the souks of Jeddah and Mecca. Wilson would not have known, however, that the French had access to the supposedly top secret *Arab Bulletin*.[4]

★   ★   ★

A major shift in the strategy of the revolt was now about to take place and Wilson had played a key role in preparing the ground. It involved in part a 200-mile march up the coast from Yenbo to attack the port of Wejh—the only major Hejaz port still in Turkish hands. If Wejh could be seized then Turkish lines of communication along the railway could be attacked, and in order to defend them the Turks would have to spread their troops thinly over hundreds of miles. This would make it less likely that they would commit large forces against Rabegh and Mecca. Feisal wanted to go on the front foot in this way, but was anxious about leaving Yenbo only lightly defended and vulnerable to Turkish attack. Wilson had resolutely grasped the nettle at Yenbo in late December and assured Feisal that the Arab Regular Army at Rabegh would cope with any such attack, with the help of the Royal Navy. There was no certainty about this, but Wilson sensed at once that, without his word of honour, the nervous and highly strung Feisal would not have moved against Wejh, and the revolt would have risked inertia and worse. Wilson's bravery in giving the assurance verged, unusually for him, on recklessness, but the stakes were very high and, as so often, Wilson was the right man in the right place at the right time.

Lawrence was also doing an important job. As liaison officer with Feisal he had discussed the Wejh scheme in some detail with the Arab leader and arranged with Captain 'Ginger' Boyle of the Red Sea Patrol for supplies to be put ashore for him. On 4 January Feisal led up to ten thousand of his Bedouin warriors, half mounted on camels, on a march from their camp at Nakhl Mubarak the short distance to Owais, inland from Yenbo where the supplies were to be landed. The spectacle of colour and sound, with brightly coloured banners and drums, must have suggested a medieval army of knights and their feudal followers on the move. Lawrence was to write:

> The order of march was rather splendid and barbaric. Feisal in front in white. Sharaf on his right, in red head cloth and henna-dyed tunic and cloak, myself on his left in white and red. Behind us three banners of purple silk, with gold spikes, behind them three drummers playing a march, and behind them a wild bouncing mass of 1,200 camels of the bodyguard, all packed as closely as they could move, the men in every variety of coloured clothes, and the camels nearly as brilliant in their trappings—and the whole crowd singing at the tops of their voices a war song in honour of Feisal and his family! It looked like a river of camels, for we filled up the Wadi to the tops of its banks, and poured along in a quarter-of-a-mile-long stream.[5]

This might have been Lawrence's swan song to his days in Arabia. Wilson had ordered him to hand over his liaison duties to Lieutenant-Colonel Newcombe. Lawrence met him near Um Lejj, halfway between Yenbo and Wejh. The extrovert Newcombe got on well with Lawrence and asked him to stay involved with Feisal up to the attack on Wejh. Lawrence was more than happy with this, but the way the port was captured was to lead to a permanent rift between him and an important member of Wilson's Jeddah circle. Enter once again the energetic Captain Norman Bray, who had met Lawrence, Wilson, and Gray a few weeks earlier at Yenbo. Bray had returned to Jeddah as Wilson's intelligence officer once more. Wilson was delighted: 'Bray is invaluable to me and I am hoping that now I shall be able to send really useful intelligence.'[6] But Bray's combat experience in the trenches of the Western Front meant that he was soon plucked from the Consulate to help lead a seaborne force of 550 Arabs who were to be landed on the far side of Wejh to prevent the Turks from escaping to the north. The plan was that the landing from HMS *Hardinge*, with other ships in support, would be timed to coincide with the main attack, that of Feisal's thousands from the south. The other officer with Bray was Major Charles Vickery, one of Newcombe's Military Mission and a gunner who, like Bray, had given brave service in France. He and Lawrence instantly formed a poor opinion of each other when they met at Um Lejj on 16 January. Vickery outranked Lawrence, who was perhaps disconcerted by the older officer speaking much better Arabic than he did. Vickery seemed to think that the revolt had not achieved much and Lawrence was put out by his offering whisky, forbidden to Muslims, to Captain 'Ginger' Boyle in Feisal's presence. Feisal diplomatically laughed this off, but Lawrence understandably saw this action as disrespectful to Feisal.[7]

The awkward meal at Feisal's camp was a foretaste of things to come. The Royal Navy flotilla arrived at Wejh on 23 January, but to Admiral Wemyss's consternation, and that of Bray and Vickery, Feisal's large force was nowhere to be seen. The careful planning of the combined operation was unravelling. A decision had to be taken. Vickery was landed with the Arab troops to reconnoitre for a position for a small naval landing party. The attack went

Figure 10. T. E. Lawrence at Wejh, probably early 1917. Lieutenant Gray was given the photograph, probably by the officer who took it (unknown, but perhaps the supplies officer Captain Raymond Goslett). The same image is at the Imperial War Museum (Q60912).

ahead, but Bray and Vickery were furious with Lawrence for not encouraging Feisal to stick to the agreed plan.[8]

Defending the town were about eight hundred Turkish soldiers and their camel corps of about five hundred Ageyl Bedouin. The seaborne Arabs were not of the best fighting quality and had never been intended to bear the brunt of the fighting. Half the Arabs refused to fight, but the other half did well, encouraged by the prospect of loot. Parts of the town had to be taken street by street, aided by gunfire from the ships and by the naval landing party. Captain Lewen Weldon and HMS *Anne* also played a role at Wejh: his seaplanes were sent up as spotters for the naval gunners and later searched for the retreating Turks who had headed inland.[9] It did not take long for the remaining small pocket of Turks to surrender. The town was in Arab hands.

The capture of Wejh was a game-changer. It marked a pivotal new phase of the revolt, whose emphasis shifted to the north and to frequent hit-and-run raids on the Hejaz Railway. The Turks were to remain on the back foot for most of the remainder of the conflict, where they were effectively confined to their garrison towns of Medina and Maan.

★   ★   ★

What on earth had gone wrong with Feisal's forces? They finally arrived with Lawrence, two days too late. The limp excuse offered was lack of water, but this should not have prevented a few hundred at least of Feisal's by then eight thousand men from keeping faith with the seaborne attackers. In fact Lawrence lied in his report on the failure, presumably in an attempt to protect the credibility of Feisal as a military leader.[10] The real reason for the Arab Army's disappearing act, and its lack of discipline, was that Abdullah's forces had captured a senior Turkish officer, Ashraf Bey, with his column of camels laden with supplies and £20,000 in gold. The Bedouin under Feisal's command simply decided to take time off to celebrate and no doubt to get their hands on some of the loot if they could. The plan coordinated with Admiral Wemyss just evaporated.

The surprise capture of Ashraf Bey happened near Wadi Ais, north of Yenbo. The gold carried by his supply column was probably intended partly as bribes to Bedouin tribes to secure their loyalty (or at least their agreement not to support King Hussein). The Turks were just as savvy as Hussein and Lawrence in their liberal showers of gold.[11] It seems highly likely that Lawrence could not resist interrogating Ashraf, finding the prospect more appealing than putting pressure on Feisal to stick to the coordinated attack

Figure 11. 44 Smith & Wesson revolver given to Lieutenant Gray by
T. E. Lawrence. Gray's contemporary inscription records that the weapon was
taken from a senior Ottoman officer, Ashraf Bey, when Lawrence captured him
and £15,000 in Turkish gold. In fact, it was Emir Abdullah who seized Ashraf;
Lawrence's role was probably to interrogate him.

on Wejh that had been agreed. We can say this because Lawrence took
charge of Ashraf's pistol, a 0.44 Smith & Wesson, complete with leather holster, and in due course gave it to the souvenir-collecting Gray. Gray described
the circumstances in his own hand on a luggage label which remains tied to
the pistol to this day:

> Presented to W. L. Gray by Col. Lawrence—bearing name in Arabic of Ashraf
> Bey. The latter & his following with £15,000 Turkish gold were captured by
> Col. Lawrence in 1916. Ashraf Bey is known to have been responsible for the
> death of some 2000 Armenians and this revolver was taken from his person.

Perhaps Gray assumed that Lawrence, rather than Abdullah, had captured
Ashraf because it was Lawrence who had handed him the pistol. If Lawrence
had been aware of Gray's misconception at the time, it would have been in
character if he had said nothing to set the record straight. Unfortunately it
would also have been in character if Lawrence had told Gray that he had
been the one to capture Ashraf. Whatever the truth of the matter, a dog-eared
luggage label has brought a tiny part of the Lawrence legend into being.[12]

Ashraf's prospects were grim. Brought to Mecca as a prisoner of war in
February, he was humiliated on Hussein's orders. A group of beggar boys led

by a ten-year-old dragged him along on a donkey through one of the town's gates, dancing around him, prodding him, beating drums, and shouting, 'Oh treacherous! Oh devil! Oh unbeliever!'[13] Worse would have followed.

★   ★   ★

By the time Bray and Vickery landed on the beach at Wejh, Gray could at last allow himself a breathing space after the most gruelling three months of his life. He had returned to Jeddah from Rabegh by 10 January to find his two assistants, Major Weldon and Lieutenant Arnold, ill with the local fever—but at least he had assistants. The Irishman Weldon, aged 43 and looking ten years older, was a 'dug-out', a clever officer brought out of retirement after ten years in journalism.[14] Another assistant, 21-year-old 2nd Lieutenant Norman 'Strewth' Hopwood, also known as Hoppy, was sent to Jeddah on 30 January from General Headquarters intelligence, Cairo. Gray introduced them all to some labour-saving innovations he had introduced into coding.[15] There was no longer a Rabegh crisis to generate its own storm of secret cables, and Gray found time in the evenings to play whist and poker and enjoy more songs played on Cochrane's gramophone. From his fiancée Mabel, his mother, and his sisters he received parcels of cakes, anchovy paste, butter, biscuits, tobacco, socks, shirts, slippers, and flypaper. He wrote to Mabel about the antics of his pet gazelle, Georgie. Gray and his colleagues were even able to play 'the golf we had invented', so called because the only clubs they had were drivers. Pearson had given Gray and Captain Marshall, the doctor, a driver each and some golf balls. Badminton equipment had also arrived. Gray had been considered the best athlete in his regiment, and had won a number of cups for boxing, fencing, and other sports. He showed his relief: 'It makes life so much more worth living to get a bit of fun or sport & not to have such a thundering lot of work to do.'[16]

Gray had a keen interest in Arabian curios. He had a shell case from the siege of Taif and, on a visit to the commandeered Austrian Consulate next door to the British one, he picked up a fragment of shell, presumably from a British seaplane or warship, with part of a wooden screen still attached to it.[17] One morning before Colonel Wilson came down for breakfast, Gray surreptitiously picked a few pieces out of a section of the previous year's Holy Carpet that Colonel Wilson had been given by King Hussein after the pilgrimage. Gray was later frustrated to learn that while he was in bed with concussion, Wilson had sent the material to his wife Beryl in Egypt. With hindsight, Gray wished he had asked Wilson for a reasonably sized piece as a souvenir or even cut a piece off.[18]

★ ★ ★

Another keen curio-collector was Major Hugh Pearson, who had been drafted in to help Wilson and hold the fort for him if necessary. Irrepressibly bouncy and half-deaf, Pearson was a short and wiry 43-year-old Royal Engineers officer who had been Director of Survey and of intelligence in the Sudan under Wingate. This was his second visit to Jeddah: in June 1916 he had arrived on HMS *Anne* with Captain Kinahan Cornwallis of the Arab Bureau on an important intelligence mission. The revolt had been underway for just two weeks, and Pearson's role had been to assess its progress and to deliver supplies to Hussein including gold.[19] In early August, Pearson had been eyewitness to about eight hundred half-starved Turkish prisoners and forty-three officers on HMS *Dufferin*.

Pearson had never taken to Jeddah, describing the town as 'poisonous'. Back now at a less dangerous time, he would have enjoyed being the life and soul of the party, as usual, if the town's atmosphere had not been so unsettling. It was clear that scope for some of his favourite pursuits, such as hunting wild beasts and fancy dress balls, was strictly limited at Jeddah. Pearson may have been outgoing, but he hated socializing with the French Military Mission. On New Year's Day he and his colleagues drank sweet champagne at the French Consulate and commented: 'these things I loathe, but it is a necessary part of one's job'.[20] The reason for his unease was his handicap of deafness: unless directly spoken to he could not tune in to general conversation at table.[21] He found communication easier when dressed in the robes and lion's mane headdress of an Abyssinian general (which he was to do at a ball in Cairo in May, complete with sprained ankle and leg in plaster).

On one occasion Pearson had 'hidden from Col. Brémond our bearded French colleague here who comes nightly, drinks two whiskies and sodas and stays hours'. Pearson's letters home, like Gray's, are inevitably bland at times because of self-censorship, but occasionally we gain insights into the challenging world of Wilson's Jeddah circle:

> Things are very weird here and one feels one is an actor in a drama. . . . A false step might so easily be of almost world-wide importance, and though of course one is but an agent, the man on the spot must have some weight in guiding Govt. action, and there are such wide considerations to be weighed in one's every action.

Wilson had left Jeddah on 18 January for a meeting with Admiral Weymss and was now in Cairo for a much-needed break. Pearson found the time to do what he had been contemplating since December. Golf was one of his many sporting passions: he had taken his golf balls with him all over the wilds of the Sudan on survey work (on one occasion they had melted in the 122- degree heat, a fate that few men could talk about). Pearson wanted more than unofficial golf at Jeddah: on 11 February work began on 'a real golf links of nine holes of a really very sporting character',[22] part of which spread over the Turkish trenches just outside the town.[23] The golf course also lay over the abandoned Royal Flying Corps (RFC) emergency landing ground and was within a fore shot of the fugitive remains of Goodchild's camel depot.

★   ★   ★

That a little piece of Surrey now lay over an unneeded RFC landing ground was a striking symbol of how far the revolt had advanced with the capture of Wejh. Arab, British, and French eyes were now turning to a longer front to the north and towards Syria. But there was a fly in the ointment. Aziz al-Masri, in command of the Arab Regular Army, had met Wilson and Wemyss and along with Vickery he thought the Arabs were incapable of concerted action and should restrict themselves to hit-and-run guerrilla raids. Lawrence had independently grasped these ideas at an early stage.

Lawrence had managed to stay at Feisal's side after Wejh fell, following a strong plea from an anxious Feisal that his liaison officer should not return as planned to Egypt.[24] In early February, Lawrence had done a most extraordinary thing which would have exposed him to a charge of treason had it been known. He told Feisal about the secret Sykes-Picot agreement between Britain and France, so that the Arab leader was in no doubt that he would have to capture Damascus and other inland cities of Syria to try to stop the interior being governed by France after the war. In effect, Lawrence was saying that the Arabs would have to fight against the British and the French as well as the Turks. In other words, he was subverting the imperialist designs of his own government. Lawrence also exposed Brémond's real purpose in pressing now for an Allied attack on the port of Aqaba, at the northern end of the Red Sea. The scheming French officer thought that a landing here would in effect contain the revolt to the Hejaz, because it would turn the tribes between Aqaba and Syria against Hussein, fearing imperial conquest. But Feisal, who was a shrewd political operator, already knew what Brémond was up to and had no intention of agreeing.

Figure 12. Lieutenant Norman Hopwood playing golf on the nine-hole course laid out at Jeddah by Major Hugh Pearson. The course lay partly over the Royal Flying Corps' emergency landing ground, abandoned when the Rabegh crisis ended in January 1917, and partly over the defensive trenches near the captured Ottoman barracks.

In late February, Pearson had a visit from Major Vickery to discuss the Arabs' strength, guerrilla warfare, and the need to cut the Hejaz Railway. Pearson wrote that Lawrence was of 'inestimable value' alongside Feisal.[25] Wingate's office agreed:

> The value of Lawrence in the position which he has made for himself with Feisal is enormous, and it is fully realised that if we could find suitable men to

act in the same way with Ali and Abdullah it would be invaluable. Such men, however, are extremely difficult to get. [26]

These comments are intriguing for two reasons. First, Lawrence was doing very important work but he was not seen as unique. Two more Lawrences were needed, for attachment to Feisal's brothers. Second, the extraordinary words, 'the position which he has made for himself': here was an unconventional junior liaison officer, who to a great extent had been left to his own devices in a remote area which very few officers in Cairo knew much about. Lawrence had the twin advantages of having his boots on the ground and having a deeper knowledge of Arabian affairs than any other British adviser in the Hejaz.

Other boots on the ground now began the much-discussed campaign against the Hejaz Railway. Lieutenant-Colonel Newcombe, Lieutenant Hornby, Lieutenant Garland, Major al-Masri, Capitaine Raho, and other Arab and French officers carried explosives and led demolition parties of Arabs from Wejh. The idea was to prevent the Turkish garrison at Medina from being properly resupplied, and to prevent Fakhri Pasha from going on the offensive again. That Hussein allowed the infidel soldiers to take part was thanks to the trust he placed in Wilson: their relationship was fundamental to the progress of the revolt. Wilson was delighted to hear in February that the maverick explosives expert, Garland, managed to blow up a moving locomotive for the first time, using a contact mine that he had apparently devised himself. This is still described today as a 'Garland mine', but in fact the fertile mind of Sir Mark Sykes had come up with the idea four months earlier—and it was a recycled idea. He had fought in the Boer War and had seen the Boers use 'a Martini rifle with the barrel cut down to 4 inches', stuffed with dynamite and with a trigger device which 'explodes the charge, bending the rail and derailing the locomotive…A man on a camel could carry 5 dozen such mines.'[27] This mechanism was precisely what Garland used and would now be called an IED or improvised explosive device.[28]

Lawrence, who had been taught by Garland how to blow things up, came to railway demolition a little later. He did not actually see the railway before March 1917, but before long was taking his own demolition parties and demonstrating his peculiar insight into how to win Bedouin hearts and minds. Ever-larger quantities of explosives, detonators, and electrical cable were brought to Wejh by the ships of the Red Sea Patrol. Colonel Pierce Joyce, in charge of logistics there, was hard-pressed to keep up with demand. A hit-and-run campaign of railway raids was setting the desert ablaze.

8

Sabotage, Golf, and Betrayal

While Garland, Lawrence, and others were causing the timetables of imperial Ottoman railways in the Hejaz to be revised on a regular basis, an old Jeddah hand was quietly involved in counter-espionage and the rooting out of subversion. Bray, fresh from his starring role in the Wejh campaign and still livid with Lawrence, was back in town. Covert jihadist groups, neutralized by Bray and Ruhi in the run-up to the autumn pilgrimage, were active once more. These organizations had the same aims as before: to muddy the waters by spreading anti-Hussein propaganda, so weakening the revolt, and to export pan-Islamic and anti-British rhetoric to destabilize India. The nightmare of the British about revolution in their jewel in the crown was perhaps overstated at times, but it had a dark and powerful hold over their psyche. It certainly stimulated Bray's imagination. His and Ruhi's special expertise was called upon again.

The two men became agent-runners once more, perhaps re-activating networks still in place. Wilson greatly appreciated the fresh contribution made by Bray, 'in direct contact as he is with the Agents of the Anjuman-i-Kaaba and other secret Pan-Islamic Societies in Jeddah and elsewhere'.[1] Wilson sent to Wingate Bray's report on his new mission, which was called *Intelligence and Notes on the Pan-Islamic Movement*.[2] It included a map showing places where pan-Islamism was being taught and where there were branches of the Anjuman-i-Kaaba. Ruhi's footprints are over this operation as over the earlier one.

Wilson was now having to cope with yet another setback. He had hoped to keep Bray on his staff for as long as possible, but fault lines were running just below the surface as his conscientious intelligence officer battled hidden demons. Wilson, by nature straightforward to the point of brusqueness, was baffled when Bray suddenly announced on 18 March that he wanted to leave Jeddah but could not explain in detail why.[3] Wilson felt let down because there was still much for an unusual man of Bray's skills to do in the Hejaz. When Wilson pressed him, Bray said he could not disclose his real reason for wanting to go without committing a breach of faith with an unspecified individual.

Wilson thought Bray had 'a kink somewhere over this Arab Question generally or else it is because he is not fit and his mind is a bit distorted.' Bray claimed that he had wanted to get away ever since he had returned to Jeddah, though Wilson had detected no hint of this. Wilson was annoyed but reluctantly felt Bray had to go because 'I'm afraid otherwise he will worry himself to death.'[4] Wilson was probably unaware that Bray's wife had a serious mental illness, which was perhaps a factor in his distress. Gray was later to praise Bray and make an intriguing but vague comment on his sudden departure from Jeddah: Bray's 'intelligence work was excellent. He insisted on leaving us and going to France again. He could not stick it here.'[5]

Why was Bray so distracted? He was clearly suffering great stress because of a conflict of interest, and felt his position was impossible because he could not serve two masters. Wilson of course was one. Intriguingly and not surprisingly, given their previous involvement, it is clear from papers buried deep in an archive that the other master, in an unofficial but real sense, was none other than the Yorkshire baronet and capricious amateur diplomat, Sir Mark Sykes. Back in Cairo and feeling in limbo, Bray wrote to Sykes: 'I have always considered rightly or wrongly that I have been working for you, and have in a very small way tried to forward your policy as I read it & I would not like to be left a wandering sheep under anyone else's orders...if my own wishes were consulted I will work for you in any way you suggest'; otherwise, he said, he would go back to his regiment.[6]

Sykes was assistant secretary to the War Cabinet, where he was known as the Mad Mullah, and was in charge of Middle Eastern affairs. He had carved out a huge fiefdom for himself, mainly because hardly anyone else in government knew much about the region. Driven by restless whimsy, at times half-baked ideas, and boundless breezy optimism—or arrogance as many saw it—Sykes could also scheme as ruthlessly as Lawrence to achieve his ends. The policy line that Bray told Wilson he felt bound to carry out must have been Sykes's policy, or at least what he believed to be Sykes's policy (at times it flipped with alarming speed). At about the time Bray was back in Jeddah, Sykes was plotting to obtain Jewish Zionist support for Palestine as a solely British protectorate, rather than being under the joint administration of Britain, France, and Russia, as set out in the Sykes–Picot Agreement.

In this way he was quite happy to deceive his partner, François Georges-Picot. Sykes was also prepared to bypass Hussein over arrangements for future French control of much of Syria. Had Bray got wind of some of this and concluded that, though he enjoyed the vicarious thrill of Sykes's high-octane diplomacy, his conscience would not let him stay attached to Wilson while some of the revolt's aspirations were being subverted? Perhaps Sykes in one of his scattergun conversations had confided in Bray, before his return to Wilson's service, about the secret agreement with the French. This could have eaten away at Bray's equilibrium.

His secondment was over too early for Wilson's liking, but, as before, Bray with Ruhi had carried out important, secret, and forgotten work in Jeddah. Most good intelligence work demands patience and a feel for when is the right time to do nothing. It is invisible during and after its execution. By contrast, the sound and fury of railway demolition work were exciting and raised morale amongst the Arabs and the British and French; they produced instant and visible results that could be appreciated by the brass hats in Cairo. The sabotage work still resonates today as iconic testament to the Arab Revolt, while many of the low-key but essential intelligence and diplomatic efforts, particularly those carried out in the fulcrum of Jeddah, remain little-known or hidden. They are a lost part of the narrative waiting to be reclaimed.

★   ★   ★

Lionel Gray's war was not troubled by agonies of conscience or the machinations of maverick diplomats. In late February, while Wilson was in Egypt, Gray visited Wejh, Yenbo, and Rabegh on what he curiously called a pleasure trip. Writing on HMS *Hardinge* notepaper from Rabegh, he tried his hand at naval gunnery, hitting his targets with the big guns.[7] He got on well with the Naval Transport Officer for Jeddah, Commander Dugdale, and with a number of ships' officers who visited the port. One was Captain W. E. Lewis of SS *Race Fisher*, a 'fleet messenger' that also carried military stores. Gray sometimes left the harbour in a sailing boat to collect the mail from her.

Gray also went out in the Consulate launch to collect stores from one of the ships.[8] He brought to the jetty large quantities of potatoes, sugar, bacon, coffee, cigarettes and tobacco, money, and revolver ammunition. The carriers, including a 90-year-old man who was grossly overloaded with a huge weight of stores, managed eventually, after a 'comic opera' series of collapses and a broken bench, to get everything to the Consulate about a mile away. Gray bought socks and tobacco for his own use from some of the ships and was also given newspapers and magazines to supplement *The Times, The Mirror, Punch*, and *John Bull*, which were sent out by his family. His mother had even sent him two golf balls she had picked up from a field bordering a golf course near her Surrey home.[9]

One day, with the pressure temporarily off, Gray watched small birds, probably bulbuls or finches, flying into his room in search of ants and places to build a nest. He was still taking quinine to ward off fever. Moving to a window, he was astonished to see the desert beyond the crumbling town wall 'quite green just like Clapham Common'.[10] Goats and donkeys were grazing, a result of the very heavy and unusual rain that had fallen recently. Gray mused that Wilson had not offered him his horse for more riding exercise since his concussion, and wondered whether Wilson blamed himself for the accident.

Mabel Holman was pleased her fiancé had given up riding, but Gray found himself in the doghouse for talking to a leper: 'You say you have seen and spoken to a leper—what a foolhardy thing to do!'[11] Nervous and highly strung, Mabel had had to endure the anticipation of repeated Zeppelin attacks near her home in Muswell Hill, north London. She was also suffering mounting dread about the survival prospects of her only brother, Gerald, who was training as a pilot in the Royal Flying Corps (RFC). She told Gray that depression was affecting her health, and complained that he should have been promoted by now: 'Being such an important person on the staff, I do think you ought to be made a captain—especially as all your assistants seem to be either Captains or Majors.'[12] Gray repeatedly did his best to try to reassure Mabel. He knew that she had the added pressure of helping her uncle, Ernest Bentley, with his classified work on code research for the government. Mabel had, astonishingly for a woman at the time, been engaged on this demanding project for about two years: a year earlier she had told Gray in confidence that she had 'helped considerably and made discoveries'.[13]

★   ★   ★

Gray knew that Wilson was a more rounded character than his stiff-necked, rather priggish attitude suggested. The colonel had come back from leave in Egypt 'full of beans'.[14] Wilson had a distinct sense of humour and he could laugh at himself. He showed this on 5 April when Jeddah was hit for two hours by a violent storm with thunder and lightning, hurricane winds, and torrential rain. Huge hailstones bounced off the verandah roof at the Consulate. The officers' rooms and mess room, left with windows open as usual, were deluged. 'The water was falling into the Colonel's room like a

cataract & he was sitting there laughing like anything. I went to the window
& he caught my eye & so did an enormous hailstone. He laughed the more.'[15]
The storm swamped the golf course under a gunmetal sky, obliterating the
fifth hole. Gray's crunch tournament match with Major John Bassett had to
be abandoned. He had already beaten Wilson, Captain Marshall the doctor,
and his ciphering colleague Captain Dixon. A few days later Gray was to
win the reconvened final match with Bassett and with it the silver spoon
presented by Colonel Wilson.[16]

Bassett had arrived as Wilson's new deputy by early April, following the
departure of Pearson on 12 March for Cairo and then Abyssinia, where he
was needed to sign an important treaty with the emperor. A 38-year-old veteran of the Boer War, Bassett was, like Wilson and Pearson, another trusted
member of General Wingate's inner circle. Over the coming months he was
to play a key diplomatic role in helping keep the revolt on an even keel.

Gray witnessed the comings and goings of the Jeddah circle and continued to conjure up vivid cameos of life in the town. Leaning out of his
first-floor window, he was transfixed by an extraordinary scene and immediately took some photographs, then rushed outside to take some more: 'In
a fight at Bir Sheba the Arabs captured a banner from the Turks . . . A procession headed by the standard-bearer of a number of the Sherif's soldiers has
been marching all round the town for 2 hours or more singing lustily their
peculiar chants.'[17]

★ ★ ★

Meanwhile from March onwards Lawrence had been busy at Wejh, helping
Feisal set up his base. Feisal was receiving many deputations from Arab
chiefs, and was knitting together potential alliances for an advance north
towards Syria. Two armoured cars with British crews had arrived under
Lieutenant Leofric Gilman. Future prospects looked sound, but then came
bombshell intelligence from the Arab Bureau: Medina would be evacuated,
because the Turks realized they would be unable to defend all of the railway.
They were to move 500 miles north to defences on the railway near Maan.
This alarmed General Murray, who was about to attack Gaza and was worried that the Turks would be able to transfer a very large force there and tip
the balance against the British. So Clayton ordered that the evacuation of
Medina must be prevented. In Newcombe's and Garland's absence on railway raids (Vickery had returned to France), Lawrence persuaded Feisal to
put his planned advance on hold. The message went out from Feisal to
Abdullah and Ali and to tribal leaders: step up the railway attacks north of

Figure 13. Sherifian bodyguard.

Medina at all costs. Lawrence set out on 10 March to Wadi Ais to hand letters from Feisal to Abdullah, whose performance in the field had been rather sluggish.

On arrival at Abdullah's camp, Lawrence just had time to explain the urgent plans before he was laid low by a serious attack of dysentery and malaria. He was confined to his sick bed, and later said this gave him the opportunity to rethink the strategy of the revolt. Wilson, Newcombe, and Vickery, like him, appreciated that the Turks would have to deploy thousands of soldiers to defend the railway against increasing demolition raids. Lawrence's insight was that there was no need for the Arabs to take Medina:

Figure 14. Mahmas, one of T. E. Lawrence's Ageyl bodyguards. The Ageyl were often outlaws but were fiercely loyal to Lawrence.

if the Turks kept their base there they would be harmless. Why not ensure that they and their weapons were immobilized in the town and along the railway? If the railway functioned intermittently, but only just well enough to provide the Turks with food, they would be neutralized, their numbers depleted by infectious diseases. So Murray's Sinai strategy would not be endangered and Feisal could still implement his plans for an advance on Syria to try to stymie the French.

Lawrence's two railway raids in late March were a success, aided by two so-called Garland mines and shelling of Abu el Naam station by trained Arabs with a mountain gun and a howitzer. This was a brave action on Lawrence's part, because he had no combat experience or even training. Lawrence later wrote of Arab guerrilla raids against the railway: 'Most wars were wars of contact...Ours should be a war of detachment. We were to contain the enemy by the silent threat of a vast unknown desert, not disclosing ourselves till we attacked.'[18]

Meanwhile Feisal had not made a good impression on Major Pierce Joyce who had arrived at Wejh on 17 March, to act as senior British officer in charge of the armoured cars and the RFC flight that would soon move up from Rabegh. Joyce was concerned that Feisal was still concentrating too much on thoughts of Syria and not enough on attacking the railway. But Feisal had been alarmed for a while about reports that the French might invade Syria, and was irritated by the machine gun instructors that Brémond had left at Wejh. Wilson had managed to calm Feisal down for the time

Figure 15. Captured Ottoman flag paraded in triumph through the streets of Jeddah, early 1918. Photograph taken by Lieutenant Lionel Gray from his Consulate balcony after he heard the celebrations.

being, no easy task since the Arab leader had moral courage but was also timid and could be as easily startled as a thoroughbred racehorse. Wilson spluttered: 'Damn Brémond and his nasty ways, he creates more beastly situations for me than one would have thought possible.'[19]

Feisal was a sophisticated political player with his own intelligence sources. Newcombe reported that, 'Feisal asked that Beduins be informed that Turkish money will not be accepted: the sooner they learn this, the

Figure 16. Sherifian soldiers drinking tea at Jeddah.

sooner will the Turks find it impossible to buy them over.'[20] But Feisal became jittery again when Brémond came to Wejh on 1 April, with a plan to increase French advisers there. The Arab leader had seen through Brémond's game. Feisal wanted to take the northern Syrian cities before the French could—Lawrence wanted the same thing to happen—and proposed taking the northern Red Sea port of Aqaba to use as a base. Clayton, though, had rejected this plan on 8 March because he did not want the Arabs controlling the port: it was too near a strategic British interest, the Suez Canal, and he wanted the British at Aqaba after the war. Lawrence now felt he was on a collision course with British policy. With steely determination and a strange kind of diffident arrogance, he decided that he would go his own way when he had sufficient intelligence and when the time was right. That time was fast approaching.

What was of great help to Lawrence in his deliberations was the chance to interrogate at Wejh eleven Ottoman prisoners of war, who had been captured at Aqaba by a Royal Navy landing party. The men included eight Syrian soldiers who said they wanted to fight for Feisal. Lawrence learned vital details about the numbers of Turkish troops at Aqaba and the surrounding areas. His interrogations of less amenable captives—and he encountered many—would probably have been like no others. His maverick nature most likely made them quirky, unpredictable, and surprising to his comrades as well as to the prisoners. A number of his friends spoke later not just of his quick intelligence but of almost a sixth sense: an insight into the hearts and minds of people. His interrogations would have breathed empathy, an innate sympathy with the predicament of Syrian and Mesopotamian prisoners who had been forced to join the Ottoman Army (unlike Ashraf Bey with his gold) and who were not offering to fight for Feisal. Many of them would have been like the villagers at Lawrence's pre-war archaeological excavations at Carchemish in northern Syria, whom he had trained and supervised and understood so well. The prisoners would not have expected this slightly built, unassuming young interrogator with the mesmerizing blue eyes, who spoke so softly and simply (even if not fluently) in their own language, and who seemed somehow to reach out to them in spite of being an enemy officer. Perhaps their relief at being treated far better than by their own Turkish officers meant that the canny Lawrence did not have to push too hard to gain information on army units, their locations and identifying symbols, their weaponry and camel transport, their state of health and morale, and so on.

Wilson was fulminating once again, but this time the object of his wrath was not Colonel Brémond. Sir Mark Sykes, a master of disinformation and deception, was engaged in intrigue no less insidious than that of the Arab factions at Jeddah and Mecca. Wilson found Sykes's manoeuvres an affront to his conscience and he took action. Wilson was aghast that, in late April, Sykes had left Hussein high and dry, in discussing with Georges-Picot and a delegation of Syrian exiles in Cairo how Syria might be run after the war. The exiles, chosen by Sykes because they were biddable, knew nothing about the Sykes-Picot terms or British promises to Hussein, and were happy to suggest only limited independence for a very small part of Syria. The whole thing was a sham and Wilson's blood pressure was rising. He had got wind of Sykes's scheme in late March and had warned Clayton against deceiving Hussein, arguing that honesty could result in 'winning the gratitude of millions of Moslems of the Empire... For Heaven's sake, let us be straight with the old man; I am convinced it will pay us in the end.'[21] Wilson's advice had not been heeded, but now he forced a meeting on Sykes by urging the king to ask him to visit Jeddah. This ploy worked and Sykes set off for Arabia on 30 April. On the way to Jeddah, he called in at Wejh on 5 May to talk briefly to Feisal. Sykes gave him a woolly account of an Anglo-French agreement on some future Arab confederation or state, including Syria. But what Sykes did not know was that Feisal was aware of the actual terms of the Sykes-Picot Agreement, as confided to him by Lawrence. Feisal kept his powder dry (he really had no choice) and knew the need to push on for Syria and claim the land was all the more urgent.

That same day Sykes went on to Jeddah and met Hussein. He gave the same mixture of half-truths and lies to the king. In a brief report, Sykes lied in stating that he had fully explained the agreement to Hussein and Feisal, and that he had dragged an acceptance from them. Wilson's optimistic but naive hopes that Sykes would play fair with Hussein were dashed. On his way back to Egypt, Sykes called in again at Wejh on 7 May where he found Lawrence. It seems that Lawrence confronted Sykes over the half-baked story he had given Feisal (neither British men made a record of the discussion). Lawrence was hostile to Sykes from that day. Sykes's cynical deception probably made Lawrence feel justified in earlier acting treasonably against his own government by telling Feisal about the Sykes-Picot terms.

Meanwhile Wilson doggedly refused to give up in his attempt to have Sykes held to account over his subterfuge. Sykes and Georges-Picot visited Jeddah on 19 May and the French diplomat's meeting with Hussein resulted in a tense stand-off: their views on the future government of Syria were diametrically opposed. Then Georges-Picot was shocked and delighted when Hussein announced that he would accept the same French role in the Syrian coastal area after the war as the British would assume in the Baghdad province of Mesopotamia. Hussein claimed he had a letter from McMahon saying Mesopotamia would go to the Arabs (apart from the port of Basra), though he could not produce the letter. But Hussein was not aware that the Sykes-Picot terms called for Baghdad province to be permanently run by the British. So Hussein was in effect agreeing to the French controlling the Lebanon part of Greater Syria and the Syrian coast to the north—the prize that France was determined to gain. The slippery Sykes was delighted: he thought Hussein's statement would begin to resolve the conflict between British promises to Hussein and the secret agreement between the British and the French.

Wilson smelt a rat and so did Newcombe. Both men had attended some of the Jeddah deliberations. Wilson was aghast at what he saw as a betrayal of Hussein. In a long and deeply felt letter to Clayton, he described the Hashemite leader as 'one of the most courteous of men, absolutely loyal to us and with complete faith in Great Britain. . . . we have not been as open and frank as we should have been at this last meeting'. When Hussein 'agreed to France having the same status in Syria as we are to have in Iraq surely the main points of our agreement re. Iraq should have been stated to prevent all chance of a misunderstanding which might have far-reaching consequences'. The point for Sykes, of course, was that a misunderstanding was precisely what he wanted. Wilson complained that Sykes and Georges-Picot had compressed their talks with Hussein into a mere four hours—far too short a time to do the subject justice.

Wilson, like Lawrence, was fearless where a matter of principle was at stake. He asked for his letter to be shown to Sykes,

> as it is what I would have told him if I had had an opportunity . . . If we are not going to see the Sherif through and we let him down badly after all his trust in us the very 'enviable' post of Pilgrimage Officer at Jeddah will be vacant because I certainly could not remain.[22]

Stewart Newcombe was also deeply anxious about hoodwinking the sherif and wrote to Clayton on similar lines as Wilson.[23] Wilson and Hussein were bound together by honour and a degree of naivety. They were swimming against a tide of amoral power politics, the reluctant spy and the self-deceiving arch-intriguer who seemed to have a blind spot about British trustworthiness. Wilson wrote: 'Is the Sherif living in a fool's paradise?' The ultimate irony was that Wilson, with a gold standard code of morality, may have inadvertently beguiled Hussein into believing that Sykes's word as an Englishman must be as good as Wilson's own word.

Meanwhile Feisal, knowing about the Sykes-Picot terms, was appalled at his father's statement about Syria and Iraq. The two men argued and Hussein, unable to doubt the honour of Great Britain, slapped Feisal down: 'These words are from a father to a son. Never doubt Great Britain's word. She is wise and trustworthy; have no fear.' The pathos of the words resonates to this day. Feisal felt he had to go on to the front foot and did so adroitly. On 28 May, he publicly called on the Syrian people to rise up, and disingenuously thanked the British and French governments for supporting Arab independence. This raised the stakes and ultimately Sykes's trickery had the effect of strengthening the schism between Arab and Allied objectives in the Middle East. Clayton, far-sighted and a genial master of *realpolitik*, felt that Hussein would simply have to accept however things panned out after the war. Sykes was to cast a long and permanent shadow.[24]

★   ★   ★

Lawrence played no part in these negotiations because by then he was deep in the desert on a covert mission. His shadow too was stalking the land.

9

Aqaba, the Arab Legion, and Jam Roly-Poly

A warm spring day in Wejh saw the groundwork for a major new phase of the Arab Revolt that would encourage the Arabs, bamboozle the British high command, confound the French, and shock the Turks. Feisal had been trying for some time to persuade Auda abu Tayi, chief of the war-like Howeitat tribe, to join the rebels. Auda, whose territory in north-west Arabia bordered the environs of Wejh, had finally came to see him. Lawrence met Auda too, on 14 April 1917. Lawrence was impressed with the chief's charisma and was to write:

> He must be nearly fifty now (he admits forty) and his black beard is tinged with white, but he is still tall and straight, loosely built, spare and powerful, and as active as a much younger man. His lined and haggard face is pure Bedouin: low forehead, high sharp hooked nose, brown-green eyes, slanting outward, large mouth... pointed beard and moustache... He has married twenty-eight times, has been wounded thirteen times... He has only reported his 'kill' since 1900, and they now stand at seventy-five Arabs; Turks are not counted.[1]

Lawrence could see at once that here was a warlord whose legendary successes could help attract more recruits from the tribes, and who could help in the planning and logistics for an attack on Aqaba. Lawrence could not help but be struck by the contrast between Feisal and Auda. Feisal had subtle political skills in keeping fractious tribes, often hereditary enemies, signed up to the revolt. His networking called for endless patience and diplomacy. Feisal was brave politically and knew what fate awaited him if the revolt failed and the Turks captured him: a public hanging in the main square of Damascus. Yet like Lawrence he was not a natural warrior and hated fighting and killing. Lawrence had given a very different impression of Feisal when he reported to his bosses soon after meeting the Arab leader the previous

October. Feisal was nervous and could vacillate and trim his sails to accommodate the views of whoever had most recently advised him. Auda abu Tayi, by contrast, was the natural and fearless fighter who would offer a better prospect of taking Aqaba.

Lawrence began discussing with Auda a daring strategy for seizing Aqaba from inland, rather than from the Red Sea as Feisal had been considering. He knew from his interrogation of Turkish prisoners from Aqaba that the defensive positions high in Wadi Itm, which was reached by a narrow track that led east from the town towards the Maan plateau, were only lightly held. But an Arab force, advancing from Aqaba after a seaborne attack, would be pinned down in Wadi Itm and find it almost impossible to break through, as the Turks would be able to bring up a large defensive force from their garrison at Maan on the railway. They would have had warning too of any assault from the sea. There would be no element of surprise and the Turks would be able permanently to block any attempted Arab move inland to Syria, with fatal consequences for Feisal's plans. On the other hand, if the Wadi Itm track could be captured by a lightning strike inland, beginning near Maan itself, the Turkish forces in that town could be blocked from moving to the defence of Aqaba. The lightly garrisoned port itself should then fall to the Hashemites without too much effort.

The scheme was outrageously bold and would have to be kept secret. Feisal did not tell his entourage in case information leaked out to Turkish spies. Colonel Brémond had to be kept out of the loop or he would try to get his government to lean on the British to block the operation, which could have alerted the Turks. Above all, Lawrence had to keep the scheme a secret from Clayton and his other colleagues, given the orders that Aqaba should not be taken by the Hashemites. Disgusted by Sykes's smoke and mirrors, and his habit of making and breaking promises on a whim, Lawrence seemed to have decided that he would need to use deception if Sykes were to be outmanoeuvred—an astonishing presumption for a junior officer. Only facts on the ground, he thought, would make up for doomed appeals to British honour. The revolt had to be taken north out of the Hejaz. Feisal would have no hope of gaining Syria unless his forces took the land, and for that a base at Aqaba, supplied by the Royal Navy, would be essential.

Feisal appointed Sherif Nasir ibn Ali, his trusted deputy, as leader of the mission and gave him the key role of winning the loyalty of the Syrian tribes. Auda was to obtain from fellow Howeitat tribesmen the camels and sheep that would be needed to transport and feed the Arab forces as they

Figure 17. The house at Wejh of Nasib al-Bakry (Emir Feisal's influential Syrian adviser) is one of those behind the Arab.

pushed into Syria. The third of Feisal's key men was Nasib al-Bakry, an Arab nationalist from Damascus. He was to canvas support from Arabs of like mind in and near Damascus who were prepared to rise up in rebellion. It is not clear whether Nasir, Auda, and Bakry thought the seizure of Aqaba was the end-game of the present mission, or whether that would be a later objective. For his part, Lawrence encouraged the perception by his British colleagues that he was accompanying a small local Arab campaign against the railway around Maan. Joyce's railway attacks were engaging the few British advisers, but Lawrence did not attract attention because Feisal could supply camels, money, stores, and explosives. Lawrence was just as adept at smoke and mirrors as Sykes. He told Wilson, his superior, that Auda would soon be going on a raid towards Maan as a first objective, and that he might be going with the Arab warlord. Auda told Wilson the same story when the two men met. Laurence was vague about the secondary objective of the small, mobile strike force that he mentioned.

Sherif Nasir, Auda, Bakry, and fewer than forty-five tribesman set off with Lawrence from Wejh, heading north-east, on 9 May. After only four days Lawrence suffered a serious outbreak of boils and high fever. On the tenth day the party blew up a section of the Hejaz Railway line near Diraa.

On 20 May they entered a fearsome, arid wasteland called El Houl, 'the terror'. Four days of near-continuous sandstorm followed, the wind 'so dry that our shrivelled lips cracked open, and the skin of our faces chapped'.[2] Lawrence was all the time troubled, knowing that if the revolt moved into Syria then Arab lives would be sacrificed for what could well already be a lost cause. He was prepared to use subterfuge and lie for tactical reasons, and could be ruthless in dealing with those who would stand in his way, but at heart he had certain deeply held moral ideas. His mental and physical state must have influenced his bizarre decision to go into the desert alone, without telling his comrades, to rescue Gasim, a Syrian Arab from Maan who had been left behind. Lawrence could easily have died in that harshest of landscapes, and his name could have become a byword for unfathomable and futile heroism.

Reaching Wadi Sirhan, a 200-mile-long depression running north-west to south-east, the force met Auda abu Tayi's Howeitat tribesmen. The wadi was notorious for poisonous snakes, which Lawrence hated; they killed three of the Wejh group. Lawrence by now was tormented by his knowledge of the Allies' plans to betray the Arabs. This seems to have prompted his extraordinary decision to go on a virtually suicidal trek, taking just two guides, into the heart of Syria to the north. He left behind a notebook with the band in Wadi Sirhan, assuming it would find its way to Clayton's hands. Inside, in a margin, he scribbled the anguished words: 'Clayton. I've decided to go off alone to Damascus, hoping to get killed on the way. For all sakes try and clear this show up before it goes any further. We are calling them to fight for us on a lie, and I can't stand it.'

Then followed a remarkable 400-mile journey that took Lawrence to the outskirts of Damascus and the border of Lebanon. He apparently led some locals in blowing up a railway bridge north of Damascus, which the Turks believed for a time heralded a local revolt. Lawrence met a number of possible Arab allies but they were very cautious: the risks of rebelling against the Turks so close to their heartland were huge. The great leader Nuri Shalaan of the influential Rualla tribe, whom Lawrence met at the oasis of Azrak, knew about British promises to Hussein and had documents that contradicted each other. He showed them to his British guest and asked which ones he should believe. Lawrence, who later said he was 'continually and bitterly ashamed', said he should put his faith in the most recent document. The alternative was to lose the support of this key chieftain (in fact Nuri Shalaan sat on the fence, for some time intriguing with the Turks, and did not come over to the revolt until near its end).

Lawrence returned to Wadi Sirhan, he later claimed, with a grim determination to help engineer facts on the ground to help the Arab cause. If the rebels could take control of Syria, perhaps they could defeat not only Turkish power but French ambition and the policies of his own government too. When the men from Wejh left the wadi on 18 June heading for the wells at Bair, they were accompanied by about 500 tribesmen, mostly Auda's Howeitat. But spies had been at work: the Turks had got wind of the rebel band and had blown up three of the wells. Fortunately one well survived. The problem now was that the Turks were likely to conclude that Aqaba was the Arabs' target. They would probably also destroy the next group of wells at Jefer, not far from the important garrison and railway town of Maan. What was needed was a major diversion to throw the Turks off the track. This began with disinformation. Local tribes were led to believe that the rebel force was still at Wadi Sirhan. The Arab leaders and Lawrence knew that this information would find its way to the Turks through their informers. Then Lawrence set off with about one hundred Bedouin for small-scale guerrilla raids, with no particular pattern, on the railway around Amman, about 150 miles to the north of Bair. He was remembering the impact of his bridge raid north of Damascus. The diversion seemed to work: the Turks were distracted and sent four hundred men to Wadi Sirhan to find what they thought would be the rebel camp.

The rebels were now confident about moving on to the wells at Jefer. The Turks had destroyed them too, but one was retrievable after repairs. A little earlier, an Arab detachment had been sent to drum up support amongst the tribes on the way to Aqaba, and had taken the Turkish blockhouse at Fuweila. Heading there, the rest of the Arab force heard that about five hundred and fifty Turkish troops were ahead of them, having been sent from Maan to relieve Fuweila. If these soldiers got to the narrow Wadi Itm track leading towards Aqaba, all Arab hopes of taking the port would be dashed.

The Turkish relief column would have to be destroyed. It happened on 2 July. Found sleeping and trapped in a mountain valley at Aba el Lissan, near Fuweila, the Turkish troops were slaughtered by a Howeitat charge. All but one hundred were killed or captured. Lawrence and Auda then had a stern test as they finally persuaded the Bedouin not to head back towards Maan in search of ready loot, which the poor port of Aqaba could not offer.

The whole operation hung in the balance, since the Turks would have been sure to make every effort to retake Maan and the way to Aqaba would then have been closed. Quick action was needed as the gold for paying the Bedouin had run out and Lawrence was issuing his own notes promising to pay when the port was in Hashemite hands.

That same day the Arabs set out on the 40-mile march to Aqaba. They moved up into the mountains and poured down the Wadi Itm, past empty Turkish defences all facing the sea. The small Turkish garrison, short of food, surrendered to Nasir's forces on 6 July after two days and very little fighting. The daring raid had succeeded but the work was far from done. Food had to be obtained for six hundred Arabs and the same number of Turkish prisoners, and British supplies and reinforcements had to be brought to Aqaba as soon as possible, to prevent the Turks from trying to retake the port.

Lawrence at once set off, with eight Bedouin, across the Sinai desert towards the Suez Canal. He covered the 150 miles in an astonishing forty-nine hours. British soldiers at the canal on 9 July were suspicious when they met the waif-like figure in tattered Arab clothing. Lawrence was fortunate, when changing trains for Cairo at Ismailia, to see Admiral Wemyss and his party on the platform. HMS *Dufferin* set off from Suez within hours with reinforcements, stores, and gold coins bound for Aqaba. Reaching Cairo, Lawrence astonished Clayton by walking into his office, describing his 1,300 miles on a camel in the last thirty days and the Arab feat at Aqaba, and producing a sketch map showing how the Syrian Arabs could advance in conjunction with the British Army in Palestine, and acting as its right arm. This bravura performance and the achievement behind it entranced the hard-headed Clayton. Lawrence became the toast of Cairo and his legend was born. His mission in Syria to gather intelligence was praised even more than the taking of Aqaba. Reginald Wingate recommended that Lawrence should be given the Victoria Cross, the highest award for bravery (this was not possible because there was no British person present as a witness).

Lawrence's influence over Feisal meant that he played an important role in planning and executing the seizure of Aqaba. But it is easy to forget the essential leadership roles of Feisal's three lieutenants and their bravery in venturing into Ottoman Syria where Turkish spies could expose them at any time. Lawrence was more than a liaison officer but this was an Arab operation implemented by Arabs.

Lawrence was now summoned to the recently appointed new commander of the Egyptian Expeditionary Force, General Edmund Allenby, who had

taken over from General Archibald Murray following his defeat at the
Second Battle of Gaza. Allenby didn't quite know what to make of this
strange, emaciated little man dressed in a white Arab robe and headdress.
Allenby, nicknamed 'Bloody Bull', was a burly giant, about the size of three
Lawrences. Lawrence showed Allenby his sketch map, which set out the
potential for seven separate Arab forces striking the Turks across Syria.
Allenby mulled over Lawrence's hugely ambitious vision for coordinated
action with the Palestine command. Later writing of himself, Lawrence
commented: 'Allenby could not make out how much was genuine performer
and how much charlatan.' The Commander-in-Chief simply said: 'Well,
I will do for you what I can.' But in fact, Allenby, who was planning a major
new advance on Gaza, was enthralled by Lawrence's proposal. He endorsed
it and the War Committee agreed the following week. A watershed in both
the Arab Revolt and the Palestine campaign had been reached.

★ ★ ★

Just as Lawrence was about to enter the arid wastes of El Houl on one of
the toughest journeys of his life, Gray was in the rather more comfortable
surroundings of the Grand Continental Hotel in Cairo. He had arrived in
Egypt on 9 May with Wilson and was on three weeks' well-deserved leave.[3]
Gray dined in Cairo with Wilson and his wife, Beryl, and also with Bray,
who was engaged on a sensitive new mission. Gray admired Bray's pluck
and said he would have been a lieutenant-colonel or dead had he not been
in the Indian Army. Gray also dined with Captain Goslett, with whom he
had shared a tent at Rabegh and who was now in charge of supplies at Wejh.
He saw General Murray, then still Commander-in-Chief of the Egyptian
Expeditionary Force, who remembered him from his cipher officer days at
Ismailia, and twice called on the Arab Bureau.

  Gray's busy social life propelled him to the end of his leave: golf and
snooker at the Sporting Club, to the Kursaal Theatre with Bray, drinks at the
Turf Club and Shepheard's Hotel, trips to the Pyramids and to a cinema for
the must-see film *Charlie Chaplin and the Tanks*. But by 3 June, Gray was frustrated by a mix-up over his return voyage to Arabia. He knew he was needed
there and went to see Cornwallis at the Arab Bureau to press for the muddle
to be sorted out. Cornwallis advised him to go direct to the intelligence
chief, General Clayton. Clayton asked Gray how he liked Jeddah: 'I said it
would be all right if it wasn't for fever, bad smells, heat, bad food, lack of
drainage, mosquitoes, flies, humidity, lack of communication with outside

world, filthy people, etc. not to mention overwork. He was very pleasant &
said he was sorry he couldn't make me a Captain just then.'[4]

Gray had to wait until 17 June before leaving Suez for Wejh. He spent a day
there with Wilson, Joyce, Davenport, Goslett, and his cipher officer colleague,
'Hoppy' Hopwood. Gray gave Hoppy the clarinet he had been asked to collect from a Cairo music shop. To the many surreal experiences of the British
in Arabia were added the faltering notes of Hoppy's clarinet at dusk as they
punctured the languorous air of Wejh. On 19 June, Gray crossed the Red Sea
on HMS *Dufferin* to Port Sudan, on an unspecified mission that perhaps
involved new ciphers.[5] By late June, he was back in 'salubrious Jeddah'.[6] Here
he became mess president, which was time-consuming, the more so as he had
only one assistant now.[7] The post involved budgeting for and ordering food
and drinks, and planning meals, including entertaining King Hussein and his
representatives, the French Military Mission, and other guests. Gray was soon
to claim that he had saved hundreds of pounds which were only wasted
before.[8] Camel caravans brought tomatoes from Mecca and sweet potatoes,
turnips, cabbages, and tomatoes from Taif. Gray's native cook produced an
imaginative steak and kidney pudding, which had the surprise ingredient of a
number of little birds.[9] The cook could also turn his hand to roast sirloin of
beef, roast mutton, scrambled eggs, omelette, porridge, onion sauce, and jam
roly-poly.[10] As with the golf course, the Consulate staff were revealing a
national characteristic: the ability of the British to recreate the Home Counties
in whatever remote part of the world they were operating.

The British often played bridge with the French Military Mission as part
of their entertaining (the French were very good at this game). Wilson played
Brémond at golf and Gray captured the moment in a photograph. Brémond's
star had been waning since April, partly thanks to Lawrence's intrigues, and
it seemed he might have to leave the Hejaz.[11] (In fact Brémond clung on
until December, which left plenty more scope for annoying Wilson.)

★   ★   ★

It was no accident that Bray had been in Cairo at the same time as Gray. His
strongly expressed wish to carry on working for his close associate, Sir Mark
Sykes, had been answered. He had been taken on again to run another
secret operation that Sykes was trying to get off the ground. Bray apparently
sold Sykes the idea for an Arab Legion to support the revolt. It would con-
sist of Arab prisoners of war from the Ottoman Army currently in camps in
Egypt, Mesopotamia, India, and Burma, together with Egyptians and volunteers from Aden.

In fact, the first batch of prisoners of war had come over from India back in September 1916 to join Nuri al-Said at Rabegh, but it was not possible to recruit enough of them.[12] The concept of an Arab Legion with proper training in Egypt promised better results. In recruiting Ottoman prisoners of war for the Arab Revolt, the British and their Hashemite allies were using against their enemies a tool the Germans had employed in the European war. The Germans had set up special camps for Muslim prisoners of war, and encouraged North Africans and Indians to defect to the Ottoman Army (though with only very limited success—the British enrolled far more Ottoman prisoners into the Arab Northern Army).

Towards the end of May, Sykes went to Britain's Aden Protectorate to discuss the matter with the Resident, the British political officer. By then Bray was heavily involved in planning and in visiting prisoner of war camps in Egypt.[13] Sykes had good hopes of raising two efficient battalions by mid-September. Major Gerard Leachman, an influential Indian Army intelligence officer and Arabist based in Mesopotamia, went to India with two Indian officers in late May to tour the prisoner of war camps and enrol recruits. Sykes told the War Office that the Legion would fight for the Arab cause on Arab soil: 'When the periodic Rabegh panic occurs, as I anticipate it may in October–November, everyone will be thankful for a fairly cohesive force whose presence in Hejaz will not compromise the reputation of the Holy Places.'[14] The Legion would promote Syrian and Arab unity and 'supply us with a rallying point for deserters...who come over through conviction and not through cowardice'.[15]

Sykes wrote: 'I am convinced that an Arab National movement is growing and that now is the moment to gain it as an asset of the Entente.'[16] He wanted the Legion to be set up and funded jointly by the British and the French. Scheming as ever, he told the War Office that the French costs were agreed purely on Georges-Picot's personal say-so and asked that this private initiative should not be raised with the French. But the French Government did become involved in the discussions, and when a British Foreign Office clique 'took an unreasoning hatred of the Arab Legion...three months' intrigue and folly' followed. Sykes put his political infighting skills to good use and, finally, in late July, he told Clayton he was confident the Arab Legion would get the go-ahead.[17]

Approval was given, but by now Bray was disillusioned. In effect part of the Sykes-Picot Mission, he had been given an office at the Arab Bureau. He had set up a committee of Arab officers from among the prisoners to advise on the formation of the Legion. But freedom for the Arab officers meant that they were able to discuss political ideas with Syrian nationalists based in Cairo. The officers got to hear rumours of the Sykes-Picot Agreement and came to Bray asking for an assurance that they would be fighting for the true independence of their country. Bray's conscience was pricking him and he knew he could not give this assurance. He went to Sykes and said he wanted to resign.[18] Sykes wanted to keep Bray, and to placate him and the Arab officers he told them that the future of the Arab peoples lay in their own hands. These weasel words could not satisfy Bray and the officers for long. Bray later wrote: 'How, then, could I be a party to a deception which I knew would dishonour the name of my country and alienate our friends of the Arab world.'[19] Like Wilson and Lawrence, Bray was not the sort of man who could keep his conscience under wraps. He resigned from his mission and returned to his regiment in France. Setting up the organization and training methods for the Arab Legion was to be the final part of Bray's legacy for the revolt. His important groundwork would be built on by another member of Wilson's influential Jeddah circle. The eccentric but competent and shrewd Major Hugh Pearson was about to appear centre-stage in Egypt and would soon be closely involved with the expanding base at Aqaba.

★   ★   ★

While Wilson was in Cairo with Gray, his deputy, Bassett, was very capably holding the fort. He had arrived at Jeddah by 6 April. Affable, tactful, and efficient, Bassett had been a governor of two provinces in the Sudan and had been a senior intelligence officer there. He was touched by the great camel crisis in September 1916, when his name was put forward as an emergency camel buyer in the Sudan. Not long after, he took up an important though short-lived role as intelligence liaison officer with the French in the eastern Mediterranean, working closely with the British Eastern Mediterranean Special Intelligence Bureau. Then followed command of the 2nd Battalion of the Imperial Camel Corps in Sinai, from November 1916 to March 1917, and a top quartermaster job with the British Military Mission in the Hejaz. Bassett continued with this role for a time at Jeddah, parallel to his diplomatic duties. He received a number of requests for supplies, in May and June, from Joyce at Wejh.

Bassett's skills were soon harnessed to the delicate art of dealing with Hussein. He met the king and Feisal with Wilson and Newcombe from time to time to discuss military strategy. Bassett noted how Wilson's steadying

and trusted influence over Hussein—sometimes reassuring, sometimes persuading—helped lubricate the revolt. For example, on 24 May, as Wilson
told Clayton: 'At Jeddah I got the Sherif to write a strong letter to Sherif Ali
telling him to buck up generally and that he should attack the railway line
at Buwait and between there and Medina and really destroy it.'[20]

Bassett and Wilson were soon to obtain intelligence on the number of spare
rails stockpiled at each station, which indicated how difficult it would be for
the Turks to repair lengthy sections that had been blown up. Not only that, but
the information would be obtained from a new and groundbreaking source:

> From the first attempt at organised military intelligence obtained through an
> Arab Intelligence Officer we hear that twenty to forty rails are kept at every
> station, 3000 rails being at Medina, and 100 to 200 at El Ula and Medain Saleh.
> There is no water at most of the stations, and it is brought to them by means
> of the trains.[21]

A network of agents, run by a Hashemite, Syrian, or Mesopotamian Arab,
must have produced this information. It is not clear to what extent the

Figure 18. House of the Kaimakam (Governor) of Wejh, who is standing in the
centre at the back, talking to Colonel John Bassett (in white topee) and Colonel
Edouard Brémond (only his helmet is visible). With Cousse (foreground) and
Pisani (wearing fez) of the French Military Mission.

British may have been involved, though Ruhi had sources in Medina. Feisal, Abdullah and Ali had their own spies; a factor which is easy to overlook in western accounts of the revolt.[22]

★   ★   ★

Bassett is one of the forty officers mentioned by Lawrence, in the Preface to *Seven Pillars of Wisdom*, as being able, like him, to tell their own stories about the Arab Revolt. While Bassett gave invaluable support to Wilson at the southern hub of the revolt, an additional hub was being assembled over six hundred miles to the north. The deserted beaches of Aqaba were being transformed as the new base soon outgrew Wejh and became the focal point of Hashemite and British ambitions.

10

Hopes and Fears

Wilson tended to be as honest with himself as with others. He recognized at once the vital role in the capture of Aqaba played by the officer he had called a 'bumptious young ass' eight months earlier, and recommended that Lawrence should be given the Distinguished Service Order. Wilson had always wanted to see a move to the north followed by an advance into Syria. He knew his dented pride at having been one of those duped by Lawrence as he set off on his circuitous route to Aqaba was unimportant. Wilson praised Lawrence's key contribution and vision, realizing they stood to give a huge boost to the progress of the revolt.

Lawrence set off on HMS *Dufferin* for Jeddah on 17 July. His stock had risen so high that it seemed obvious that he should be the officer to broach a controversial subject in person with King Hussein—a meeting that would never have been entertained two months before. Allenby had agreed to Lawrence's suggestion that Feisal, advised by Lawrence, should report directly to the British commander-in-chief, and become his right arm on the far side of the River Jordan. Lawrence had sold Allenby and Clayton a plausible piece of wishful thinking—that the Syrian leaders were keen to rally round Feisal and look to the Hashemites (distrusted by many) to obtain their independence. Nuri Shalaan, for one, would have given a hollow laugh at the prospect. But Lawrence, not always letting the truth get in the way of a good story, now seemed bent on shaping the narrative of the revolt to suit his ideas. The Syrians would rally round because he said they would.

Lawrence's scheme promised to enhance the prospects of Allenby's proposed move up through Palestine, in distracting and perhaps tying down Turkish troops in Syria that might otherwise be diverted to Palestine. Feisal had written to his father endorsing the transfer of his army to Allenby's command. But Hussein, as Wilson and now Bassett knew all too well, was the most suspicious of leaders, jealous of even his own sons and wanting to exercise all control himself. This could have been one of Lawrence's trickiest assignments. Fortunately he had all of Wilson's experience and influence over Hussein to count on. On 22 July Lawrence arrived at Jeddah. Wilson was ready to discuss personnel for the Aqaba base with him: it had already been decided that Stewart Newcombe, to whom Lawrence owed much, would not get the commandant's role, which went to Major Pierce Joyce. Newcombe had never been able to reconcile himself to the Arabs' lack of discipline and inability to act like the British Army.

When Lawrence met King Hussein with Wilson on 28 July, it was Lawrence's first encounter with the Hashemite leader. Hussein quickly accepted the proposed new role for Feisal. Part of the Arab regular army would soon be on its way to Aqaba and the rest, under Jafar al-Askari, would go there in late August with Feisal. At a meeting the following day, Hussein made it clear to Lawrence and Wilson at some length how worried he was by the austere Wahhabi branch of Islam that was followed by his arch-rival Ibn Saud. Wilson and Bassett would have to deal with these concerns before many weeks had elapsed.

For now, Lawrence had to react urgently to some stunning and disturbing news from an intercepted Turkish cable.[1] Auda abu Tayi, his partner in the Aqaba campaign, was secretly talking to the Turks and contemplating joining them. Lawrence returned to Aqaba at once, then travelled inland to meet the Howeitat chief at Guweira, an important village between Aqaba and Maan. The stakes were high because the Turks had already recaptured Aba el Lissan and were bombing the Arabs at Aqaba. It was vitally important that the Howeitat stuck to their positions or the Turks could retake the Wadi Itm, with fatal consequences for the Syrian campaign. In an inspired stream of elliptical references to Auda's wisdom and successes as a great raider, and to more gold coins to come, Lawrence the shy showman somehow retrieved the situation and drew Auda back into Feisal's orbit. He had the spark of insight, an Arab's instinct for what to say and how to say it, an extraordinary empathy that made him an outstanding intelligence officer. Conjuring up more smoke and mirrors, Lawrence blithely told Cairo the Auda affair had all been just a misunderstanding.

Lawrence had protected his credibility and that of his vision. He was prepared to lie not just for his country but also to his country. Above all, he was prepared to lie for himself. If pressed, he would probably have given his trademark impish grin and spoken softly of constructive ambiguity. But inside him was a hard kernel of utterly focused and ruthless will which sat uneasily and enigmatically with the sensitivities of a deeply moral man. In practical terms, Lawrence continued to get away with his extraordinary trick of being at the same time an intelligence officer, a shaper and implementer of policy, and a combatant in the field.

Lawrence's travels now took him to Cairo for a week, where he met Wilson again to discuss the northern campaign with Clayton and others at the Arab Bureau. Funding, supplies, and strategy needed to be thrashed out. At this time Lawrence wrote some remarkable guidelines called 'Twenty-seven Articles', which succinctly set out how to influence the intensely proud and independent Bedouin without appearing to do so: 'The less apparent your interferences the more your influence. They are willing to follow your advice and do what you wish, but they do not mean you or anyone else to be aware of that.'[2]

The way was now clear for a huge military build-up at the Aqaba base. Lawrence returned there on 17 August, the day after his twenty-ninth birthday. This backwater of a port was transformed by the constant arrival of ships of the Red Sea Patrol offloading huge quantities of supplies, animals, weapons, gold sovereigns, and thousands of fighters. The day after Lawrence arrived, HMS *Hardinge* brought Jafar al-Askari and eight hundred Arab regulars. Feisal's men were also ferried from the base at Wejh and were joined by new recruits trekking in from the mountains to the east. But all was not plain sailing. There were many supply and other logistical problems because of the very large numbers of men. Lawrence threw himself into a host of tasks in what he called 'the maddest campaign ever run'. For the present it was 'heavy and slow, weary work'.[3] The flight of Royal Flying Corps planes from Yenbo was quickly brought up the coast to counter the Turkish aircraft from Maan that were regularly bombing Aqaba.

★   ★   ★

Cyril Wilson was gratified to receive a letter in the first week of September from Major Lawrence, as he had become. Lawrence praised Wilson's role in the 'Hejaz show', saying his good experiences of it were 'largely due to you, of course'. Lawrence added that people

> do not seem always to appreciate that while we hop about the Railway and places smashing things up, and enjoying ourselves, someone else has to sit and stew in Jidda keeping the head of the affair on the rails. You would be glad to hear sometimes how Feisul and the rest speak of you.[4]

Wilson had by then been stewing in Jeddah for the past fifteen months, stoically drawing on reserves of patience, diplomacy, and endurance. He had also travelled up and down the coast, into the interior, and across the Red Sea to Cairo. He had been keeping not merely King Hussein 'on the rails' but also the very revolt itself. Lawrence probably recognized this and knew that without those metaphorical rails, all the railway tracks blown up in the desert would have counted for nothing.

Wilson, supported by Bassett, now had one of his stiffest tests in bolstering Hussein and keeping the Arab Revolt show on the road. Jeddah was the beating heart of the revolt but its rhythm was irregular. The warning signs were there back on 29 July at Jeddah, when Hussein showed Wilson and Lawrence just how anxious he was about the threat from the hard-line Wahhabis in the Nejd, the central Arabian territory of his great rival, the warlord Ibn Saud. The cantankerous Hussein was becoming seriously distracted by his formidable opponent. Ibn Saud, like all the tribal chiefs in the Arabian Peninsula, was constantly looking over his shoulder in case there was a Turkish recovery. He was happy to run with the hare and hunt with the hounds, even though he received a subsidy from British India, and took a canny long-term view. He encouraged the Wahhabi zealots as a counterpoise to King Hussein's overambitious bid for empire. The pro-Turk, Ibn Rashid, rival of both leaders and warlord of the large Shammar confederation of tribes in north-central Arabia, was the other main player. The British knew that there had never been a precedent for a united Arabia, where sectarianism and fierce independence ruled—and there was no prospect for one, whatever the outcome of the Hashemite revolt.

These facts came home powerfully to Wilson and made his pilgrimage liaison man, William Cochrane, apprehensive during the September Hajj when Hussein's noisy neighbours turned up in town. Ibn Saud's brother, Mohamed, was escorted to Mecca by 7,000 armed Wahhabi tribesmen. This show of power unnerved Hussein. He was already downcast from the time, soon after the capture of Aqaba, when he lost the loyalty of the tribes along the Jeddah to Mecca road.[5] This had caused him to drop his support for Feisal's planned move from Wejh to Aqaba. Wilson had helped talk him round. Hussein was prone to vacillation at the best of times and his old suspicions returned. He wanted to keep the revolt in his own hands and now, worried about the threat from Ibn Saud, he was getting cold feet about the planned Hashemite push from Aqaba into Syria. He refused to give Feisal the large sum of about a million francs that the French at Mecca had given him.[6]

Hussein's negative mood and contrariness were now dragging Feisal down into depression. Feisal was also fearful of a Turkish attack at a time when the supply chain to Aqaba was disjointed. He even talked of suicide.[7] He despaired too of his own brothers, Ali and Abdullah, who like Hussein were not interested in the Syrian movement. Feisal suspected that Abdullah and his father did not want to capture Medina because then British payments to Hussein would end. This belief was encouraged some weeks later, when Wilson heard that Hussein declined an offer from Fakhri Pasha to withdraw from Medina and set off for Damascus.[8]

In the anti-climax after the capture of Aqaba, the momentum of the revolt was slowing dangerously. The risk that it could unravel could not be ignored. At this time Wilson and Bassett were the vital men who helped pull Hussein back from the brink of despair. Their patient and open dealings with him were a bedrock of the revolt. They knew that if they could persuade Hussein to hold his nerve and to keep paying Feisal from his British subsidy, then Feisal would be more likely to regain his equilibrium and courage, and the prospects for a Syrian advance would be improved. Wilson and Bassett managed to traverse this diplomatic minefield and in doing so steered the revolt back on course. Their role was indispensable.

★ ★ ★

Another officer contributing to the Aqaba build-up was Wilson's old Jeddah colleague, the golf-mad Pearson, who now enters the story again. Many more recruits were needed for Feisal's Northern Arab Army. With Sir Mark Sykes's return to London to deal with his political enemies, and Bray's unwillingness to continue with the Ottoman prisoner of war training programme, Pearson was drafted in from the Sudan in August to pick up the baton. General Wingate had a high opinion of Pearson, 'who has done consistently good work in all the special missions on which he has been employed'.[9] Writing of the Arab Legion work, he told Sykes that Pearson was 'an ideal man for it—full of energy, charming manners and already greatly liked and trusted by the French officers'. The prisoners of war kept cooped up in Cairo while the powers-that-be debated whether to go ahead with the scheme were 'fed up and in a nasty frame of mind', so Wingate decided not to start with them but to wait for the thirty officers and 420 men who were due to leave India for Egypt at the end of August: 'They will form the nucleus...Pearson is dead keen on a success, and I hope that in three weeks or a month we shall have an infantry battalion and a four gun battery in being'.[10]

Pearson sailed to Aden on 4 September with a French officer, Colonel Coulombre, to meet the prisoners, then travelled back with them, using the time to get to know them. Pearson told Clayton that they were disappointed at not being landed in the Hejaz, as they hoped to fight for Sherif Hussein immediately. Most of the Arab prisoners claimed that they had been forced to fight for the Turks. Clayton continued: 'Faisal is very anxious for them to go straight to him at Akaba, but I have told him that they will be much better & more easily trained at Ismailia and that he will get them when they are ready for service.'[11] On 24 September the contingent marched through Ismailia, with the sherif's flag borne in front of them, to its camp at Ferry Post East beside the Suez Canal. In all there were three British and two French advisory officers, with an escort from the Warwickshire Regiment for security.[12]

Just two days later Pearson was facing up to the realities of his role:

> I am afraid we have got an uphill task here to make the men obey their officers...
> We have won the men all right...But their own officers are appalling and
> I suppose it is not to be wondered at after over two years of life as prisoners
> of war.

Pearson's ideas on how to raise the morale of the Arab officers did not all come from the training manual: 'They have got to get back their self-respect and we have given them a nice mess [rooms for relaxing and eating in], really smart uniforms and they have got to buy themselves sticks [officers' swagger sticks], slap their legs and stare at the girls.'[13] He was amused to see that nearly all the soldiers passed themselves off as at least a grade higher than their rank in the Ottoman Army.

Pearson's natural ebullience was soon to the fore. Within a week he could write:

> We have really made an astonishing start and are going to be a success beyond,
> I think, the expectation and almost the wishes of Great Britain and France. It is
> all right now but such a spirit has arisen that future difficulties may be in store,
> when Arabs will consider themselves capable of running their own affairs.

Pearson was typical of most British officers in finding full Arab independence impossible to imagine. The training camp had a visit from delegates from Sherif Hussein and a telegram from him read out on parade 'created such enthusiasm and astonishment that the delegates talked of our numbers reaching 20,000'.[14]

Pearson's reference to future difficulties was a clue that he was now wrestling with his conscience about the Sykes-Picot Agreement. He had listened to a private and to three or four officers from the prisoners of war volunteers who had all spoken enthusiastically on parade about Arab unity and Arab independence. It was a fired-up Nuri al-Said, Feisal's Mesopotamian chief of staff (and former officer in the Ottoman Army), who mentioned the figure of 20,000 to Pearson after these speeches. The heady optimism, if such it was, matched Hussein's own unrealistic hopes for an Arab empire under his control. The arrival of the king's delegates was designed to boost morale amongst the prisoner volunteers. But Pearson was troubled and in a private letter to Clayton wondered,

> how awkward it would be if the question was put as to what was intended with regard to Syria and Baghdad. In anything I have said I have been most awfully careful to steer clear of such things, but I cannot help feeling that we are not absolutely straight with these people.

Fuad el Khatib, Hussein's secretary, had made a measured speech to the volunteer soldiers, which set Pearson thinking: 'Fuad, I suppose, knows the arrangement after the war and he was very temperate, but I am not quite easy about the whole thing, as I feel sure we do not mean all that they mean and that we are letting them think we mean.'[15]

Clayton sent Sir Mark Sykes just an extract from Pearson's letter. He told Sykes that 'owing chiefly to the energy and tact of Pearson and Coulombre, the Legion settled down and has steadily improved...I have explained to Pearson the situation and the fears which he expressed...have been allayed'. This was a prime example of the shrewd spymaster's command of bureaucratic language. Whether Pearson saw things the same way as Clayton is hard to judge, but what is clear is that the prisoners of war felt anxious in case the Legion were to be used outside the Arab front. Clayton said he thought it was essential to use the Legion soldiers entirely in Arab areas and under their own officers and, to ally any misgivings, 'a considerable detachment should be sent to Akaba to join Emir Feisal's operations as soon as possible'. Clayton added that to use the Legion in Palestine or in any operations along the Syrian coast (which the French had been considering) would lead to very considerable trouble.

Then, in a breathtakingly disingenuous passage with his usual tone of calm reasonableness, Clayton remarked:

> After all, it is for the cause of Arab freedom that we formed the Legion, and it would be very unfortunate if we allowed any impression to arise that we were using it for our own purposes...the Legion under its own flag would have an excellent effect in impressing on the Syrians the fact that the Arab is really fighting in earnest for his freedom and independence.

Clayton's approach was subtle and devious. He knew the value of encouraging perceptions in the minds of people with strong aspirations.

Perhaps Clayton pulled the wool over Pearson's eyes; perhaps Pearson let this happen. He carried on, describing the men with a strange mixture of condescension and affection:

> We look smart, we don't get drunk or cause trouble in the towns, we have a soldierly bearing…We really look rather fine wild men…and most of us have been under fire and though most of us, it is true, have been prisoners of war, we have very quickly thrown all that off and now own the streets as free men, ready to cut the throat of any Turk who comes along. We had a route march this morning, rather ridiculous, but we have four buglers who can bugle a weird march at the head of the battalion and we have a flag with a red half diamond and black green and white stripes distinctive of the Arab race.[16]

Not surprisingly, there were tensions at the training camp. The Arab Legion's commanding officer, Major Kholki, was terrified of the men and constantly asking for four or five to be shot, and when Pearson stopped him doing so, Kholki complained that he was insulting his authority and the honour of the Arab flag.[17] At the end of October, Pearson made some revealing comments to his sister, Ursula:

> I am running a motley crowd, mostly Bagdadis [sic]…as the first beginnings of an independent Arab Army, uniting the Arabs of the Persian Gulf,…of the Hadramut, of Aden, the Yemen, Asir and the Hedjaz, and Palestine, Syria, Mesopotamia, and central Arabian Arabs all fanatically against the Turk. Religion does not nominally creep in, and we have Christians and Jew Arabs as well as Moslems, actually there are of course squabbles…Sir Mark Sykes and M. Picot hide in London and Paris and leave us to stand the racquet [sic]. Revolutions are of only about twice a week occurrence now instead of daily.[18]

Pearson was pleased to see the back of the first batch of the Arab Legion. There was a frustrating twenty-four-hour delay as the men were about to march off for Suez. This led to serious insubordination and Pearson blamed the Legion's commanding officer for fomenting trouble. SS *Ada* left Suez for Aqaba on 19 November, with thirty officers and three hundred men.[19] One of the officers now based at Aqaba to oversee their further training and deployment was the adventurous former camel buyer with Goodchild at Jeddah, the Australian Major, Harold Suttor. Pearson looked forward to a less troublesome detachment to come, but thought the Legion was started too late because the war would be over soon (he was to be proved wrong). A contingent arrived from Aden; they and the Yemenis were far less trouble than the men from Mesopotamia.[20]

Pearson arranged a soccer league with a team from each of the five sections of the Legion and a band with drums and bugles to encourage *esprit de corps*.[21] As an Assistant Political Officer, and having to self-censor his own letters, he was remarkably indiscreet in his letters home. Of the Arabs conscripted into the Turkish Army,

> many of them have had their homes looted by Turks and Germans, so they were very fanatically anti-Turk and German, though by no means particularly pro-Allies. They were for Arabia for the Arab and Arab independence. If asked whether they would sooner have Turks or English over them, many would probably say Turks, as after all they are their fellow religionists. But they are fanatically against having anything to do with either...Of course they are quite incapable of governing themselves, and their ideals are incapable of realisation probably for many decades.[22]

Pearson would have preferred to have been doing the job on his own, without the French, but knew this was a political rather than a military arrangement. The French were forming the *Détachement Français de Palestine et de Syrie*, including four battalions of Armenians, two of which formed the *Légion d'Orient*.

> You may ask what the French are doing here, and everybody wants to know. There are big political matters at stake though and by allowing participation here we can claim things more important elsewhere....I shall have well earned my military medal from the French for having a gin and bitters daily before lunch, a cognac after lunch, two whiskies and sodas before dinner and another gin and bitters and cognac after dinner. And yet I have a very clear eye and ditto head, and if it does mean an earlier grave, I am after all dying slowly for my country.[23]

A further contingent of the Arab Legion sailed for Aqaba on 16 December. By 26 December there were another 575 volunteers and as many more were expected. Feisal was heavily involved. A secret cable from Aqaba to the Arab Bureau read: 'Feisal will be glad of all volunteers. These should be fully armed and equipped before leaving Cairo even if this causes slight delay. Officers are also required but please submit names before appointing them in order to obtain Feisal's approval.'[24] Feisal was using his intelligence networks to identify Ottoman spies amidst potential officers of the Legion. By now Pearson had left for political officer duties on the Palestine front, where he would liaise with the Arab forces under Feisal and with Lawrence. For his

Figure 19. Arab Regular Army, part of which was trained by Major Hugh Pearson in Egypt, under the Hejaz flag at Aqaba.

Figure 20. Jafar al-Askari, former Ottoman Army officer and chief of the Arab Regular Army, with Lieutenant Lamotte of the French Military Mission at Jiddah oasis, inland from Wejh.

work training the Legion and adding to Feisal's men, Pearson was awarded the Distinguished Service Order on 1 January 1918. He had played a major role in a forgotten but important episode of the Arab Revolt.

Far to the south at Jeddah, Gray was feeling the pace after many months of concentrated ciphering work and intermittent ill health. He was finding it hard at times to focus on his challenging routine with its lonely rigour. He was also a world away from the frontline action that he once more craved.[25] Meanwhile Lawrence had what Gray longed for. But it came at great cost as his world spiralled into despair and post-traumatic stress.

11

Great Escapes

On 7 September, five days after praising Wilson for his key role in the Arab Revolt, Lawrence set off from Aqaba heading for the railway south of Maan. He intended to attack Mudawwara station, which had vitally important water supplies on the line of communication to Medina. A blow here would knock out the only large source of water for more than 240 kilometres and would cripple the railway. It would also distract the Turks from trying to retake Aqaba and would boost flagging Arab morale. But Lawrence was able to raise only a third of the Bedouin he wanted, because Auda abu Tayi's Howeitat at Guweira were blowing hot and cold about supporting Feisal and some were moaning about not being paid. So instead of Mudawwara, Lawrence's band attacked a ten-carriage train on a bridge on 18 September. He used an electric exploder for the first time, rather than a contact mine. The train's two engines and the first carriage were blasted into the culvert under the collapsed bridge. The devastating effects were complemented by deadly fire from two Lewis machine guns and a Stokes trench mortar on a rocky outcrop, operated by two instructors from Aqaba.[1] The Lewis guns slaughtered a number of stunned Turkish soldiers sitting on the roofs of the seven carriages that had not collapsed into the culvert. Then a mortar shell caused more carnage.

While the one hundred or so Howeitat fighters moved in to loot and take the traditional spoils of a desert raid, Lawrence also rushed down to the train. He was confronted by the hellish sights and sounds of carriages full of civilians. There were refugees and the families of Turkish officers going back to Damascus, 'thirty or forty hysterical woman...tearing their clothes and hair, shrieking themselves distracted'. Lawrence, who hated any physical contact even among friends, was appalled when some of the women's husbands 'seized my feet in a very agony of terror of instant death...I kicked them off as well as I could with bare feet'. The nightmare for this sensitive man who had no combat training got worse when he discovered a wrecked carriage full of patients bound for hospital. The carriage was upended in the culvert below, the dead and dying with their stretchers and the hot metal all mangled up together. Lawrence heard, 'Typhus!', a delirious cry, 'So I wedged shut the door and left them there, alone.'[2]

On his return to Aqaba, Lawrence wrote to an old friend:

> I'm not going to last out this game much longer: nerves going and temper wearing thin....I hope when this nightmare ends that I will wake up and become alive again. This killing and killing of Turks is horrible. When you charge in at the finish and find them all over the place in bits, and still alive many of them, and you know that you have done hundreds in the same way before, and must do hundreds more if you can.[3]

Something insidious and debilitating was beginning to snake its way into Lawrence's mind. Many decades later it would come to be called post-traumatic stress disorder, and it was to cripple him for the rest of his time in Arabia and for the rest of his life.

The day after Lawrence described his horror, he wrote jauntily to a fellow officer of the thrill of the raid: 'two beautiful shots' with the Stokes mortar killed twelve Turks on the spot and, in Bedouin style, he grabbed some loot, a 'superfine red Baluch prayer-rug'. He continued: 'I hope this sounds the fun it is. The only pity is...the wild scramble while it lasts. It's the most amateurish, Buffalo Billy sort of performance, and the only people who do it well are the Bedouin.'[4] Lawrence was whistling in the dark, trying to keep his demons at bay.

Those demons were to jostle him remorselessly as the autumn wore on. Barely a week after Lawrence's return from the blood-bath of the train raid, his Arab Bureau friend, George Lloyd, now Chief Intelligence Officer at General Headquarters (GHQ),[5] told Clayton: 'He is overworked and he must be overstrained.'[6] Lloyd's tone suggests he thought Lawrence was at serious risk of burnout.

Even as Lloyd was writing about his worries, Lawrence was on his way with Captain Pisani, the French gunner, to smash up another engine. But the Howeitat raiders began arguing amongst themselves and with other tribes, and Lawrence found himself judge, jury, witness, counsellor, and probation officer, claiming that in six days he 'had to adjudicate in twelve cases of assault with weapons, four camel-thefts, one marriage settlement, fourteen feuds, two evil eyes, and a bewitchment'.[7] Lawrence could blithely lie, exaggerate, and transpose incidents in *Seven Pillars of Wisdom*, but there is no reason to doubt the broader truth of his involvement in tribal affairs. He saw this, though, as 'false authority', because he was 'without experience, with my very imperfect knowledge of the Arabic language'.[8]

Just a few days after getting back to Aqaba from his most recent raid, Lawrence was summoned by aeroplane to a crucial meeting at GHQ near El Arish on the Sinai coast. The top brass were waiting for him on 12 October: General Allenby, General Wingate, and his mentor, David Hogarth, from the Arab Bureau. Allenby wanted to discuss with Lawrence how Feisal's Northern Arab Army could assist the long-awaited British advance on Gaza. An Arab uprising in Syria to distract the Turks there would be a bonus for Allenby, but, as Clayton warned, could lead to disaster for the Arabs if Allenby's advance was hamstrung, leaving the tribesmen exposed to a merciless Turkish onslaught. Lawrence agreed and came up with a daunting plan for a deep penetration raid to destroy one of the large railway bridges in the Yarmuk gorge, to the west of Deraa. The idea was to wreck the Turkish line of communication to Palestine, since Deraa was the junction of two lines, one from Damascus to Haifa and Jerusalem, and the other the Hejaz Railway from Damascus to Maan and Medina. Allenby wanted the bridge to be blown up on 5 November or one of the following three days, to be timed with his planned attack on Gaza following a lightning strike on Beersheba to the east. If Allenby's advance was successful and then continued, perhaps then the Syrian Arabs would have the confidence to rise up.

Lawrence proposed taking just a small Bedouin raiding group far into enemy territory, past villages with potential informers and vulnerable to the long reach of Turkish intelligence. This was a hugely risky venture and, as Lawrence returned to Aqaba on 15 October to prepare for it, his colleagues had deep reservations about the chances of a successful raid and of his very survival. George Lloyd, who had been given the go-ahead to accompany Lawrence at least some of the way, told Clayton that Lawrence was,

> much oppressed by the risk and magnitude of the job before him. He opened his heart to me last night and told me that he felt there was so much for him still to do in this world . . . that seemed horrible to have it all cut off . . . for he feels that, while he may do the job, he has little or no chance of getting away himself. . . . He is really a very remarkable fellow—not the least fearless like some who do brave things, but, as he told me last night, each time he starts out on these stunts he simply hates it for two or three days before.[9]

In choosing to do something very dangerous that he hated, Lawrence was showing outstanding bravery. And he had yet more pressure on his over-loaded mind and body: the impossible task, as he saw it, of being loyal at the same time to Allenby and to Feisal. He simply could not accept that his primary loyalty was to Allenby. It is almost as if, in his comments to Lloyd, Lawrence was in the same frame of mind as when he left his 'farewell' note to Clayton before setting off in despair on the long journey that ended with the taking of Aqaba.

Clayton replied to Lloyd: 'I am very anxious about Lawrence. He has taken on a really colossal job and I can see that it is well-nigh weighing him down. He has a lion's heart, but even so the strain must be very great.'[10] But pragmatic and far-sighted as ever, Clayton thought Lawrence should not be withdrawn just yet, because his mission impossible was needed as support for Allenby's advance. If Lawrence was to be sacrificed, so be it.

Lawrence and Lloyd set off on 24 October with Sherif Ali ibn Hussein as Arab leader of the party. For a time, as moonlight bathed the spectacular mountain backdrop to Wadi Rumm, Lawrence seemed to relax and even spoke about his family and his Oxford past—unheard of, for this most taci-turn of men. Perhaps he sensed this would be his last trip, or he wanted it to be so. But there were strange discordances. Colonel Brémond had warned Lawrence at Aqaba that Abd el Kader, the Algerian exile travelling with him and Lloyd who had promised to deliver raiders in the Yarmuk area, was a traitor in Turkish pay. Lawrence chose to ignore this advice from his old French rival and did not tell George Lloyd.

Another member of the raiding party, Lieutenant Charles Wood of the Royal Engineers, was an explosives expert and would have taken over from Lawrence if he had been injured or killed. Wood was the base engineer at Aqaba and was the only sapper available. In agreeing to be a member of the team, Wood was selfless and brave—not only had he been declared unfit for active service because of a deep bullet wound in the back of his head (inflicted at Ypres in 1915), but he was also suffering from dysentery and influenza. He struggled on, at times delirious and falling behind, in low spirits. Completing the party were a number of Captain Norman Bray's Indian machine-gunners.

This unlikely band of saboteurs pressed on, dogged by more ill omens. Lawrence got lost on two occasions. Lloyd had to insist on using his com-pass rather than following Orion in the night sky, the method Lawrence was convinced would lead to the railway.[11] An additional reason for disquiet was the fact that it was hard to attract Arab raiders for the mission—smashing up a train was fine because of the prospect of loot, but lumps of stone from a demolished bridge did not have the same allure.

Lloyd offered to stay on with Lawrence, who declined because Lloyd was not a demolition expert. The real reason was recorded by Lloyd: 'He would like me to go home to England, for he felt that there was a risk that all his work would be ruined politically in Whitehall and he thought I could save this.' Lloyd went with Lawrence as far as Jefer, 'in case he breaks down again'[12] (perhaps a reference to Lawrence's state of mind at Aqaba). Lloyd then returned to Aqaba on 29 October. He sensed that the war-weary Lawrence was anticipating death, that perhaps he felt the continuation of his own life was unimportant.

Delays in recruiting local Sirhan tribesmen meant that Lawrence's party did not reach the eastern end of the Yarmuk gorge until the evening of 7 November. Then disaster struck as one of the band dropped a rifle up by the bridge at Tell al Shehab. Turkish sentries began shooting, and the Sirhan dropped their bags of explosive into the ravine, fearful of a massive explosion if they were hit. The raid was doomed. To raise Arab morale, Lawrence bizarrely chose instead to attack a train at Minifir, south of Amman, with an inadequate length of electric cable (most had been lost in the Yarmuk gorge). He sat with his detonator behind a small bush only 50 yards from the track—he was in full view of the soldiers on a troop train, who thought they were looking at a small Arab. Sent flying by the blast, a bloodied Lawrence then limped away from the destroyed engine while Turkish soldiers shot at him, grazing him by his own account at least five times. Lawrence seemed careless about his own life. More surprisingly, he had lost his deep-seated concern for the lives of his men. He had pitched his force of sixty against four hundred Turks. Twenty of his group were shot down, including seven who were killed in the act of rescuing him. The rest had a narrow escape, back up the wadi and on to their camels. For Lawrence there was no escape, though, from the reality that the Turkish line of communication between Syria and Palestine, which Allenby had asked him to smash, was intact. He was deeply ashamed of his failure.

★   ★   ★

At the quiet hub of the revolt, Wilson continued with his vital but thankless task. His intelligence-gathering role was important and included both intercepted Turkish radio messages and the network of agents run by Hussein Ruhi.

Many reports in *The Arab Bulletin* deal with desertions from the Turkish Army, and with lack of supplies, disease, and morale at its Medina base. Wilson wrote to Wingate in September that two or three Turks as well as Syrian Arabs were deserting every day and were in a weak condition from malnourishment. He reported that the railway line was so damaged that no trains had entered Medina for fifty days. He praised the demolition work of Captain Norman Clayton and Captain William Davenport, both in the Egyptian Army. They operated in Abdullah's and Ali's territory, to the south, and the raid that put the track out of action for so long was carried out in July while Lawrence was homing in on Aqaba. Davenport and Newcombe raided Qal'at Zumrud, 140 miles north of Medina, and destroyed 3 miles of railway line; a stunning feat which was one of the most successful raids of the whole campaign. The damage was done by detachments of Egyptians, Algerians in the French Army, and Indian machine-gunners from Bray's regiment—the same Indians who were to accompany Sherif Ali and Lawrence on the Yarmuk raid. The southern campaign tends not to receive the same attention as the eye-catching raids by Lawrence and others in the north, but in keeping the Turkish garrison at Medina on the back foot, it was essential for the success of the operations in Syria.

Wilson then turned in his letter to a subject close to his heart, and one which suggested his health at the time was bearing up. He looked forward to playing golf again with Wingate: 'I hope to be able to give you a better game as I went round in 39 the other day, our bogie (9 holes) is 36.'[13]

Wilson's non-golfing efforts were recognized with the award of the Distinguished Service Order in the autumn. Later in the year, General Wingate as General Officer Commanding, Hejaz Operations, wrote to the War Office in London pressing in vain for Wilson's promotion to brigadier-general. Wingate mentioned Wilson's 'close personal relations with the King of the Hejaz', the bedrock of the revolt. He argued that the higher rank would help 'ensure the efficient discharge of Colonel Wilson's onerous and, frequently, very difficult duties'. Wingate also felt that promotion would give Wilson a degree of one-upmanship in dealing with the wily French and even more kudos in his relationship with Hussein vis-à-vis the French.[14]

Meanwhile dark clouds were gathering again over the revolt. Abdullah's and Ali's lukewarm attitude to raiding had worsened when they heard in early November about the Balfour Declaration, which gave British support for a Jewish homeland in Palestine. Then at the end of the month, the Bolsheviks in Russia leaked full details of the Sykes-Picot Agreement. Cemal

Pasha, the Turkish Governor of Syria, played on Arab doubts about their alliance with the British by announcing an amnesty for their treachery and offering gold to buy them back. When a train north of al 'Ula was ambushed, it was found to be carrying a conciliatory letter from the Turks to Hussein and £24,000 in gold.

Wilson decided to try to stiffen Abdullah's resolve in late December 1917. He set off by camel on a journey of more than 100 miles from Yenbo to the emir's camp. If he felt his good round of golf presaged a general improvement in his health, he was to be sorely mistaken. In Gray's later words: 'He was going inland to help to buck them up a bit but had not got many days in when he contracted dysentery & just got back with his life.'[15] Wilson typically tried to stick to his post at Yenbo and it was some days before he could be persuaded to transfer to the nearest hospital at Suez. The delay nearly killed him. He was carried on to HMS *Hardinge* and his anxious wife, Beryl, fearing the worst, was waiting for him at Suez. She went on board early on New Year's Day 1918, as soon as the ship docked. Beryl was shocked at her husband's weak and gaunt state.[16] Gray later wrote that Wilson's serious illness had affected his heart; recuperation in Egypt would take more than four months.[17] Fortunately, Bassett was on hand at Jeddah to step into the breach as a new crisis loomed.

★   ★   ★

Gray had been shocked to hear of his colonel's brush with death. His experiences continued to be exotic and tedious, stimulating and frustrating. He described the discomfort and weirdness of life in Jeddah, with snapshots of quirky moments and vivid images frozen in time. A welcome breeze blew biscuits off the plates and glasses off the tables on the Consulate balcony.[18] The sounds of Arab music and rifle shots carried across the water from the bay beside the golf links.[19]

A strange sing-song voice suddenly interrupted Gray's writing. The town crier was calling out the timetable and routes for the Khedivial Mail Line steamers, whose captains were sometimes entrusted with secret documents to and from the Arab Bureau. Gazing across from his balcony, Gray watched the old man on his plodding donkey, holding his umbrella up against the sun. His view also took in four or five villages.[20]

Throughout the searingly hot summer of 1917, Gray took quinine to ward off Jeddah fever (Major Marshall, the doctor, could find no evidence for the malaria that Gray had originally feared) and also spread diluted carbolic acid on his skin to counter prickly heat. Consolation arrived on 17 September, when he was mentioned in despatches.[21] The award was perhaps for his special mission at Rabegh with its attendant dangers. Young and Cochrane, however, received the same award, an acknowledgement of their tireless contribution to the vital work of Wilson's Jeddah circle, so Gray's recognition may also have been for his efforts at the Consulate.

At this time, Gray was very conscious of his fiancée Mabel's suffering. Her worst fears had been realized when her 20-year-old brother Gerald, a rookie pilot in the Royal Flying Corps, had been shot down in France in September. Mabel knew there was no real hope that Gerald was alive. In November, she told Gray: 'All joy has gone out of my life.'[22] (He would have taken this stoically.) Gray had commented earlier of Mabel: 'What with having to put up with nearly getting blown up [the Zeppelin and aeroplane attacks] & then this is about as much as anyone can be expected to stand.'[23] Gray sent Mabel some flowers from Eve's tomb, the monument outside the town walls that he could see from his balcony.

In November 1917, Gray painted a vivid picture of the link between Jeddah and Aqaba:

> We went to a reception before breakfast at the Governor's house on the occasion of the arrival of men of three tribes for reinforcements to the tribes fighting in the North at Akaba & district. They were very picturesque & all arrived from Mecca chanting their native chants as they marched and danced along brandishing their guns & rifles. They formed up in lines & rings outside the Governor's house dancing & singing.[24]

In the same month, Gray received an invitation in Arabic from Sherif Mohsen to a sunset dinner in the fasting month of Ramadan, to honour the arrival of Italian delegates from Eritrea in north-east Africa.[25]

Gray had no patience with Jeddah's beggars, whose chanting and foot stomping below his window broke his concentration when ciphering.[26] His duties now included the mess accounts, which had become 'all mixed up. . . . Funny things, accounts'. A number of these original accounts survive. Fortunately a new Army Service Corps officer, Captain Horace Fox, who had just arrived to take charge of supplies at Jeddah and Wejh, had been a chartered accountant before the war. He set right Gray's mistake and saved him further worry. Gray's gratitude did not extend as far as the golf course, where he beat Fox comprehensively, winning the first five holes out of nine. Gray's other leisure pursuits included going out riding with Kaisuni, King Hussein's Minister of War.

By early December, Gray was now censor as well as chief cipher officer and mess president. Across his desk passed everything from secret intelligence directives to the mundane 'Order for Intoxicating Liquors, whisky, 2 cases' (which might have continued 'Brémond, for the use of', in the mind of the sociable French colonel). One of the secret documents, sent by the pre-war psychical researcher, Commander Everard Feilding of the Arab Bureau, specified recognition prefixes distinguishing cables from General Clayton (Director), Colonel Dawnay (Intelligence and Operations) and Major Wordie (Supplies and Personnel).[27]

★   ★   ★

After the failure of the Yarmuk bridge raid and the near-suicidal attack on the troop train, Lawrence and Wood set off for the commanding medieval fortress of Azrak, to the east of Amman in what is now Jordan. Lawrence had met Nuri Shalaan, the powerful leader of the great Rualla tribe, there in June. This oasis in its harsh and empty wasteland was an ideal forward base for the Syrian campaign. Lawrence spent a few days there, then set off with three men to reconnoitre the Hauran area for a possible uprising. On this trip he slipped into the important railway junction of Deraa to gather intelligence, passing himself off as a fair-skinned Circassian. Two years later he claimed he had endured an appalling and brutal ordeal of torture and rape here, at the hands of the Ottoman Bey (governor) and his guards. Viciously lashed, bloody, and beaten, he managed to escape and got back to Azrak. He sent Wood on ahead, then two days later, with a broken body barely able to ride, made an astonishing three-day camel journey to Aqaba, covering a scarcely credible 86 miles a day. Lawrence tore out his diary entry for the day in Deraa (which has led some to question whether he was there at all)[28] and only mentioned the story, in 1919, for political reasons when he wished to discredit a pan-Islamist who was causing trouble for Feisal in Syria. Lawrence later admitted that his extraordinarily candid and almost exultant description of the Deraa incident in *Seven Pillars of Wisdom* was a deception (which is not the same as saying that it lacks any elements of truth). As George Bernard Shaw wrote of Lawrence, 'He told me that his account of the affair is not true. I forebore to ask him what actually happened.'[29]

It is tempting to try to cut a path through Lawrence's dense psychic undergrowth and easy to get lost in the attempt. It seems likely, though impossible to prove, that something traumatic, painful, and humiliating involving sexual surrender took place at Deraa. It is also clear that Lawrence was mortified by his failure to blow up the bridge and to raise the revolt in

Syria, and perhaps he embroidered whatever happened at Deraa to project his periodic feelings of worthlessness and need for masochistic punishment. Ultimately Lawrence is no different from everyone else: in essence his unknowable self lies deep within him, out of reach.

★ ★ ★

When Lawrence returned to Aqaba in late November he heard of Allenby's seizure of Gaza and of his rapid advance—though with considerable losses— through Palestine to take Jerusalem. Lawrence travelled to the city and was in a group of officers walking behind Allenby as he made his low-key entrance on 11 December. Curiously, less than three weeks after the ordeal Lawrence described, Hogarth wrote that he was 'looking fitter and better than when I saw him last'[30] (though Lawrence was of course good at dissembling). The short film of Allenby's entry, made by a War Office cinematographer, allows a fleeting glimpse of Lawrence's broad grin. Lawrence's old friend Ronald Storrs was appointed military governor of the city. Meanwhile his old adversary, Colonel Brémond, had finally been dismissed from the Hejaz, a victim partly of Lawrence's machinations.

Lawrence was back at Aqaba when Wilson lay dangerously close to death at Yenbo. Meanwhile Wilson's deputy John Bassett was having to cope with worrying crises that once again had Sherif Hussein at their epicentre.

12

'Someone you once knew and a King'

Bassett, like Wilson, was by now familiar with the wiles of the arch-intriguer and power broker, Sherif Mohsen. In late 1917 Bassett had to warn the Arab Bureau that Mohsen, Governor of Jeddah and hereditary emir of the Harb tribe, was behind the unrest of his own followers. Hussein had stopped paying the Harb, in an attempt to get an increase in his British subsidy, and this rankled because as *The Arab Bulletin* reported, the Harb 'have robbed all and sundry for centuries on the Medina–Mecca roads' and they still expected to be bought off as in the past. An additional problem was that Ottoman intelligence was encouraging divisions in the fragile Hashemite tribal alliance. Some of the Harb were coming under the influence of two pro-Turk leaders. Ibn Rashid, leader of the Shammar confederation of tribes in north-central Arabia and, for the time being, camped near Medina, was one. The other was Sheikh Hussein Mubeirik, who occupied the hilly ground behind Rabegh.[1] He had been a menace when Gray visited Rabegh with Wilson back in December 1916.

Harb raiders had even attacked a French military party and stolen some of Emir Ali's supplies. Bassett worked hard with Hussein to bring this disturbing development to a rapid end. Within two weeks of his report, he was able to send the Arab Bureau copies of letters from Hussein, signed by many Harb chiefs, professing loyalty to the Hashemite leader.[2] It seems likely that Bassett persuaded Hussein to deliver to the Harb leaders some of the bags of British gold sovereigns that he had been hoarding. Bassett was genial and unfussy and had struck up a good relationship with Hussein. He was amused on one occasion to receive a request from the Hashemite leader in what he called Hussein's 'official epistolary style': 'And now, O excellent Agent! would you allow me to ask whether the despatch or two or four aeroplanes would make any appreciable difference to Great Britain's total of aeroplanes, which are like the locusts in number?'[3] There was already a flight of the hard-pressed Royal Flying Corps outside Aqaba, and the locust simile did not go down well with the Arab Bureau.

The second Christmas Day of the revolt had arrived and Bassett, Gray, and four colleagues enjoyed a glass of port in the morning with the special cake sent by Mrs Beryl Wilson. Later they emptied the three bottles of champagne left behind by Cochrane, who was on leave in Cairo. For Gray it was mostly work and not much play: there were many incoming cables and the wires were particularly bad and full of wrong figures,[4] which entailed extra hours of meticulous deciphering. There was now a new wireless staff at the Consulate.

★   ★   ★

On the day a dangerously ill Wilson was carefully carried on to HMS *Hardinge*, bound for hospital at Suez, one of the dominating personalities amongst British Arabists unexpectedly arrived by camel at Jeddah. Gray ran to get his camera to record the event. It was 31 December 1917 and 32-year-old Harry St John Bridger Philby, bearded and clad in his usual Arab robes, was the last man Sherif Hussein wished to see in his territory. Philby was the champion of Ibn Saud, Emir of the puritanical Wahhabis of Nejd in central Arabia and great rival of the sherif. Philby was a Political Officer for the Government of India, which opposed British support for Hussein and was paying Ibn Saud £60,000 per year as part of an earlier treaty arrangement. Philby was also quite open in his belief that Ibn Saud would make a better leader than Hussein against the Ottomans. Hussein was outraged when he was told that Philby's escort from Riyadh, Ibn Saud's base, included some die-hard Wahhabis and a detachment of Ibn Saud's personal bodyguards.

Bassett had to cope with the diplomatic fallout. He made great efforts to steady Hussein, who was sulking in Mecca and refused to meet Philby. Philby claimed that he wanted to mediate between Ibn Saud and Hussein, on the basis that a friendly relationship would be in Britain's best interests, and his pretext for turning up was that a meeting had to be in the Hejaz because Hussein had refused to allow a team of negotiators from Cairo to pass through his territory to Riyadh. The British moved swiftly to repair the damage. Commander David Hogarth (former director of the Arab Bureau) was despatched to Jeddah just two days after Philby's arrival—standing in for Ronald Storrs, whose new duties kept him in Palestine. By the time Hogarth arrived a few days later, Bassett had been mollifying Hussein for nearly a week and had also had the difficult task of entertaining his unexpected British guest, who had no intention of moving on.[5] Hussein was already reeling from the double whammy of the Balfour Declaration about British support for a Jewish homeland in Palestine, and the Bolsheviks' spilling of the beans about the full details of the Sykes-Picot Agreement. Bassett was vitally important as the man on the spot because Hussein's feathers had been badly ruffled and he had talked despairingly of suicide.

Bassett was under no illusion about the magnitude of his own role. His old Sudan boss General Wingate, in his second year as High Commissioner of Egypt, told him that Hogarth would discuss the wider political issues with Hussein, and that Bassett might have to explain this to Philby and to impress upon him the fact that Hogarth had 'certain instructions from me which may necessitate private interviews between him and the King'.[6] This was code for keeping the outspoken Philby away from discussion of the Balfour Declaration and the Sykes-Picot Agreement.

The first item on Hogarth's agenda was smoothing over the rivalry between Hussein and Ibn Saud. This could only be a patching-up operation, given that Hogarth wrote of Hussein that Philby's 'advocacy of Ibn Saud roused him to considerable heat'. Hussein refused to believe that Ibn Saud was not in cahoots with Fakhri Pasha, the Turkish Commandant at Medina (time would show that Hussein's suspicion was justified). The discussions went around in circles, with Ruhi as interpreter, between 8 and 14 January 1918. Finally Hogarth had to resort to 'some plain words about our treaty obligations to Ibn Saud', which he said were well received by Hussein.[7] What Hussein really thought about Hogarth's words is not recorded.

Meanwhile Hogarth had had a lot of explaining to do to Hussein. The Hashemite leader had regarded Palestine as part of his broader Arab kingdom, following the anticipated defeat of the Ottomans. The Balfour Declaration, made public on 7 November 1917, stated that Britain would use its best endeavours to establish 'a national home for the Jewish people' in Palestine. At the same time nothing was to be done 'which may prejudice the civil and religious rights of existing non-Jewish communities'. But in supporting Zionism, what Britain really wanted was the support of influential American and Russian Jews to keep those countries engaged in the war. In addition, Britain wanted to administer Palestine after the war, to keep it as a buffer zone between the strategically vital Suez Canal and their old imperial rivals, the French, who would be uncomfortably close in Lebanon and much of Syria. Britain thought the Balfour Declaration would make Zionists favour British administration of Palestine. As with the Hussein–McMahon Correspondence and the Sykes-Picot Agreement, British concerns were pragmatic—to do what was necessary to win the war. Awkward ambiguities and contradictions could be ironed out once the Ottomans were defeated.[8]

Hussein must have feared for his ambitious bid to grab an empire when he heard Hogarth's urbane comments on the case for Jewish settlement in Palestine. Hogarth reported that the sherif 'welcomed Jews to all Arab lands', but this was perhaps a tactical ploy by Hussein to retain Britain's support against the French in a post-war settlement. Hussein seemed to believe that Britain's power and good faith were unbounded. But Hogarth also sensed something else with which Wilson and Bassett were very familiar. For all his courage and astute intelligence, there was a vulnerability about Hussein,

> [who] admits there is murmuring against him in Mecca and Jeddah as well as elsewhere…His chief preoccupation is money; and he conceives fantastic schemes for swelling his budget…He has hardly a man of ability whom he can trust, let alone a man of any experience or knowledge of government.

Hogarth's conclusion was penetrating: 'He is born to rule, but, probably, not to rule much farther than his eyes can see.'[9]

The British gave their frail ally the red carpet treatment, putting on an imperial show as a distraction from Hussein's burdens. The old ruler was invited on board HMS *Hardinge*. He spoke to Indian Muslim crew members and had a midday prayer on the bridge. Gray, the keen photographer, was present and took some stunning images of the royal tour of the warship, including one of Hussein firing the most powerful gun at a target, under the watchful and nervous eye of Commander Thomas Linberry. There is also a photograph of Gray standing proudly beside Hussein. His poignant caption for Mabel on the back shows their strained relationship: 'Someone you once knew and a King.'

Philby does not appear, no doubt for diplomatic reasons, in Gray's superb group photograph of Hussein flanked by Bassett, Hogarth, Linberry, the spy/interpreter Ruhi, and assorted other British and Arab officers on the deck of the *Hardinge*. Hussein obstinately refused to allow Philby, who was so obviously championing Ibn Saud, to return overland to Riyadh through the Hejaz, so the political officer had to travel to Egypt on the *Hardinge* when Hogarth returned, on 14 January.[10]

★ ★ ★

Bassett would have breathed a sigh of relief when he and Ruhi stepped on to the Consulate launch to return to the Jeddah quayside, leaving Hogarth

Figure 21. On board HMS *Hardinge* off Jeddah, January 1918, following Bassett's and Hogarth's crisis talks with a wavering Hussein. From third left: Captain Linberry, Suleiman Qabil, Sherif Hussein, Commander David Hogarth, Colonel John Bassett, Hussein Ruhi. This image illustrates both the vital importance of diplomatic work at Jeddah and the political value of Red Sea Patrol ships and captains.

and Philby on board the *Hardinge* for their trip to Suez. Hogarth took with him a letter from Bassett for General Wingate. Wingate's reply showed how much he valued Bassett's key role in helping keep the revolt on an even keel: 'From all Hogarth tells me you have "made good" with the King and are carrying on the Wilson tradition most successfully.' Bassett had stepped into the breach, brokering a number of vital meetings spread out over two weeks, sidestepping diplomatic snares before Hogarth's arrival and, together with Hogarth, helping steer Hussein back from the brink. Bassett was relieved to hear in the same letter that Wingate was resisting Ronald Storrs' attempt to poach Ruhi for service with him in Jerusalem—the Persian's intelligence work in the Hejaz was too important to be lost.[11]

The immediate crisis with Hussein may have been over but the Hashemite leader remained in fragile spirits, vulnerable to plunging despair. The stakes were high and Bassett was the man in the hot seat. He was asked by Wingate in early February to send Hussein a telegram drafted by the Foreign Office in London. The object was clearly to boost Hussein's morale. The sherif was

Figure 22. Sherif Hussein firing a large gun on HMS *Hardinge*, with Commander Linberry watching on anxiously.

praised for having decided to forward to the High Commissioner the letters addressed by the Turkish commander-in-chief in Syria to Feisal and Jafar al-Askari: 'The Turkish policy is to create dissension by luring the Arabs into believing that the Allied Powers have designs on the Arab countries.'[12] It is not clear whether Hussein believed this breathtaking example of patrician double-speak, but the British certainly knew that he wanted to believe, as Wingate put it to Bassett, 'that the British are people of their word and that he need have no fear that we shall ever break any actual pledges we have given to support the Arab Cause and his position'. Perhaps Bassett was as cynical as Wilson would have been about the guile that oozed from the use of 'actual'.

Wingate was impressed by Bassett's letter setting out Hussein's anxieties and despondency, and sent an extract to Sir Mark Sykes, then in charge of the new Middle East Bureau at the Foreign Office. Referring to Hussein, Wingate over-optimistically hoped that Sykes's recent speeches about Syria 'will go some way towards soothing the King's ruffled feelings and will cause him to put all ideas of "suicide" out of his head'. Wingate congratulated Bassett for the efficient way he was carrying out Wilson's work.[13] Bassett was carrying on Wilson's tradition of discreetly sustaining and shaping the Arab Revolt. Both men were probably unaware of a stunning process that could have undermined them and Hussein alike: the British had secretly been meeting the Turks in Switzerland to discuss a possible peace deal. It came to nothing.

★ ★ ★

Meanwhile, as Wingate told Bassett, Wilson himself was making slow progress and would go before a medical board over the next few weeks. There was no certainty that he would be passed fit to return to Jeddah.[14] A month later, in late February, Wilson was still looking very shaken. He was about to go to Helouan near Cairo for a few weeks' convalescence.[15]

Wilson was supposed to be recuperating at Helouan, but he could not resist writing to Hussein to say how disappointed he was that Abdullah had not pressed ahead with demolition raids on the railway, leaving the southern campaign mainly to Davenport. Wilson said he was feeling much better but was frustrated that he would probably not be allowed back to the Hejaz for another two months.[16]

Wilson had by now been awarded a high honour, the CMG (Companion of the Order of St Michael and St George). He had already received the *Légion d'Honneur* from his *bêtes noires*, the French. Gray wrote to congratulate

Figure 23. Sherif Hussein's house at Jeddah, with guard of honour for Lieutenant Lionel Gray who had been invited by Hussein to photograph him.

him and, in his reply, Wilson regretted not being able to play golf because 'my new flesh is very stiff'—a pointer to a serious medical intervention of some kind. Wilson praised Gray generously: 'No-one knows better than myself that without the loyal support and hard work of my staff (of which you are one of the oldest now) I would be able to accomplish very little.'[17]

While Wilson kept in touch with Hussein from Egypt, Gray was helping Bassett in the delicate task of dealing with Hussein's brittle confidence—and therefore in keeping the revolt on an even keel. Gray had gained Hussein's trust. Soon after the crucial January meetings between Hussein, Bassett, and Philby, the cipher Lieutenant's relationship with the Hashemite leader bore remarkable fruit. The photographs of Hussein that Gray had taken on board HMS *Hardinge* probably smoothed the way. It all began at an official reception for the ruler at the Consulate, when Hussein entertained the bemused British with a long and richly embroidered story about his recent dream and what he thought it meant. Ruhi did his best to translate. When the monologue was over, Gray saw an opportunity and steeled himself to approach Hussein when the time was right. He wanted to take some close-up portraits of the leader, but how would Hussein react to his presumption? Gray told Mabel that he simply asked if he could photograph the Hashemite leader, who said the following morning would be fine. But Gray had too much work then and, extraordinarily, telephoned Hussein to delay the meeting by another day. As Gray put it, 'I found the old boy not in the least reluctant to have his photo done, as I thought he might be, being against their religion'.[18] These extraordinary images are trap-doors to the past and resonate across the years.

Mabel admired the photographs: 'What a pity I do not know if I can publish this . . . Ask him if he minds their being in the papers.'[19] She wanted to escape, if only briefly, the privations and stresses of rationing and a depressed economy, and the dread of German air raids. She and her family and friends on the Home Front were now approaching a fourth year of uncertainty and pain.

Gray tactfully told Mabel nothing about the variety of food available at Jeddah, though he did let his mother know how pleased he was with a meal he organized for the French Military Mission. The allies and rivals praised his Red Sea trout, chicken, and spinach garnished with eggs; custard pudding; Turkish coffee; liqueurs; and cigars. Bassett, now promoted to Colonel, told Gray it was the best dinner ever served at Jeddah.[20] But in spite of his growing influence in the Jeddah circle and the kudos of being Hussein's photographer, Gray was disgruntled in the first few months of 1918. Both Wilson and Bassett had put his name forward for promotion to Captain, but incompetent bureaucracy at General Headquarters Cairo had blocked this, and the officer who could have acknowledged the error refused to do so.[21] Mabel commiserated with him on the shenanigans[22] but was alarmed that he seemed to be missing a life of action with his old comrades in the Westminster Dragoons: 'you would be very silly to throw up a staff job...fellows who are sticking to their posts in far-off countries under bad conditions of climate etc. are in every way as much a hero as those in front-line trenches'.[23] Gray's humour would not have been improved when Mabel wrote: 'I note the honours your Colonel received, also C.B. [Companion of the Order of the Bath] to Lawrence—where's yours?...I think you ought to have something.'[24]

★   ★   ★

Medals were always the last thing on Lawrence's mind (he was later to award his *Croix de Guerre* to Hogarth's dog, which trotted around the streets of Oxford with it around its neck). Lawrence and others were busy planning more loud explosions and bright lights, while Bassett and Gray, Young and Cochrane, and Ruhi carried out their quiet diplomatic and intelligence work in the shadows. The period from December 1917 briefly brought optimism after the military disappointments of November. Lawrence, Joyce, and others saw the potential of the Rolls-Royce armoured cars and the Talbot cars mounted with light artillery, and experimented with them over different terrain. Depots were set up at Guweira, where there was an advance headquarters for Feisal's army, and other places east of Aqaba, in the realization that a small number of cars could pack a considerable punch in long-range raids.

On 26 December, Lawrence and Joyce felt the moment had come. Joyce led a mobile force that set off for the important railway station at Mudawwara. Its defences were too strong, but Joyce's men, with Lawrence who came along for the ride as an observer, were able to smash up the Tell Shawm station and some railway wagons to the north. Valuable lessons were learned. Lawrence enjoyed this style of warfare, later calling it 'fighting de luxe, for our troops, being steel-covered, could come to no hurt'.[25]

Two weeks later, on 15 January 1918, a mixed force of five hundred of Pearson's Arab Legion men and Sherif Nasir's Bani Sakhr tribesmen swept into Tafileh, a little town north of Maan that the Arabs needed to safeguard the right flank of Allenby's army. Lawrence arrived five days later, to find sullen townspeople who hated the Bedouin whom they saw as rapacious marauders. The population of Tafileh knew that the Turks would carry out reprisals against them if, on retaking the town, they believed its inhabitants had been feeding the rebels, so they hoarded their food even more than usual. There was an edgy, dangerous stand-off. Then came the worst possible news, on 23 January: a large Turkish force was on its way from Kerak, to the north, to recapture Tafileh. Kerak was the very town, together with Madeba, that the Arabs had wanted to control in order then to press on to the northern shore of the Dead Sea. Here, near Jericho, they could have linked up with Allenby's men in Jerusalem not far to the south—and they could then for the first time have been a significant force as Allenby's right arm. The clear danger from up to one thousand Turkish troops meant that these plans had to be shelved. The Arab Legion made a tactical retreat, but after the Turks took a bluff outside the town, the Arabs' mountain guns rained mortar fire on them. Lawrence set up a pincer attack, with small mobile bands attacking behind enemy lines. The Turks wilted and rushed for what they thought was the safety of the Wadi Hesa gorge. They were mistaken—set upon in a three-pronged attack, the Turks lost around three hundred killed and over two hundred and fifty captured. Mountain Arabs picked off many more in the gorge.

The battle of Tafileh was significant for being a major, if almost forgotten, achievement of the Arab Army. Hugh Pearson, with his engaging enthusiasm, would have been proud to have heard in Jerusalem what the Arab Legion had achieved. Norman Bray, who claimed the credit for setting up the Legion, was far away with his regiment in the trenches of France, and his troubled mind would probably have shied away from any news of the battle.

Meanwhile Lawrence's wounded psyche could give him no peace. He was beyond feeling even the slightest satisfaction that his tactics had been successful. His old empathy for the defeated enemy had evaporated, and many wounded Turks were left out in a night-time snowstorm, to be found dead in the morning. He wrote a report on Tafileh verging on satire, but was still awarded the Distinguished Service Order medal and was about to be promoted to colonel. By now Lawrence's exhaustion was accompanied by a growing disillusion. The £30,000 that he had obtained for Zeid, Feisal's younger brother, intended for the new northern campaign to take Kerak and Madeba, with the prospect then of meeting Allenby's army in the Jordan valley, had all been dissipated in back-pay and bribes to keep tribes neutral. Lawrence was appalled, the spectre of another failure like Yarmuk looming over him. He told Clayton: 'These Arabs are the most ghastly material to build into a design . . . I am getting shy of adventures' and 'sooner or later must go bust'. For nearly a year and a half he had been 'riding a thousand miles each month upon camels, with added nervous hours in crazy aeroplanes or rushing across country in powerful cars. In my last five actions, I had been hit, and my body so dreaded further pain that now I had to force myself under fire'.[26]

Haunted by the massacre at Tafileh, weighed down by almost intolerable psychic burdens, Lawrence was enduring more and more 'the rankling fraudulence which had to be my mind's habit: that pretence to lead the national uprising of another race, the daily posturing in alien dress, preaching in alien speech . . . My will had gone, and I feared longer to be alone'.[27]

Yet there was to be no escape for Lawrence. He had set off by camel for Allenby's headquarters at Ramleh in Palestine, hoping to be released from his heavy responsibilities. His hopes were dashed because he was too valuable to Allenby, who had been tasked in late February to lead an assault on Syria as a top priority and needed the Hashemite rebels as his right arm. The collapse of the Russians on the Eastern Front had made an advance in the Middle East all the more vital, since Allied war planners wanted to try to distract the Germans from an all-out assault on the Western Front. Lawrence was resigned: 'I must take up again my mantle of fraud in the East.'[28]

By mid-March Lawrence was in Cairo for a hectic round of meetings. There is no evidence that he called on a convalescing Wilson—perhaps he simply lacked the motivation, running on empty as he was. The first few months of 1918 had brought despair, the spectre of betrayal, and acute war-weariness to Hussein, Feisal, and Lawrence alike—with Bassett and Wilson from his sickbed having to cope with much of the fallout, while Gray did his bit to help as his disillusionment grew. Involvement in the Arab Revolt was now a heavy weight on all these hard-pressed men.

13

'Blood brother of the Bedouins'

In early April 1918, Lionel Gray was at last given a change of scene. He was transferred to 'Red Sea Littoral, Base C'—military language for the base at Yenbo, 200 miles north of Jeddah. He took with him his 17-year-old Sudanese servant, Yahya. Yenbo was 100 miles west of Ottoman-held Medina and was important for supplying weapons, explosives, food, and gold to the Bedouin forces of Emirs Abdullah and Ali, who were camped inland and were carrying out their sometimes insipid attacks on the southern section of the Hejaz Railway.

The commandant at Yenbo was the tall figure of 39-year-old Captain Henry ('Harry') Goldie, a banker before the war, who had been engaged on important railway demolition work in the southern sector with Captain Herbert Garland. Garland, the maverick demolition expert who had taught Lawrence how to make an improvised explosive device, was also at Yenbo for the time being. Lieutenant Henry Hornby, Lieutenant Norman Clayton, Captain William Davenport, and Lieutenant Harry Garrood were other officers attached to Abdullah's Southern Army. The fact that so many expert saboteurs were out in the desert is an expression of just how much support the Arab forces needed. Gray liaised closely with the men of the Yenbo wireless station. Set up in January 1918, it played a key role in the receipt and transmission of secret messages between the port and Jeddah, Aqaba, Suez, and Cairo.

Gray was to get no closer to the combat action that he missed than the perennial fight against flies and bugs. Gray told his mother about the first British detachment at Yenbo: 'It is a dirty little place & I believe they had a lot of trouble with bugs...but I sent them 4 gallons of creosol which should have settled a few millions'.[1] He said, only half in jest, that he had trained a crack squad of powerful red ants to kill flies at Jeddah and wondered whether he could arrange to escort them on board ship to Yenbo to do battle against the bugs there. If they needed extra training, he was ready for the challenge.

Gray was resilient by nature and like many soldiers he used levity as a sort of antidote to the grim reality of debilitating fevers and seemingly endless separation from loved ones. Lieutenant 'Hoppy' Hopwood, one of Gray's ciphering assistants, had been delirious with fever at Yenbo in January; though he had recovered.[2] Gray was replacing him and would soon come to prefer the dry heat there to the humidity of Jeddah. The town, with its crumbling walls and towers, sat on a flat coral reef about twenty feet above the sea. Gray's billet was in a ramshackle house in which his ciphering office also served as sitting room, bedroom, and bathroom. He shared the space with his tame gazelle, Georgie, who with a commendable sense of security got into the spirit of intelligence work by eating the waste paper Gray discarded during his ciphering work. Georgie's favourite food was boiled rice with a little curry, followed by tea leaves and marmalade, with cigarette ends as a savoury.[3]

The supply ships that dropped anchor at Yenbo delivered a constant stream of gelatine, detonators, and fuses, as well as the equipment needed for contact mines. They also brought tibben (compressed barley straw) for camels, bran and oats, veterinary stores, and signal stores. Gray was an eyewitness to the loading near the quayside of huge numbers of baggage camels heading for the remote desert camps: 'I see the great caravans starting out to Abdullah & Ali with supplies etc.'[4]

Some of the exotic everyday sounds at Yenbo conjured up the familiar: 'It is evening now and the natives are tom-tomming in the town somewhere with occasional rifle shots. It sounds like two railway stations in the distance...'[5] Georgie the gazelle was dead barely more than a month after arriving at Yenbo, but he was soon replaced by a young gazelle given to Gray as a present by a sheikh.[6] Another omnivore, he had to be kept away from Garland's *Daily Mirror* and Gray's *Daily Express* newspapers. There was no golf this time but Gray was able to get daily exercise by horse riding.[7] He hoped to get his own horse with the help of his friend and riding companion, Kaisuni, the Egyptian Army Captain who was Hussein's Minister of War. The two men discussed Hussein's administration which Gray dismissed as comical: there was a minister of public works and a minister of agriculture in a land where there were no public works and no agriculture. Gray's summary was predictably harsh for a westerner of his time—it was 'a Fred Karno's Government'.[8]

Wilson had been expected back by 1 May after four months' recuperation, but instead he was at Alexandria:

> His cure is not complete & he should not come back to this hole of a country at all. It takes all the go out of anyone & everyone complains of loss of memory after being here a while. Maybe it is owing to ill effects of continually drinking condensed water.[9]

But Wilson was not to have to wait much longer to be back in the land of memory loss and fever, and also to be reunited with his ponies, which Gray had been training for him at Yenbo (together with those of Colonel Sadik, Wilson's Egyptian Staff Officer in the Hejaz). Wilson left Suez on SS *Borulos* on 10 May, in company with Joyce, Dawnay, and other army and Royal Air Force officers, who were all headed for Aqaba.[10] Wilson went to Feisal's Aba el Lissan base on 13 May to meet him and Joyce, where he heard of tension between Feisal and the suspicious Hussein. He then went on to Yenbo a few days later. The long-serving 'Pilgrimage Officer' was at once pitched into a round of diplomatic and military meetings. Gray explained to his sister, Cecil, that Wilson had arrived looking fit after his illness. The two men lunched and dined with Garland on board *Borulos* and later visited 'various notables of Yenbo including Kaimakam (like our Lord Mayor), Egyptian Army detachment, school, wireless station and so on.'

Gray must have been reminded of his encounters with officers of the Red Sea Patrol at Rabegh during the height of the crisis over British troops, nearly a year and a half earlier: 'after seeing the Stokes Mortar team which we had trained we went aboard the little ship and had a whisky & soda with the Colonel'. Wilson left for Jeddah the next morning and missed what Gray described as the 'Anniversary of the Arab Revolt' celebrations. He said in his letter of 22 May that these had recently taken place; an oddly timed anniversary, since the revolt broke out sporadically on 5 June and then officially on 10 June. This intriguingly suggests that whatever may have happened in mid-May 1916 held considerable significance for Hussein.

Gray gave a revealing eyewitness description of the celebration dinner that he and Herbert Garland attended in a large tent, to which the French and others were also invited. To avoid diplomatic embarrassment over the seating arrangements, Hussein had decreed that there should be a round table with informal seating. After the soup came 'a huge dish just like my

Figure 24. A recently unladen dhow at Yenbo, with Red Sea Patrol vessel in the background.

Figure 25. Bedouin forces at the port of Yenbo, 1917.

Figure 26. Lieutenant Gray's pet gazelle at Yenbo with his Sudanese servant, Yahya. The gazelle had a commendable sense of security: Gray recorded that it ate the screwed-up balls of paper that he discarded on the floor during his painstaking enciphering and deciphering work.

bath in which was a whole sheep stuffed and roasted and curled around', followed by other courses including rice and salted almonds. For the entertainment, the guests sat in front of an open space partially covered with carpets and matting, on which a group of about thirty men then sat down in a ring. A singer stood in the centre of the ring and chanted hypnotically (a 'monotonous dirge') while the chorus chimed in first from one side, then the other, alternately jumping up and squatting down. There was much 'bowing to and fro, until it made us feel giddy to watch them under the bright moon and the fire lamps'.

There were other demonstrations of religious zeal, including a fire-eater and a pair who began 'throwing themselves down on their heads until they became insensible'. There was dancing and drumming round little fires which warmed the drums and improved their sound. Gray described what sounds like Shia observances at this 'funny kind of fair... the Kaimakam told us they used to stick knives into themselves and scratch themselves to show their faith but he stopped that by order of the King'. At the end of a long day, Gray was 'lulled to sleep by the distant sound of the tom toms'.[11]

By early June, Gray was fed up because his eyes were full of dust (a remorseless wind had been blowing for over two weeks) and his face and neck were smothered with flies; thousands of them had a single-minded devotion to lapping up the moisture around his mouth and eyes. The flies were well and truly in the ointment: Gray had spread the fly cream sent to him by his sister, Cecil, over his skin, but the flies had treated it like jam. The fly spray, though equally ineffective, 'has made the loveliest hair-tonic spray I have ever had' when mixed in equal quantities with eau de cologne. Gray was doing what all soldiers did, using ingenuity to try to keep his spirits up in the face of shortages and discomfort. And at least he now had something to look forward to: he had just heard that he would probably get three weeks' leave in July.[12]

★ ★ ★

While Gray was tormented by flies, the officers in the desert, including Lawrence, were plagued by lice and camel ticks. Lawrence found that the ticks would creep under his sheepskin bedding, after drinking the blood of the tethered camels, and burst open with splatters of blood when he rolled on them in the night.[13] But at least in early April, about the time Gray arrived in Yenbo, Lawrence was on a camel again (it was the first time in over a month, and the change did him good). The British war planners had realized that their strategy to move north on Damascus was hamstrung by the abandonment of the plan for the Arabs to take Kerak and Madeba, and then press on up the eastern side of the Dead Sea and River Jordan. Zeid's irresponsible use of the £30,000 brought to him had put paid to that idea. If Allenby's men were to move on Damascus, their long eastern flank— everywhere east of the Jordan—would be vulnerable to attack from the Turks who still held the land. So the plan now was that Lawrence would form one element of an attack on the vitally important railway town of

Maan, as a preliminary to an attempt on the most important objective, Damascus. To act as cover and prevent Turkish reinforcements reaching Maan, British cavalry would push across the River Jordan, north of the Dead Sea, and attack the Hejaz Railway near Amman. If the Arabs could take Maan, Turkish troops to the south, including those in Medina, would be permanently cut off from Damascus. The way would be clear for Allenby's forces and the Arabs, on either side of the Jordan, to advance together to take that glittering prize.

But more frustration was to dog Lawrence, the British in Palestine, and the Arabs alike. Lawrence's role was fairly minor and he was not one of the British advisers present at the attack on Maan. His task was to ride with a small Bedouin force to the Atatir valley, about a hundred miles north from the Arabs' advance base at Guweira, then with other tribesmen to conduct guerrilla raids against the Turks near Amman. These nuisance raids would be timed to coincide with the British cavalry attacks. The British, however, were bogged down. Turkish and German defenders were waiting for them at the hill town of Salt, about ten miles west of Amman. Suffering a shocking two thousand casualties, the British took Salt, but a raid on the railway at Amman was beaten back by more determined enemy units. To make matters worse, the Turks had dislodged the British from Salt and were pursuing them across the Jordan.

The reason for Lawrence's presence at Atatir had now evaporated. He set off with fifteen of his bodyguards to be present at the Arab attack on Maan, arriving there on 13 April, which was the day it started. The Arabs had high hopes: about three thousand men of their Regular Army—many former prisoners of war from the Arab Legion trained in Egypt by the irrepressible Pearson—had set off from their camp at Aqaba. The railway north and south of Maan had been cut. The Arab Regulars were led by Jafar al-Askari, who had to resort to his volcanic temper and vitriolic abuse to encourage the Bedouin cavalry to support his infantry when their attack stalled. As ever the Turks were tenacious fighters when defending entrenched positions. The attackers captured some outer defensive posts, but could not make headway against the large Turkish garrison and the railway station. Five hundred Arab townsmen, fearful of Bedouin looters should Maan fall, fought side by side with the Turks to repel the Arab attackers: a striking commentary on the complexity of alliances during the revolt.[14] After four days' fierce fighting, the Arab Army was broken and retreated from a shattering defeat. The Arabs had to settle for a siege of Maan that would last until the end of the war.

Lawrence stayed in the area for a time to help other officers cut the railway further, to the south of Maan. About 60 miles of track were damaged, but this could not make amends for the failure to capture Maan and its garrison. Lawrence now headed for Allenby's headquarters at Ramleh in Palestine. He arrived on 2 May and was given more bad news. Allenby's second advance on Amman had been repulsed in late April, and he had had to send about sixty thousand of his best troops, about half his army, to France to try to counter massive German attacks. They were replaced, but only by inexperienced troops. An assault on the Syrian front was now off the agenda for the time being. Two weeks later, on 15 May, Lawrence saw the glimmer of an opportunity when Allenby told him about two thousand fine riding camels that would be available in two or three months' time, with the planned disbanding of the Imperial Camel Corps. He persuaded Allenby to give him the camels for Feisal's men, on the basis that they would make possible an attack on the strategic railway junction town of Deraa, and the demolition of the Yarmuk bridges—which would be redemption for Lawrence's earlier failure.

Lawrence and Feisal were re-energized. Baggage and riding camels were in short supply: many had already been bought by the British, but perhaps the main reason was Turkish intrigue with tribal leaders. Now, Lawrence could foresee the Arabs winning Syria independent of Allenby's forces. As he put it, the camels would be 'a gift of unlimited mobility. The Arabs could now win their war when and where they liked.'[15] For the time being, Lawrence became involved (in ways that are not clear) in secret negotiations between Feisal and the Turks, prompted by two messages that Feisal had received from General Mehmet Djemal, the Commander of the Turkish Fourth Army at Damascus. As Britain was quietly discussing a possible peace settlement with Turkish representatives in Switzerland, the Foreign Office could hardly complain or try to take the moral high ground. Lawrence was sailing close to the wind and was keen to exploit any strategic advantage for the Hashemites, in case, as seemed likely, they were betrayed by the British.

★ ★ ★

Through all the twists and turns of the Arab Revolt in the first half of 1918, with its despair and fears and dashed hopes, a young intelligence officer and friend of Gray was living an extraordinary and hidden life amongst Bedouin tribesmen. His forgotten story has never before been told. Twenty-three-year-old Lieutenant Leslie Leonard Bright—known to his friends as Leo—was fresh-faced, five foot ten inches tall, and a Bimbashi, or Major, in the

Egyptian Army (the lowest rank given to British officers). Bright had fought with the Suffolk Regiment at the catastrophic Battle of Loos in Belgium in October 1915, where he was severely injured in one eye leading a bombing attack.[16] Unfit for further service in the trenches because of his eye, Bright was transferred to Egypt in late 1916. He showed an aptitude for intelligence work and learned Arabic. In late 1917 he was sent as commandant to the British base (known as Base B) at Wejh, the little port whose capture in January that year had caused so much bad blood between Lawrence and Bray.[17] Bright lived in the crumbling British mission house, a large two-storey structure with many heavily shuttered windows. He built up a good relationship with the Kaimakan or governor, and liaised with Wilson before the colonel's desert journey brought on that near-fatal attack of dysentery. Bright was a semi-detached member of Wilson's Jeddah circle. He was well aware of the pitfalls of working in 'this land of intrigue', to use Wilson's phrase. An intercepted wireless message had told the British a few months earlier that Suleiman Rifada, a pro-Turkish Sheikh, had 'a good agent at Wejh who supplies fairly accurate reports of Arab plans and movements'.[18]

Bright's intelligence work was seen by the Arab Bureau as part of a jigsaw that would help to bring order and cohesion to a mass of agent reports, gossip, front-line reports, stolen or captured documents, newspaper stories, aerial photographs, prisoner of war interrogations, the all-important radio intercepts, and more. Following analysis of the raw data, including much that was still coming from the indefatigable Hussein Ruhi, Operations would be given intelligence reports on enemy units and the sometimes shifting alliances of tribes. But Bright brought something special to this mix: his great strength was his aptitude for melting into the desert and living with the tribes deep in the interior, gaining vital information for the Arab Bureau. He was in touch particularly with the Billi, whose land lay to the west of the Hejaz Railway and across to the coast, and with the adjacent Moahib, whose area had been cut through by the railway.

Bright was what in modern British intelligence parlance is called a 'camel driver': a doer in the field rather than an analyst behind a desk. But he was also able to work penetrating analysis into his many reports to the Arab Bureau, which were considered so valuable that they were printed intact in its highly secret *Arab Bulletin*. Bright's heavily thumbed notebook, with 'Tribes of Centre' inscribed by him on the front cover, is crammed with intelligence nuggets written by him in pencil. Covering much more than the Billi and Moahib, he listed the tribes and their sheikhs, with numbers of tents, armed men, camels, and horses, and the location of their winter and summer quarters (his spelling is used here). There are notes on the Anazeh, 'hereditary foes of the Shammar' (significant because the Shammar were Ibn Rashid's tribal confederation and he was actively pro-Turk). Explaining why the great warlord Nuri Shalaan was still cautious about not committing to the Sherifian forces before he could be sure they would win, Bright wrote: 'Ruweilah are entirely dependent on Damascus for provisions as they raise no crops. Nuri Shalaan could put into field about 1,500 to 2,000 men, armed and mounted on camels with small proportion of horses. The Anazeh average 50 camels per tent.'

Bright knew how important Nuri Shalaan would be to the Hashemite cause. On the back of a sheet of loose paper he wrote a pen portrait of Nuri's son, Nawaf: 'A convinced adherent of Pan-Arab party. Though more colourless than his father is better educated and considered by Arab Unionist Party in Damascus as more advanced political thinker in the desert.'

Bright's attention to detail included describing the various war cries of the tribes, with notes on how to distinguish them. The war cries of Ibn Saud's Wahhabi warriors are included. The sons of various sheikhs are named. A section that would make the camel-buying Captain Goodchild green with envy goes into considerable detail about the numbers of camels owned by particular tribes, with the major camel breeders—further evidence of the importance the Arab Bureau attached to intelligence on this vital military asset. The Anazeh, for example, the biggest confederation of tribes in the region,[19] had a massive total of 300,000 camels; the Shammar and Ateibah had 80,000 each, the Harb around Mecca and Jeddah 50,000, and the Howeitat 10,000. These and other tribes, including the Rualla or Ruweilah (who were part of the Anazeh), are all listed as noted camel breeders. Bright took the trouble to underline, 'The Duleim are not camel breeders'.

An intriguing section of this stunning notebook gives details about Sherif Hussein's enemy, Ibn Rashid. The different quarters of his fortress at Hail are listed, and his khalifa or agent, his three flag bearers, and his agent at Baghdad are all named. The quarters of Ibn Rashid's oasis of Jauf are also described: Bright probably knew that Nawaf Shalaan was keen to conquer this settlement.[20]

Bright, like Lawrence, brings to mind a triumphalist passage in John Buchan's thriller *Greenmantle*: 'We are the only race on earth that can produce men capable of getting inside the skin of remote peoples' (though the French, the Germans, and the Austro-Hungarians also did this pretty well in

Arabia).[21] Bright was producing gold dust. His reports to the Arab Bureau included intelligence both from living with the tribes and from his administrative and liaison duties as base commandant at Wejh. One of his key roles was dealing with Sherif Sheraf, who was based at Wejh in late 1917 and for much of 1918. Sheraf was Feisal's cousin and one of his most trusted lieutenants; he had led railway demolition raids and Lawrence had fought with him. Lawrence was later to call him 'perhaps the most capable of all the Sherifs in the army... very clear-headed, wise and kind'. Sheraf had been chief justice of Sherif Hussein's court, and 'knew and handled tribesmen better than any man, and they feared him, for he was severe and impartial, and his face was sinister, with a left eyebrow which drooped (the effect of an old blow) and gave him an air of forbidding hardness'.[22]

Bright worked hard with Sheraf to try to persuade the sheikhs of the Billi tribe to provide camels and men—not an easy task since some of the Billi had been fighting for the Turks. Sheraf asked Bright to get hold of Turkish ammunition for about 1,200 rifles belonging to Bedouins who had left the Turks to fight for Hussein.[23] In June 1918, as well as a small detachment of the Egyptian Army, there were some seven hundred and forty soldiers of the Arab Regular Army under three officers living in the old fort at Wejh—a mixture of Harb, Hudheil and other tribesmen, Meccans, Syrians, and Baghdadis. Bright reported that 'small parties of them trained in demolition, are attached to the Bedus [Bedouin] for raiding expeditions'. He provided political intelligence on which sheikhs were the most reliable in Sherif Sheraf's operations. He and Sheraf were supervising every month the distribution of 8,400 sacks of rice or flour to seven tribal groups—further testimony to the vital role of the Royal Navy in supporting the revolt. Quoting Bright's report, *The Arab Bulletin* in late June referred to tribes 'with whom he has now lived for some months'.[24]

Bright was conscious all the time of the expert scheming of Turkish intelligence, a very influential organization called the Teşkilât-i Mahsusa (Special Organization).[25] In March, an alarmed Feisal at Aqaba had had a cable sent to Bright: 'Following for Sherif Sheraf from King begins. Our flags have been used by enemy camel corps against us to deceive the Arabs. Against this warn everybody to be on their guard.'[26] Bright was on his guard at Wejh until at least late August.

Lawrence held Bright in high regard and later called him 'blood brother of the Bedouins', giving him his own two-volume set of a classic of Arabist literature, Charles Doughty's *Travels in Arabia Deserta*.[27] Lawrence listed Bright amongst the forty officers who could tell their own important stories of the revolt. Bright's forgotten story reminds us that Lawrence was not the only officer to understand and live on equal terms with the Arabs. And unlike Newcombe, Garland, Vickery, and many other officers, he had Lawrence's insight and empathy for the Arabs and their culture. This meant that Bright had Lawrence's ability 'to exert influence in subtle ways and suppress any inclination to be a major figure in his own right'.[28] A colleague, almost certainly Garland, later wrote of Bright: 'He did a great work in a quiet way.'[29] This simple tribute might also have been paid to most of the men who worked in the shadows in Wilson's Jeddah circle.

★ ★ ★

Wilson himself and Bassett would soon be severely tested yet again, as a highly strung Sherif Hussein seemed likely to tip the revolt into meltdown. In the meantime, following the failure to capture Maan and its garrison, railway raids were stepped up, the armoured car section caused increasing mayhem, and Gray at last felt within touching distance of the combat action he craved.

14

Alarms and Excursions

Gray was on the move again, pleased to have another change of scene. Wilson wrote to him in early June, saying that if the Aqaba base still wanted a cipher officer, he would let Gray go there for a month before a period of leave in Egypt.[1] Gray was to leave as soon as Major Davenport arrived to take charge at Yenbo. Aqaba did want a cipher officer and Gray arrived with his servant Yahya at the bustling Aqaba base on SS *River Fisher* by 11 June.[2]

Aqaba was officially 'Red Sea Littoral Base A': the military censors were not renowned for their imagination. Since its capture about a year before, huge quantities of supplies, weapons, gold sovereigns for paying the Northern Arab Army and bribing Bedouin tribes, and reinforcements for Feisal's men had poured into the port from the ships of the Royal Navy. Aqaba was a base for an armoured car section, a mobile artillery battery, and X Flight of the Royal Air Force ((RAF) as the Royal Flying Corps (RFC) had become on 1 April 1918). Gray was struck by its distinctive surroundings, so different from those of Jeddah and Yenbo: 'There is grass here, at least…a kind of scrub mixed with a little grass, & the hills which undulate just like Salisbury Plain are quite green'.[3] Gray's skills were missed at his old bases. Bassett wrote from Jeddah: 'It is a blow to find you have definitely severed your connections with this charming sea-side resort.'[4] He was pleased for Gray that with the move came higher grading (Staff Lieutenant, 1st Class); though the skulduggery at General Headquarters that had deprived Gray of his captaincy still rankled.

Wilson was well aware that Gray was desperate to see some action beyond the rolling hills and mountains. He told Gray that he had put in a request for him to be sent to Feisal's camp at Aba el Lissan for 'as long as possible to help in the show'.[5] Gray's eyes would have lit up, as 'show' was a military term for combat action. Aba el Lissan, about 50 miles north-east of Aqaba, was Feisal's forward base and a hive of activity. It was only about 14 miles from Turkish-held Maan. Lawrence was at Aba el Lissan on 8 June and Lieutenant-Colonel Pierce Joyce, in charge of Hedgehog, the British mission, was often there too.

Gray wasted no time telling Wilson that he would love to take part in combat action, because he had had some experience of explosives work. Joyce was happy to have him at Guweira, on the way to Aba el Lissan, which was also a base for Feisal's Northern Arab Army.[6] Gray was chafing at the bit at Aqaba because he first had to train his newly arrived assistant cipher officer. But Gray was soon released and went off with the Armoured Car Battery, hoping to take part in a railway demolition 'stunt'. They travelled to Guweira, and 'the journey up to this show was the most wonderful thing I have ever undertaken'.[7] He passed through the dramatic Wadi Itm on the way to Guweira. 'Going up the mountain on a car was what I should have described an impossibility were it not a fact.... There were places where a false move would have bounced us like a tennis ball to the bottom.'

The sense of freedom and anticipation that he felt on his trip with the armoured cars, after eighteen months of intense ciphering work at unhealthy Jeddah and Yenbo, is almost palpable. Mabel was concerned that her fiancé was in fighting mode.

> I note you are out for blood & I cannot understand why an Intelligence officer is sent on such a stunt...I cannot reconcile the interesting photos you sent of the railway with your being again in the fighting, but I hope you will come through it all with flying colours & bent double with honours as a reward for your pluck & initiative.[8]

Hit and run attacks on the Hejaz Railway would have been a strange concept to Mabel, after nearly four years of reading about the grim horrors of static or slow-moving trench warfare on the Western Front.[9]

Gray's dreams of action, however, were to be short-lived. He could be spared from his ciphering duties for only a short time and his availability seems not to have coincided with a raid. Gray had to return to Aqaba because his assistant was overwhelmed by the work. To Gray's chagrin he had practically been within sight of Maan on the Hejaz Railway before having to give up his 'warlike ideas'.[10] Gray found a mountain of work waiting for him—a situation with which he was wearily familiar from his Jeddah days in particular.[11] He was once more restricted to the old work pattern of long desk-bound hours, reordering groups of numbers and fathoming errors with endless patience and attention to detail. Intriguingly, Mabel had sent him some more ciphers, a product of her contribution to her uncle Ernest Bentley's top secret work for the government.[12] At face value, this was a strange security breach that would have caused more than sharply raised eyebrows in military intelligence or the Secret Service Bureau (later to be called the Secret Intelligence Service or MI6) in London.

★ ★ ★

Gray had described the photographs of the railway that he sent to Mabel as very rare. He had just managed to get them before the owner went on sick leave to Ceylon. The three photographs showed a massive explosion and its after-effects during a raid, in April that year, on the ten-culvert bridge below Mudawwara on the railway. The photographer was Lieutenant Leofric Gilman, who had led that 'stunt' and whose armoured cars section had given Gray those brief hopes of combat.[13] Gray got on well with the stoical and even-tempered Gilman in their short time together. Both men had been through the fire of combat and shared an expertise as machine-gunners. They were both keen photographers and had a self-deprecating sense of humour. Gilman was a red-haired 37-year-old, the son of a vicar, who had worked with the old family firm in Hong Kong before the war. He had fought at Mons in October 1914, where he won the Mons Star, and had been gassed and shell-shocked at the Somme.

Service in Egypt followed. Gilman and another officer, Lieutenant Ernest Wade, were sent down the Red Sea to Wejh in late February 1917 to test two Rolls-Royce armoured cars. Gilman modified the armour plating and stripped it off when softer sand needed a lighter load. He also introduced double tyres to gain better purchase over the ground. The unit was sent to Aqaba in November 1917, and also had Crossley tenders from the RFC (good for larger loads) and Talbot trucks to transport the ten pounder guns of the Royal Field Artillery detachment.[14]

On one of the long-range reconnaissance trips to the railway with Lawrence in late December, Gilman led two armoured cars across the flat desert, chasing a gazelle on the way. It was New Year's Eve 1917. Lawrence loved the freedom of sweeping along at high speed. The group stopped at a remote desert camp a few miles from the strategically important Mudawwara railway station, with its large water tanks. Gilman's and the RAF's official War Diary entries mention Tooth Hill, and Lawrence later referred to an 'old camp behind the toothed hill facing Tell Shahm station'. He wrote: 'We slept there that chilly night, happy with bully beef and tea and biscuit, with

English talk and laughter round the fire, golden with its shower of sparks from the fierce brushwood.... For me it was a holiday, with not an Arab near, before whom I must play out my tedious part.'[15]

Ninety-five years later, in November 2012, British archaeologists from the Great Arab Revolt Project walked into the camp. They had identified it from one of Gilman's photographs showing his armoured cars in front of a toothed hill, followed by a search of satellite images.[16] They discovered a remarkable time capsule that made their hearts leap. There were two fireplaces complete with brushwood ashes, bully beef and condensed milk tins, fragments of Gordon's gin bottles and army-issue rum jars. There were old

Figure 27. Lieutenant Leofric Gilman, leader of the Hejaz Armoured Car Battery, which offered mobility and offensive power both alone and in joint special forces operations.

Figure 28. Lieutenant Leofric Gilman, far right, and the remains of the many-culverted bridge blown up near the Hejaz Railway station at Mudawwara, April 1918.

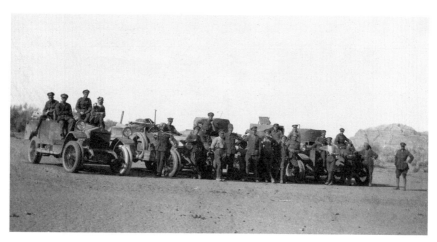

Figure 29. Hejaz Armoured Car Battery, with the odd man out Lawrence looking to his right (standing to the left).

spark plugs and about fifty spent bullet casings, of the 0.303 type used for Vickers machine guns mounted in the armoured cars. The cartridges had probably been swept from one of the cars following a raid. The camp site looked as if Gilman's men and Lawrence had left it the day before: a moment frozen in time. More accurately, a sequence of moments, as Gilman was to return to the camp in January 1918 and then in April, when his photograph of the men and armoured cars posed in front of Tooth Hill was taken.

A raid on 21 April, not long after the failed attempt by the Arab Army to storm the station and garrison at Maan, came within a whisper of claiming Lawrence's life—and that of Gilman and the others. The story has never been told before. Here are Gilman's own words, from his unpublished hand-written memoir:[17]

A full-scale attack on the Turkish railway line north of Mudowara had been planned by Colonel Dawnay of the Grenadier Guards... It was known as Dawnay's show and though Lawrence did come on the scene when the attack was in full swing, the success of it was due to Dawnay's careful planning. My Armoured Cars, Peake's camel men, Brodie's mountain guns all took part and there were no Arabs involved. We reached the line, took prisoners and had a field day blowing up rails and stations. It was then decided to cross the railroad and have a look at Mudowara itself—a very important watering place for locomotives. It was well fortified. Several attempts had already been made, without success, to capture this position.

It was decided that I should come and that an open Rolls-Royce tender carrying high-ranking officers would accompany us. The tender carried Colonel Dawnay, Lawrence, Captain Peake, Major Young. There was quite a big open plain leading up to Mudowara station, and we approached across this to get a better view of the Turkish position. The Turks were pooping [sic] off at us with a gun that was out of range so we approached nearer. We then stopped and got out of the car to discuss what we would do next. We were standing in a group when all of a sudden the wily Turk opened up with a long-range gun of which we did not know the existence. Shells fell uncomfortably near for the Turks quickly got our range. I shouted for everybody to get back to the cars and we beat it for all we were worth on a zig-zagging course. My armoured car was following the tender to act as a screen when I distinctly saw a shell land immediately in front of the tender now travelling at over 70 m.p.h. The shell was a dud and did not go off and I saw it sticking in the sand as I passed. Had this shell exploded it must have killed everybody in the tender. Had this happened "The Seven Pillars of Wisdom" [sic] would never have been written nor many other books on Lawrence, and the film "Lawrence of Arabia" would never have been shot. I do not suppose any of my crew noticed the incident and the occupants of the tender were not in a position to.

Lawrence was so annoyed at having been caught by this wily Turkish trick he wanted to get back at them. So he guided the party by a detour to a many culvert [sic] bridge below Mudowara, and out of range of all the Turkish guns, where we laid heavy charges and blew the whole structure sky high. I got a photo of it going up. This completed that day's work and we withdrew to a point some miles above Mudowara and camped for the night. I slept alongside Lawrence that night and in a discussion on what we had done that day, I mentioned the incident of the dud shell. I do not think it made much impression on him for I never heard him mention the subject again or discuss it with others. We were both very tired and sleepy. After all, I had had quite a bit of experience of dud shells on other fronts. Don't anybody say you can't see a shell arrive, you can you know.

It is tempting to argue that the outcome of the Arab Revolt might have turned on this single random incident, an unexploded Turkish shell that highlights the fragile and paper-thin divide between life and death. Gilman drew a sketch map, also never before published, documenting these dramatic events. It shows the railway stations, the men's camps including Tooth Hill (though not named as such), the location of the Turks' hidden long-range guns, a captured Turkish post, and a long area of track blown up north of Tell Shahm station after the narrow brush with death. Gilman wrote above the sketch map: 'The Turks were never able to repair the railway again.'[18] Lawrence was later to deal summarily with the escape from the Turkish shelling: 'we made off in undignified haste to some distant hollows'.[19] Not surprisingly, Gilman was another of the forty officers Lawrence said could write a story of the revolt as well as he could.

By the time Gilman gave Gray the photographs of the demolished ten-culvert bridge, in July or August 1918, the armoured cars officer was close to collapse. Gray had seen the pain in his friend's eyes, the numbing exhaustion of post-traumatic stress, the careless mannerisms of a brave man, like Lawrence, running on empty. Gilman recorded the disintegration in his memoir:

About August 1918 when the final advance on Damascus was to take place I suddenly realised that I was on the point of cracking up. My long years of continuous service in France and Flanders, and now the desert had sapped my endurance. I went to Colonel Joyce the head of the expedition and told him of my fears and that I did not feel competent any more to take men into battle without, perhaps, endangering their lives . . . It was heartbreaking that I was not to see the final act when I and my unit had done so much of the spadework.

The day after I arrived [at Cairo] I was standing on the verandah of Shepheard's Hotel where I was staying when, without warning, something snapped in the back of my head and I fell like a log... The walls of the bedroom seemed to be whispering and talking gibberish to me and I spent a dreadful night... Lawrence came to see me and was most upset that I had not been given a rest sooner.[20] There it was, I had delayed just that much too long, and now what had happened was to take me years to fight and get over... While I was at Colombo I received a cable from the Arab Bureau, Cairo, informing me that I had been awarded the Military Cross.

★   ★   ★

While Gilman was on the verge of a nervous breakdown, there were more signs that Lawrence was heading for a collapse. He remained under acute strain but forced himself to carry on, the fragility of existence inescapable. He had briefly managed to elude his demons while sitting around the brushwood fires at Tooth Hill. The words he chose tell us everything about his mental state there: he enjoyed 'English talk and laughter... with not an Arab near'. He was bone-weary of acting a part, anguished by the fraudulence he felt he was inflicting on the Bedouin and consumed by guilt. On 15 July he wrote to his friend Vyvyan Richards:

> I have been so violently uprooted and plunged so deeply into a job too big for me, that everything feels unreal. I have dropped everything I ever did, and live only as a thief of opportunity... It's a kind of foreign stage on which one plays day and night, in fancy dress, in a strange language, with the price of failure on one's head if the part is not well filled.

He would 'remain always unsatisfied. I hate being in front and I hate being back, and I don't like responsibility and I don't obey orders. Altogether no good just now.'[21]

It was telling that Lawrence was so detached and morose at a time when he might have felt uplifted by the news from Allenby. Just four days earlier, on 11 July, visiting the Commander-in-Chief's headquarters, Lawrence had heard that 19 September was the date chosen for the start of the huge Egyptian Expeditionary Force offensive. Lawrence had already worked up some plans with Colonel Alan Dawnay, who now coordinated military operations with Feisal's Northern Arab Army, for the Arabs to advance into Syria. Now there was no need to risk an independent operation—in Lawrence's mind, Feisal could still at least try to stake a claim to Syria through ridding the land of Turks, while moving forward in tandem with Allenby's advance to the west of the River Jordan.

★   ★   ★

But the best-laid plans during the Arab Revolt could be knocked off-kilter in an instant. Sherif Hussein had been increasingly jittery since early summer, and Wilson and Bassett were worried. Back in early May, before Wilson's return from recuperation, Bassett had an uncomfortable dispute with a suspicious sherif over the ciphers that he and his family used. The British had been rocked earlier in the year when they realized that the Turks in Maan seemed to have clear foreknowledge of the Arabs' movements. Bassett tried to persuade Hussein to switch to the more sophisticated British codes, explaining that the British used 'very much fewer groups of figures than is the case in Your Highness's own cypher'.[22] The British knew their codes were more secure: they had been breaking the sherif's own unwieldy codes and reading his messages for almost two years (how long the Turks had been breaking them is not clear). Hussein's suspicion mounted. The British wanted easier access to messages between him and his sons, because relations between them were becoming more and more strained. Bassett had managed to derail a cable from an irritable Hussein to Feisal, but others hit their target. After a dispute between Hussein and Feisal in early May, Bassett forwarded a message to Aqaba in which the old leader curtly told his son to 'die at Maan or capture it' before he would consider seeing him again.[23]

Wilson had cut short his time at Yenbo, and his reunion with Gray, to hurry back to Jeddah to resume his dealings with Hussein. Wilson had just seen Feisal at Aba el Lissan and wanted to try to persuade Hussein to see his son to talk through their dispute. Wilson was also aware that since his absence on sick leave, British officials in Cairo had become more critical of Hussein. They knew he had been unpopular with the more liberal Syrians for some time, because he had introduced Sharia law in the Hejaz soon after the revolt broke out, and because he claimed that Syria should be ruled by him as King. Clayton recognized a very real fear among the Syrians: 'They realise that reactionary principles from which the Sharif of Mecca cannot break loose are incompatible with progress on modern lines.'[24]

Wilson had tried, apparently in vain, to persuade Hussein to stop the practice of beating Turkish prisoners and putting them to work in chain gangs. He also protested against Sharia punishments, including cutting off hands and feet.[25] Wilson had this difficult conversation with Hussein on 27 May, his first meeting with the sherif that year. He was moved by Hussein's concern for his health, when the old leader insisted that Wilson should not climb the stairs all the way to the cool rooftop chamber where he normally held his meetings. Instead, Hussein met him on a lower floor of his Jeddah house. Wilson recorded: 'For the most part of the interview the King had an arm round my shoulders, which attitude though affectionate made one rather warm.'[26]

The next day Wilson felt the time was right to ask whether Hussein would see Feisal. When Hussein was evasive, Wilson bluntly asked what the problem was. When Hussein replied that others might see Feisal's return to the Hejaz as a sign of his defeat, Wilson explained that Feisal just wanted to discuss his plans. Wilson skilfully persuaded Hussein to relent, then was hit by a bombshell. Wilson was furious when he discovered that Feisal was about to meet Chaim Weizmann, the Zionist leader. The British thought that the Hashemites might be better placed to realize their ambitions if Hussein supported the Zionists in their bid for limited Jewish immigration to Palestine. In return for that Arab support, the Jews would support the creation of a vaguely defined Arab Kingdom. In addition, Jewish agricultural and other expertise might help in the development of Palestine. Wilson was incandescent because he knew how Hussein would react when he discovered that Feisal was negotiating with the Zionists without first clearing the matter with him. The Arab Bureau asked Wilson to keep Hussein in the dark, which the Colonel hated doing.

Wilson now had to grapple with another problem. On 1 June Hussein complained to him that his title, 'King of the Hejaz', was meaningless, and threatened to resign. He wanted to restore an Arab caliphate (which he thought the British had agreed to in the Hussein-McMahon Correspondence) and wanted to rule all the Arabs through his own Arab Government. He also told a startled Wilson that all Arab chiefs would have to recognize him—a hint that he would fight his old rival Ibn Saud if necessary.

Wilson was deeply concerned by this revelation. Hussein and Ibn Saud were at daggers drawn over the disputed territory of Khurma, an oasis 120 miles east of Mecca. If Feisal went home to help his father in a war with his rival, Allenby would have no support on his eastern flank, which could have been disastrous for his advance into Syria. Wilson knew that Ibn Saud was the stronger of the two leaders. He wrote to Wingate on

5 June with his usual forthright realism, saying that Britain would soon have to decide whether to back Hussein or Ibn Saud.[27] In late June the Khurma oasis dispute looked set to turn into open warfare and, on 18 July, Hussein visited Wilson in Jeddah, pressing for a decision on whether Britain supported his leadership of all the Arabs. Wilson replied in the only way he could: the British Government had 'a strong hope and desire for eventual Arab Union', but 'had never guaranteed the formation of an Arab Kingdom under the Kingship or Suzerainty of himself or any other individual'.[28]

Hussein was affronted, or at least gave the appearance of being affronted, and once more threatened to resign. Wilson's feet had scarcely touched the ground since his return to Jeddah, as diplomatic crises rolled in like waves battering a coastline. When Wilson heard that the sherif had sent Sherif Shakir and his men with machine guns to Khurma, he felt he had to confront Hussein. He knew that warfare could undermine the planned Arab push into Syria. At a meeting on 20 July, Hussein became angry and defensive. A serial resigner, he yet again offered to go. Wilson doggedly stood his ground and the British Government backed his line. Convinced that Britain would never accept him as ruler of all the Arabs, Hussein dramatically put his resignation in writing on 28 July.

Bassett thought this was a bluff by the 'increasingly nervous and highly-strung' sherif. Yet he and Wilson were well aware that the stakes could not be higher. Hussein threatened to withdraw Arab troops from Syria for the fighting in Khurma—the doomsday scenario that the British most feared. Bassett wrote to the sherif, with backing from London, disingenuously blaming Turkish intrigue for the trouble between him and Ibn Saud, and smoothly adding: 'HMG [Her Majesty's Government] regard your leadership of the Arab movement in the war as vitally necessary.'[29] Allenby himself then intervened, supporting Wilson's and Bassett's line and pressing Whitehall to back Hussein openly and pressurize Ibn Saud to withdraw from Khurma. The Cabinet agreed, the policy worked, and the crisis was over, at least for the time being.

Wilson's key relationship with Hussein, tested in the fire of previous disputes over the course of more than two years, was fundamental to the resolution of this potentially fatal crisis. Hussein had edged close to the brink and perhaps the only man who could have coaxed him back was Wilson, ably helped by the diplomatic skills of Bassett. Hussein was indignant and overwrought but ultimately, as in their previous dealings, he responded to

Wilson's persuasive blend of unflinching realism and honourable straight dealing. The two officers had kept their nerve when it mattered most. Their contribution behind the scenes had once again been vital to keeping the rocky course of the revolt on track.

★   ★   ★

Wilson and Bassett were well aware that their demanding work at Jeddah supported the other hub of the revolt at Aqaba, more than 630 miles to the north. The bustling port with its ever-increasing influx of men and military supplies would be pivotal to a successful outcome as the endgame seemed tantalizingly near. Gray was gaining rare insights into the detailed intelligence, planning, and logistics work that helped steer the course of the revolt. He would also get to know an intriguing cast of characters at the expanding base, and find that a tormented Lawrence wanted to confide in him.

15
Aqaba Calling

Lionel Gray was well used to the antics of bats, lizards, gazelles, and ants. At Aqaba he was introduced to tarantulas, scorpions, dogs, and a mischievous monkey, known to all as the Aqaba ape. The monkey was a kind of mascot and often perched on a wooden frame on the beach, attached to a long chain. On 12 July 1918, barely a month into Gray's service at Aqaba, it managed to cast off its fetters and gleefully cavorted around the large camp, chasing its usual victim, Bob the terrier, and causing mayhem in its wake.[1] Its freedom was short-lived and it seems soon to have been back on its customary perch, an experience with which Gray was only too familiar.

Gray's frustrated bid for action with the armoured cars in the desert had taken place while Major Robert Scott, the Commandant, was away in Egypt—he had attended a conference at the Arab Bureau on 8 May and was liaising at General Headquarters (GHQ) in Palestine until 28 June. It was Scott's dapper deputy who was keen on the menagerie and Gray was pleased to be reunited with him. He had shared a tent with Captain Raymond Goslett on the beach at Rabegh, at the heart of the crisis over the threatened Turkish offensive that might have strangled the revolt. Goslett went on to be in charge of supplies at the port of Wejh. His skills were in logistics and at Aqaba, now 32 years old, he was the key man for getting supplies to Feisal and his army, Lawrence and other officers, Gilman's armoured cars, and the Royal Air Force (RAF). He had been the first base commandant at Aqaba, before Scott's arrival in February 1918. Goslett kept two salukis, called Snorter and Musa, fleet-footed Arab hunting dogs that were a familiar sight around the British officers' tents. Scott, by contrast, had a small dog of indeterminate origin that he called his 'Bulgarian weasel-hound'.[2]

Scott was a 39-year-old ex-solicitor and staunch Protestant, who before the war became Deputy Grand Master of the Orange Order in Ireland. He not only raised a company of the armed Ulster Volunteer Force, to resist home rule for Ireland, but also used the family car for gun-running. He had served with the Royal Inniskilling Fusiliers at Gallipoli and Salonica, and was mentioned in despatches in both campaigns. At Salonica he contracted the malaria that was to dog him in Arabia. The lanky, pipe-smoking Scott was easy-going, affable, and popular, and Gray, who had a similar character, got on well with him. The two men shared a grim combat experience, both having fought the Turks at Chocolate Hill, Gallipoli.

Scott had arrived at Aqaba on 7 February 1918 on board SS *River Fisher*. Dhows and lighters were offloading supplies under the watchful gaze of the monitor M31, a small guard ship that protected the port.[3] The palm-fronded beach was studded with dozens of tents for officers and men, two large hospital marquees, a YMCA canteen in another very large marquee, vast piles of supplies and equipment, mountains of fodder for camels and horses, and flocks of anxious sheep brought over from Suez as food for Feisal's men. Near the wireless station with its tall mast were swirling groups of Armenian refugees seeking sanctuary from the Turks or being trained to fight them, Royal Flying Corps (RFC) men from the nearby base playing football, and the Aqaba ape plotting his escape. Egyptian Labour Corps men constructing a pier jostled with Turkish prisoners brought in for interrogation before being sent to camps near Cairo. The sights, sounds, and smells of this bustling military base, with up to three thousand people, were beyond anything Scott had anticipated.

Scott was briefed by Colonels Dawnay and Joyce, and by his predecessor, Captain Goslett. He soon met a key visitor to the port, Sheikh Youssef, who was quartermaster to Feisal and who could sometimes be found sitting on a chair outside the gate of Aqaba's crumbling stone fort, supervising supplies for the Arab Army that were taken in and out of the building. Alongside the fort, which had been bombarded by the Royal Navy back in November 1914, run-down, mud-brick houses straggled along the town's only main street, which the British called Bond Street. Scott rarely ventured there. He spent much time taking charge of boxes of gold sovereigns that were regularly delivered by Royal Navy ships, most of them for Feisal's men. Only two days after Scott's arrival, the monthly grant for February of nearly £104,000 was handed over to him.[4] Scott spent hours counting and distributing the money to Youssef, giving him £15,000 just three days after he arrived as commandant. He did much of the accounts on board the M31 monitor and his diary mentions 'doing gold' no fewer than thirty-four times until the end of October—once with Lawrence and also with Goslett and Major

Figure 30. Major Robert Scott, commandant of the Aqaba base from February 1918. Scott kept a diary that documented the comings and goings of Lawrence and other officers, the many supply ships, and the American Lowell Thomas whose post-war shows turned Lawrence into an international hero and icon.

Figure 31. Fort at Aqaba, used by the British, French, and Arab forces to store supplies.

Figure 32. Sheikh Youssef, Emir Feisal's quartermaster, keeping a watchful eye on the entrance to the fort at Aqaba, where supplies for the Northern Arab Army were stored.

Figure 33. Royal Flying Corps/Royal Air Force landing ground at Disi, north-east of Aqaba.

Maynard, Joyce's deputy. On 7 April one of Gilman's armoured cars arrived to collect some gold for the interior, and on 27 September he wrote: 'Sent cars up with £50,000.' Scott also maintained what was called the Special Grant: he drew £10,000 from it on 26 February and it seems that this was in part used for intelligence operations including funding agents.

Like many British officers, Scott found his cultural differences from the Arabs difficult to bridge. In some notes jotted down on loose sheets he wrote:

> Our job to train the Arabs to fight, discipline, etc. and a job it was, they treat everything as a huge joke and say Inshalla Bukra [God willing, tomorrow] & Maaleesh [never mind] to everything...Bedouin Arabs good at scavenging only, grave robbers...Sherifian Arab quite different.[5]

Scott was helped from 9 April by a new Staff officer, the Egyptian Shafik. In his first few weeks, Scott sometimes found the time to play bridge, Baccarat, and poker with his fellow officers, and recorded his winnings and losses in his diary. He drove with others up to the breathtaking Wadi Itm on 9 March, where they shot pigeons and partridges with rifles, and on 4 April observed a fish bombing party (the British had found that dropping a Mills bomb into the sea and stunning large numbers of fish was less time-consuming, if more dangerous, than using a rod and line).

★   ★   ★

Scott's duties were inextricably linked with those of the tireless Red Sea Patrol of the Royal Navy. Twenty different ships are named in Scott's diary, and there are 110 mentions of ships throughout the seven months of his diary when he was in Aqaba.[6] Scott recorded twelve ships' movements, in and out, in April alone. Mixing business and pleasure with the Royal Navy was an enjoyable part of Scott's role. He dined with ships' officers, both on board and at the base. On 22 February he went on a motoring trip 'away into the wild mountains' with Commander Crocker of HMS *Petracosta*, Captain Goslett, and Lieutenant Montagu Leith, Lionel Gray's predecessor as cipher officer.

The Red Sea Patrol carried fairly large numbers of Armenian refugees to and from Aqaba. There are seven references in Scott's diary to Armenian men signing on to fight for Feisal's cause. They tended to join the French *Légion d'Orient*. Traumatized Armenian children and women in their brightly coloured dresses were a common sight on the beach. They and men unable to fight were transported by sea to Egypt. The scale of Armenian emigration to escape persecution and death in Syria and Turkey was such that an Armenian

Mission arrived at Aqaba in July 1918. Its Chief was Abah Bedrossian, who represented the Armenian National Union as well as the refugees. Scott liaised closely with him and attended Armenian committee meetings. Gray's friend and golfing and bridge partner from Jeddah days, Major Marshall the doctor, cared equally for sick and starving Armenians as for injured British and Arab combatants. Bedrossian showed his appreciation by giving Scott a fine wristwatch, but unfortunately it was for a woman and too small, so after the war he gave it to his grandmother who was delighted to wear it from that day.[7]

On one occasion the Armenian dimension brought Scott a dilemma. Abah Bedrossian wrote to him about a Syrian Armenian woman at Aqaba:

> We received her in our camp as a woman and a Christian. But I am sorry to say she has not shown a good conduct, and has been in immoral relations with the doctor of the Turkish prisoners. You know well that her base conduct is not a good example for the camp and, especially, for the honour of the Armenian woman. Now I send her to you and beg you to do whatever your rules and orders command.[8]

British military rules could be numbingly restrictive, but not even they could have anticipated an Armenian woman having an affair with a Turkish doctor at a British base.

★　★　★

By late March, Scott was well settled into a stimulating pattern of work that mixed the routine with the unpredictable. Lawrence, constantly on the move, had turned up since early February on seven occasions—on SS *Borulos*, by air, and by camel. He described Scott as 'a perfect Irishman' who 'had good temper, capacity, spirit'.[9] Scott was another of the officers listed by Lawrence in *Seven Pillars of Wisdom* who could give a good personal account of his experience of the revolt. Lawrence had dinner with Scott and the other officers on 5 March: Lawrence was ascetic and shy, never truly convivial, but he was a master at putting on an act and perhaps the occasion even pushed away his feelings of being a fraud for a short time, as at Tooth Hill in the desert. After more comings and goings, he returned early on the morning of 22 March. The Aqaba ape and those already stirring from their tents on the beach would have seen a familiar slight figure in white Arab dress on a fine camel, surrounded by at least twenty of his Ageyl bodyguards in their brilliantly coloured robes that flashed in the rising sun. Feisal called in from his advanced base at Aba el Lissan to see Lawrence and Scott the next day, and Lawrence went through the gold accounts with the commandant on 25 March.

Two days later saw some unexpected visitors. Scott's diary for 27 March simply includes: 'Two Americans arrived.' Lawrence had met Lowell Thomas, an ambitious journalist, and his photographer, Harry Chase, in Jerusalem in mid-January. Lawrence's old friend Ronald Storrs, the Military Governor there, had introduced them. Thomas had heard about the Arab Revolt and was looking for a stirring story to get the American public behind the war effort. He planned a touring 'travelogue', a mix of lectures, actors, and film. Lawrence jumped at the opportunity to publicize the revolt—in another age he would have been a master of social media—and knew that American opinion could be very important in shaping the map of the Middle East after the war. His softly spoken and fluent comments, his charisma, and his exotic Arab dress intrigued Thomas. After Lawrence had left Jerusalem he persuaded Allenby to let Chase and himself visit Aqaba. Lawrence was apparently surprised to see them, but agreed to let Chase take some more portraits of him (one had already been taken in Jerusalem). Chase took other excellent photographs of Arabs and their leaders and of Gilman's armoured cars. Scott's diary shows that Thomas and Chase saw Lawrence for less than three days before he travelled inland. Lawrence was unaware that the canny Thomas had a hidden agenda: the Arab movement would be just a backdrop to his real story, that of a scholarly British archaeologist who had become the 'uncrowned King of Arabia' (Storrs had introduced Lawrence to Thomas in this way, and the American was not one to let irony get in the way of a good story). Lawrence, typically, would not say a lot about himself, so Thomas got much information from his fellow British officers, 'all of whom did magnificent work in Arabia'.[10] Thomas and Chase went inland with Feisal on 31 March and returned to Aqaba on 14 April, their Arabian adventure over, for a voyage to Suez on HMS *Hardinge*.

★   ★   ★

Lowell Thomas wrote of the amiable Scott: 'Scott specialised in mirth and money . . . In Scott's tent were boxes of sovereigns, gold conscripted from every corner of the Empire . . . The only guardian of all these boxes of golden "goblins" was a dog about the size of a squirrel'.[11] Scott and his unmistakable 'Bulgarian weasel-hound' were a familiar presence around the officers and men of the RFC (which became, on 1 April 1918, the

Royal Air Force). Scott recorded dinners with the RFC and, on 16 March, Lieutenant Siddons flew him and an important message up to the forward base at Guweira in his BE2e. The RFC, in the shape of X Flight of 14 Squadron, had arrived at Aqaba from Egypt on 9 September 1917, following pressure from Lawrence for aeroplanes to support Feisal's Northern Arab Army. There had already been bombing raids on Maan and other railway attacks. Captain Stent, in command of X Flight, continued these missions, under the overall orders of Lieutenant-Colonel Joyce, who coordinated the use of aircraft with ground forces. Six aeroplanes were originally sent to Aqaba.

On 1 November 1917 a slightly built young RFC man, lately in Egypt, was having an unusual conversation on board HMS *Hardinge* as the ship approached Aqaba. A ground crew mechanic, 2nd Aircraftman R. Jackson, was talking to one of the former prisoners of war, trained by Pearson near Cairo, who was on his way to fight for Feisal—'a Turkish officer re-enlisted in Arab Legion, very intelligent fellow'.[12] Jackson and eight other ground crew were on their way from the Aboukir camp to boost X Flight's complement. Jackson watched the 'unloading by searchlight' at around midnight, as the 2-mile-long 'border of date palms fringed to sea shore . . . became a hive of activity'. The following morning he observed: 'In the rear of the tree finger is an Arab camp and right over to the west of the bay is the RFC camp, through the glasses 4 tents, 4 marquees and 2 hangars are visible.'

Jackson was inoculated against cholera and sent to the workshops, repairing and overhauling engines and aircraft—work that was vital for the frequent bombing and reconnaissance missions. On 4 November a 'boat arrived with the Prince Feisal and his army aboard, a salute was fired by the Arab Legion artillery stationed here'. Thirty-seven more RFC men arrived from Aboukir on 8 November, making the total between fifty and sixty. Jackson's duties included repairing the engine of a Crossley tender and road testing the car past the camp of the French Algerians. For some reason he took strongly against Lieutenant Siddons, who held a religious service alongside a fighter bomber in a hangar on 25 November: 'The quintessence of sanctimonious conceit! An empty bomb box covered by an Arabian headcloth for an "altar".' Lowell Thomas met Siddons and was later to call him 'an embryo parson'.[13]

Jackson met Lawrence for the first time on 6 December, when there was concern over a missing aircraft that should have collected him from Aqaba to take him to Egypt and Palestine: 'this was the instance when Sergeant

Stokes failed to recognise him purely on the "Arab" [Lawrence] failing to heed the warning of danger from the machine just coming in…[and] pushed him away to the side of the runway, a typical instance of the "Imp's" sense of humour.'[14]

The rhythm of Jackson's life is revealed in his diary. Pistons broke and fell into sumps, workshop lorries got stuck in the sand, ships endlessly came and went (including patched-up old HMS *Fox*, Wilson's sweltering home off Jeddah all those long months ago). A Greek merchant opened a food store on the beach (Del Monte peaches and Nestlé's milk), the RFC played HMS *Humber* at football and won, SS *Burriana* arrived on Christmas Day—'Told they had brought £20,000 for the Sherif.' At the Boxing Day sports, 'Sherif Said—second son of King of Hejaz [in fact the fourth son]—gave prizes to winners.' Above all, Jackson's diary shines a rare light on the vital work of ordinary RFC ground crew in extraordinary circumstances, men who quite literally kept some of the wheels of the revolt turning.[15]

★   ★   ★

Gray was able to renew his acquaintance with Lawrence while working for Scott at Aqaba. Twenty-one long months had passed since their voyage together to Arabia. Gray enjoyed his discussions with his enigmatic comrade, later recalling:

> We came to see quite a lot of each other…One of our topics of discussion was what is the ideal of life. Lawrence told me that he thought the ideal life was lived by the ordinary private soldier. He had enough money to live on, he said. All he had to do was to be smart and to obey orders for which he was not responsible. If they were wrong he would not get the blame.[16]

Lawrence's journeys with Gilman and the armoured cars, and with the RFC, seem to have given him the idea to enlist in the ranks after the war. Lawrence would have made these poignant remarks before the end of summer 1918, which was the last time Gray saw him, making this the earliest concrete evidence of Lawrence's hankering after a new identity.[17]

Lawrence and Gray both got to know an unusual fellow officer at Aqaba. Captain Gerald Omar Rushie Grey of the Royal Army Veterinary Corps was from Jamaica and was almost certainly the only black British officer in the Middle East. He was also distinctive in being, at only 5 foot 2 inches tall, even shorter than Lawrence—which must have been of some comfort to Lawrence, who was sensitive about his height, when the men were close together. This was precisely how they found themselves on an uncomfortable train rattling down to Suez from Cairo on 18 May 1918. Their mission, with a few other officers including Captain Philip Graves of the Arab Bureau, was to board HMS *Imogene* the next day bound for Aqaba. Rushie Grey was struck by two things: the piercing blue eyes of the shy little officer beside him, and his apparent affectation in reading an ancient Greek classic in the original (this would have been the Aristophanes that Lawrence took with him throughout the war). Rushie Grey was not sure whether Lawrence was only pretending to understand what he was reading.[18]

Rushie Grey had seen earlier service near Gaza in Palestine. His task now was to run a veterinary hospital at Aqaba and care for large numbers of camels and horses, getting them back on their legs if they were ill or injured. A hundred extra camels had arrived on 9 April. The Camel Transport Corps took food and equipment of all kinds up Wadi Itm and over the mountains to the forward bases. The three hundred men of Colonel Robin Buxton's Imperial Camel Corps trekked down from Sinai and arrived at Aqaba on 30 July. While Lawrence addressed the men, warning them frankly of the difficult campaign ahead, Rushie Grey addressed the mange and other afflictions of the camels.

The plan was to launch a daring long-distance attack on the strategically important railway station at Mudawwara, the scene of earlier frustration for Lawrence, Gilman, and others. Lawrence was not present at the assault. At 5.30 on the morning of 8 August, Very lights shot up as a signal and the dismounted Imperial Camel Corps attacked with machine guns, Mills bombs, and rifles, taking the southern Turkish redoubt or fortified post. Lieutenant Brodie and his mountain gun artillery had to be brought in to overpower the fiercely defended northern redoubt, helped by Lieutenant Siddons and two of his RAF planes that bombed it and the station in a coordinated attack. The water towers were blown up, so the locomotives now had no water on a 150-mile-long stretch of track. Twenty-one Turks were killed and one hundred prisoners taken. The British lost four killed and about fourteen wounded including three officers. The Arabic-speaking doctor, Major Marshall, set up a field hospital in the ruined Ottoman fort. He also negotiated safe passage for the Turkish prisoners (their Bedouin escort would have killed them had they not been promised the balance of their pay only when the Turks reached Aqaba safely). Marshall also wrote two messages to Scott that winged their way to him by carrier pigeon. The first confirmed the capture of Mudawwara; in the second Marshall asked for a fellow doctor, Captain Frederick McKibbin, to be sent to the forward base at Guweira to care for the wounded, who were to be taken there in a medical hamla or camel convoy. Marshall also asked the RAF to lend some of their tenders to convey the wounded to Aqaba.[19]

Captain Rushie Grey's veterinary experience was tested to the limit less than three weeks after the spectacular success at Mudawwara. Major Scott wrote an urgent message for Gray to encipher and send to the Arab Bureau: 'Two hostile aeroplanes bombed Akaba on 26th August. Casualties 13 killed, 18 wounded also 18 animals killed & wounded. Aeroplanes came from direction of Tebuk area. Our aeroplanes operating from Guweira failed to get into touch with them.'[20] Scott's diary confirms that the dead were all Bedouin fighters and that the animals were camels. Rushie Grey could have done very little for most of the injured ones.

For Gray the attack was the first experience of enemy action since his time fighting the Senussi in the Western Desert of Egypt. He had recently returned from three weeks' long-awaited leave in Cairo, the first he had had in nearly two years' service in Arabia. He devised some more codes while in Egypt for his cipher colleagues at GHQ and went up in an aeroplane.[21] Gray was delighted to see his old friend, Major Marshall, again at Aqaba. Marshall enjoyed Gray's companionable good humour.[22]

★ ★ ★

Gray would have loved to have been with his friend in amongst the action at Mudawwara, but even had he not been on leave in Cairo at the time, he could probably not have been spared by Major Scott. Gray seemed fated to stick to the path of stern duty—which led unwaveringly from enciphering to deciphering and back again. Meanwhile Mudawwara, with its well-planned joint ground and air attacks by the British, showed how far the desert war had evolved from hit-and-run raids on the railway. It also fed into the final, decisive phase of the Arab Revolt as it headed for a climax.

The vibrant Aqaba base, together with the forward bases at Guweira and Aba el Lissan, played an essential part. The interconnecting skills of a wide range of men at Aqaba gave the campaign gradually increasing strength, and made it greater than the sum of its parts. It could so easily not have been so: from the Rabegh crisis over a Turkish counter-attack to the alarming prevarication and despair of Sherif Hussein, the revolt at times hung on a knife-edge. It kept its momentum in part because of the collaboration between base commandants, the Regular Arab Army and its trainers, demolition experts, armoured car and artillery men, pilots and air mechanics, intelligence officers and agents, and others. The vision and logistical skills of Colonel Alan Dawnay in particular, and the touch of genius of Lawrence with his abilities to inspire and persuade as well as achieve, were fundamental. But all these men were only able to operate thanks to the essential diplomatic work carried out by Wilson and Bassett at that other hub of the Arab Revolt—a much quieter one than Aqaba—at Jeddah. Without their key contribution the work of everyone else, Lawrence included, would have been in vain.

★   ★   ★

And there was another overarching theme of the revolt. The Red Sea Patrol of the Royal Navy was integral to the genesis and dynamics of the revolt and made possible the achievements of Wilson and his men.

16

Fairy Godmothers to
the Arab Revolt

Captain Henry Brocklehurst, a Royal Air Force (RAF) liaison officer, was not impressed with the ship he found himself on for his first and only trip to Arabia. It was 10 May 1918 and SS *Borulos*, sailing from Suez to Aqaba under a Maltese skipper, was as crowded and noisy as most of the merchant navy ships that had been taken over for the war effort. In his diary Brocklehurst gives a rare insight into what it was actually like to be a passenger on one of these vessels: 'it is packed with Arabs, English details [servicemen from the ranks], sheep, ducks, fowls, rabbits & every conceivable thing. One observer for Aqaba, the absolute limit & several NCOs who have risen to the dizzy heights of 2nd. Lieut. so the conversation savours somewhat of the Corporals' Mess.' The fastidious Brocklehurst, sounding like Ronald Storrs, was used to an orderly RAF officers' mess in Egypt and was outside his comfort zone. He recorded the names of the three colonels on board 'but I don't know them'. They happened to be, with Lawrence, the most influential colonels involved in the Arab Revolt: Wilson, on his first trip back to Arabia after his long convalescence, Dawnay, and Joyce.[1]

Brocklehurst's comments reveal how what was going on down the Red Sea in Arabia was a closed book to many of the British and Dominion combatants in Egypt. This 'otherness' of the secret Arabian campaign is borne out by his comments on Captain Frederick Furness Williams, the officer commanding the RAF's 'X' Flight at Aqaba: 'FW is an appalling man . . . never shaves & doesn't look as if he washes & is altogether most repulsive'.[2] Like many other officers, Furness Williams had adapted to local conditions: he wore the Arab headdress or keffiya, and did a very demanding job in a debilitating climate, so naturally he would never look like the perfectly turned-out officer in his Cairo mess.[3]

By the time of Brocklehurst's voyage, the Royal Navy had been in control of the Red Sea for over two years. The protection of Egypt and the Suez
Canal, that essential lifeline to British India that ran down to the northern
shore of the Red Sea, was a vital strategic objective. The Royal Navy ships were
also a powerful visual symbol of British imperial might and the advantages
that might flow to the Arabs as its allies. The Red Sea Patrol's indispensable
role in the Arab Revolt, however, began well before the start of the rebellion
and always had much more than symbolic importance.

Colonel Alfred Parker, chief of intelligence in the Hejaz, depended heavily on the Royal Navy. Rangy and slim and the nephew of Lord Kitchener
(whose inescapable gaze and pointing finger were familiar to millions who
had seen the recruiting poster back home), Parker had been governor of
Sinai before the war. Like Pearson, he was passionate about football, believing
it was 'good for the soul', and insisted that everyone under him should turn
out to play three times a week.[4] He found that opportunities for the sport
were strictly limited back in January 1915, just two months after the Ottoman
Empire took the side of Germany and Austria-Hungary in the war, when he
spent a number of days on HMS *Northbrook* as the ship explored the Red Sea
coast. Messages were passed to the sheikhs of the coastal towns, but their
replies betrayed Turkish influence and Parker realized that he was being
played.[5] He would have needed the 'great fund of humour and unlimited
patience' attributed to him by a colleague.[6] Parker slipped into the Hejaz
to recruit agents and a number of their names appear in his diary. He and
Lieutenant-Colonel Stewart Newcombe reported to General 'Bertie' Clayton
in Cairo, and were in charge of reconnaissance and agent-dropping too.
Parker commanded a motley band of Royal Navy reserve officers, whose
ships were often German cargo steamers commandeered at the beginning of
the war. They were converted for use as troop carriers, to carry the seaplanes
of the Royal Naval Air Service, and to transport secret agents or emissaries to
Sherif Hussein. In December 1914, the very first messenger from Kitchener,
as High Commissioner of Egypt, to Hussein to explore a possible Arab revolt
was Hussein Ruhi's father-in-law, Ali Effendi, who had estates in Egypt. The
secret world ran deep in his family.

Some of the Red Sea Patrol ships were fitted with powerful radio trans-
mitters and receivers to intercept enemy signals.[7] The vessels also scoured
the Red Sea coast to monitor the movements of Bedouin tribesmen and
Turkish soldiers. An outstanding commander at this time was Captain
Lewen Weldon, in charge of the *Aenne Rickmers*, a converted spy ship that

dropped agents along the unlit coast in often uncharted waters. He later described another side of his work, 'a queer amphibian [sic] job cruising in a makeshift sea-plane carrier manned by a Levantine crew and carrying French planes, French pilots and British observers'.[8] The men serving under him were given an extra allowance, called 'hard lying', because of the hazards of the job. In January 1915 he took the *Aenne Rickmers* into the Gulf of Aqaba, from where the frail Henri Farman seaplanes set off for a dangerous flight over the mountains of Moab to observe the Turkish garrison at Maan on the Hejaz Railway. The loss of a plane and its French pilot in an accident stopped further missions for a time.

Lieutenant George Wyman Bury was another important officer who had intelligence duties in the Red Sea Patrol. Officially a political officer from autumn 1915, he was heavily involved with the blockade of the Hejaz and other Red Sea ports which began in March 1916. As Bury later explained, the purpose was 'to blockade the Arabian coast against the Turk while allowing dhow-traffic with foodstuffs consigned to Arab merchants, and steamer-cargoes of food for the alleged use of pilgrims, to go through'. This was not quite the whole picture, though. Sherif Hussein had asked the British for a blockade, reckoning that insufficient food would get through to the troublesome Mecca townsfolk who hated his autocratic rule and who were nervous about an alliance with the British. Hussein hoped they would be starved into cooperation with his planned revolt.[9] Fast armed boarding steamers such as HMS *Lama*, HMS *Perth*, and HMS *Lunka*, and the auxiliary cruiser HMS *Suva*, converted from passenger and cargo steamers, were ideal for a blockade role. Bury also had to keep the eastern highway free of mines and transportable submarines, and prevent the passage of spies between Arabia and Egypt. But he soon became aware of the deep-seated corruption in this part of Arabia: 'the Hejazi merchants were selling direct to the Turks and letting their fellow-countrymen have what was left at the highest possible price'.[10] Wilson and his Jeddah colleagues would soon become all too familiar with this factor.

As Bury put it: 'There was always trouble off Jeddah—the approaches to that reef-girt harbour lend themselves to blockade-running dhows' carrying contraband for the Turks.'[11] His ship would often have to open fire with rifle or shrapnel to discourage the Arab dhows. In early spring 1916 Bury and his colleagues persuaded the Arab Bureau to sanction a higher level of offensive action. On 21 March he was on board HMS *Fox*, the oldest ship in the Red Sea Patrol, which bombarded a well-manned Turkish fort and the customs house, without damaging the mosque, at the little port of Um-Lejj. One of Bury's agents, a fisherman, had come on board to pinpoint the position of these buildings, which were hidden from view outside the town. The fisherman-spy was terrified by the noise of the 6-inch gun, as he lay curled up on the bridge with some ineffective cotton wool stuffed in his ears. The fort at Wejh was also badly damaged, though the Ottomans were later to reinforce it. In this way limited amphibious warfare with well-defined aims became part of the Red Sea Patrol's mission. The Royal Navy was seeking to degrade Ottoman military forces, if at all possible without offending the religious sensibilities of the Arabs.

By May, it was clear that the blockade was not tight enough: the Hejazi tribesmen were opportunistically taking money from the British, Sherif Hussein, and the Turks, while at the same time being fed by supplies from the dhows. So on 15 May Bury and his colleagues implemented a total blockade. No landings were allowed on the Arabian coast unless the British had specifically sanctioned them. This tipped the Mecca merchants into grudging cooperation with Hussein, though tensions simmered not far below the surface and never went away.

★　★　★

By mid-1916 Captain 'Ginger' Boyle's force comprised two old cruisers (including HMS *Fox*, on which Wilson had sweltered before moving to the Jeddah Consulate with Young and Cochrane), four Royal Indian Marine ships, two sloops, six armed boarding steamers, an armed tug, and a launch.[12] One of the Red Sea Patrol's offensive operations was the seizure of Kunfida, the main port of Asir, which was the region lying south of the Hejaz. Asir's leader, the Idrissi, was jealous of Hussein and the British thought he could not be trusted to support the sherif. The coastal towns were under Turkish control and had to be neutralized, not least to maintain a buffer zone between the Hejaz and Turkish-controlled Yemen to the south of Asir. So on 8 July a number of Captain Boyle's ships bombarded Kunfida. The Turkish garrison there soon surrendered. Wilson did important diplomatic work behind the scenes, as he did so often in his career, building up a good relationship with the Idrissi who had been persuaded that the Red Sea Patrol had captured Kunfida on his behalf.

Wingate wrote to Wilson: 'The success of the Kunfida negotiations is entirely due to the firm attitude you took up and to the support which Boyle rendered.'[13] Wilson's relationship with Boyle was of crucial importance to the outcome of the Arab Revolt and has often not received the attention it deserves.

Figure 34. Captain Boyle (left) and Commander Linberry of the Red Sea Patrol.

★ ★ ★

The relationship between Wilson and Boyle was one manifestation of a broader political role for the Red Sea Patrol. The British were always alert to Muslim sensibilities, both in Arabia and also in India, about the use of military might so near the holy cities of Mecca and Medina. So a delicate balance had to be maintained between the use of targeted naval force where appropriate and the non-lethal projection of British power and goodwill to achieve political objectives. Boyle was particularly well suited to striking this kind of balance. His extensive pre-war experience in the Pacific had

Figure 35. Lieutenant Lionel Gray (far left) on board a ship of the Red Sea Patrol with two unidentified colleagues. The officer on the far right gives the inadvertent impression of auditioning for a film part.

given him broad political responsibilities needing high leadership and nego-tiating abilities.[14]

Boyle was highly valued by another key individual, his commanding officer Rear-Admiral Rosslyn E. Wemyss. Wemyss was genial and astute and had consummate political skills. In January 1916, when he assumed overall charge of the Red Sea Patrol, he had moved decisively to sweep away another bizarre example of British imperial bureaucracy. He found the Red Sea Patrol divided into two distinct parts, one working politically under Egypt and the other under the Government of British India, with no liaison or cohesion between them. He amalgamated the two sections, and was soon able to say that Boyle, his senior officer, was 'doing splendidly'.[15]

Wemyss was promoted to vice-admiral on 6 December 1916, not least for his political acumen. He wrote to his wife off Rabegh on 20 January 1917, showing that he had a firm grasp of the complexities of the revolt: 'The more one learns of this Hedjaz business, the more does one realise how intricate it is and how various people and parties are taking, or attempting to take, a part in it for many divers reasons. India, and Indian secret societies, Syrians, Turks of all parties.'[16] Wilson, Bray, Ruhi, and others at Jeddah would have heartily agreed with him.

The Red Sea Patrol was a key overarching theme of the Arab Revolt, and had been pivotal in sustaining its early and fragile momentum through offensive power, the ready provision of merchant supply ships, the continued interception of Ottoman wireless communications, and diplomatic support. Wemyss was always prepared to take swift action when it was needed: he had instantly approved the despatch of food, stores, and £16,000 in gold sovereigns to the hungry and unpaid Bedouin fighters at Aqaba, as soon as Lawrence had requested them following the capture of the port.

The Red Sea Patrol also considerably improved British knowledge of the coastline from Aqaba to Aden. In a post-war lecture, Commander David Hogarth, Lawrence's mentor and former director of the Arab Bureau, said that before the war much of the eastern shoreline of the Red Sea was scarcely better known in detail than the shores of the Antarctic. Royal Navy support for the revolt meant that safe passage for its ships and smaller supply vessels had to be found through the formidable line of triple coral reefs.[17]

★   ★   ★

In contrast to the strategic and political work of Wemyss and Boyle, Gray gives some intriguing insights into how other Red Sea Patrol officers interacted with him and his colleagues. Commander Frank Dugdale, the Naval Transport Officer responsible for ships' timetables and cargoes, was based at Jeddah, for part of 1917 at least. He ate and drank and played bridge with Gray and the others, and his mess bill for two weeks in October 1917 survives.[18] Dugdale was also a keen golf player on the Jeddah course: he left Gray a note, asking him to get hold of some golf clubs while on leave in Cairo, which Wilson had offered to bring back with him.[19] While based at Yenbo, Gray enjoyed dining with Captain W. E. Lewis of SS *River Fisher*, which was a 'fleet messenger' used by the Arab Bureau to carry stores for the Arabian campaign. Lewis kept the Yenbo contingent amused with his fund of unlikely stories.[20] These accounts and others are rare glimpses into the hidden everyday world of Red Sea Patrol officers who have fallen below the radar of historians.

★   ★   ★

General Wingate appreciated the invaluable help of the Red Sea Patrol and stated that without its unstinting cooperation, under the command of Captain William Boyle, a successful revolt would have been impossible.[21]

Lawrence too was well aware of the importance for the Arab Revolt of British control of the Red Sea. He wrote to his mother from Wejh on

12 February 1917, soon after its capture: 'The Arab Movement is a curious thing. It is really very small and weak in its beginning, and anybody who had command of the sea could put an end to it in three or four days'.[22] Like Wilson, Lawrence greatly admired Wemyss and Boyle. He wrote of Wemyss:

> I found that his active and broad intelligence had engaged his interest in the Arab Revolt from the beginning. He had come down again and again in his flagship to lend a hand when things were critical, and had gone out of his way twenty times to help the shore, which properly was Army business. He had given the Arabs guns and machine-guns, landing parties and technical help, with unlimited transport and naval co-operation, always making a real pleasure of requests, and fulfilling them in overflowing measure.
>
> Had it not been for Admiral Wemyss' good will, and prescience, and the admirable way in which Captain Boyle carried out his wishes, the jealousy of Sir Archibald Murray might have wrecked the Sherif's rebellion at its start. As it was, Sir Rosslyn Wemyss acted godfather till the Arabs were on their feet.[23]

Lawrence gave a graphic summary of the role of the Red Sea Patrol, with a variation on the godfather theme:

> The Red Sea patrol-ships were the fairy-godmothers of the Revolt. They carried our food, our arms, our ammunition, our stores, our animals. They built our piers, armed our defences, served as our coast artillery, lent us seaplanes, provided all our wireless communication, landed landing parties, mended and made everything. I couldn't spend the time writing down a tenth of their services...The Admiral was hearteningly useful. His support, in the high place, made all the naval ships our active helpers.[24]

★ ★ ★

The remarkable number of 'Ginger' Boyle's ships that regularly anchored off Aqaba to discharge supplies and men, and take refugees and prisoners back to Suez, staggered everyone at first from visiting liaison officers to aircraft mechanics like young Jackson and the former prisoners of war in Pearson's Arab Legion. But an unexpected arrival in early 1918 turned up at the bustling base not by sea as usual but overland. His bizarre story would flummox senior officers at Aqaba and cause consternation among intelligence chiefs at the Arab Bureau.

17

'Use great caution'

The Curious Case of Agent Maurice

In early June 1918 Gray discovered the fragments of a very strange spy story. He had found them soon after his transfer to the Aqaba base, buried in one of three much-thumbed and rather dog-eared notebooks that his cipher officer predecessor had left behind for him. The notebooks held an extraordinary record of hundreds of decrypted secret cables and messages about to be encrypted, spanning the period November 1917 to March 1918.[1]

A travel-worn man who looked like an Arab had ridden unannounced into Aqaba with two Bedouin sheikhs on 21 January 1918. This alone was enough to raise security concerns, but it was when the man claimed to be an important British spy who had previously been based in Switzerland that British officers' antennae began to twitch in earnest. They cabled the Arab Bureau that same day with the new arrival's extraordinary story:

> Rafai Bey who passed in Switzerland by name of Edward Maurice has arrived at Sherif Feisal's HQ via Damascus and Hammad [sic - i.e. Hama] & has brought with him some Bedouin chiefs, Shaiman son of Hasseni, Sheikh Hussein of the Walad Ali tribe, he wishes to leave for Cairo with important information. Please wire permit to Akaba for him to leave by first boat and should he bring Bedouin chiefs. Please inform General Clayton and Colonel Deedes.

The next day, 22 January, Aqaba cabled the Arab Bureau with further details of Rafai/Maurice's astounding claims:[2]

> Resumé of information given me by Rafai as follows. Travelled from Switzerland via Austria, Bulgaria, Constantinople and visited Hamma & Aleppo & Homs, he fled from Damascus & came here via Jauf, he reports all Northern Bedouin tribes had declared against Turks. The Beni Muslim, Beni Khaled with exception

of their chief Abdel Kherim Pasha, the Fowara & Shasshas all in Haddad district—these & other tribes declare their willingness to operate against Turks as may be directed. Turks are endeavouring to organise Bedouin force to act against Sherif & £200,000 has arrived at Damascus for forwarding schemes which according to Rafai will not be accepted by Bedouins. About 6 weeks ago a Turkish division arrived at Constantinople from Romanian front & left for Palestine front. Another division has been withdrawn from Caucasus & was destined for Palestine also a cavalry brigade under Mohammed Ali Bey. He heard at Constantinople that 3 German divisions had been promised for Palestine, also 2 Austrian divisions & 24 batteries, the advance party of about 2000 men & 159 officers had already arrived at Bizanti. 10 armoured cars have arrived at Damascus. He reports that indications of Bedouin activity in north against Turks are excellent.

Maurice appeared to be a superspy, a man who could travel through enemy territory and even visit Constantinople, a man with top-grade intelligence on Ottoman and German/Austrian military strategy as well as on Bedouin tribal alliances and intentions. Was this all too good to be true?

Gray would have been intrigued as the story developed. The initial response from Cairo on 23 January was terse: 'Maurice may come but not the two Sheikhs, telegraph what day he leaves and under what name.' Another report full of curiously specific intelligence from Maurice, which he claimed to have received within the last few hours, was then sent to the Arab Bureau on the same day, 23 January:

> Further information received today from Monsieur Maurice from a Bedouin. Important conference between Bedri Bey Governor Aleppo, Asmi Bey Governor Beirut, Gailual Governor Adana, Ismail Hazki Bey Governor Lebanon, Tassim Bey Governor Damascus... This conference tried to raise volunteer army of Maoweilla & Beni Mislim Bedouins paying for cavalry £15 Turkish, camels £8 to £10 Turkish, Infantry £5 to £6 in gold. Emir Abdul Kadr & Sheikh Nassani & others were sent but not a single Bedouin accepted these terms. Tassim Bey sent messages to Nuri Shalaan inviting him to come to Damascus with 500 camels to take money, supplies etc. Nuri Shalaan has warned that this was a trap. Further information that 5000 troops arrived by Jan. 1st at Kiochla for Damascus. Turks have heavily reinforced & fortified round Nablus & intend an offensive there.
>
> Maurice very impatient to get to Cairo as he has important information on the Sherifian campaign from Damascus & Aleppo.

The most likely explanation for Maurice's reports is that they were neither the Crown Jewels from a confident and resourceful spy, nor a breathtaking tour de force of disinformation. It is hard to verify them, but his assertions seem to be a mixture of personal observations, hearsay, and rumours, with a leavening of pure fabrication to bolster his own reputation. Maurice's reports seem to be more misinformation, rather than carefully calculated disinformation sent to confuse the British. The Arab Bureau was certainly wary, cabling on 25 January: 'You should use great caution with Maurice. His good faith very suspicious & he magnifies enormously his own import-ance. He should be treated politely but not made much of. Please inform Captain of ship which brings him & warn him to tell officers not to give him any information.' So the Arab Bureau wanted to get their hands on Maurice without alerting him to their suspicions. Gray noticed the implied acknowledgement by the Bureau that Maurice was a British agent (he was considered to have had some importance, or why say that he hugely magnified it?).

That same day Maurice was put on a ship for Suez. After a couple of days interrogating him, the Arab Bureau sought as much detail as possible about the spy's backstory or legend, cabling on 29 January: 'Have you or Major Lawrence obtained any new information about Maurice. What do Feisal & the Arabs generally think of him and his journey. Reply urgent.' This seemed a wise if somewhat belated request, given that Feisal was a sophisticated operator and had a good intelligence system. The reply the following day was dismissive: 'Feisal & Arabs I have spoken to look upon Maurice with mistrust & give little credence to information he produced. Had he not been proceeding direct to Arab Bureau he would probably have been detained in custody. Am making further enquiries.' The only real surprise here is the word 'probably', which suggests a degree of backtracking: per-haps the Aqaba officers had at first thought Maurice would never have had the gall to invent such an audaciously unlikely narrative.

In fact the Arab Bureau had apparently already made up its mind about Maurice six days earlier, on 23 January, just two days after the first cable from Aqaba. The subsequent messages were all about filling in details and joining up dots. Gray would not have known of the entry in General Headquarters' (GHQ's) official War Diary, Political Intelligence for 23 January:

> The Arab Bureau telegraphed the Director of Military Intelligence, England, with regard to the action to be taken re. "Maurice". This man has travelled from Switzerland (where he was an Intelligence agent) via Austria, Bulgaria, Constantinople, Hama, Aleppo and Homs, and has given information concerning the Turkish endeavour to enlist the sympathies of the Bedouins, and also as to the movement of the Turkish troops. He is reported to be in German pay.[3]

Those final eight words have an almost incidental ring, but for the British intelligence establishment they would have had a terrible resonance. They would have been desperate to find out how long Maurice had been paid by the Germans, if the report was accurate. Unpicking and assessing the damage inflicted by an agent they had seen as a mother lode of top-class intelligence would be a painful and lengthy process. Maurice was in modern parlance a fabricator, at least to a certain extent, though it seems unlikely that he had been a false-flag penetration by enemy intelligence from the start. Every piece of intelligence sent in by him, including material from any sub-agents, would have to be treated as suspect unless there was clear evidence of its reliability—and even then, nagging doubts would flash in what would later be called a wilderness of mirrors. With this sort of bleak mindset, good intelligence was liable to be discounted. What on earth had gone wrong?

★   ★   ★

As so often in this sort of case, describing is easier than explaining. The stakes could not have been higher. Maurice had been endorsed by none other than the chief of intelligence at Cairo, General 'Bertie' Clayton and by the hyperactive politician and 'Mr Fixit' of Middle Eastern policy, Sir Mark Sykes. Following the paper trail back to early 1916 reveals intriguing insights into the wider intelligence duel between the British and their formidable adversaries, the Germans and Ottoman intelligence.[4] The earliest reference to Maurice seems to be in late January 1916 when, using the cryptonym 'Mustafa', he reported on the imminent arrival of enemy planes at the Sinai border with Egypt.[5] In March 1916 he was dropped in Syria by a French ship from the island of Arwad, an intelligence base off the coast. He toured Palestine as well as Syria, and reported on troop concentrations as 'Mustafa'. He was later returned to Arwad.[6]

The fateful entanglement of Maurice, Clayton, and Sykes is laid bare in a bombshell letter dated 26 December 1916 from the intelligence general to Sykes. Clayton thanked Sykes for his letter of 20 November,

> sending the outline of the scheme which you discussed with Maurice. I am glad to have it by me, as it is a guide at any rate to what we should prepare for and be ready to put into operation should the opportunity arise. At present I feel that we cannot do very much until our forward movement in Sinai has got along a bit & can move a little more quickly. The approach of our troops will give heart to any revolution & we shall be in a better position to support it.

Clayton agreed with Sykes that the Entente with France was all-important and that attempts to score off Britain's allies were 'sickening'. It seems from this that Maurice may have promoted a scheme—or at least agreed that it was feasible—for an uprising of tribes against the Turks in Syria, to complement the Arab Revolt in the Hejaz. There is also a hint that Maurice did not like the French. For now, Clayton felt a Syrian revolution was too risky because the Turks could suppress it in the absence of British troops to give support from Palestine.

There is no suggestion that Clayton suspected Maurice of wanting to provoke a tribal rising that would play into the Turks' hands. Far from it: he had had lengthy discussions with the man he clearly saw as his agent, and told Sykes that he had sent Maurice to Switzerland where he could do useful work.[7]

Neutral Switzerland was a country teeming with spies, would-be spies, disinformation, and rumour. Every belligerent power had its operatives and agents there, though the Swiss were not at all happy that their country should be used as 'a kind of intelligence clearing-house where spies . . . engaged in an espionage free-for-all'.[8] Some British and other networks had been broken up by the Swiss authorities, but by 1916 the sheer number of players involved meant the genie could not be put back in the bottle. What interested Clayton in particular was that Switzerland was a melting pot for various Ottoman factions, both those supporting the ruling Committee of Union and Progress and liberal groups that wanted to overthrow it. There were anti-British, pan-Islamic groups there too: Bray had gone there in 1913 to investigate them. Clayton knew there was a good likelihood that Maurice could serve him well in Switzerland.

Following Maurice's trail in that country uncovers an intriguing pattern. In May 1917 he reported that the Turks and Germans were very anxious about the Anazeh and Rualla tribes in Syria, whom they feared would rise in support of Sherif Hussein—so much so that the Germans were sending agents to them to try to deflect them.[9] In June it was reported that: 'Arrangements made with E.M.S.I.B. [Eastern Mediterranean Special Intelligence Bureau] to supply information to an agent of theirs who is proceeding via Switzerland to Turkey.' This is about the time that Maurice claimed he went to Turkey and so he could have been the agent in question, though perhaps another agent was involved as Maurice was unlikely to have worked for the EMSIB as well as for Clayton. But if Maurice was supplying information to the EMSIB agent, there was scope for dangerous disinformation to be given.

In August a British Army intelligence document mentioned 'our representative in Switzerland' who reported on four leading Turks who were in
Switzerland. This person thought that three of them were moderate members of the ruling party, 'the sort of men who might be selected to make
overtures for a separate peace'. Again, this could have been disinformation
on the part of the Turks.[10]

★   ★   ★

Maurice's detailed story, given under lengthy interrogation once the Arab
Bureau had him securely at Cairo, was eye-poppingly bizarre. It reads like
an ambitious synopsis for a Buchanesque spy thriller that was rejected for
being too far-fetched. It seems to be a story of hubris, disenchantment with
the British, and delusions of grandeur as well as betrayal. The GHQ Political
Intelligence War Diary shows that Maurice was still asking to see Feisal at
Aqaba (he would have been unaware of the Arab leader's damning put-
down). The report continues:

> According to his own account he stayed five months in Switzerland, and then
> in order to get to Syria, having failed to obtain our permission, pretended that
> he had quarrelled with his British employers, and entered the German Secret
> Service. He was received with open arms by Fuad Selim, who arranged that
> Maurice should go to Berlin, and subsequently interview Talaat Pasha [one of
> the ruling triumvirate] at Constantinople.
>
> He was entertained on a lavish scale at Berlin. Soon after his arrival he was
> taken to Army HQ...He was asked his opinion as to the best way of retaking
> Baghdad...Maurice told [Kuhlmann, at the Ministry of Foreign Affairs] that
> he had only worked for the British to get rid of Khalil and Jemal [another of
> the three Ottoman leaders].
>
> At Constantinople he was taken to see Talaat at the Sublime Porte. Talaat
> asked numerous questions about the possibility of peace with England...He
> also asked Maurice if he considered it possible to make peace with the Sherif,
> or if not, to raise a volunteer army against him. On the same day Maurice met
> Jemal, who spoke very vindictively against the Sherif, and talked of crushing
> him. Later in the afternoon Maurice was taken to see Enver [the third of the
> ruling three]...In a second interview, Talaat informed Maurice that certain
> peace overtures had been made by the Arabs, but they had been rejected,
> because one of the conditions was that the Sherif of Mecca should be Caliph.
>
> Maurice was present at the station when the Kaiser arrived in Constantinople...
> Maurice heard that the reasons for this Imperial visit [included]...the partition
> of territory after the war...Maurice went to Damascus on November 2nd....
> Apparently [Enver] had a violent quarrel with Falkenhayn, who deliberately
> told him the Turkish army was rotten. Efforts were then made to induce

Maurice to raise a force of Bedouins, but it was at this juncture that, according to his account, he began to work on our behalf in Arabia.

Maurice was told at Damascus that the Turks would soon have 30 to 35 Divisions on the two fronts—Palestine and Mesopotamia. He paid visits to all the major centres in Syria. Suspicion began to fall on him, and he had considerable difficulty in escaping from Damascus as a sum of £20,000 was being offered for his apprehension. He claims to have visited most of the leading tribes, and to have induced the Sheikhs and notables, some 2000 in number, to swear upon the Koran that they would never draw sword against the British or the Sherif. After these efforts he crossed the Hejaz Railway, and joined up with the Sherif Feisal and Lieutenant-Colonel Joyce, who telegraphed to ask if Maurice might come to Cairo.

So Maurice's superhuman abilities extended to joining German intelligence as a double agent while remaining a triple agent for the British; meeting top German army officers and officials in Berlin; meeting all three of the ruling Ottoman triumvirate in Constantinople and Damascus; being made party to the most confidential high-level intelligence by them; being at Constantinople railway station when Kaiser Wilhelm arrived and being briefed on his detailed objectives; escaping from Damascus in the nick of time; eluding a huge manhunt; and, even more improbable, persuading two thousand sheikhs and notables to swear allegiance on the Koran to the British and Sherif Hussein (who had had difficulty in getting a handful of tribes to support him consistently).

Bertie Clayton, the consummate intelligence professional, would have been mortified at Maurice's deception. He would have been used to agents exaggerating and fabricating in their reports, giving their handlers what they thought they wanted to hear, but the mention of Maurice being in German pay would have hit Clayton hard. It is impossible to be sure, without a full paper trail, just how much damage Rafai/Maurice inflicted on the British.[11] We are left with the smooth mandarin tone and classic English understatement of the conclusion of the report on Maurice: 'The consensus of opinion with regard to Maurice is that he is not reliable and that a recommendation should be made for his internment'.[12]

In a telling postscript, the British could not bring themselves to admit more widely to the Maurice debacle. A War Office report on the Arab Revolt dated 31 August 1918 includes the following: 'Maurice (a British secret agent) visited Berlin and Syria before emerging at Akaba. He gave information indicating that the Germans were endeavouring to reconcile the Turks with the Arabs.'[13] The words do their intended job: they conjure fog in the guise of clarity, while the real story lies masked in their hinterland.

★ ★ ★

The curious case of agent Maurice allows a light to be shone on a tiny part of the secret world. Cyril Wilson, Lionel Gray, T. E. Lawrence, John Bassett, Hugh Pearson, Norman Bray, Hussein Ruhi, John Young, Thomas Goodchild, and Leslie Bright were all caught up, to some extent, in the hidden war between British intelligence and their Ottoman and German counterparts. None was ever party to more than a few fragments of the whole picture; the whole picture would, in any case, always stay elusive, out of reach even to the Arab Bureau chiefs. All the cast of characters here were aware, though, that their secret adversaries were a constant presence, eddying around Jeddah, Aqaba, and elsewhere and sometimes leaving ripples in their wake.

It was the nature of Gray's work that he was given more glimpses into the secret war than his colleagues, though they were mostly snapshots rather than detailed canvases. The cable notebooks left behind for him are a gateway to hidden corners of the revolt, a rich seam of evidence for both strategic and more everyday concerns. Lawrence was called upon by the Arab Bureau on 20 January 1918 to set up a spy network in Syria.[14] A few weeks earlier, Lawrence had been put firmly in his place by his mentor David Hogarth of the Bureau: 'From Hogarth for Major Lawrence. Sir Percy Cox [Chief Political Officer, Mesopotamia] objects decidedly to your proposal about Mesopotamian tribes joining Sherif. If you go to Jauf el Amr or talk to Feisal do not proceed with the matter.'[15] Cox reported to the British Indian Government: this was another example of tension between the Foreign Office and India over the Arab Revolt.

The strength of Feisal's Northern Arab Army is given on 26 January 1918 as: '108 officers, 9 sub-officers, 3057 ORs [other ranks], 1.5 inch How[itzer], 2 18 pounder field guns, 2 15 pounder field guns, 4 EA [Egyptian Army] 2.95 mountain guns, 4 Indian ten pounder mountain guns, 2 [illegible] & 25 MGs [machine guns].' There were also five officers and 148 other ranks of the Egyptian Army at Aqaba. The French at this time had one officer and seventy-eight other ranks there; there were also two officers and sixty-four other ranks at bases at Wadi Musa and Ghadia Abu Sowana.[16]

A number of cables deal with sensitive ciphering issues. On 26 February 1918 the Red Sea Patrol reported: 'Arab Bureau Cairo code compromised. Only to be used when essential & if contents are not secret.' On 29 January the Arab Bureau cabled: 'GHQ inform me their wireless stations can intercept messages from Aqaba. They instruct you to send all messages about intelligence or operations... to double address viz Arbur [Arab Bureau] &

Egypforce, a code word or number should be used & indicator made as usual at end of text...K92 has been allotted as code for Chief Political Officer GHQ.'

On rare occasions, natural forces could damage the railway line as much as explosive charges: 'Reliable information reports great damage done to railway line by rains S. of Tebuk. All culverts over Wadi Akhdar & Wadi Ghudei have been washed away & no train has passed this sector for 15 days.'[17] 'Reliable information' was one level of dependability. 'A most reliable source' was the highest level and was code for intercepted wireless messages, as was 'Agent Y reports'. Ottoman wireless communications and those from German Pascha units had been regularly intercepted from April 1916. The Special Wireless Section of the Signal Branch of Egyptian Expeditionary Force even had a central interception station on top of the Great Pyramid at Giza. Codebreaking staff in Egypt worked on encrypted material intercepted both by land-based stations and by Red Sea Patrol ships.[18] Agent reports were assessed by analysts who used words like 'rumour' and 'hearsay evidence', and on one occasion, shortly before the Arab Revolt broke out: 'Report by honest but stupid agent.'[19] A gloss by one intelligence officer read: 'I consider this man's statement unreliable & think he is probably a Turkish officer.'[20]

While wireless intelligence was the most important means of information gathering for the British, the role of human intelligence—operatives and their agents—should not be underestimated. The same applies to the risks these men ran. Lieutenant Ashley Powell was attached to the Eastern Mediterranean Special Intelligence Bureau, like his friend and fellow Irishman, Captain Lewen Weldon. He was sent to Arabia in May 1918, in the words of *The Arab Bulletin*, 'to collect intelligence from Feisal's camp'. On 12 June Powell nearly paid with his life.

> Lieut. Powell had accompanied Major Maynard and his armoured cars to the neighbourhood of Jurf ed-Derwish, and momentarily lost touch with the party. While he was alone, he was accosted by five stray Bedouins, who finding him resist them, stabbed and beat him, stripped off his clothes, and took a considerable sum in gold. His wounds were less serious than they easily might have been.[21]

Powell was treated at Major Marshall's makeshift Aqaba hospital, and left for recuperation in Egypt on SS *Borulos* on 23 June.[22]

Secret cable messages in the Aqaba notebooks did not always deal with high-level intelligence, and Lawrence could not escape the more mundane requests. An outgoing message on 15 December 1917 read: 'For Lawrence. Can you bring us 3 primus stoves when you return.' Lawrence was also asked whether his youngest brother, Arnold, would like to join the Arab Bureau.[23]

In the intelligence war the British were always looking to exploit Turkish weaknesses. They were involved with a 'desertion organisation' in Syria, the brainchild of Commandant Sarrou of French intelligence. The desertion rate in the Ottoman Army was high, and the Allies stood both to gain intelligence from interrogations and to damage the morale of the Turkish Army. The governor of Ruad Island (also known as Arwad) off the Syrian coast was a French agent, and he recruited 'principal agents for each desertion sector selected from chiefs'. There were also special agents to encourage desertion where there were most soldiers, such as at depots. Deserters were to be paid and routes were carefully worked out leading to small boats at embarkation points at Ruad, Alexandretta, and Beirut.[24] The enterprising governor of Ruad also approached British intelligence, asking for £100 per month in gold in return for setting up and running an agent in the telegraph office at Aleppo. And in one of the more striking euphemisms for a brothel, he also asked for four Egyptian women 'to form an establishment for the benefit of his Garrison', after his Syrian Christian men had caused trouble over local Muslim women.[25]

It is easy to overlook the significance of the Arab rebels' own intelligence system. Gray was aware of this as he read the secret Aqaba cable notebooks. A message reached Aqaba on 27 January 1918 (the source is not clear—perhaps it was Lieutenant Leslie Bright at Wejh): 'Abdullah told me today to inform you he has information that a man named Yousuf el Besaim from Syria is in Hail with £25,000 buying supplies in Kuwait... & camels from Nejd. Man is agent of Jemal Pasha & stores & supplies are intended for Syria.' But it seems the real objective was to help the Ottoman garrison at Medina, because two letters dated 18 February, captured by Abdullah's Arabs, showed that Bessam (i.e. Besaim) 'had arrived there from Hail with a caravan'.[26]

Feisal always seemed clear as to who he could trust. His quartermaster Sheikh Youssef had a cable sent to Bright for the Kaimakam or governor of Wejh, naming a number of untrustworthy sherifs (meaning sheikhs?) who were due to arrive by land: 'Please send them back to Aqaba at once under

a guard, by orders from Feisal.'[27] Their fate was probably sealed, as Feisal had
earlier given orders for the execution of traitors and deserters. In late 1917
Clayton had written that there seemed 'little doubt that Feisal has a traitor
in his councils and one who is well-informed'.[28]

And there was another headache for Feisal and the British. By early
1918 Pierce Joyce at Aqaba knew that the Turks had managed to break a
British cipher. Colonel Alan Dawnay, who liaised between the EEF and
the revolt, wrote to Joyce: 'The compromised cipher is a most unfortunate business, but there is absolutely no doubt that the Turks have lately
been getting certain of our messages. There is just a chance that this may
be traceable to dirty work by somebody at Akaba.'[29] Perhaps this was a
parting shot from Maurice, or the 'dirty work' was done by the traitor
close to Feisal.

There is no doubt that the 'special organisation', the Teşkilât-i Mahsusa,
was a powerful secret service, and Ottoman military intelligence was also
active and competent. Some Ottoman intelligence accounts, apparently
covering the last few months of 1917, were uncovered by Colonel John
Bassett, Wilson's trusted deputy. They record payments to agents, deserters,
and tribal sheikhs, including the Emir of the Juneina and two sections
of the Harb, the Hawazim, and Beni Amr. Gold watches were given in
December 1917 to the brother and uncle of the pro-Turk Ibn Rashid.
Payments went to the son and followers of Sheikh Mubeirik of Rabegh, a
perennial thorn in the side to Sherif Hussein and the British, who 'seem
to have come into Medina more than once and to have been entertained
lavishly and paid handsomely'.[30]

Not surprisingly, Ottoman intelligence was mirroring the activities of
the British. Bassett discovered that documents taken from prisoners of war
included detailed descriptions of Hejaz tribes: 'The tribal divisions are much
more numerous than those given in the Handbook of Hejaz [produced by
the Arab Bureau], whilst the names of the Sheikhs differ in almost every
case.' In a campaign in which disinformation was rife, perhaps some of the
Bedouin informants were playing the same game. The Ottomans could be
ruthless: the Arab Bureau believed that Fawwaz el-Faiz, Sheikh of the Beni
Sakhr, was killed by them in August 1917, 'on account of his pro-Sherif
leanings, by poison given in a cup of coffee'. The Sheikh made the mistake
of going to Amman at the invitation of Jemal Pasha, one of the ruling
Ottoman triumvirate.

★   ★   ★

These few accounts give a flavour of the complexity of the Arab Revolt, whose reality was far removed from the legend of the Bedouin tribes rising as one behind 'Lawrence of Arabia'—a legend still reluctant to leave public consciousness. The hidden intelligence war had underpinned and shaped the revolt for over two years.[31] Now, as the summer of 1918 wore on, the plans and missions of the belligerents were moving rapidly to the endgame. Wilson and his Jeddah circle, with Gray and Scott at Aqaba, knew that the next few weeks would be crucial.

18

Endgame

The long-suffering Wilson must have thought that Sherif Hussein was on a permanent mission of self-destruction. Barely two weeks after he and Bassett had made strenuous efforts to help preserve the facade of Arab unity by diluting the dangerous tension between Hussein and Ibn Saud over Khurma, a brief newspaper announcement threatened meltdown. *Al Qibla*, a newspaper that was tightly controlled by Hussein, stated on 19 August 1918 that Jafar al-Askari, the energetic ex-Ottoman Army officer, had never been commander-in-chief of Hussein's Northern Arab Army. Jafar was deeply offended and resigned. While he sulked in his tent, his combat-toughened commanders, Mesopotamians and Syrians, resigned with him. They had always resented Hussein and mistrusted his bid for an Arab empire under the Hejaz. Feisal, pressed by his commanders and offended by his father's action, resigned as well on 29 August. Hussein called him a traitor and appointed his youngest son, Zeid, to succeed him. Zeid refused. Meanwhile Hussein's secret messages to Feisal became incandescent with rage.

With the likely paralysis of the Arab Army, disaster loomed. The timing could not have been worse: on the very day of the *Qibla*'s publication, Allenby announced that he was bringing forward his great offensive and that the Arab raids had to be coordinated to take place no later than 16 September, three days before his attack. He planned to use the Arabs as part of a deception strategy: they would attack the crucial railway junction at Deraa, drawing the Turks to the east of the Jordan and away from his real initial target, the Mediterranean coast. Buxton's Imperial Camel Corps, after their success at Mudawwara on 8 August, had already played a part in this deception. They had ridden north towards Amman and on to Azrak. Turkish and German intelligence concluded that Allenby's main target would be Amman—an Arab raid on Deraa would fit that scenario. With the change to the timetable, Lieutenant-Colonel Pierce Joyce, in command of the British forces at Aqaba, and his efficient quartermaster, Captain Hubert Young, were both alarmed. Young now had only seven days in which to organize two huge convoys of baggage camels for the Deraa raid. They would need to set off from Aqaba for Azrak, en route to Deraa, on 26 and 28 August. Young threw himself into the project, which was a daunting logistical task in such a short time.

Meanwhile it was vital for the row between Feisal and Hussein to be patched up. Lawrence realized that Feisal would only be happy with an apology from his father, and also that the chances of the patriarchal Hussein giving one quickly were about as likely as Wilson converting to Islam. Lawrence reckoned that he had just four days to pull the leading players back from the brink. Bringing Hussein round could have taken weeks, so Lawrence resorted to subterfuge to get what he wanted. He was in an ideal position for this because he was both seeing and advising Feisal, and also reading the heated messages that Feisal and Hussein were exchanging between Mecca and Aqaba. Lawrence and Joyce understood the Arab ciphers, so Lawrence did what he did so well—he bent reality, in this case to adjust the perceptions of father and son. He secretly decoded Hussein's messages, then turned the most offensive passages into nonsense and enciphered them again, before giving them to Feisal. Feisal was naturally mystified and asked his father for clarification. There was a gradual thaw in the frosty relationship, since as Lawrence pointed out, Hussein never repeated the scrambled sections but each 'fresh version [was] toned down at each re-editing from the previous harshness'. Finally came a cable from Mecca with good news and bad news—in Lawrence's words 'the first half a lame apology and withdrawal of the mischievous proclamation, the second half a repetition of the offence in a new form. I suppressed the tail, and took the head marked "very urgent" to Feisal's tent.' After his secretary had done the deciphering, Feisal 'gazed wonderingly' at Lawrence, 'for the meek words were unlike his father's querulous obstinacy'. Feisal suspected Lawrence's deception but, sophisticated politician that he was, saw a way out. He read the apology aloud and announced, 'The telegraph has saved all our honour.'[1] Lawrence was fuming, later hitting out harshly at Hussein: 'It was intolerable to be at the mercy of so crass a person.'[2]

Lawrence had used stratagems of which the slippery Sir Mark Sykes would have been proud. He had shown again his capacity to be ruthlessly manipulative when the stakes were high. Lawrence, typically, later played down the efforts of Wilson in cajoling Hussein to soften his hard-line attitude to Feisal. He summarily referred to the attempt to get Hussein to apologize: 'Allenby and Wilson were doing their best, engrossing the cables.'[3] When the commander-in-chief himself got involved, things happened—witness the earlier resolution of the flare-up between Hussein and Ibn Saud over Khurma. It was disingenuous of Lawrence merely to state that Allenby and Wilson did their best.

In the meantime, during Lawrence's inspired burst of creative diplomacy, Hubert Young had been desperately busy at Aqaba getting the baggage camel convoys ready to set off for the Deraa raid. He wrote: 'The place was one seething, snarling, sweating mass of camels and Arabs, each as difficult as the other to control.'[4] Young had to assemble two convoys of six hundred baggage camels each. He managed to send them on their way, in line with the new timetable. Reaching the Aba el Lissan base, 70 miles north of Aqaba, four hundred and fifty were converted to riding camels for Feisal's men. Here Feisal, in his new green Vauxhall motor car, reviewed his troops before they set off for Azrak. There were the four hundred and fifty camel-mounted Arab soldiers, French mountain guns under Captain Pisani with his Algerian gunners, three British armoured cars (sadly without their brave but burnt-out leader, Lieutenant Leofric Gilman), Captain Frederick Peake's Egyptian Camel Corps, and some camel-mounted Gurkhas. All these units, together with the baggage camel convoys, reached the remote fortress of Azrak by 12 September. To keep to Allenby's timetable they would have to set out for the raid on Deraa the next day. The game was afoot.

★   ★   ★

Gray's perspective on the mass of camels at Aqaba was rather different from Hubert Young's. Buxton's Imperial Camel Corps had arrived on 30 July, before the attack on Mudawwara.[5] By the time Young's baggage camels arrived for the march to Azrak, Gray was blaming them for his *bêtes noires* in Arabia—the flies that had stalked him from Jeddah to Wejh and from Yenbo to Aqaba.[6]

At least in his half-finished new house and office, built of mud bricks, Gray and his colleagues could cope with the flies better as the windows had netting instead of glass. What had been completed so far, in mid-September, were the mess room, Major Scott's combined room and office, and Gray's own combined room and office. Gray mentioned two cases of bubonic plague at the base. Mabel would hardly have been reassured by her fiancé's lighthearted comments: 'Don't get scared that I shall get it. . . . I don't think white people get it . . . What fun it would be, wouldn't it. I wonder what it does to one.'[7] The plague had been diagnosed by Gray's old golfing partner at Jeddah, the doctor Major William Marshall.

Gray's sense of humour, so appreciated by Marshall, remained buoyant. He wrote a little spoof holiday leaflet, *Sunny Akaba: an Appreciation*, 'published by Red Sea Littoral Publicity Society, Northern Hejaz, 1918', using coloured crayons for effect. It begins: 'Where shall we go for the holidays?...Have you ever thought of Sunny Akaba? Magnificently situated...surrounded by the most superb mountain scenery, Akaba may well be styled "The Queen of the Red Sea Littoral".' Digs at military bureaucracy and penny-pinching creep in: 'The Corporation with the public-spirited energy for which they are famous are erecting a magnificent hotel, which should shortly be completed [doubtless a reference to the officers' mud brick house]...in a prominent position facing the sea'. Gray, an unwitting prophet, would have been astonished to see the modern transformation of unhealthy Aqaba to a sanitized, major tourist resort full of hotels, shopping centres, and nightclubs.[8]

Gray still had bursts of intense ciphering, not least linked to Sherif Hussein's near-derailing of both Allenby's deception strategy and of the Arab Revolt itself. Yet the end-of-term air at Aqaba was inescapable, even though the outcome of the revolt was still unclear as the raiding party made its way to Deraa.

★ ★ ★

Gray's old Jeddah colleagues, on the other hand, were in far from celebratory mode. Bassett had done what he could when the crisis over Sherif Hussein's row with Feisal blew up; he had been dealing with the old leader's crabby and perverse outbursts as well as his occasional near-suicidal depression (or so it seemed) for nearly a year and a half. In early August Bassett had to listen to Hussein's limp explanation for the return from the north of eight hundred Ateibah fighters, whose tribal area lay well to the east of Medina in the south. Spies in Jeddah reported to the Consulate that the tribesmen had recently left the Northern Arab Army because Feisal had not paid them. 'The King's version of the affair, given to Colonel Bassett, is that the Ateibah are unable to stand the northern climate, and are being sent back for service in the southern Hejaz!'[9] Perhaps it was more likely that the parsimonious and suspicious Hussein had withheld funds from Feisal.

Another of Gray's old Jeddah comrades, Hussein Ruhi, had now been intimately involved in the Arab Revolt and its gestation for two and a half years. On 21 August 1918, probably after some leave in Egypt, he returned to Jeddah on SS *Borulos*, apparently with his wife and a daughter or two: 'Mr Ruhi and family', together with Gray's cipher assistant, 'Hoppy' Hopwood, were on board.[10] The presence of family members in Arabia with a serving officer (military or not) would have been very unusual. Perhaps Ruhi's wife and children were en route to another destination. Ruhi was still ferreting out useful intelligence: he left Jeddah on 9 September for Mecca to obtain as much information as possible on an unspecified subject requested by the Director of the Arab Bureau, Colonel Kinahan Cornwallis.[11] Perhaps his trip concerned a very sensitive matter that was still troubling the British: King Hussein's dispute with Ibn Saud over the Khurma territory. Ruhi certainly had agents who had access to Hussein's thinking and motivation on this flashpoint, which was still of concern into October. As the *Arab Bulletin* put it: 'Hussein Effendi Ruhi reports that he learns from a trustworthy source that the King has imposed moderate counsels on [Sherif] Shakir, who proposed to advance on Khurma.'[12]

★   ★   ★

Some 790 miles to the north-west of Jeddah, on 16 September as planned, Allenby launched the main phase of his deception strategy east of the River Jordan. His aim, using the Arab forces, was to disrupt Ottoman communications and persuade the 63-year-old German General, Liman von Sanders, who commanded the combined Turkish-German forces, that that was where the British attack would be concentrated. Bedouin tribesmen massed at Azrak seemed to presage a raid on Amman. Lawrence and the Arabs, with an armoured car detachment, attacked the railway south of Deraa, wrecking a bridge near Mafraq. Meanwhile Peake's Egyptian Camel Corps and Hubert Young caused devastation on the railway with 'tulip' mines, which forced the rails up and twisted them into the shape of a tulip bud, impossible to straighten. With the railway destroyed to the north and south of Deraa, the Turkish garrison at the town was cut off. The garrison made strenuous efforts to repair the line, but to no avail: 6 kilometres of line were destroyed and more bridges were blown up. Lawrence and Pisani also captured and blew up two railway stations at Mezerib, a large depot that supplied the Turks' Palestine front. Not content with that, Lawrence and Hubert Young climbed on to the roof of one of the stations to cut the vital telegraph link between Syria and Palestine. On 18 September Lawrence learned of a setback: hard-working German troops had managed to rig up a working bridge north of Mafraq, to replace the one blown up by him two days before. Lawrence and his men took swift action. With the French gunners' help, they stormed a Turkish force at Nesib on the railway to the north and demolished the bridge.

With railway and telegraphic communications to Palestine cut, Allenby struck with overpowering force on 19 September. Just before dawn he launched a massive artillery bombardment of Turkish lines north of Jaffa on the Mediterranean coast: the Battle of Megiddo had begun. A huge infantry attack followed. The Turks were completely wrong-footed: Allenby's flair for deception, encouraged by his intelligence advisers, had even extended to building 15,000 life-size models of horses. They replaced the real horses, which had been withdrawn from the Jordan Valley and the Judean Hills to the coast, where they had been hidden from enemy aerial reconnaissance in camouflaged tents. Sleighs pulled by mules had been drawn across the Jordan Valley to give the impression of dusty cavalry manoeuvres.[13] When Allenby launched his cavalry to supplement the infantry breakthrough, the effects were devastating. His infantry had already advanced 7,000 yards in the first two and a half hours. Now the cavalry swept inland through northern Palestine behind the Turkish lines, capturing key towns.

Just twenty-four hours after his campaign began, Allenby intended to use the element of surprise to capture Liman von Sanders and his staff in his head-quarters at Nazareth.[14] Lieutenant Ashley Powell of the Eastern Mediterranean Special Intelligence Bureau, who had been so nearly stabbed to death by Bedouins in a secret desert operation in June, seems to have played a key role. He had returned to Arabia on 7 August.[15] He sent a stunning piece of oper-ational intelligence, by carrier pigeon, from Feisal's camp at Aba el Lissan to Major Scott at Aqaba, for transmission to Allenby's headquarters: 'ex-chief of Regie [taxation official] Deraa states Sanders' rooms in upper floor Casa Nova Hotel south side. Entrance by private door and stairs on south side of hotel in garden. Lt. A Powell.' Unfortunately the message, which is in Powell's hand, is not dated, but it was sent in reply to a specific request for information and must relate to Allenby's plan to send in a snatch squad to seize Liman von Sanders before he could react to the lightning British push. The value of human intelligence as well as radio interceptions is dramatically clear.[16]

Liman von Sanders escaped capture by a whisker. Warned by tough street fighting, he left the Casanova Hotel in Nazareth, his headquarters, a few hours before Allenby's cavalry arrived at three o'clock on the morning of 20 September. By then key towns such as the crossroads of Tulkarm, Baisan, and Afula had been captured, and the Ottoman Seventh and Eighth Armies had been completely encircled. When the British captured the main railway bridge over the River Jordan at Jisr al-Majami, there was no escape route from Palestine to Transjordan. Tens of thousands of Turkish soldiers surrendered. With the seizure of the ports of Acre and Haifa on 23 September, the conquest of Palestine was complete.

★ ★ ★

Colonel Dawnay had sent an aircraft to Azrak, where Lawrence was waiting, on 21 September. It brought orders from Allenby, who did 'NOT wish Feisal to dash off, on his own, to Damascus'. This was of course a reference to the Sykes-Picot Agreement. Yet the British did not wish to make life easy for the French in Syria. Referring to Feisal, Allenby had written: 'we shall soon be able to put him there [Damascus] as part of our own operations'.[17] Lawrence was a passenger on the aircraft's return to Allenby's headquarters at Bir Salem in Palestine. Allenby was delighted with the Arabs' operations but told Lawrence that he and the Arabs were to play a support role in taking Damascus. It would have to be a joint operation with Allenby's army. Lawrence still hoped, however, that Arab boots on the ground just might increase their bargaining power when the Ottoman Empire was dismembered.

The end was now near. Allenby dealt with Transjordan by sending the New Zealand Mounted Brigade to capture Salt and Amman. Four thousand soldiers from Maan, on their way to Amman, surrendered to the 2nd Australian Light Horse Brigade. The Arab Army took Deraa on 27 September. On the same day, Turkish atrocities at Tafas were followed by an Arab loss of control in which few if any prisoners were taken. It remains unclear whether Lawrence sanctioned the bloodbath, which remained seared in his memory for the rest of his life. Now Allenby's cavalry and the Arab Army drove towards Damascus, harrying the Ottoman Fourth Army, which fell back before an unstoppable tide. The battle was unequal: the best Turkish troops had been diverted to the Caucasus in a rash campaign to secure Baku and a new pro-Ottoman state of Azerbaijan, and the threadbare Fourth Army was riven by low morale, desertions, inadequate munitions, and malnutrition. It had no chance against Allenby's overpowering superiority in manpower and armour. The climax of the Palestine campaign and of the Arab Revolt approached.

Contrary to what he later claimed, Lawrence was not the first to enter Damascus. The 3rd Australian Light Horse Brigade beat him to it, passing through the city, unopposed, at dawn on 1 October while aiming to cut the Turkish line of retreat to the north. The Turks had not even bothered to defend Damascus.[18] The British made a political point by letting Feisal's Arab Army accept the city's formal surrender. Sherif Nasir entered Damascus on behalf of Sherif Hussein later on 1 October. With him were two power-ful Bedouin warlords, Auda Abu Tayi and Nuri Shalaan, the latter having climbed off the fence for a significant contribution to the last act of the revolt. Feisal arrived on horseback with a large band of his fighters on 3 October. At the Victoria Hotel, with Lawrence as his interpreter, Feisal had to listen to Allenby laying down the terms of the imperial victors. France would be the 'protecting power' over Syria, excluding Palestine and Lebanon: in these two areas the Arab administration would have no status. In the rest of Greater Syria, Feisal would be a mere administrator under French guidance and with French financial backing. He would have no control of the coastal area and reportedly complained: 'I am in a house with no door'.[19] It was the very success of the revolt, with Feisal reaching Damascus, that had brought to a sharp focus all the tangled contradictions and bad faith in the various promises that the British had made.[20]

Feisal was downcast. He and Lawrence alike were caught in a web of nervous tension and despair. Lawrence, mentally and physically exhausted, damaged by all he had undergone, had been running on empty for months. He had been disenchanted with the Arabs and their infighting for nearly a year. Most of all he was disenchanted with himself; sick at heart for what he knew would be the British betrayal of the Arabs and for a more personal, visceral betrayal. He knew that Arabs believed in people, not governments or organizations. The rebels, at least many of them, believed in him, and it cut him to the core that he had deceived them about the planned carving up of the Middle East after the war. Why he should have presumed to take all the cares of geopolitics on his own shoulders is an intriguing subject. He agonized over British and French deceit yet condoned episodes of duplicity on the part of Hussein and his sons.[21] What mattered, though, was that Lawrence believed he had brought dishonour to the rebels and to himself. Burnt out, feeling he could achieve nothing in Damascus, he left for Cairo on 4 October, intending to try to fight for the Arab case in Europe.

Lawrence probably had little interest in the subsequent British capture of the other main cities in Syria and Lebanon. The campaign ended when Aleppo fell on 26 October. Because of the collapse of their Syrian army, the Ottomans would soon be forced out of the war. At one level, Lawrence's tortured psyche had forced him out of engagement with the Arab Revolt and its hollow victory. In a telling and poignant phrase confided to his notebook on 2 October, he had written: 'I knew I was worn tool lying in darkness under bench [sic].'[22] The tool would, however, still be capable of doing good work.

★   ★   ★

Back in Aqaba, Gray's war appeared to be coming to an end. The contrast with the cutting edge of *realpolitik* in Damascus could not have been greater. By mid-October Aqaba had become a port of embarkation as more and more serviceman left by steamer for Suez. Gray and some comrades sailed 350 yards across the bay to Solomon's Island (also known as Pharaoh's Island), towing behind them a rowing boat full of Royal Flying Corps and other men who were soon to leave for Egypt. They scrambled over the twelfth-century Crusader castle and went for a swim in the very deep water, which was 'great fun but we clean forgot about the sharks which might have easily got someone'.[23]

Captain Marshall, known as 'the fighting bacteriologist', was a great friend of Gray's and 'not half the man he was'.[24] Marshall was exhausted after nearly two years of intensive, draining duties, including stressful battlefield medical work, and left Aqaba for Egypt on 16 October for urgently needed leave. So many brave and dedicated officers in the Arabian campaign went the same way.

Gray had been craving action and risk-taking for so long. The opportunity finally came by accident on 29 October, with the war nearly over. A chance event showed the absurdity and fragility that are inescapable at some stage in all human lives. Gray somehow contrived the very difficult feat of almost blowing himself up while fishing. Gray and a number of his comrades had been driving along the west side of Aqaba bay, just to see how far they could get, when their thoughts turned to dinner. As Gray told his sister, Cecil, 'I am the chief fisherman and my bait is a bag of bombs.' They caught over a hundred fish and had to dive to the bottom in ten feet of water to retrieve some, but,

> I nearly blew myself up when I was lighting the skipper's bomb while I foolishly had another guncotton bomb in my hand. A spark touched my bomb & set it on fire in my hand & it blazed up in a flame. I instantly chucked it into the water and it went out...I had to be quick and risk a severe burn to save our lives.[25]

Gray ended the letter two days later: 'Oct. 31st. Great news! The war with the Turks is finished.' An armistice had been signed.[26]

Scott's important role at Aqaba, and also Gray's, had been acknowledged by Lieutenant-Colonel Pierce Joyce, who had written to Scott on 2 October from outside Deraa, the day after Nasir and Auda had entered Damascus: 'I do not know how to thank you & your staff for all you have done to help the show along. You have run a damn good show & relieved me of oceans of work & responsibility.'[27] Scott's diary records on 31 October that he had been ordered to evacuate Aqaba. On 11 November he said goodbye to Sheikh Youssef, Feisal's quartermaster, and boarded SS *Borulos* for the last time. On the voyage to Suez he heard with great excitement that peace had been declared.

Gray was hoping for some well-earned leave, but just eight days after his hair-raising fish-bombing escapade, he heard that he would soon be sent to Cairo and then General Headquarters (GHQ) Palestine; his ultimate destination was unclear.[28] Like hundreds of other officers, his active service was to continue for many more months. One of his last actions at Aqaba was to write a revealing document for Captain Frederick Peake of the Egyptian Camel Corps on 11 November, the day Scott left and Peake took over from him as Commandant. Gray itemized with their notations all the secret ciphers, including Arab Bureau and naval ciphers and secret letters of instruction, and formally handed them over to Peake, who signed for them.[29]

Gray boarded SS *Borulos* for Suez on 13 November. In due course he reached Jaffa on the Palestine coast and on 1 December he arrived as cipher officer at GHQ, Bir Salem near Ramleh. His plans to have a couple of sight-seeing days in Jerusalem, later spending Christmas in Egypt, were dashed when on 18 December he was abruptly ordered to catch the first train to Aleppo in northern Syria.[30] Gray did not know it at the time, but he was destined to spend many months at Aleppo.

★   ★   ★

Meanwhile Wilson, the unassuming officer who had been central to the survival of the Arab Revolt on so many occasions, coped steadfastly as ever with the misery of dysentery and with Sherif Hussein's insecurities and outbursts, in the face of disappointments at Damascus and the threat from Ibn Saud. Wilson was steeped in a sad irony as 1918 came to an end with an armistice and celebration of victory. He had a similar if much less complex moral compass to Lawrence. This most dutiful and honest of men must have been anguished, just like Lawrence, when the Arab ship whose course he had helped steer for so long hit the rocks of British and French imperial interests—as Wilson had resolutely predicted would happen. He would be needed for some time further at Jeddah to manage the aftermath of that collision.

19

Aftermath

When Lawrence slipped out of Damascus in a Rolls-Royce tender called *Blue Mist*, on 4 October 1918, he was near breaking point from post-traumatic stress and self-loathing. His iron will, however, was still sufficiently strong for him to promote Arab claims for self-determination. Reaching London before the end of October, he wrote a report called *The Reconstruction of Arabia* for the Eastern Committee of the Cabinet. At a private audience with George V he did an unheard-of thing, startling the King by turning down the awards of Knight Commander of the Bath (which would have made him Sir Thomas Lawrence) and Distinguished Service Order—he would not accept them because he felt his government was about to betray its former Arab allies. As we have seen, although Lawrence had reluctantly accepted the *Croix de Guerre* from the French, he decided that his mentor David Hogarth's dog was a more worthy recipient.

In January 1919 Lawrence went to the Paris Peace Conference as Emir Feisal's interpreter and adviser. Lawrence did his best to influence European and American politicians and opinion-formers, but Arab claims were sidelined. The French tried to freeze Feisal out: they even omitted his name from the official list of delegates. Feisal did not get the chance to speak until 6 February. In March, with no agreement on the Middle East, President Wilson of the USA suggested an international commission to canvass the views of the people of Greater Syria (including Lebanon, Transjordan, and Palestine). As both the French and the British refused to take part, it became called the King-Crane Commission, after the names of its only two members who were Americans. Lawrence and Feisal were dismayed because the French position was too strong. Lloyd George, the British Prime Minister, was determined to have the oil of Mosul and the rest of Mesopotamia. He also wanted Britain to administer Palestine, to keep the French away from Sinai and the all-important Suez Canal that bounded it. In return, the British would not oppose a unified French administration in the whole of

Syria and Lebanon. Clemenceau, the French premier, had been quick to agree, having feared he would have to concede more. This was *realpolitik* red in tooth and claw. Lawrence said: 'Those five months in Paris were the worst I have lived through—and they were worse for Feisal.'[1]

Feisal was a sophisticated politician but his gentle and considerate temperament did not suit him to the hard-headed world of geopolitics at the Paris Peace Conference. He got nowhere at a meeting with Clemenceau in mid-April, because of the French understanding with the British over dividing up Mesopotamia, Palestine, and Syria. Inevitably Feisal failed to get recognition as king of the whole of Syria: instead, he became the precarious steward of a small inland kingdom. As for Lawrence, he realized that he was currently no longer useful to the British Government, but he stayed on in Paris and stepped up the writing he had begun in quiet periods during the conference. The first draft of his account of the desert campaign, *Seven Pillars of Wisdom*, began to take shape. Lawrence did not know it, but he would have a chance later to influence the changing map of the Middle East in a profound way.

★ ★ ★

The story of Wilson and his Jeddah circle was also interwoven with the dramatic aftermath of the Arab Revolt. Gray had left Allenby's headquarters at Ramleh in Palestine by car on 19 December 1918. At Deraa he transferred to the Hejaz Railway for Damascus and the Victoria Hotel, meeting some of Gilman's armoured cars section. He then travelled on by rail to the burnt-out station at Rayak, part of a huge swathe of destruction caused by the retreating Turks: 'Appalling damage meets the eye everywhere and amongst the wreckage are 30 aeroplanes and at least 30 large railway engines, trains, ammunition dumps, stores, ordnance, guns, etc.'[2] He saw 'two fine railway bridges...destroyed...(I thought it was Lawrence but it wasn't)'.[3] Christmas Day found him being entertained at dinner by some Australians at the headquarters of the Desert Mounted Corps. Shortly before New Year's Day he reached Aleppo, which he found terribly cold, via Homs and Hama.

Gray's new boss was Colonel Sir Mark Sykes, who had been in Syria as Chief Political Officer since at least November. He and the Frenchman whose name would forever be bound together with his, Georges-Picot, had both been sent out to arrange for some political officers to be appointed in view of the tension between the British, the French, and the Arabs. But Sykes's stock had fallen. Hogarth told Clayton: 'His shares are unsaleable here [i.e. London] and he has been sent out (at his own request) to get him away.'[4] Gray wrote that Sykes had 'just been returned [as a Member of Parliament at the General Election] with about 10,000 majority. He calls it a jingo & roast beef & plum pudding election.'[5] Gray was soon busy preparing for the visit of General Allenby on 4 January 1919, though he had time to visit the hospital where he met the distinguished senior physician, Dr Altounyan.

Gray was one of a number of officers who had been moved into the Occupied Enemy Territory Administration, or OETA, which was a joint British and French affair. Syria was awash with refugees, muddle, confusion, and, of course, imperial rivalry. Gray was in charge of ciphering and in due course became assistant liaison officer. His duties also included repatriating demobilized Turkish soldiers and giving relief aid to desperate Armenians, who had suffered a series of appalling deportations and massacres at the hands of the Turks since the late nineteenth century. The busy office was no good for cipher security: 'I cannot stay there with secret ciphers so have to do them in my room or in dining room.'[6] The uneasy *entente* with the French did not stop the British intercepting their cables. On 16 January, for example, they intercepted a cable from Georges-Picot himself, regarding the repatriation of Armenians.[7]

A number of Gray's secret cables relate to Sykes's investigation of Armenian massacres. Sykes sent a message to the War Office in London on 10 January, naming the organizer of massacres at Kharput as the former Vali (Governor), Sabit Bey, and naming his chief lieutenants. Conditions at Diarbekir were far worse: Sykes lists the names of seven men, including Attar Zade Hakke Pasha, who were 'alleged chief murderers of children'. There are more horrors: 'Eyewitness states that former Vali Dr Rashid Pasha responsible for crucifixion and burning of Bishop Magerditch Wartabet in mosque.'[8]

In late January 1919 Sir Mark Sykes left Aleppo for Paris and the Peace Conference. Within about three weeks he was dead, yet another victim of the worldwide Spanish Flu pandemic. Gray was greatly shocked at the news of Sykes's death on 16 February. He could easily have suffered the same fate, as Sykes nearly took him to Paris as his assistant, but Gray's ciphering skills were urgently needed at Aleppo. He had clearly warmed to Sykes:

> Full of energy. He would rush into the house after having seen lots of people, talk about several subjects at once, ask questions, talk about something else while the answer was being given, change his clothes, draw a funny picture & be off again all in about 10 minutes. I used to call him the 'whirlwind'.[9]

In March Gray saw his old friend, the doctor Major William Marshall, then based in Damascus. Gray was delighted to hear about Mabel, as Marshall had met her in London while he was there in December, helping to escort Feisal on his visits to London and Glasgow. Gray was also reunited with his old colleague, Lieutenant-Colonel Joyce, from Aqaba days, who stayed at Aleppo on political intelligence work with Colonel Cornwallis of the Arab Bureau until at least early April.[10]

Another old Jeddah colleague to appear in Aleppo, by 7 February 1919, was Wilson's former deputy, Colonel (as he had become) Hugh Pearson. Pearson too was helping cope with the aftermath of the Arab Revolt and the defeat of the Ottoman Army. After training former Ottoman prisoners of war in Egypt for Feisal's Northern Arab Army, falling out with Sykes, and doing political work in Palestine he had at last had the action in the field that he had been craving for years. Pearson had become commandant of Allenby's Royal Engineers in Palestine, building roads and bridges and sweeping forward with the Desert Mounted Corps, delighted to be part of the 'most successful cavalry force in history'.[11] His brief in north Syria was to ensure a water supply for the summer months, rebuild shattered bridges and roads, and build huts for the troops. He also built wharves along the Euphrates River and laid on the motor launches that would use them. He managed a river trip passing Carchemish, the ancient Hittite site by the Euphrates where Lawrence the archaeologist had worked during some of his happiest years, before the war.[12]

Of course Pearson would not have been Pearson without throwing himself wholeheartedly into every sporting endeavour under the sun. This irrepressible officer managed to start on three tennis courts and also organized horse racing for the Desert Mounted Corps,[13] polo, cricket, and a Social Club. And he did not neglect his great sporting passion, golf: 'I have made two golf courses in the war, Jeddah and Aleppo and think my [métier?] is a golf course architect.'[14] Pearson stayed at Aleppo until May, when he returned to Egypt and had lunch with the Allenbys.

★　★　★

Gray and his comrades needed sporting distractions as a temporary respite from the harsh reality of life in north Syria, which pressed in upon them constantly. The misery of the Ottoman Armenians in particular was inescapable, and secret cables show that the British were spending £25,000 per month on relief work including food and supplies. The scale of suffering for those Armenians who had survived the deportations and massacres is all too clear from a cable sent on 2 January by Captain Everard Feilding of the Arab Bureau, who had been sent to Aleppo to help organize Armenian relief.[15] It was Feilding who took over from Sykes when he left on his fateful journey to Paris.

Gray's secret telegrams and letters reveal an extraordinary narrative of an Armenian massacre, the dashed hopes of the Arabs, and Feisal's fears of betrayal. On 28 February he witnessed a sudden massacre, a 'spontaneous combustion' that spread like wildfire at which fifty Armenians were killed and more than one hundred injured: 'if it had not been for British troops there would not have been a Christian...left alive in Aleppo'.[16] Gray believed the massacre was provoked by Arabs (though they may have been Kurds) who found a pretext for attacking the Armenians, their original motive being 'purely robbery with murder if necessary'.[17]

Lawrence had said that Feisal bore the heaviest burden in the aftermath of the Arab Revolt. The Emir returned to Damascus to prepare for the King-Crane Commission's arrival. On 8 June Feisal arrived at Aleppo railway station, where Gray was keenly waiting to greet him with his boss, Major Brayne. Gray had organized a reception for this most important guest, his experience running the officers' mess at Aleppo (as at Jeddah and Aqaba) being put to good use.[18]

Feisal was understandably very concerned about the outcome of the American Commission on Syria. Gray was as usual privy to the most sensitive secret messages, sending a cipher telegram on Feisal's behalf to Allenby on 11 June. Feisal asked

> whether the League of Nations is prepared to put into force the recommendations made by the Commission, and whether the Commission is authorised to recommend the giving of the mandate to any Power wanted by the great majority of the population...the vast majority of Syrians want Britain.

He went on to state that if ordinary Syrians knew that Britain was not going to accept a mandate and the league would not allow complete independence, then Syria would ask for America in preference to France. Feisal was a shrewd and sophisticated politician, and could see the writing on the wall: 'I have been told that this Commission is only a show, and that the fate of the country has already been decided. I feel sure this is incorrect, but at this crisis in the history of Syria, a clear pronouncement on this point is of the greatest importance.'[19]

Feisal's pessimism was fully justified. In this first ever survey of Arab public opinion, the majority in what is now Syria asked for a US mandate. But the determined French claim to Syria, linked to the British need for the oil of Mesopotamia, remained too strong. The views of the commission were ignored and the report was put on a shelf to gather dust (it was not published until 1922). Feisal was hung out to dry, as he and Lawrence had anticipated.

Meanwhile Feisal fought on as best he could. Just before leaving Aleppo for Beirut, he asked Gray to send two further secret telegrams to officials, asking them to 'collect in writing all oppressive measures taken by French officials in your area' (Beirut) and likewise in other parts of Lebanon and Syria.[20]

★ ★ ★

Gray's support role as the harsh legacy of the Arab Revolt unfolded had now lasted seven months. But he also had to bear more personal concerns and pain. He had no idea what he would do with his life after the army no longer needed him. He did not really want to return to Ernest Bentley's code business in London, and had thought about an import–export business of some kind in Syria, or perhaps working in East Africa. More to the point, he was uncertain about Mabel's wishes. Misgivings and a loss of self-confidence had crept upon her from grief and depression, and the weary years of separation. She had written to say that she could not tell what her feelings about the future would be until she had seen him: 'five years is a long time to be away from anyone'.[21] Gray left the Middle East for good in mid-August 1919 and headed back to Egypt, then home on leave, anxious about his prospects for a happy future with Mabel. In a world convulsed and changed forever, the outlook for Gray, as for the ancient land of Syria, hung precariously in the balance.

★ ★ ★

Far to the south-east, across vast wastes of gravel and sand, the aftermath of the Arab Revolt was also unfolding in its heartland. Wilson, Bassett, and the rest of their Jeddah circle worked tirelessly on in their backwater of the Ottoman Empire. The dispute between Sherif Hussein and Ibn Saud over the Khurma region, that old flashpoint, was still causing dangerous instability, and the British officers had to use all their diplomatic skills. Lawrence on one occasion seemed to fan the flames by recommending, extraordinarily, that tanks should be sent to Arabia to help Hussein, an intervention that must have exasperated Wilson. General Headquarters in Egypt sent a cable to Troopers (the War Office): 'Re. tanks required by Lawrence for small force which Feisal wishes to send from Jeddah to Khurma. Considers request should be met.'[22] Lawrence did not see eye to eye with Philby, who was Ibn Saud's champion from the India Office. Perhaps this bizarre recommendation for tanks, which was not acted upon, reflected their rivalry.

Wilson's mood would have been improved by a key event that happened at about the same time as that unwelcome cable. Fakhri Pasha, the tough-minded commandant of the Turkish garrison at Medina, had carried on resisting after the armistice with the Turks. By 9 January he had had enough, the mutiny of some of his own officers tipping the balance. He was escorted to the desert outpost of Bir Derwish outside Medina, where the formal surrender took place on 13 January. Wilson sent Bassett to interrogate Fakhri; Bassett took with him Hussein Ruhi and Lieutenant Leslie Bright, the intelligence officer friend of Lawrence who had done such important work at Wejh and living with the tribes. Fakhri, a proud man, explained to Bassett that it had been beneath his dignity, after the armistice, to surrender to the maverick explosives expert Herbert Garland, who was a mere captain. Garland had been attached to Emir Abdullah's forces in the south. Fakhri also thought it would have been dishonourable to surrender to the Arabs. Bassett was struck by the commandant's physical and mental distress: 'during the last phase, illness, melancholia and religious fanaticism brought him to a state verging on insanity'.

Bassett knew from Garland's report that Fakhri had been communicating with Ibn Saud, but found no evidence of any concerted plan of action between Ibn Saud and Fakhri. Fakhri even claimed that Ibn Saud had been 'a serious thorn in his side'. But Bassett's perceptiveness and his intelligence background persuaded him that Fakhri was keeping something back. As we have seen, Bassett had seized Fakhri's diary and his intelligence service accounts. He knew that Fakhri 'conducted all correspondence with Ibn Saud personally…keeping no copies', and that Ibn Saud's messengers had been brought in to Medina under special escort, with items of £3 on several occasions paid to messengers from Nejd.[23] Bassett inferred that Fakhri and Ibn Saud had each been hoping to use the other, keeping their options open for a possible alliance against the Sherifians. Perhaps this was the real reason for the delay in Fakhri's surrender. Ibn Saud, for his part, was certainly adept at playing a long game, looking for ways to encroach on Sherif Hussein's territory and outmanoeuvre his old rival.

Bassett had done another important job interrogating, sifting the evidence, and drawing up a more detailed account of Turkish intelligence operations and of the often hidden role played by the India Office's preferred top Arab, Ibn Saud. As time went on it became clear that Ibn Saud was the elephant in the room during the Arab Revolt, and also that both he and

Sherif Hussein were using the British for their own political intrigues, at least as much as the British were using the Arab leaders.

★ ★ ★

Leslie Bright and Ruhi were both present at Medina, with Herbert Garland, just after the surrender. Bright or Ruhi took some striking photographs, including one showing Emirs Abdullah and Ali proudly standing at open windows on the balcony of a building, a number of Hejazi flags of the Arab Revolt fluttering below them. Another fine image shows the two Emirs accepting an exhausted Fakhri's surrender at Bir Derwish.[24] Bright and Ruhi saw some appalling sights in Medina. Twenty per cent of the garrison were very debilitated, and more than one thousand were sick with amoebic dysentery, malaria, nephritis, and influenza. Civilians were also in a very poor way.[25] To make matters worse, the Bedouin had gone on the rampage in the town as soon as they entered it, on 15 January. They looted more than four thousand eight hundred locked houses, about seven-eighths of the total number; some even belonged to the Ashraf, fellow sherifs in Hussein's family. The Bedouin treated the loot from Medina like the spoils of any other tribal raid. More surprisingly, eighty per cent of the Baghdadi and Syrian officers of the regular Arab Army joined in.[26] An Egyptian Army officer with Abdullah, Miralai (Colonel) Yahya, and a French Muslim with Ali's forces, Capitaine Depui, both witnessed the devastation. They wrote reports which were given to camel-borne messengers, but conveniently for Abdullah and Ali, they never reached Jeddah. Bassett smelt a cover-up, writing of the small camel train: 'there is reason to believe it was purposely held up by order of His Highness Emir Ali'.[27]

After the surrender of Medina, Wilson entrusted Bright with the challenging task of escorting eight thousand Turkish prisoners across the desert on camel-back to the port of Yenbo, where they were to be evacuated to Egypt. Bright set about this with his usual calm, good humour and logistical skills. Eight batches of one thousand set off on the four and a half day journey, once enough camels could be found, from 10 January to 13 February.[28] The job was dangerous for Bright because of the infectious diseases swirling around Medina, and also for the prisoners because on the journey to Yenbo the Bedouin lurking in the desert had to be prevented from picking them off and doing their usual scavenging. The Red Sea Patrol laid on SS *Abbassieh*, SS *Pentakota*, and SS *Purnea* as transport ships, with a military escort.[29] Up to fourteen thousand blankets had been shipped to Yenbo, because the health of the Turkish soldiers who had surrendered in the run-up to Fakhri's formal surrender was so bad.[30] Bright finally returned to Egypt on 5 March 1919, on SS *Abbassia*.[31]

Bright was later given high praise by an unnamed colleague, almost certainly Herbert Garland:

> He evacuated 8000 through Yenbo, and had only Bedouins to help him. I warmly recommended him for his work…I was inland keeping the Arab tribes quiet while the Turkish force was moving down to the coast on camels. He did a great work in a quiet way. Every native he came in contact with liked him, and he could do what he liked with them.[32]

It seems that Leslie Bright had the Lawrence touch, to a certain extent at least. He had an empathy with the Bedouin that Garland, Newcombe, and most other British officers lacked.

★　★　★

Wilson remained a lightning conductor and source of reassurance for Hussein, but, after the hollow victory of the Arab Revolt, the old leader's world was beginning to disintegrate before his eyes. Wilson tried to help him cope with growing dejection as his great rival Ibn Saud pounced, grabbing land in the disputed territory of Khurma. Ruhi, as active as ever, went with Hussein to meet Abdullah and his army to the north-east of Mecca. Hussein gave a rallying speech pardoning all deserters who had crossed over to Ibn Saud. About ten thousand tribesmen arrived, claiming they had been forced into Ibn Saud's army, but this did not ring true.[33] Abdullah's army was defeated on 25–6 May at Tarabah, where the Ikhwan (Brotherhood) of Ibn Saud killed about two hundred and fifty Sherifians. *The Arab Bulletin* reported: '10,000 Bedouin originally reported to be with Abdullah seem to have melted away, and as Colonel Bassett remarks, "everything points to the majority of the tribal elements which profess allegiance to King Hussein being absolutely unreliable"'.[34] Wilson and Bassett once again had to coax Hussein away from the cliff edge of abdication following this serious setback.[35]

The escalation of the toxic dispute between Hussein and Ibn Saud was as much part of the aftermath of the Arab Revolt as the surrender of the Medina garrison or the wrecked infrastructure and hopes of Syria and its people. Ibn Saud could sense the weakness of his rival's position. Wilson feared that the writing was on the wall for the tragic figure of Hussein and his family. The long-serving 'Pilgrimage Officer' dutifully stuck to his post until mid-1919. Wilson's assistant, William Cochrane, who had been with him from the beginning, had left Jeddah in January 1919. His hard work had helped to bring about a successful pilgrimage in 1916 when failure could have brought disaster to the revolt. Ruhi stayed for rather longer: he was to go on the Hajj pilgrimage to Mecca that autumn (and doubtless make use of the opportunity for more espionage). Bassett, another important officer lost to public consciousness, left Jeddah on 19 July, travelling to Suez on SS *Baron Beck*.[36]

★　★　★

Wilson's Jeddah circle had shaped the Arab Revolt and was then intimately involved with its immediate aftermath. Wilson's resilience and sheer pluck had brought him and the revolt through wobbly episodes and heart-stopping crises. He would never talk or write of his crucial role, so far as we know, and never became a name known to the public. But those intimately involved with the revolt knew the truth. As we have seen, Captain Boyle of the Red Sea Patrol wrote that the ultimate success of the revolt was principally due to Wilson. Lawrence naturally introduced a little smoke and a mirror or two, claiming from centre stage that Wilson was a 'powerful help' to him and that 'especially he helped me with the King'. Lawrence did, however, have the grace to write (though not in the main editions of *Seven Pillars of Wisdom*): 'Wilson had a wonderful influence in his [Hussein's] councils because the Arabs always trusted him, sure of his single eye to their best interests. He was the King's touchstone.'[37]

Gray showed tenacity and resilience of a different order. While he was not a major player, his intriguing story throws light on unknown and unexpected corners of the revolt, and he acts as a foil to the high-powered political involvement of Wilson and Lawrence. Other officers in Wilson's circle—principally John Bassett, Hugh Pearson, John Young, William Cochrane, and Norman Bray—had played key roles during the revolt with Pearson, like Bassett, also involved in its aftermath.

Having said all this about Wilson and his men, there is no doubt that Lawrence's contribution to the Arab Revolt was extraordinary and indispensable. That it is necessary to state this at all may seem odd, but so many attempts have been made to debunk the overblown Lawrence legend, and also the man himself, that at times the historical record of his achievements seems to be given less significance than the compulsion to explain the 'real' Lawrence. Promoting a single thesis at the expense of the many-layered complexity of the man can never really be helpful.[38] The irony is that searching for the 'real' Lawrence by dissecting the legend can actually add to the legend and help spread it, through claims that may not stand scrutiny but which are added to the groaning Lawrence-related bookshelves.[39]

The eye-catching desert warfare run by him and others put boots on the ground at Aqaba and ultimately Damascus, and played a part—if arguably not a major role—in helping Allenby defeat the Ottoman Army. Lawrence's skills in organizing and coordinating, his daring and courage, his intuitive grasp of guerrilla warfare and how to harness it, and his talent for manipulating his own leaders if necessary were all crucial. Lawrence's influence over Feisal, and his wise empathy in exerting it, was of huge importance for the way the revolt put out tendrils and grew.

But there was an overarching nexus of influence that has stayed below the radar. Without Wilson's extended influence over Hussein, from the very beginning of the revolt, the campaign would have been at mortal risk of withering on the vine. Wilson and Bassett shored up the revolt on a number of occasions when collapse was a serious threat. Their lost stories, with those of others in their circle, show that the Arab Revolt could not have had its hollow success without their unsung interventions. Without them there would have been no call for Lowell Thomas to promote Lawrence as a hero, no iconic 1960s film, and libraries around the world would have had space for other subjects. As it happened, Wilson and Lawrence had more in common than might appear at first sight: both men acted heroically in the face of what seemed like overwhelming adversity and—particularly for Lawrence—acute mental strain. Wilson would have downplayed any talk of having been a hero (as Lawrence did), but he had done more than enough to live up to his father's brave attempt to relieve General Gordon at Khartoum.

The compelling story of Wilson and his close-knit band points to an inescapable conclusion: the Jeddah Consulate was a vitally important hub of the revolt whose influence has been considerably undervalued. It is helpful to draw our eyes away from the desert campaign from time to time to appreciate this rather startling concept. Jeddah with its artery to Mecca and Sherif Hussein frequently seemed to be the beating heart of the revolt, whose irregular rhythm needed remedial action. Wilson was the crucial man on the spot who had the touch of a pacemaker.

Wilson was the outstanding forgotten shaper and sustainer of the revolt. Wingate used the word 'self-sacrifice' of him, and this was accurate in more than one sense: Wilson lost a leg to blood poisoning caused by his long-standing dysentery and his refusal to leave what he saw as the path of duty. The ultimate legacy of the Arab Revolt for Wilson, in a personal sense, was probably the inescapable pain that all of his principled dealings with Hussein counted for nothing in the end. Imperial interests overrode everything else, as they had always done; in the aftermath of the revolt, their bleak amorality spread like water through cracks.[40]

Epilogue

It was 29 March 1920. Commander David Hogarth, former Director of the Arab Bureau, had just given a magisterial lecture on 'War and Discovery in Arabia' at the Royal Geographical Society in London. During the discussion, an awkward silence had descended when a diminutive member of the audience refused to comment after he had been invited to do so. Sir Henry McMahon, former High Commissioner in Egypt and fateful correspondent with Sherif Hussein when the British were promoting a Hashemite revolt, rose to his feet in frustration and stunned those present. He flung a sneering barb at his shy colleague: 'There are others whom you would much rather hear, but they are not courageous enough to get up.'[1] The silent and slighted man in the audience, whose work had just been given many mentions by Hogarth, his mentor, was Colonel T. E. Lawrence.

The post-traumatic stress that had crippled Lawrence for nearly a year before he entered Damascus had stalked him remorselessly—when combined with his natural shyness and dislike of public speaking, his apparent detachment amounting to rudeness at the lecture meeting is understandable. Lawrence seemed unable to shake the dust of Syria and its sorrows from his feet, in spite of telling friends that he had done so. Like a moth drawn to a flame, he returned to situations that would stir up his demons. It was as if he wanted to punish himself through dreadful memories of carnage and through public humiliation.

It was a supreme irony that less than a year after the end of the revolt, when he said he was a 'worn tool', Lawrence was turned into an international superstar by Lowell Thomas's lecture and film show, which played to millions in Britain and the USA. There was an appetite for a romantic hero who appeared to have won freedom for the Arabs, to allow people to escape the horror of so many lost to the mechanized slaughter on the Western Front. While crowds flocked to see the extravaganza at the Royal

Albert Hall in London and other huge venues, their hero, though burnt out and sick of his experiences, once or twice crept in as unobtrusively as he could to a seat at the back. Lawrence affected disapproval of Thomas, yet part of him could not resist the realization that he had been put on a pedestal like the heroes of classical antiquity he had so admired as a boy.[2] As Thomas put it, Lawrence seemed to have a compulsion for 'backing into the limelight'.[3]

After the crushing disappointment of the Paris Peace Conference, Lawrence had immersed himself in writing *Seven Pillars of Wisdom*, his personal account of the Arab Revolt. Although he now had no official position, he carried on campaigning against the Middle Eastern settlement. In 1920 the imperial powers were challenged when frustrated Arab leaders claimed Syria for Feisal and Iraq for his brother Abdullah. The French forced Feisal out of Damascus and the British were confronted by a serious rising in Iraq. Lawrence wrote compelling letters to *The Times* supporting Arab independence. His influence was growing and in December the call came from the Cabinet: it wanted Lawrence to be adviser on Middle East affairs to the new Colonial Secretary, Winston Churchill. The two men, with Gertrude Bell, foremost intelligence expert on Iraq, and others, attended a conference at Cairo in March 1921. A plan was rapidly drawn up and Lawrence was sent to Transjordan and Palestine to sell it to Feisal and Abdullah. It worked: Feisal was offered Iraq and Abdullah was given Transjordan. These were extraordinary concessions from an imperial power, even though the new rulers were likely to be strongly pro-British.

Lawrence now wanted once more to put the Middle East behind him, but he could not escape another job. He was sent to Jeddah in late July 1921, to negotiate a treaty with the ageing King Hussein of the Hejaz. Lawrence became exasperated and angry at Hussein's perverse intransigence and unrealistic demands for everything from control of all Arab states to extra cargoes of the British gold sovereigns to which he had become so attached. Lawrence now must have appreciated the extraordinary weight that had been on Wilson's shoulders for so long, as Hussein slipped into a familiar pattern of theatricality, followed by threats of abdication and suicide. Lawrence could not come to an agreement with him. Hussein really did abdicate in 1924 after a military defeat by Ibn Saud's forces. His son Ali was King for just over a year, then fled to Iraq when Ibn Saud overran the Hejaz in December 1925. The Hejaz was incorporated into the Kingdom of Saudi Arabia in 1932.

By the spring of 1922 Lawrence had helped establish Abdullah as Emir in Transjordan and was an even bigger celebrity. After the Cairo conference, some at least of Britain's vague promises to the Arabs, he felt, had been honoured. Yet he could never escape the deceit he had practised during the revolt. He loathed his wartime role, and refused all offers of high-profile official posts. To the astonishment of his friends, he enlisted in the ranks of the RAF, doing just what he had told the cipher officer Lionel Gray, four years earlier, that he would like to do. This was Lawrence's rabbit hole to escape. He wanted what he called 'brain-sleep'[4] and had a desperate need to elude the debilitating mental strain to which he had subjected himself. On 30 August 1922, he took on a new identity as Aircraftman, 2nd Class, John Hume Ross. A spell in the Army ranks as Private T. E. Shaw followed, then a return to the RAF. Lawrence went on to complement his military and diplomatic achievements with others, principally in literature and in the improved design of power boats for the rescue of RAF crew who had to ditch at sea.

★ ★ ★

It is no surprise that historians often tend not to know what to make of Lawrence. Pierce Joyce called him a 'mass of contradictions'[5] and Robert Graves, who also knew him well, mentioned his 'exasperatingly complex personality'.[6] This complexity pervades his extraordinary *Seven Pillars of Wisdom*, which has sometimes given rise to confusion and red herrings— Lawrence's favourite fish. Lawrence described the book as 'a personal narrative pieced out of memory'.[7] His friend, the writer E. M. Forster, gave one of the best summaries of the book: 'Round this tent-pole of a military chronicle, T. E. has hung an unexampled fabric of portraits, descriptions, philosophies, emotions, adventures, dreams.'[8] As far as the main phases of the Arab Revolt are concerned, and much of the detail too, the archives bear out the book's broad accuracy. But the publication had a political role, to endorse Feisal's claim to self-government. With this in mind, Lawrence at times lied and misled, as well as teased and bemused. He was a master of half-truths, denigration by inference and omission; a shape-shifter who had a touch of genius in his mastery of smoke and mirrors as well as of guerrilla warfare. These factors are relevant to the low profile he gives to Wilson.

It seems that Lawrence tried to be truthful as much as he could—at heart he was a deeply moral man—but he was subject to the huge pressures of divided loyalties and these led him to distort some historical events into the shape of propaganda that would help his cause. Some lies are relatively minor but they all bear discussion because they throw light on Lawrence's agenda. Lieutenant-General Sir Harry Chauvel, the Australian commander of the Desert Mounted Corps, identified a number of inaccuracies in *Seven Pillars of Wisdom*. Lawrence was wrong in saying that the Arab forces, rather than the Australian 10th Light Horse Brigade, were the first into Damascus; he lied in telling Chauvel that Shukri Pasha had been elected Military Governor of Damascus by a majority vote of its citizens (he had not been— only the minority from the Hejaz wanted him); he was wrong in saying that Chauvel asked his permission to drive through Damascus (a ridiculous concept); he lied in telling Allenby that he did not know about the Sykes-Picot Agreement and therefore could not have told Feisal about it.[9] Lawrence also wrote that Colonel Alfred Parker, chief of intelligence in the Hejaz, was a mere liaison officer with Sherif Ali at Rabegh.[10]

As we have seen, Lawrence admitted after the publication of *Seven Pillars of Wisdom* that his account of the torture and rape at Deraa was not true (though it seems that something very traumatic did happen there, and that he was telling some kind of emotional truth). As for half-truths and omissions, Lawrence gives little emphasis, for example, to the key roles played by Lieutenant-Colonel Pierce Joyce, his commanding officer, and by Jafar al-Askari, Commander of Feisal's Northern Arab Army. He omits from his account the significant fact that Bray was the first to recommend Feisal as military leader for the revolt, and is dismissive of Bray's and Vickery's important roles in the seizure of Wejh. Lawrence also glosses over atrocities by Arabs on Turks.

In this context, his lack of recognition of Wilson and his Jeddah circle's crucial impact on the revolt is part of a pattern and is comprehensible. Yet it seems disingenuous of Lawrence to excuse himself, as it were, by stating in the Preface that the book is no more than a personal memoir of the revolt. He understood much of the bigger picture better than most, and shaped some of it. As a consummate former intelligence officer he knew that perceptions were as important as 'facts'. His omissions have big repercussions, because they mean a balanced and rounded understanding of the progress of the revolt cannot be gained from *Seven Pillars of Wisdom*. To downplay the indispensable diplomatic and intelligence roles played by Wilson, Bassett, and others in the Jeddah circle has to be seen as another layer of deception. This layer, with the others, fed into Lawrence's key objective: to create the perception that his stirring story must inevitably justify self-determination for Feisal; and that his deeds and Feisal's were inextricably bound to each other. Other considerations were secondary. Recognition of, in particular, Wilson's essential role would be unhelpful in that it would dilute the impact of the Lawrence-centred narrative.[11]

We have to remember that Lawrence went to extraordinary lengths to encourage Feisal to stake a claim to Damascus as soon as possible. Lawrence had in effect committed treason and subverted the imperialist designs of his own government, pitching the Emir against Britain and France as well as the Turks when he told him about the Sykes-Picot Agreement in early 1917.[12] Lawrence was not concerned that it was, arguably, Allenby's massive conventional force that really won Damascus and defeated the Turks. Lawrence would have shrugged off the Egyptian Expeditionary Force's words in 1920: 'It should be remembered that the Arab successes in the late war have been greatly exaggerated. Their victories were generally very easy ones.'[13] A man with Lawrence's indomitable willpower would not let his chosen narrative be thrown off course by qualms about being unfair to Wilson.

The defects of *Seven Pillars of Wisdom* should not be stressed too much. The book is accurate in most key areas, and where it is inaccurate it does, after all, reflect the truth of who Lawrence was and his complex motivations and thoughts.[14] It will probably live forever as world-class literature. And as Lawrence intended, the book and his other writings encouraged strong perceptions of the Arabs' achievements and place on the world stage: they came out of the war with a hugely raised profile, thanks to a great extent to him. Yet the limelight falling on Lawrence and the book for four generations has inevitably created a hinterland of deep shadows. New light shone here on Wilson and his band as they emerge from those shadows, and the centrality of Jeddah to the running of the Arab Revolt, has revealed another, surprising narrative that supplements and enriches the standard story.

Perhaps Wilson resented the public lack of recognition for him. More likely he would have been content just to have done his duty as best he could. When, near the end of Wilson's life, General Wingate wrote to him praising his indispensable role and his 'great work' in the Arab Revolt, without which it could never have succeeded, Wilson might have brushed aside these plaudits with equanimity, believing the truth was more complex.[15] But he and his circle deserve to be commemorated, a century after their vital work fell through the cracks of history. It is not unreasonable to believe that some part of Lawrence's unfathomable make-up would have acknowledged that this was so.

★   ★   ★

The Arab Revolt was a war of unintended consequences, and its painful leg-acy continues to reverberate to this day. Lawrence's insight told him that the lines on the sand drawn up by the Sykes-Picot Agreement, splitting much of the Ottoman Empire between Britain and France, would not work, that the French would ultimately be kicked out of Syria. Sir Mark Sykes, flour-ishing a map in a typically grandiose gesture, had said at the end of 1915 that he wanted a line drawn from the Mediterranean to northern Iraq, literally from the 'e' of 'Acre' to the last 'k' of 'Kirkuk'. Georges-Picot, with an eye to French imperial interests, had no objection. The point here is that the frontiers of the new map were totally artificial. At the Paris Peace Conference in 1919, Lawrence had produced a very different map that would have split the area (with some exceptions) into Sunni, Shia, and Kurdish zones, to be ruled by Sherif Hussein's sons.[16] He recognized the ethnic and religious ties that bound these groups together—that the Sunnis in Syria, for example, had their counterparts in Lebanon, Iraq, and Transjordan, just as the Shias and Alawites in Syria had their counterparts in Lebanon and Iraq.

However, the British wish to control oil in Iraq condemned Lawrence's idea. The British were not willing to accept an Arab Government at the time because they thought outside investors in the oil industry would lose confidence. The Sykes-Picot Agreement still haunts the Middle East and further afield. The words have a resonance in the great Arab cities of Damascus, Baghdad, Beirut, and Cairo and have become a sort of code for British perfidy. This sense of betrayal was augmented by the fateful Balfour Declaration at the end of 1917, which promised a national home for the Jewish people in Palestine. The Sykes-Picot Agreement had left the future of Palestine uncertain, so the British thought that by encouraging the Zionists, who wanted Palestine, they could disguise their own imperialist ambition: this was to have a buffer zone to keep the French away from Sinai and the strategically vital Suez Canal, Britain's lifeline to India. The Balfour Declaration stated that 'nothing shall be done which may prejudice the civil and religious rights of existing non-Jewish communities in Palestine'. The trampling underfoot of this provision has delivered another harsh legacy.

In fact the Sykes-Picot Agreement had become rather nebulous by as early as 1918, and the borders of the modern Middle East differ in many areas from the Sykes-Picot borders. But, as so often, it is perceptions that exercise a powerful hold. Sykes and Georges-Picot are now rooted in a jihadist lexicon of hate. Islamic State (IS) announced in 2014, after its capture of Mosul and other territory in Iraq and Syria, that it was actively seeking to reverse the effects of the Sykes-Picot Agreement. An IS jihadist in a video called *End of Sykes-Picot* warned of borders to be broken.[17] Another fighter explained 'how a ninety-eight-year-old colonial map created today's conflict'.[18] A further IS video appeared to have its leader Abu Bakr al-Baghdadi speak of eliminating borders: 'this blessed advance will not stop until we hit the last nail in the coffin of the Sykes-Picot conspiracy'.[19] Lawrence would have found their methods sickening, but he would have understood the insidious effects of IS's propaganda and its exploitation of perceptions. Norman Bray, who continued to fight and warn against jihadists long after the Arab Revolt, would be turning in his grave to see the explosion of jihadism in the region and its malign influence in the cities and towns of Europe, the USA, and beyond.

IS, with its unprecedented, Khmer Rouge-like assault on all non-Islamic cultures, past as well as present, made a rapid advance after 2014. The Kurds also made territorial gains in Iraq and Syria. Lawrence foresaw the need to accommodate them as a distinct ethnic and cultural group; their settlements are spread between parts of Syria, Iraq, Iran, Turkey, and Armenia. Syrian Kurds have fought both IS and Sunni Arabs whom they see as IS supporters. Gains in Kurdish territory are dismaying Turkey and any involvement of the Turkish army against a Syrian Kurdish enclave would raise the stakes dramatically.

Another issue that has reared its head, going well beyond the lines on the Sykes-Picot map, is the big geo-political game that is being played throughout the Middle East. Sunni Saudi Arabia and the Gulf States are battling their rivals Shia Iran for influence in Syria, Iraq, and Yemen, with both camps using proxies, sectarianism, and multi-layered civil wars to further their cause. The Sunni group Jabhat Fatah al-Sham, set up in July 2016, was previously an al-Qaida affiliate called al-Nusra Front, and was not far behind the extreme violence of IS. Al-Nusra Front was backed by Saudi Arabia, Turkey, and Qatar in the murky war to stem Iranian-backed Shia advances, and its new incarnation (which has not necessarily cut all links with al-Qaida) could well receive the same support.[20]

At the time of writing (November 2016) the area occupied by IS in Iraq has shrunk dramatically. This could result, perversely, in one of its main objectives—the descent into ever more serious sectarian strife as Sunni tribes, who looked to IS for support against a majority Shia government, feel threatened by Shia incursions. Whatever the future of IS, it seems as though the Middle East and Libya (which has three competing governments, a prominent IS presence, and many militia groups) will suffer a sustained period of bloody conflict and instability, with continued challenges to state control. And IS retains a fearsome capacity to mobilize suicide bombers in those areas, and bring terror and the threat of social breakdown to Europe, the USA, and around the world.

Any enduring settlement in the Middle East may, ironically, take vision and imagination on a Sykes-like scale, by all those living in the region, to lift heads from the present gloom and to reverse the tides of hatred. Lawrence and a few others, such as Gertrude Bell and General 'Bertie' Clayton, foresaw the inevitable outcome of the territorial settlement after the First World War. The disregard shown then for sectarian, ethnic, and tribal considerations and sensitivities is now taking its full toll. As what is left of the Sykes-Picot borders becomes more porous and crisscrossed by jihadists, militias, and armies, Lawrence's shade—and perhaps Cyril Wilson's too—might be heard to murmur 'I told you so'. Lawrence knew a century ago that the impetus for lasting peace must come from the nations and peoples involved. Whether this will prove feasible remains to be seen.[21]

Post-Arab Revolt Biographies

Lieutenant-Colonel John Bassett ('Jack' to his family) carried out political intelligence work in 1919 in Asir, the territory bordering the Hejaz and Yemen, whose ruler was intriguing against King Hussein. Bassett was awarded the OBE in 1919. Back in Egypt, he saw much of Lionel Gray and the Arab Bureau offices, and told Gray he had had enough of Jeddah. Bassett married Evelyn Mary Gillman Burgess in 1929, and became step-father to Guy Burgess, the future Soviet spy and defector. His great-nephew remembers that Bassett was 'incandescent with rage' about the defection, especially for its effect on Burgess's mother. A keen race goer, Bassett lived at Ascot and subsequently at Newbury and then London. He died in 1961, aged 83.

Captain Norman Bray (known to his family as Evelyn) was put in charge of Kerbela in Mesopotamia in 1918 and, by his own account, managed to defuse a rebellion by 140,000 Arabs. He then joined the Indian Political Service and went to Bahrein as British Agent. Bray wrote reports on what he saw as the pan-Islamic and Bolshevik threat that was sweeping across the whole of Asia, the Middle East, and North Africa. Later, living abroad with their two sons in search of a cure for his wife's insanity, he became passport control officer (usually Secret Intelligence Service cover) in Copenhagen and Geneva. While in Geneva he apparently thwarted a revolution in Egypt and had various hair-raising adventures. Bray became a political campaigner and met Hitler in Berlin, earning him a rebuke from the Chief of SIS, Sir Hugh Sinclair. During the Second World War, Bray served as ground crew during the Battle of Britain. His second wife was his sons' Danish nanny, who had gone with the family to Geneva, and by whom he had two further children. His third wife tried to burn their house down after a row; many photographs and other documents were lost, probably including his manuscript autobiography which had the unfortunate title *Divine Harmony*. Bray died in 1962, aged 77.

Captain Lionel Bright returned to Cairo where he socialized with Lionel Gray, Major Marshall the doctor, and other comrades from the Arabian war. Wanting to improve his bank balance, he set off up the White Nile in early 1920 to join the Equatorial Battalion of the Egyptian Army. He was based at Mongolla, in what is now South Sudan, and was in charge of training and frontier defence. On his way back to England on leave, in autumn 1922, he made a surprisingly wide detour, visiting Damascus, Aleppo, Smyrna, Constantinople, Rome, and Paris, presumably partly on intelligence duties. After a month in England, he was on his way by ship back to Egypt when tragedy struck. The blackwater fever that had killed Major Hugh Pearson had infected Bright too. He died in Spain in January 1923. He was just 28 years old.

Captain William Cochrane resigned his commission in 1919 and went back to work for his pre-war employers, the shipping agents Gellatly Hankey. Before he left for home he could be seen driving a smart car around Cairo. He married in 1925 and had two sons. Cochrane retired in the 1930s just before he was due to be appointed to the board of directors: his son recalls that this was a matter of principle, as he had been asked to do things he considered unethical. In the Constable Country of Essex, Cochrane grew vegetables and fruit in a large garden, and joined the Home Guard in the Second World War, advising his unit on strategy, training, and communications. He died suddenly of a brain tumour in 1947, aged 69.

Lieutenant Leofric Gilman left the British Army as Captain. He married the widow of his brother, Harold, founder of the influential Camden Town Group of artists, in Paris in 1920. Harold had died of the influenza pandemic in 1919. The Gilmans brought up the son of that marriage and also had a daughter of their own. Gilman, known to his family as Leof, worked for companies involved in road construction in France and England, and later became secretary of the Christmas Island Phosphate Company. Gilman's daughter and great-niece remember a man who was down to earth with an engaging sense of humour, a man who was visibly moved when he saw the sculptor Eric Kennington's effigy of Lawrence at St Martin's Church, Wareham. Gilman had no words and simply placed his hand gently on the smooth Portland stone. He died in 1977, aged 96.

Captain Thomas Goodchild went on further camel-buying trips, to the Western Desert of Egypt and Somaliland. He was briefly with the Occupied Enemy Territory Administration in Palestine, and ended his army service as Major Goodchild, OBE. From 1923 to 1943 he was secretary of the prestigious Alexandria Sporting Club, where he met King Farouk. A contemporary described Goodchild as efficient and charming though sometimes given to bouts of drinking. In 1938 he discovered the dead body of the Club Treasurer, who had shot himself, slumped across his desk. He had left Goodchild a note of apology, knowing he was about to be exposed as an embezzler. Goodchild died in Alexandria, aged 65, in 1943. He and his wife, Valerie, were childless. After extraordinary First World War service in Egypt, England, and France, and Second World War heroics in Alexandria too, Valerie died in that city in 1979, aged 95. Thomas and Valerie Goodchild lie, forgotten, in a neglected part of the British Protestant Cemetery in Alexandria.

Lieutenant Lionel Gray was decommissioned as Captain and worked on ciphers and codes at Cox's Shipping Agency in Alexandria. He kept in touch in Egypt with many of his old Arab Revolt comrades. He married his wartime fiancée, Mabel Holman, in Cairo in 1920. For a time Gray ran his own codes business in Alexandria. Mabel's illness in 1922 led them and their baby son to board a ship for England at a day's notice. In 1923 Gray opened the first commercial radio shop in the world, at Muswell Hill in London, and he was the first agent of the Marconiphone Company.

His daughter remembers Gray's patience and kindness to the children who were keen to listen to the radio, the new 'must-have' electronic gadget. Gray served as an air raid warden, based at Hornsey, in the Second World War. He died in north London in 1963, aged 80.

Captain Gerald Omar Rushie Grey returned to his homeland, Jamaica. For his war service he was rewarded with 60 acres of land in the Blue Mountains, near Newcastle. Employed as a Government of Jamaica veterinary officer and manager of a slaughterhouse, he also became a distinguished breeder of thoroughbred racehorses, his second wife managing the stud farm. Rushie Grey founded the Thoroughbred Owners and Breeders Association of Jamaica in 1952 and became its first president. His daughter remembers a kind man with a strong moral compass who liked telling stories about Lawrence. Rushie Grey died in Jamaica in 1960, aged 68.

Colonel Thomas Edward Lawrence sought a kind of oblivion and became Aircraftman John Hume Ross, Royal Air Force (RAF) in 1922. From 1924 he was Private T. E. Shaw of the Royal Army's Tank Corps, and in 1925 he rejoined the RAF. The subscribers' edition of *Seven Pillars of Wisdom* was published in 1926. He wrote other books, corresponded with a wide range of friends, showed great generosity when they needed financial or other help, and did pioneering work on high-speed rescue boats for the RAF (which alone would have secured his reputation had he done nothing else). Lawrence retired from the RAF in 1935 and had a fatal motorcycle accident a few months later, aged 46.

Agent Maurice, whose real name may or may not have been Rafai Bey, apparently slips from the historical record soon after his interrogation by the Arab Bureau in Cairo. We will probably never know for sure where Maurice's 'real' loyalties lay, if he had any. Perhaps the rest of his story is latent and lives on, fragmented in archives or family photograph albums or memories passed down.

We understand much more about Lawrence than about Maurice. But the workings of the human heart are so complex, and the strands of character and motivation so hard to unravel, that for both, deep within, there is a kernel of impenetrable self. This will remain true for Lawrence, in spite of the shelves full of books that have been written about him. For the whole of this cast of characters, as for Lawrence, the core of their personality lies out of reach.

Major Hugh Pearson, as Lieutenant-Colonel, resumed his duties as director of survey in the Sudan. In 1919 in London he married Blanche Grigg, the daughter of an Indian Army officer whom he had first met in India twenty years earlier. They were to have less than three years together. Pearson was British representative on the Wadai-Darfur Boundary Commission, which delimited the boundary between the Sudan and French Equatorial Africa. On this project he contracted blackwater fever and died, aged 49 and childless, in 1922 in Western Darfur. It was the day before he was due to sign the boundary agreement. A grave slab marks his burial in a remote corner of the hideously war-torn Central African Republic. The author is liaising with the British Honorary Consul there, who would like to repatriate Pearson's body, if the political situation allows, to the family plot in a Sussex churchyard.

Lieutenant Ashley Powell returned to Egypt in December 1918 from intelligence duties in Damascus. He was in and out of hospital for further treatment in early 1919, following multiple stab wounds at the hands of Bedouin in June 1918. Powell returned to his pre-war work for the Egyptian Government as a judge in the Native Courts. His passport shows that he travelled to Cyprus and Switzerland in 1919 and 1920, perhaps pointing to further intelligence work. He married in 1922 at County Wicklow in his native Ireland. Two children were born in Egypt and, after the Powell's return to Ireland in 1928, two further children followed. In 1926 Powell had co-authored *A Manual of Egyptian Arabic*. He was Reid Professor of Law at Trinity College, Dublin from 1931 to 1936, then a barrister. Powell died in 1967, aged 82.

Hussein Ruhi went back to Cairo on his retirement from government service and set up a school. By the mid-1920s he was working in the Department of Education at Jerusalem, where he was reunited with his old handler, Sir Ronald Storrs, who was governor of the city until 1926. Ruhi married three times and had twelve children; at least two of them followed his profession as a teacher. Ruhi died in 1960, aged 75; his grandchildren live in Amman, Jordan.

Major Robert Scott had frequent bouts of malaria and was invalided out of the army in January 1919. He was awarded the OBE, and resumed married life with his wife and three children in Dublin. In the run-up to Irish independence, Scott's brother, Harry, an inspector in the Royal Irish Constabulary, was warned in 1922 by the Irish Republican Army to leave Ireland within twenty-four hours or be shot dead. Scott looked like Harry and was warned to leave the country too. He went immediately and lived with his family in France, then in Kent, finally moving to Portrush in County Antrim, Northern Ireland. His health had been wrecked by the war, beginning with the malaria contracted at Gallipoli and Salonica, and he seems to have been haunted by the horrors of Gallipoli in particular. Scott died in 1933, aged just 55.

Colonel Cyril Wilson resumed his pre-war duties as governor of the Red Sea Province in the Sudan for a time, then retired to Hampshire. The Wilsons' only child, a daughter, Joan, had been born in 1919. Wilson remembered how Lawrence, who had ridden on his motorcycle from Dorset, got down on his knees to play with her. When she was 26, Joan married a 61-year-old widower from a neighbouring village. She died, childless, in 1977. The author's attempt to trace the large quantity of Arab Revolt papers that Wilson said he had in the 1930s led him to many of Joan's acquaintances, but the trail ran cold. Wilson probably gave his papers to his old colleague Lieutenant-Colonel Pierce Joyce, who was thinking of writing a book on the revolt. Wilson died in 1938, aged 65.

Captain John Young returned to Upper Egypt as an inspector in the Survey Department. His manuscript memoirs give his eyewitness accounts of riots by Egyptians seeking independence from Britain. He was involved in interrogations following some of them. In 1922 he had six weeks' holiday in Libya and Tunisia. This was almost certainly cover for further intelligence work. In 1924 he went to

Palestine as financial controller for the Orthodox Patriarchate of Jerusalem, then co-chaired a commission to report on squabbling between that body and the Christian Orthodox Arabs. As a result he was hugely unpopular with everyone, which would probably not have bothered him unduly. He died in London, unmarried, in 1954, aged 80.

Notes

PREFACE

1. LHCMA, King's College, London, Joyce Papers, 1/M/42, 21/2/36, Wingate to Wilson, 21 February 1936.
2. Earl of Cork and Orrery, *My Naval Life* (1942), p. 98.
3. T. E. Lawrence, *Seven Pillars of Wisdom* (1935), p. 6.

CHAPTER I

1. Wilson would probably have read, when a little older, a book based on his father's relief expedition. This was *The Dash for Khartoum: a Tale of the Nile Expedition* (1892) by George Henty, prolific author of boys' adventure stories.
2. The Sudan, bordering Egypt to the south, was of strategic importance to the British. Since Egypt under the Ottomans had nominally exerted authority there, the Sudan had effectively become British-run following Britain's occupation of Egypt in 1882. In theory the Sudan was an Anglo-Egyptian condominium from 1899, but the Egyptian khedive or viceroy had no real power and the British had full control. From November 1914, when the Ottoman Empire joined the war on Germany and Austria-Hungary's side, Britain declared that the nominal ties of Egypt and the Sudan to the Ottoman Empire were dissolved.
3. Henry Newbolt's poem, *Vitae Lampada* (1897), published in Henry Newbolt, *Collected Poems 1897–1907* (no date given, but 1910); description of 'Newbolt man' by Patrick Howarth quoted in Paul Fussell, *The Great War and Modern Memory* (1975), p. 26.
4. SAD, Wingate Papers, 199/1/4, letter from Wilson to General Reginald Wingate, Governor-General of the Sudan, 2 January 1916.
5. Many of the details in this and the preceding paragraph are taken from the letters and photographs sent from Jeddah to his family and fiancée by the intelligence officer Lieutenant Lionel Gray.
6. Sherif Mohsen of the Harb tribe was a member of Sherif Hussein's family and his representative at Jeddah.
7. In fact British help for the Arab Revolt in June 1916 brought about the last in a sequence of dashed Ottoman and German hopes for serious widespread jihad. Earlier setbacks in 1915–16 were the failure to take the Suez Canal, the Indian

princes' declaration for Britain, and the defeat of the Senussi warriors in the Western Desert of Egypt. But the jihadist bogey still had power: we should remember that only three months before the Arab Revolt broke out, in March 1916, the British had been sufficiently alarmed by the perceived threat to earmark two army divisions in Egypt 'to reinforce India in the event of a general rising on the North-West frontier accompanied by hostilities on the part of Afghanistan': AWM 4, 1/4/12, War Diary, General Staff, General Headquarters (GHQ), Egyptian Expeditionary Force (EEF), 11 March 1916, secret cipher report from chief of the Imperial General Staff to chief of Medforce.

8. The Hussein–McMahon Correspondence lasted from 14 July 1915 to 10 March 1916.

9. The entry is for 11 June. There was also an underground hospital connected to the trenches near the barracks.

10. 'One of the English men wanted to go too close to the garrison but he was stopped by Sheikh Oreifan [a British agent and go-between with Sherif Hussein] because he might be harmed by the Turks or by Turkish informers' (12 June). Extracts from the diary are published here in English for the first time (the periods before 8 May and after 14 June are missing). The original manuscript is entitled *Qitaa min Rihlat Sharif Makka Hussein*, and is listed as M1413/2 in a catalogue of Islamic manuscripts in Cyprus, published in 1995 by the Research Centre for Islamic History, Art, and Culture (IRCICA) in Istanbul. The diary was published in Arabic as *Min watha'iq al-thawra al-`arabiyya al-kubra: al-rahla al-rabi`a* (From the Documents of the Great Arab Revolt: The Fourth Journey by Husayn Ruhi), edited by Salah Jarar (no date given, but 1997). Sir Ronald Storrs, Ruhi's old handler, was governor of Cyprus, 1926–32, and Ruhi had worked with him in Jerusalem after the First World War. It is conceivable that Ruhi and his diary found their way to Cyprus; perhaps he was involved in more secret work for his old handler (or he may have given the diary to Storrs earlier). Another possibility is that King Hussein (as he became) retained the diary for some reason and brought it with him to exile in Cyprus. I am very grateful to Jacob Rosen for providing a copy of Salah Jarar's book.

11. Pembroke College, University of Cambridge, Storrs Papers, Reel 5, Box 2, folder 4, manuscript letter, Hussein Ruhi to Storrs, 15 June 1916.

12. HMS *Anne* was the new name for Captain Lewen Weldon's *Aenne Rickmers*, which had been captured from the Germans in German East Africa. The British liked to give their spoils of war what they considered more appropriate names.

13. Not surprisingly, Hussein's telephone number was Mecca 1.

14. SAD, Wingate Papers, 139/4/20, Wilson to Wingate, 16 August 1916.

15. Respectively Captain Aubrey Herbert and Lieutenant Francis Everard Feilding.

16. IWM, Private Papers of Major-General Sir Arthur Lynden-Bell, Documents.7826, 224–5, Lynden-Bell to Major-General Frederick Maurice, Director of Military Operations, War Office, 10 November 1916.

17. TNA, FO 141/803/3273/12, Sir Henry McMahon, British High Commissioner in Egypt to Wingate, 23 July 1916.

18. SAD, Wingate Papers, 139/5/88, Wilson to Wingate, 23 August 1916.

19. Letter from T. E. Lawrence to John Young, no full date but February 1921, MECA, GB 165-0177, DS, 43.1.L.18/12 Thomas Edward Lawrence Collection.

20. Ronald Storrs, *Orientations* (1943), p. 168.

21. MECA, St Antony's College, Oxford, GB165-0310, J. W. A. Young, *A Little to the East: Experiences of an Anglo-Egyptian Official, 1899–1925*, undated typescript memoir, J. W. A. Young Collection, p. 167.

22. SAD, Wingate Papers, 139/5/88, Wilson to Wingate, 23 August 1916.

23. TNA, FO 882/4/312, C. E. Wilson, 'Report on Meeting with Sherif Feisal Bey at Yanbo [sic] August 27th and 28th 1916'.

24. SAD, Wingate Papers, 139/7/113, Wilson to Wingate, 31 August 1916.

25. SAD, Wingate Papers, 139/7/114–15, C. E. Wilson, 'Provisional Arrangements for Capturing Coastal Towns', 31 August 1916.

26. Wilson reported that 'during the last month gold has been lavished right and left among the tribes'. TNA, FO 882/4/312, C. E. Wilson, 'Report on Meeting with Sherif Feisal Bey at Yanbo [sic] August 27th and 28th 1916'.

27. SAD, Wingate Papers, 139/7/113, Wilson to Wingate, 31 August 1916. Wilson added: 'just got over my second go of diarrhoea and I honestly don't think my heart will stand the worry and strain much longer'. With classic English understatement he ended 'This job is certainly no bed of roses.'

28. IWM, Private Papers of Major-General Sir Arthur Lynden-Bell, Documents.7826, 176–7, Lynden-Bell to Major-General Frederick Maurice, Director of Military Operations, War Office, 31 August 1916.

29. IWM, Private Papers of Major-General Sir Arthur Lynden-Bell, Documents.7826, 183–4, Lynden-Bell to Major-General Frederick Maurice, Director of Military Operations, War Office, 11 September 1916. Lynden-Bell did acknowledge that helping the revolt was 'an extraordinarily difficult show to run': on that point at least Wilson would have agreed with him.

30. IWM, Private Papers of Major-General Sir Arthur Lynden-Bell, Documents.7826, 193–4, Lynden-Bell to Major-General Frederick Maurice, Director of Military Operations, War Office, 29 September 1916.

31. SAD, Wingate Papers, 139/2/113, Wingate to Wilson, 10 August 1916. Wingate also praised Wilson for 'the thoroughly sound and capable way in which you are managing a most difficult and intricate situation . . . I am delighted at the good relations you have established with the Sherif.'

32. SAD, Wingate Papers, 140/5/24–8, Wilson to Wingate, 20–2 September 1916.

33. SAD, Wingate Papers, 140/6/57–8, Clayton to Wingate, 24 September 1916.

34. SAD, Clayton Papers, 470/7/17–18, Cornwallis at Jeddah to Clayton, 28 November 1917, quoted in Joshua Teitelbaum, *The Rise and Fall of the Hashemite Kingdom of Arabia* (2001), p. 257.

35. SAD, Wingate Papers, 140/6/58, Clayton to Wingate, 24 September 1916.

CHAPTER 2

1. Sherif Hussein was insistent that there should be a police guard to protect the Consulate. The Sudanese force of about twenty-five men was under the command of the Egyptian Mamour (District Inspector), Raouf Bey, and his assistant, Kamel Effendi. SAD, Wingate Papers, 139/4/25 Wilson to Wingate, 17 August 1916.

2. SAD, Wingate Papers, 140/5/29–31, Wilson to Wingate, letter commencing 20 September 1916 at Red Sea and ending 25 September at Jeddah.

3. Christophe Leclerc, 'The French Soldiers in the Arab Revolt: Some Aspects of Their Contribution', in *Journal of the T. E. Lawrence Society*, Vol. IX, No. 1 (Autumn 1999), p. 11.

4. Russia, Turkey's great rival, was to have a zone in Mesopotamia and also part of Persia (which lay outside the Ottoman Empire). Sean McMeekin has pointed out that Sergei Sazonov, the Russian foreign minister, was the 'real driving force behind the carve-up of the Ottoman Empire, a Russian project par excellence': Sean McMeekin, *The Ottoman Endgame: War, Revolution and the Making of the Modern Middle East, 1908–1923* (2015), p. xvi. The Russians lost interest after the Bolshevik Revolution and their separate peace agreement with Germany in 1918. Their earlier key role in a future land-grab from the Ottomans faded from historical consciousness, and the 1916 agreement was named solely after Sykes for the British and Georges-Picot for the French.

5. MECA, St Antony's College, Oxford, GB165-0310, J. W. A. Young, unpublished typescript, *A Little to the East: Experiences of an Anglo-Egyptian Official, 1899–1925*, p. 12. Cochrane later told his son of his dislike of sheeps' eyes, which for diplomatic reasons he felt sometimes had to be eaten (personal communication to author). This was not the custom in Jeddah, however (personal communication, Sir Mark Allen to author), so they would not have been on the menu for the French Mission.

6. SAD, Wingate Papers, 141/3/12, Wilson to Wingate, 5 October 1916.

7. SAD, Wingate Papers, 139/8/25, Arab Bureau to Wingate, 5 August 1916.

8. Catalogue note, Sotheby's sale, London, lot 201, 16 November 2006.

9. MECA, St Antony's College, Oxford, GB165-0310, J. W. A. Young, memoir, *A Little to the East: Experiences of an Anglo-Egyptian Official 1899–1925*, p. 7.

10. MECA, St Antony's College, Oxford, GB165-0310, J. W. A. Young, memoir, *Three Months in Jedda, 1916*, pp. 2–3. Ahmed Hegazi was secretary to Sherif Ali Haidar, named emir of Mecca by the furious Ottomans when Hussein launched his revolt. Ahmed was Ali Haidar's representative at Jeddah and had been intriguing against Hussein for two years before the revolt. Hussein's revenge had been to order the looting of Ahmed's house when Jeddah was seized.

11. Young also kept a detailed diary, but, if it has survived, its whereabouts are a mystery. Its contents may have been even more sensational than his memoirs. The diary is mentioned in a letter sent from Jeddah by Lieutenant Lionel Gray to his sister, Cecil, 12 February 1917.

12. *The Arab Bulletin*, No. 23, 26 September 1916, in R. Bidwell (ed.), *The Arab Bulletin 1916–19*, Vols I–IV (1986), p. 303.

13. The British campaign in Arabia was a precarious venture. At least three hundred thousand Arabs served in the Ottoman Army, by no means all of them poor conscripts with very few rights. Many Arab soldiers stayed loyal to the sultan/caliph in Constantinople, and had no interest in joining the revolt of the Hashemite family of Sherif Hussein. There is a strong case for referring to the Hashemite Revolt rather than to the Arab Revolt.

14. *Pilgrimage 1917*, typescript report by W. P. Cochrane, 21 November 1917, with annotations and 'Rough copy' in his own hand. Includes references to the 1916 pilgrimage. Cochrane collection.

15. We know of Cochrane's musical tastes from a letter sent a few months later by Gray from Jeddah to his sister, Cecil, on 12 January 1917. Cochrane also enjoyed listening to the operatic singers Luisa Tetrazzini, Nellie Melba, and Enrico Caruso.

16. Manuscript dedication by Young on Cochrane's personal copy of *Three Months in Jeddah*.

17. The medal, photograph, Hussein's effusive letter, and other documents are owned by Cochrane's son. The sword was sold many years ago by Cochrane's widow.

CHAPTER 3

1. SAD, Wingate Papers, 139/4/69, secret telegram from Wilson to director, Arab Bureau, 18 August 1916.

2. Bray kept a meticulously detailed and coloured trench map, which he had drawn himself, of the area near Thiepval. He was to leave this map in Jeddah, and it eventually found its way to a colleague's house in the London suburbs.

3. N. N. E. Bray, *Shifting Sands* (1934), pp. 74–6.

4. TNA, AIR 30/235, 22 November 1944, Bray's petition to King George VI regarding his alleged fascist sympathies and denial of his request to be given further intelligence duties in the Middle East. Bray's pre-First World War escapades read like one of John Buchan's contemporary thrillers. In Lebanon he 'was dogged by Secret Service Agents; shot at from an ambush...—and finally, poisoned by arsenic, my life being barely saved by a Polish lady doctor'.

5. We should treat Bray's words with caution. Even if the secret German document he saw was not a plant, it perhaps reflected no more than von Hochwaechter's best guess about a start-date for war. The kaiser and most senior armed services officers were looking to the summer of 1914 rather than to a specific month.

6. Tilman Lüdke, *Jihad Made in Germany: Ottoman and German Propaganda and Intelligence Operations in the First World War* (2005), p. 207.

7. HUA, Papers of Sir Mark Sykes, 1879–1919: The Sykes-Picot Agreement and the Middle East, U DDSY2/4/117, letter from Sykes to Sir John Hewett, 30 September 1916.

8. Mahmud Hassan had apparently been the seminary's first student in 1866. Deobandis is the name given to the largest Islamic group (at the time of writing) in the United Kingdom; they control over 40% of mosques and have a near monopoly on Islamic seminaries.

9. Ruhi also at some stage became an inspector of English Studies at the Egyptian Department of Education. I am grateful to Jacob Rosen for sharing his information on Ruhi.

10. According to Storrs, Ruhi's third wife, Aishah, bore a number of daughters all named after continents—they were missing only Australasia from the full set: Ronald Storrs, *Orientations* (1943), p. 150.

11. British Library, IOR/L/PS/11/129—P 5015/1917. Arabia: British Agency, Jeddah—Services of Hussein Effendi Ruhi. Letter from Captain N. N. E. Bray to Colonel Cyril Wilson, 11 April 1917.

12. Storrs wrote to Cyril Wilson on 1 August 1916: 'I have told Ruhi that he is delivered over to you body and soul. He is to consider himself not only your eyes and ears but also if necessary your hands and feet. He may even, should an especially unsavoury occasion present itself, be called upon to represent your nose.' Ronald Storrs, *Orientations* (1943), pp. 164–5.

13. Pembroke College, University of Cambridge, Storrs Papers, Reel 5, Box 2, folder 4, manuscript report, Hussein Ruhi to Storrs, 6 August 1916.

14. T. E. Lawrence, *Seven Pillars of Wisdom* (1935), p. 66. Wingate too sometimes looked askance at the Persian, telling Wilson, 'I have noticed a good many little attempts on the part of our friend Ruhi to "grind his own axe" at the expense of others.' SAD, Wingate Papers 143/6/86, Wingate to Wilson, 26 November 1916.

15. Robin Bidwell (ed.), *Arabian Personalities of the Early Twentieth Century* (1986). Reprint of 1917 first edition. The Arab Bureau regarded the Persian consul as 'pro-English . . . well-educated and intelligent' (p. 15). The merchant and shipping agent was of the Zeini Ali Riza family (p. 21).

16. Storrs wrote at the bottom of a barely legible letter from Ruhi, 'From poor little Ruhi, my most trustworthy Persian emissary, who has just left at some real risk to his life, on a confidential mission from me to Mecca.' This mission was probably an earlier one, before Bray's arrival, but Storrs' words point up the dangers.

17. N. N. E. Bray, *Shifting Sands* (1934), p. 79.

18. British Library, Arabia: Report on Mecca, f. 299, IOR/L/PS/11/113—P 4946/1916.

19. British Library, Arabia, British Agency, Jeddah: Services of Hussein Effendi Ruhi, IOR/L/PS/11/129—P 5015/1917. Letter from Bray to Wilson, 11 April 1917.

20. SAD, Wingate Papers, 140/5/23, Wilson to Wingate, letter begun 20 September and completed 25 September 1916.

21. Churchill College, Cambridge, Wemyss Papers, WMYS 4/1, report by Wemyss, undated but soon after 29 September 1916, when he left Rabegh after a visit to Hussein's son, Ali.

22. TNA, FO 371/2775, 205736/42233, Wilson's despatch no. 5 to Sir A. H. McMahon, High Commissioner, Egypt, 28 September 1916.

23. Pembroke College, University of Cambridge, Storrs Papers, Reel 5, Box 2, folder 4, typed 'Extract from diary, Jeddah, 27-IX-16'.

24. Pembroke College, University of Cambridge, Storrs Papers, Reel 5, Box 2, folder 4, typed 'Extract from diary, Jeddah, 27-IX-16'.

25. Ronald Storrs, *Orientations* (1943), p. 167.

26. MECA, St Antony's College, University of Oxford, GB 165–0310, John Young, *A Little to the East: Experiences of an Anglo-Egyptian Official, 1899–1925*, p. 14.

CHAPTER 4

1. The previously unknown meeting between Gray and Lawrence is revealed in an interview with Gray, 'Man Who Worked With Lawrence', printed in *The Hornsey Journal*, 24 May 1935, five days after Lawrence's death.

2. SAD, Wingate Papers, 141/4/780, telegram, 13 October 1916, Arab Bureau to Wilson and Wingate. The references are to Captain William 'Ginger' Boyle of HMS *Suva* and Colonel Alfred C. Parker, intelligence officer at the Red Sea port of Rabegh. Lawrence's role as a cipher courier to Jeddah is told here for the first time.

3. Russell McGuirk, *The Sanusi's Little War* (2007), p. 155.

4. Diary of Captain Thomas Goodchild, 12 October 1916, Walker collection.

5. SAD, Wingate Papers, 142/9/440, telegram from Arab Bureau to Wilson, 15 October 1916.

6. TNA WO 95/4390, official war diary, command paymaster in Egypt (EEF), Vol. 20.

7. Gray was well regarded and had nearly gone to Khartoum as General Wingate's cipher officer, but red tape put an end to that idea. Letter from Gray to his mother, 5 September 1916, Gray collection.

8. Gray's claim for travelling expenses, Army Form o. 1771, 15 September 1916. He arrived at Salonica on 6 August and stayed for just one night.

9. Taken from the memoir of Captain Lewen Weldon of the Eastern Mediterranean Special Intelligence Bureau, pp. 242–3, Weldon collection. Weldon later captained spy ships in the Mediterranean and the Red Sea. The typescript document is privately owned by his family and the reference to Lawrence is published here for the first time.

10. *Seven Pillars of Wisdom* (1935), p. 63.

11. *Seven Pillars of Wisdom* (1935), p. 58.

12. Bentley wrote to Gray: 'I am doing some very special work of a most peculiar description...I cannot tell you exactly its nature, because I feel bound to keep it very private—all I can say is it is of the highest importance to the Government.' Letter from E. L. Bentley to Gray, 24 February 1916, Gray collection. Bentley's work probably related to the cryptographic branch of the War Office, MI i(b), or of the Admiralty, known as Room 40. Equally, he may have been working for Mansfield Cumming's fast-growing Secret Service Bureau, founded in 1909 (which became the Secret Intelligence Service (SIS), MI6, in the 1920s). The Secret Service Bureau was fighting a turf war with military intelligence. Cumming signed his name 'C', and every chief of SIS since has been given the same designation.

13. Telegram, Bentley to Gray, 24 February 1916, Gray collection. In a letter to Gray dated 4 May 1916, Bentley said the pressure on him in London was 'perfectly crazy', but it was vital work 'which no-one else has accomplished'.

14. Letter from Gray to his sister, Cecelia (known as Cecil), 12 October 1916, Gray collection. Gray's servant was probably Private Alfred Le Monnier of the 1st Duke of Cornwall's Light Infantry. Gray had applied to Colonel Holdich to take Le Monnier with him on his 'special duty'. Copy of written request (undated but September/October 1916) in the huge Gray collection of Arab Revolt letters, photographs, and military and intelligence documents. At the time of writing the collection was still owned by the Gray family and had been in the same house, unknown to the world outside, for nearly seventy years.

15. SAD, Wingate papers, 142/9/41, Arab Bureau to Wilson, 14 October 1916; SAD 142/9/47, Arab Bureau to Wilson, 15 October 1916. The British spymaster was Colonel Alfred Chevallier Parker, who reported to General Clayton. He was the senior British intelligence officer in the Hejaz when the revolt broke out, and British liaison officer with the sherifian army until Lieutenant-Colonel Pierce Joyce took over from him on 5 December 1916. Hajj Abbas was a Persian agent; he would become Parker's messenger to and from Lawrence.

16. Storrs' diary referred to 'little Lawrence my super-cerebral companion': Ronald Storrs, *Orientations* (1943), p. 171.

17. Ronald Storrs, *Orientations* (1943), p. 171.

18. Andrew Shepherdson, Suttor's grandson living in Tasmania, Australia, told me that there are no family stories of Suttor having shared a cabin with Lawrence (telephone conversation, 8 August 2009). Had he done so, these would surely have survived and would have gone into Shepherdson's book, which is based on Suttor's diaries and letters home: *Journeys of a Light Horseman* (2002). It would have been appropriate for Goodchild and Lawrence, as officers of the same rank, to share a cabin.

19. Ronald Storrs, *Orientations* (1943), p. 172.

20. T. E. Lawrence, *Seven Pillars of Wisdom* (1935), p. 65. Storrs' Muslim servant, Said, had been seasick a number of times and could not help him much; he had not felt any better when Storrs told him he would be blessed if he died, even from excessive vomiting, so near the holy land of the Hejaz: Ronald Storrs, *Orientations* (1943), p. 172.

21. Ronald Storrs, *Orientations* (1943), p. 172.

22. Letter from Gray to his sister, Cecil, 12 October 1916, Gray collection.

23. Perhaps all this sailing close to the wind was a way of masking a lack of self-confidence, as was suggested by Ralph H. Isham in A. W. Lawrence (ed.), *T. E. Lawrence by his Friends* (1937), p. 295.

24. Storrs wrote: 'Mastered from Lawrence the theory and practice of the Playfair Cypher.' Ronald Storrs, *Orientations* (1943), p. 172. The Playfair cipher, invented in 1854 and named after Lord Playfair who promoted its use, encrypted pairs of letters and so was much harder to break than the simple substitution cipher with single letters. At the same time it was reasonably fast to use.

25. TNA, ADM 53/45985. Log book of HMS *Lama*, 16 October 1916.

26. T. E. Lawrence, *Seven Pillars of Wisdom* (1935), p. 65.

27. These details are included in annotations, in Gray's hand, on the back of a photograph he took of the Consulate with his Brownie Box camera. This is one of hundreds of his Arab Revolt photographs to have survived; none has been seen before.

28. Letter from Gray to his mother, 18 October 1916, Gray collection.

29. Ronald Storrs, *Orientations* (1943), p. 172.

30. Wilson had told Clayton the day before Gray arrived: 'Thank heavens a cipher officer is coming tomorrow...I honestly don't think my head would have stood much more.' SAD 141/3/64, Wilson to Clayton, 15 October 1916.

31. SAD, Clayton Papers, 470/5/4, Wilson to Clayton, 18 October 1916.

32. Letter from Gray to his mother, Margaret Gray, 18 October 1916, Gray collection. Gray would not have been aware that Hussein loved the band's music: he had rung the Consulate from Mecca, heard the band playing in the courtyard, then ordered all the windows there to be flung open while he sat with the receiver to his ear. Ronald Storrs, *Orientations* (1943), pp. 178–9.

33. Pembroke College, University of Cambridge, Storrs Papers, Lawrence to Clayton, 18 October 1916.

34. MECA, St Antony's College, Oxford, GB165-0310, J. W. A. Young, *A Little to the East: Experiences of an Anglo-Egyptian Official, 1899–1925*, unpublished typescript, p. 152. Lawrence used a Swan fountain pen to write his reports; he took two with him to Arabia and later gave them to Sergeant Tom Beaumont, the armoured car machine-gunner who served with him. Beaumont still had the pens on 5 February 1990, when he was interviewed by Michael Hammerson (copy of unpublished transcript given to the author by the interviewer).

35. T. E. Lawrence, *Seven Pillars of Wisdom* (1935), p. 91.

36. TNA, FO 882/5/17, Bray's report of 18 October 1916, sent to Clayton.

CHAPTER 5

1. Pembroke College, University of Cambridge, Storrs Papers, diary entry, 16 October 1916.

2. SAD, Clayton Papers, 470/5, Wilson to Clayton, 22 November 1916.

3. Ronald Storrs, *Orientations* (1943), pp. 189, 441. Lawrence and the Arab Bureau were also indebted to the Arabist and explorer, Gertrude Bell, whose expert mapping of tribes and information on their sheikhs was highly valued by Clayton. She joined the Arab Bureau in Cairo on 30 November 1915 and spent two months there, before her transfer to Mesopotamia and the vital diplomatic and intelligence work that made her name.

4. Letter from Gray to his mother, 22 October 1916, Gray collection.

5. Letter from Gray to his sister, Cecil, 12 May 1916.

6. As demonstrated by Polly A. Mohs in *Military Intelligence and the Arab Revolt. The First Modern Intelligence War* (2008), p. 157, n. 44.

7. Letter from Mabel Holman, his fiancée, to Gray, 19 December 1916.

8. The Arab Bureau told Wingate: 'GHQ has been able to decipher intercepted wireless messages from the Turks round Medina. We will send you the gist of anything interesting': SAD, Wingate Papers, 141/2/37, Arab Bureau to Wingate, 18 October 1916.

9. Wingate told Clayton: 'this [Hussein's new title] is giving us a good deal of trouble and our wretched cipher officers are having a very thin time'. SAD, Wingate Papers, 143/5/32, Wingate to Clayton, 16 November 1916.

10. Letter from Gray to Mabel, 3 November 1916.

11. Gray told his mother, 'I shall be able to get a grand collection of photos if I can only get enough films.' He succeeded on both counts. Letter from Gray to his mother, 6 November 1916.

12. Letter from Gray to Mabel, 3 November 1916.

13. Letter from Gray to his mother, 25 October 1916.

14. Lieutenant Evan MacRury of GHQ intelligence at the Savoy Hotel, Cairo, who was to travel to Arabia four months later with a vital piece of signals intelligence for Lawrence, had been quick off the mark with a begging letter: 'very grateful if you could procure me a few Sherif stamps…They are being sold in Jeddah, I am told, already at 2 or 3 times their face value.' Letter from Lieutenant E. MacRury to Gray, 4 November 1916. Gray found time to send specimens of the Hejaz stamps to his mother and also to Mabel: letter from Gray to his mother, 22 October 1916.

15. Letter from Gray to his mother, 6 November 1916. Gray had told Mabel on 3 November that Wilson insisted he should go out for exercise at least every other day, 'as he would sooner be without me for a couple of hours than I should crock up and be no good for a month'.

16. Entry in Goodchild's diary, 11 November 1916, Walker collection.

17. Letter from Gray to his mother, 23 November 1916. Although ill himself, Wilson took the trouble to take part personally in caring for Gray, bathing his head with eau de cologne: letter from Mabel to Gray, 9 January 1917.

18. Wilson reported that 'Young and Cochrane work A1 but they are both absolutely inexperienced in this work.' SAD, Wingate Papers, 143/5/33, Wilson to Wingate, 16 November 1916.

19. SAD, Wingate Papers, 143/5/47, Wingate to Wilson, 19 November 1916.

20. SAD, Wingate Papers, 144/5/75, Wingate to Chief Egypforce [sic], 9 December 1916.

21. SAD, Wingate Papers, 144/2/60, Egypforce [sic] to Wingate, 13 December 1916.

22. TNA, FO 882/5/41. T. E. Lawrence, 'The Sherifs', 27 October 1916.

23. Earl of Cork and Orrery (William Boyle), *My Naval Life* (1942), p. 99.

24. H. V. F. Winstone, *The Diaries of Parker Pasha* (1983), pp. 172–4.

25. H. V. F. Winstone, *The Diaries of Parker Pasha* (1983), pp. 175–6.

26. SAD, Wingate Papers, 144/3/19, Wingate to Wilson, 3 December 1916.

27. Virtually all the shares in the Ottoman Bank had in fact been owned for some decades by British and French interests: Eugene Rogan, *The Fall of the Ottomans: The Great War in the Middle East, 1914–1920* (2015), p. 12.

28. TNA WO 158/604/222A, Lloyd to Wingate, 8 December 1916. Lloyd, who was also a Member of Parliament, was an expert on Turkey and on economic affairs. He had an additional role: to report to Clayton on the progress of the revolt.

29. Letter from Gray to his former boss, Ernest Bentley, 14 December 1916.

30. Letter from Gray to his mother, 'about middle December 1916' (the vagueness of the date probably a result of the 'Jeddah fever' he mentions).

31. A continuation of the letter to Bentley of 14 December 1916, which Gray had begun at Jeddah before his trip to Rabegh.

32. SAD, Wingate Papers, 144/3/45, Wingate to Clayton, 10 December 1916.

33. Captain Stanhope in the stage play *Journey's End* by R. C. Sherriff, 1928.

34. Letter from Gray to his mother, 24 December 1916.

35. Though Pearson's report from Jeddah said that the Subh tribe had defected to the Turks: AWM, Intelligence Diary, GHQ Egypt, 1/8/8, 25 December 1916.

36. Letter from Gray to his sister, Alice, 24 December 1916.

37. CAC, Papers of George Lloyd, GLLD 9/8, Wilson to George Lloyd, 31 December 1916.

38. CAC, Papers of George Lloyd, GLLD 9/8, Wilson to George Lloyd, 2 January 1917.

39. CAC, Papers of George Lloyd, GLLD 9/13, George Lloyd to Colonel Deedes of the Arab Bureau, 29 December 1916.

CHAPTER 6

1. Cambridge University Library, GBR/0115/RCMS 356, Letters of Hugh Drummond Pearson, Pearson to his mother, 27 December 1916. The mast on the Consulate roof would have been part of a Marconi radiotelegraph system.

2. 1881 census.

3. *The London Gazette*, 10 September 1897, p. 5095, confirms the bankruptcy that had occurred some years earlier. Goodchild was at Lancing College; his elder brother also had to leave.

4. Goodchild's uncle was John Mason Cook, known as 'the second greatest man in Egypt'. He was the son of Thomas Cook, the founder of the travel company, which had close links with the British High Commissioner in Egypt and with the British Government and military. John Mason Cook led excursions to Egypt and it is tempting to speculate that he encouraged Goodchild to move to Cairo and apply for work there.

5. Official war diary, Director of Remounts (Egypt, Palestine, and Syria), Vol. 8, 7 July 1916 and *passim*, TNA, WO 95/4390.

6. IWM, Dawnay MSS 69/21/2, quoted in David B. Woodward, *Forgotten Soldiers of the First World War* (2006), p. 51. An officer of the Camel Transport Corps was to describe a procession of baggage camels an astonishing 7 or 8 miles long during the Sinai campaign: Barry Carman and John McPherson (eds), *Bimbashi McPherson, A Life in Egypt* (1983), p. 166.

7. The huge scale of the operation is reflected by General Lynden-Bell, scourge of Wilson at General Headquarters and Norman Bray's uncle-by-marriage, who said: 'I am moving heaven and earth to get camels from everywhere. We have got camel buyers in every quarter of the globe.' IWM, Private Papers of Major-General Sir Arthur Lynden-Bell, Documents.7826, 0/1/1, Letter, Lynden-Bell to Major-General Sir F. Maurice, 31 August 1916.

8. Sir L. J. Blenkinsop and J. W. Rainey, *History of the Great War based on Official Documents. Veterinary Series* (1925), p. 157.

9. The Marquess of Anglesey, *A History of the British Cavalry 1816–1919*, Vol. 5: 1914–1919, Egypt, Palestine and Syria (1994), p. 35.

10. Storrs later wrote, 'I recommended him [Abdullah] to do all in his power to expedite the business of our camel-buyers.' Ronald Storrs, *Orientations* (1943), p. 178.

11. TNA, FO 686/54, Wilson to Remounts, EEF, 28 September 1916.

12. Andrew Shepherdson, *Journeys of a Light Horseman* (2002), pp. 94, 95, 118. Andrew is Suttor's grandson and has told his story based partly on letters home, diaries, and photographs. I am very grateful to Andrew for our helpful and enjoyable discussions.

13. Ronald Storrs, *Orientations* (1943) (see n.30), p. 148.

14. Official war diary, command paymaster in Egypt (EEF), Vol. 20, TNA, WO 95/4390.

15. TNA, WO 95/4390, Vol. 21.

16. SAD, Wingate Papers, 140/8/120, Arab Bureau to Colonel Wilson, 30 September 1916.

17. SAD, Wingate Papers, 141/6/83, Sir Percy Cox, Chief Political Officer at Basra, to Ibn Saud, 18 October 1916. Cox was the representative of the Government of India, which paid a retainer to Ibn Saud, Hussein's rival. So the British were backing two horses which they saw as joint favourites in Arabia. Cox's words refer back to his earlier letter of 29 August.

18. SAD, Wingate Papers, 141/2/143, Arab Bureau to Wilson, 27 September 1916.

19. MECA, St Antony's College, Oxford, GB165-0310, J. W. A. Young, memoir, *A Little to the East: Experiences of an Anglo-Egyptian Official 1899–1925*, p. 8.

20. SAD, Wingate Papers, 143/5/33, Wilson to Wingate, 16 November 1916.

21. Goodchild's diary, 30 November 1916, Walker collection.

22. SAD, Wingate Papers, 143/6/76, Wilson to Wingate, 25 November 1916.

23. SAD, Wingate Papers, 141/3/69, Wilson to Wingate, 24 October 1916.

24. Goodchild refers to this treatment many times in his diary. It is an understandably little-known fact that Lawrence mentions camel mange six times in *Seven*

Pillars of Wisdom: he was well aware of the disease's debilitating and sometimes fatal effects.

25. SAD, Wingate Papers, 143/3/80, chief of EEF to Wingate, 18 November 1916.

26. SAD, Wingate Papers, 143/3/131–2, Wilson to Wingate, 20 November 1916.

27. SAD, Wingate Papers, 143/4/68, Wilson to Wingate, 24 November 1916.

28. SAD, Wingate Papers, 143/4/175, Wilson to Wingate, 24 November 1916.

29. Robin Bidwell (ed.), *Arabian Personalities of the Early Twentieth Century* (1986), p. 11. Reprint of 1917 first edition.

30. SAD, Wingate Papers, 138/16/31, Pearson to Wingate, 29 July 1916. Pearson had visited the Hejaz in the second month of the revolt on an intelligence mission.

31. SAD, Wingate Papers, 144/2/136, Egyptforce to Wingate, 17 December 1916. Ottoman attempts to buy tribesmen's camels are suggested a year later by the comments of Major John Bassett, Wilson's deputy: Hussein 'has great difficulty in persuading Arabs to let their camels go'. Cable from Bassett at Jeddah to British base, Aqaba, 21 December 1917, in secret message notebook taken over by Gray at Aqaba in summer 1918 (private collection).

32. Parker's letter to Arab Bureau, 23 October 1916, in H. V. F. Winstone, *The Diaries of Parker Pasha* (1983), p. 154.

33. Parker's diary entry for 4 November 1916, in H. V. F. Winstone, *The Diaries of Parker Pasha* (1983), p. 171.

34. SAD, Wingate Papers, 140/6/57, Clayton to Wingate, 24 September 1916.

35. TNA, WO 158/604/210A, Arab Bureau to Wilson and Wingate, 13 December 1916.

36. TNA, FO 141/803/3273/31, Arab Bureau to High Commissioner, 30 October 1916.

37. TNA, WO 95/4390, Official war diary, command paymaster in Egypt (EEF), Vol. 21, 7 November 1916.

38. TNA, WO 95/4390, Official war diary, command paymaster in Egypt (EEF), Vol. 21, 21 December 1916. The Arab Bureau was usually adept at getting its hands on other departments' funds. The Treasury discovered in 1918 that the bureau, whose budget was £3,000, had in fact been spending £14,000 annually: Priya Satia, *Spies in Arabia* (2008), p. 47.

39. Trooper John Robertson, Imperial Camel Corps, *Cameliers and camels at war*, URL: https://nzhistory.govt.nz/war/camel-corps/camels-and-cameliers (2009).

40. TNA, FO 686/56/106-7, Royal Flying Corps (RFC) report, 10 October 1916. Goodchild may have done unofficial intelligence work in Jeddah. His diary records that he sent a letter by Khedivial Mail Ship (one of the secure ways used by the Consulate to get reports to Egypt) to 'Lawrence' on 12 November. The recipient may have been T. E. Lawrence, who was back in Cairo at that time (no evidence has come to light that Goodchild had a relative or friend with that name).

41. The story is told not in Goodchild's diary but in Gray's letter of 1 May 1917 to his mother.

42. TNA, WO 95/4451, official war diary of the deputy director of Veterinary Services, EEF, Vol. 3, 4 January 1917.
43. TNA, FO 882/6, HRG 16/93, Wilson to Wingate, 28 December 1916.

CHAPTER 7

1. Wilson wrote: 'The Sherif is convinced that at present he would run huge risks if Christian troops came & he must know best…It is a damned shame to put everything down to the Sherif. HMG has changed its mind just as, if not more, frequently.' SAD, Clayton Papers, 470/6/9, Wilson to Clayton, 16 January 1917.
2. Wilson also wrote of Newcombe's ideas: 'this show is like nothing on earth now or before & if we "butt" in now it would do incalculable harm'. SAD, Clayton Papers, 470/6/9, Wilson to Clayton, 16 January 1917.
3. SAD, Clayton Papers, 470/6/9, Wilson to Clayton, 16 January 1917.
4. Christophe Leclerc, 'French Eye-Witness Accounts of Lawrence and the Arab Revolt, Part 1', in *Journal of the T. E. Lawrence Society*, Vol. XX, No. 1 (2010/11), endnote 3, pp. 69–70.
5. TNA, FO 882/6, pp. 127–8, Lawrence to Wilson, report, 8 January 1917. Sherif Sheraf was a friend of Hussein, an expert on tribal custom and chief of staff in Feisal's army.
6. SAD, Clayton Papers, 470/6/4, Wilson to Clayton, 5 January 1917.
7. In fact Vickery was doing his best to help Boyle, offering the nearest liquid that came to hand when he saw that Boyle was struggling to swallow some unappetizing meat.
8. Vickery's daughter remembers how her father called Lawrence a charlatan, was offended by the tone and claims of *Seven Pillars of Wisdom*, and had few good words for him: personal communication to the author, 2013. Vickery was a fine soldier of the old school but did not have Lawrence's sensitivities towards Arab culture. Lawrence later unfairly accused him of being a medal-chaser just interested in promotion.
9. Captain L. B. Weldon, *Hard Lying* (1925), pp. 157–9.
10. *Um Lejj to Wejh*, Lawrence's report in *The Arab Bulletin,* No. 41, 6 February 1917, in R. Bidwell (ed.), *The Arab Bulletin 1916–19*, Vols I–IV (1986), p. 66.
11. Ashraf was on his way from Medina to Asir, south of the Hejaz, where the Turks were trying to re-establish communication with their isolated 21st Division. Some of the gold may have been intended for these troops. War Office, 'Extracts from Summary of the Hejaz Revolt, War office, London 1918': extract published in *Journal of the T. E. Lawrence Society*, Vol. III, No. 1 (Summer 1993), n. 19, p. 39.
12. The amount of gold and the date on Gray's label seem to be simple mistakes. Gray's daughter remembered her father saying that Lawrence had told him the pistol had been used to kill many Armenians: personal communication, February 2013. Lawrence's assertion would have resonated later with Gray, who worked as a political liaison officer with Sir Mark Sykes in Aleppo in late December to January 1919 and who was eyewitness to a massacre of Armenians there.

13. MECA, St Antony's College, Oxford, GB165-0310, J. W. A. Young, memoir, *Three Months in Jedda,* 1916, p. 9. That Ashraf was the prisoner in question is confirmed in Young's *Local Personalities: Jedda and Mecca,* a manuscript exercise book (one of two) sold at Sotheby's, London, 16 November 2006, Lot 201.

14. Letter from Gray to his mother, 30 January 1917.

15. Referred to in Mabel Holman's letter to Gray, 31 January 1917.

16. Letter from Gray to his mother, 21 January 1917.

17. Letter from Gray to his mother, 30 January 1917.

18. Letter from Gray to his mother, 21 January 1917.

19. As we have seen, HMS *Anne* was the new name for Captain Lewen Weldon's *Aenne Rickmers,* which had been captured from the Germans. The British liked to give their spoils of war what they considered more appropriate names.

20. Cambridge University Library, Letters of Hugh Drummond Pearson, GBR/0115/RCMS 356, letter from Pearson to his mother, 1 January 1917.

21. Cambridge University Library, Letters of Hugh Drummond Pearson, GBR/0115/RCMS 356, letter from Pearson to his mother, 28 March 1917.

22. Letter from Gray to his sister, Cecil, 12 February 1917.

23. Pearson thought the golf course would become 'a form of entertainment for visiting ships … Our naval wireless operators are now taking to it.' Cambridge University Library, Letters of Hugh Drummond Pearson, GBR/0115/RCMS 356, letter from Pearson to his mother, 18 February 1917.

24. FO 141/736/2475, telegram from Major Weldon, the cipher officer at Jeddah, to Arab Bureau, 25 January 1917.

25. SAD, Wingate Papers, 145/3/1–7, Pearson to Wingate, undated but late February 1917.

26. SAD, Wingate Papers, 145/3/10, unsigned copy, sent on behalf of Wingate by perhaps Clayton, 2 March 1917.

27. HUA, Papers of Sir Mark Sykes, U DDSY2/4/118, Letter from Sykes in London to Colonel Elkington, 3 October 1916.

28. Garland was a brave man and one of those British men whose health was permanently ruined in Arabia.

CHAPTER 8

1. The papers of Charles Hardinge, 1st Baron Hardinge of Penhurst, Cambridge University Library, Department of Manuscripts and University Archives, GBR/012/MS.Hardinge, f.266, letter from Wingate to Hardinge, 17 April 1917. Hardinge was permanent under-secretary of state at the Foreign Office and former viceroy of India.

2. TNA, FO 141/773/6, date given as 1917 only but before 17 April 1917.

3. Wilson wrote that Bray 'utterly surprised me by asking if I could let him go back to his Regiment in France. I asked him why and he said his job was not the one he thought he was coming to do and that for some reason he could not feel he could stay as he could not give me loyal & frank advice which I had a

right to expect. I asked him what it was he was getting at and he said he could not tell me but that it was nothing to do with me personally...he said he was bound to carry out some line of policy and that it did not agree with the policy being followed.' SAD, Wingate Papers, 470/6/21–2, Wilson to Clayton, 20 March 1917.

4. SAD, Wingate Papers, 470/6/21–2, Wilson to Clayton, 20 March 1917.

5. Letter from Gray to his sister, Cecil, 16 October 1917.

6. HUA, Papers of Sir Mark Sykes, U DDSY2/11/33, Letter from Bray to Sykes, not dated but from internal evidence probably 29 April 1917.

7. Letter from Gray to his mother, 26 February 1917.

8. Letter from Gray to Mabel Holman, 25 April 1917, sent with two sets of first issue, used Hejaz stamps.

9. Letter to Gray from his mother, 1 March 1917.

10. Letter from Gray to his mother, 30 January 1917.

11. Letter from Mabel to Gray, 14 March 1917.

12. Letter from Gray to Mabel, 28 February 1917.

13. Letter from Mabel to Gray, 17 January 1916.

14. Letters of Hugh Drummond Pearson, Cambridge University Library, Royal Commonwealth Society, GBR/0115/RCMS 356, letter from Pearson to his mother, 11 March 1917.

15. Letter from Gray to his mother, 5 April 1917.

16. Letter from Gray to his mother, 16 April 1917.

17. Letter from Gray to Mabel, 27 April 1917. Gray actually held up the procession, so keen was he to record this forgotten drama. He had sent some of his earlier photographs to Ronald Storrs, who wrote thanking Gray for the photographs on 17 February 1917, recommending that he wrote captions on the back (Gray usually did so) and hoping that 'Jeddah in the winter is an almost endurable place'.

18. T. E. Lawrence, *Seven Pillars of Wisdom* (1935), p. 194.

19. SAD, Clayton Papers, 470/6/18, Wilson to Clayton, 5 March 1917.

20. CAC, The Papers of George Lloyd, GLLD 9/9, report by Lieutenant-Colonel S. F. Newcombe, 4 February 1917.

21. TNA, FO 882/12, f.199–201, Wilson to Clayton, 21 March 1917.

22. CAC, Papers of George Lloyd, GLLD 9/9, Wilson to Clayton, begun on 21 May and finished on 24 May 1917.

23. CAC, Papers of George Lloyd, GLLD 9/9, Newcombe, 'Note' on Sykes's and Georges-Picot's meeting with King Hussein, 20 May 1917.

24. Jeremy Wilson and Scott Anderson give excellent accounts of this key stage of the Arab Revolt.

CHAPTER 9

1. T. E. Lawrence, 'The Howeitat and their Chiefs', *The Arab Bulletin,* No. 57, 24 July 1917, in R. Bidwell (ed.), *The Arab Bulletin 1916–19,* Vols I–IV (1986), pp. 309–10.

2. T. E. Lawrence, *Seven Pillars of Wisdom* (1935), p. 247.

3. Writing by a window to the sound of a band playing in the nearby Esbekia Gardens, he told Mabel about some shirts he had seen in the souks made of what he thought was a mysterious new material called viyella (it had been around for well over a hundred years). Gray felt he was on safer ground in buying a new suit made of something like alpaca wool. Letter from Gray to Mabel Holman, 13 May 1917.

4. Details given in a later letter from Gray to his mother, 11 August 1917. The other references to Gray's activities in Cairo are taken from the diary that Mabel had sent him; it is still in the ownership of his family.

5. Letter from Gray to his sister, Cecil, written in the Red Sea, 19 June 1917.

6. Letter from Gray to Mabel, 25 June 1917.

7. Letter from Gray to Cecil, 2 July 1917.

8. Letter from Gray to Cecil, 11 September 1917.

9. Letter from Gray to Cecil, 21 November 1917.

10. Letter from Gray to his sister, Alice, 20 November 1917.

11. Wingate wrote to Wilson: 'You will be sorry to lose your partner at golf.' SAD, Wingate Papers, 145/4/97–8, Wingate to Wilson, 9 April 1917. Wingate was an autograph collector and was keen to have Hussein's signature, adding in a touching postscript to the letter: 'I am sending on some photographs of the King in the hopes that you will be able to induce him to sign them. You can ... say how very greatly I should value his autograph'.

12. See Eugene Rogan, *The Fall of the Ottomans: The Great War in the Middle East, 1914–1920* (2015), pp. 302–3.

13. HUA, Papers of Sir Mark Sykes, U DDSY2/11/39, telegram from Arab Bureau (quoting Bray's report) to British Resident, Aden for Sykes's attention 'on arrival', 20 May 1917.

14. HUA, Papers of Sir Mark Sykes, U DDSY2/11/39, telegram from Sykes to War Office, beginning 'Hope Arab Legion will be sanctioned without delay', apparently 2 June 1917 (a question mark follows the date). Why Sykes thought there would be another 'Rabegh panic', a most unlikely scenario given the weakened position of the Turkish garrison at Medina, is unclear: this could be another example of his habit of bamboozling people to achieve his ends.

15. HUA, Papers of Sir Mark Sykes, U DDSY2/11/39, memo from Sykes to chief of EEF, 28 April 1917.

16. HUA, Papers of Sir Mark Sykes, U DDSY2/11/39, manuscript notes by Sykes, 17 June 1917.

17. HUA, Papers of Sir Mark Sykes, U DDSY2/11/61, letter from Sykes to Clayton, 22 July 1917.

18. Sykes 'sprang up as if he had been stung by a wasp, overturning his chair. "Impossible! Impossible!" he bellowed.' N. N. E. Bray, *Shifting Sands* (1934), p. 150.

19. TNA, AIR 30/235, 22 November 1944, Bray's petition to King George VI regarding his alleged fascist sympathies and denial of his request to be given

further intelligence duties in the Middle East. See also *A Note on the Mohammedan Question—Its Bearing on events in India and Arabia. The Future of the Great Islamic Revival now that Turkey ceases to be the power on which the hopes of the Moslem world were placed*, in Bray to Wilson, 27 March 1917, in Wilson to Wingate, 29 March 1917, secret, TNA, FO 371/3057/103481.

20. CAC, Papers of George Lloyd, GLLD 9/9, Wilson to Clayton, 30 May 1917.

21. The *Arab Bulletin*, No. 56, 9 July 1917, in R. Bidwell (ed.), *The Arab Bulletin 1916–19*, Vols I–IV (1986), pp. 302–3.

22. Lawrence claimed that he had full access to Feisal's own agents, but he wrote very little about them or the intelligence they provided. See, for example, the letter from Lawrence to Wilson, 6 December 1916, in M. R. Lawrence (ed.), *The Home Letters of T. E. Lawrence and His Brothers* (1954), p. 212.

CHAPTER 10

1. For security, Clayton used the code-name 'Agent Y' for intercepted Turkish wireless messages relating to the Hejaz. Another indicator of this source was the phrase 'an absolutely reliable source'. See Yigal Sheffy, *British Military Intelligence in the Palestine Campaign, 1914–1918* (1998), p. 252.

2. From Article 14. TNA, FO 882/7, f. 93–7. Published in the same month in R. Bidwell (ed.), *The Arab Bulletin 1916–19*, Vols I–IV (1986), pp. 347–53.

3. M. R. Lawrence (ed.), *The Home Letters of T. E. Lawrence and His Brothers* (1954), p. 338, 12 August 1917.

4. Letter from Lawrence to Wilson, 2 September 1917, in David Garnett (ed.), *The Letters of T. E. Lawrence* (1938), pp. 236–7.

5. Joshua Teitelbaum, *The Rise and Fall of the Hashemite Kingdom of Arabia* (2001), p. 284.

6. Edouard Brémond, *Le Hedjaz dans la guerre mondiale* (1931), p. 179.

7. TNA, WO 158/634, report by Captain Snagge of HMS *Humber*, 1 October 1917.

8. TNA, WO 158/634, Jeddah to Arab Bureau, 26 November 1917.

9. SAD, Wingate Papers, 145/8/91, Wingate to Graham, Foreign Office, 26 June 1917.

10. HUA, Papers of Sir Mark Sykes, U DDSY2/11/67, letter from Wingate to Sykes, 20 August 1917.

11. HUA, Papers of Sir Mark Sykes, U DDSY2/11/69, letter from Clayton to Sykes, 20 September 1917.

12. Australian War Memorial 4, War Diary, Political Intelligence, 1/10/9, 27 September 1917.

13. Letters of Hugh Drummond Pearson, Cambridge University Library, Royal Commonwealth Society, GBR/0115/RCMS 356, Pearson to his sister, Ursula, 26 September 1917.

14. Letters of Hugh Drummond Pearson, Cambridge University Library, Royal Commonwealth Society, GBR/0115/RCMS 356, Pearson to his mother, 3 October 1917.

15. HUA, Papers of Sir Mark Sykes, U DDSY2/4/160, 'extracts from Col. Pearson's letter dated 5/10/17', part of a 'private letter' sent by Pearson to Clayton and enclosed with letter from Clayton to Sykes, 18 October 1917. It would be intriguing to see what was in the rest of Pearson's letter, the part deemed by Clayton to be inappropriate for Sykes to see.

16. Letters of Hugh Drummond Pearson, Cambridge University Library, Royal Commonwealth Society, GBR/0115/RCMS 356, Pearson to his mother, 11 October 1917.

17. Letters of Hugh Drummond Pearson, Cambridge University Library, Royal Commonwealth Society, GBR/0115/RCMS 356, Pearson to his mother, 21 October 1917.

18. Letters of Hugh Drummond Pearson, Cambridge University Library, Royal Commonwealth Society, GBR/0115/RCMS 356, Pearson to his sister, Ursula, 30 October 1917.

19. Entry for 19 November 1917 in secret cipher message notebook left at Aqaba for Lieutenant Lionel Gray when he was transferred there in summer 1918.

20. Letters of Hugh Drummond Pearson, Cambridge University Library, Royal Commonwealth Society, GBR/0115/RCMS 356, Pearson to his mother, 18 November 1917.

21. Pearson, ready as ever to throw himself into any sporting activity, had to conclude that at nearly 45 years old, 'I am getting too old for football. This afternoon I trod on the ball, came down on my knee, barked my chin and shook my jaw and sprained my wrist and swallowed a lot of gravel.' He was still annoyed with himself for scoring only one goal when he should have scored three. Letters of Hugh Drummond Pearson, Cambridge University Library, Royal Commonwealth Society, GBR/0115/RCMS 356, Pearson to his mother, 26 November 1917.

22. Letters of Hugh Drummond Pearson, Cambridge University Library, Royal Commonwealth Society, GBR/0115/RCMS 356, Pearson to his mother, 26 November 1917, second section written on 28 November.

23. Letters of Hugh Drummond Pearson, Cambridge University Library, Royal Commonwealth Society, GBR/0115/RCMS 356, Pearson to his mother, 30 November 1917.

24. Entry for 27 December 1917 in secret cipher message notebook taken over by Gray at Aqaba.

25. Almost a year to the day since arriving in Arabia, restless at not having a front-line fighting role as before, Gray envied a friend battling the Turks at Gaza: 'What luck they are all having. I am itching for a fight again behind my machine gun.' Letter from Gray to his sister, Cecil, 14 October 1917.

CHAPTER 11

1. Lawrence called the Australian instructor 'Lewis' and the British one 'Stokes'.

2. T. E. Lawrence, *Seven Pillars of Wisdom* (1935), pp. 368–9.

3. Lawrence to his old Oxford friend E. T. Leeds, 24 September 1917, in David Garnett (ed.), *The Letters of T. E. Lawrence* (1938), p. 238.

4. Lawrence to Major W. F. Stirling, 25 September 1917, in Malcolm Brown (ed.), *Lawrence of Arabia: The Selected Letters* (2005), p. 133.

5. CAC, Papers of George Lloyd, GLLD 9/12, Daily Intelligence Summaries, August 1917.

6. Lloyd and Lawrence got on well and Lloyd thought he could lighten the load on the younger man by accompanying Lawrence on his 'stunts' in the desert, 'to help to keep his genius a few weeks longer'. CAC, Papers of George Lloyd, GLLD 9/13, Lloyd to Clayton, 30 September 1917.

7. TNA, FO 882/7, Lawrence to Clayton, 10 October 1917.

8. Jeremy Wilson, *Lawrence of Arabia: the Authorised Biography of T. E. Lawrence* (1989), endnote 26, Chapter 21. The quotation is from the 1922 draft *Seven Pillars*, known as the 'Oxford' text, Chapter 74.

9. CAC, Papers of George Lloyd, GLLD 9/13, Lloyd to Clayton, 20 October 1917.

10. CAC, Papers of George Lloyd, GLLD 9/10, Clayton to Lloyd, 25 October 1917.

11. As Lloyd wrote in his diary: 'Lawrence who had professed to know the way was in reality completely ignorant of it.' CAC, Papers of George Lloyd, GLLD 9/11, Lloyd's diary, 27–8 October 1917.

12. CAC, Papers of George Lloyd, GLLD 9/11, Lloyd's diary, 27–8 October 1917.

13. SAD, Wingate Papers, 146/4/44–5, Wilson to Wingate, 8 September 1917.

14. TNA, WO 158/615, GHQ Cairo, British Personnel, Reports by Captain T. R. G. Bennett, February–April 1918. At this time, Wingate as High Commissioner was in control of British operations conducted from the southern bases of Jeddah, Yenbo, and Wejh. Northern operations based at Aqaba came under the EEF: same source, letter from Captain Bennett of the Arab Bureau, 3 March 1918, to GHQ EEF.

15. Letter from Gray to his mother, 25 February 1918. Gray had wanted to go with Wilson on the camel ride to Abdullah's camp, telling his mother 'I thought I might get a trip with the Colonel'.

16. Letter from Beryl Marie Wilson to Gray from the Hotel Bel-Air, Suez, 11 January 1918.

17. Letter from Gray to Mabel Holman, 5 April 1918, sent from Yenbo.

18. Letter from Gray to his mother, 5 August 1917.

19. Letter from Gray to his sister, Cecil, 11 September 1917.

20. 'Jeddah people are not allowed in their villages but the residents call here. The reason is that so much corruption goes on in them, especially the two near the coast where a lot of smuggling is done, that they don't let strangers go near to pry. Lots of slaves are here and illicit slave trading is done in the villages.' Letter from Gray to his sister, Cecil, 11 September 1917.

21. Letter from Gray to his sister, 16 October 1917.

22. Letter from Mabel to Gray, 9 November 1917. To compound Mabel's miseries, her grandmother died on 28 November (her letter to Gray, 4 December 1917).

Gerald shared the fate of T. E. Lawrence's younger brother, Will, an observer with the RFC, who had been killed two years earlier.

23. Letter from Gray to his mother, 20 October 1917. Mabel's nerves had been shattered in July 1917, when all the windows of the family house at Muswell Hill had been blown in by a bomb from a German air raid.

24. Letter from Gray to his sister, Cecil, 11 November 1917.

25. 2 November 1917. An English translation, in Gray's hand but probably the work of Ruhi, accompanies the Arabic invitation to 'the Honourable Gray'.

26. Letter from Gray to Mabel, 10 December 1917.

27. Typed instruction from Lieutenant Everard Feilding, 6 December 1917. In 1919 Feilding married a Polish spiritualist medium. It is hard to resist speculation (probably pointless) as to whether his pre-war skill in exposing fraudulent mediums was an asset in his intelligence work.

28. See, in particular, James Barr, *Setting the Desert on Fire* (2007), pp. 195–200.

29. George Bernard Shaw wrote this in the flyleaf of his wife Charlotte's copy of the subscribers' edition of *Seven Pillars of Wisdom*. John E. Mack, *A Prince of Our Disorder: The Life of T. E. Lawrence* (1976), p. 229. The copy of *Seven Pillars of Wisdom* is in the Arents Collection, New York Public Library.

30. MECA, St Antony's College, Oxford, Hogarth collection, GB165-0147, 2/28, letter from Hogarth to his son, Billy, 16 December 1917. Quoted by Lawrence James, *The Golden Warrior* (2008), p. 214, n. 17.

CHAPTER 12

1. *Arab Bulletin*, No. 70, 21 November 1917, in R. Bidwell (ed.), *The Arab Bulletin 1916–19*, Vols I–IV (1986), p. 466.

2. *Arab Bulletin*, No. 72, 5 December 1917, in R. Bidwell (ed.), *The Arab Bulletin 1916–19*, Vols I–IV (1986), p. 492.

3. *The Arab Bulletin*, No. 72, 5 December 1917, in R. Bidwell (ed.), *The Arab Bulletin 1916–19*, Vols I–IV (1986), p. 488.

4. Letter from Gray to his mother, 28 December 1917.

5. In one of those elegant quirks of history, Philby, father of the future Soviet spy Kim Philby, had difficult discussions with Bassett, future step-father of the Soviet agent, Guy Burgess. Less than two decades later, at Trinity College, the notorious Cambridge spy ring would take shape. The son and step-son would be friends and would have more in common than the two men who were thrown together awkwardly in Jeddah.

6. SAD, Wingate Papers, 145/1/1–2, Wingate to Bassett, 1 January 1918 (incorrectly dated 1917).

7. *The Arab Bulletin*, No. 77, 27 January 1918, in R. Bidwell (ed.), *The Arab Bulletin 1916–19*, Vols I–IV (1986), p. 24.

8. See Eugene Rogan, *The Fall of the Ottomans: The Great War in the Middle East, 1914–1920* (2015), pp. 348–50.

9. *The Arab Bulletin*, No. 77, 27 January 1918, in R. Bidwell (ed.), *The Arab Bulletin 1916–19*, Vols I–IV (1986), pp. 23–4.

10. Philby later replied from central Arabia to a letter from Gray, and thanked him for the 'wholly unexpected gift of 10/- [ten shillings] which I don't remember winning and also for the photos'. Letter from Philby to Gray, sent from Wadi Darwash, 4 June 1918. Gray's letter dated 3 February had taken four months to find Philby, who had been 'wandering about in this strange country, quite enjoying myself'. In sending 'love to Bassett', Philby wrote: 'I wish I could fix up to pay you another surprise visit—perhaps some day later on!' King Hussein would have been heartily relieved that this never happened. The Jeddah men enjoyed card games, especially poker and bridge, and it seems that the uninvited guest had been happy to join in.

11. SAD, Wingate Papers, 167/1/308–9, Wingate to Bassett, 24 January 1918.

12. 8 February 1918. See George Antonius, *The Arab Awakening* (1938), pp. 431–2. The English translation is by Antonius, but the original communication was in Arabic, perhaps translated from the Foreign Office English by Ruhi at Jeddah. King Hussein later made a photostat copy available to the Arab world.

13. 'You are doing capitally and I can see that King Hussein has entire confidence in you—Buck him up and don't let him get depressed about anything.' SAD, Wingate Papers, 167/2/343–5, Wingate to Bassett, 24 February 1918.

14. SAD, Wingate Papers, 167/1/308–9, Wingate to Bassett, 24 January 1918.

15. SAD, Wingate Papers, 167/2/345, Wingate to Bassett, 24 February 1918.

16. TNA, FO 882/19/172, dated 'Helouan 14th 1918': from the context of related documents, written on 14 March 1918.

17. Letter from Wilson to Gray, 14 March 1918, from the Grand Hotel Helouan. One of a number of letters written by Wilson to Gray.

18. Gray took six photographs of Hussein sitting on a window seat, then, as if he were a wedding photographer shepherding the in-laws, 'moved him from one position to another to get a better view in difficult light...He was very Kingly & moved his features very little. If you saw him looking solemn & smiling you would think they were different people.' Letter from Gray to Mabel, 20 January 1918. Photographs of Hussein are rare. Hussein's great-great-grandson is the present King Abdullah II of Jordan.

19. From two letters from Mabel Holman to Gray, 20 February 1918 and 27 February 1918.

20. Letter from Gray to his mother, 11 February 1918.

21. Letter from Gray to Mabel, 20 January 1918.

22. Letter from Mabel to Gray, 27 February 1918.

23. Letter from Mabel to Gray, 2 March 1918.

24. Letter from Mabel to Gray, 20 March 1918. Lawrence, typically, rejected his decoration.

25. T. E. Lawrence, *Seven Pillars of Wisdom* (1935), p. 459.

26. TNA, FO 882/7, f. 267, Lawrence to Clayton, 12 February 1918.

27. T. E. Lawrence, *Seven Pillars of Wisdom* (1935), p. 502.

28. T. E. Lawrence, *Seven Pillars of Wisdom* (1935), p. 503. See also Scott Anderson, *Lawrence in Arabia. War, Deceit, Imperial Folly and the Making of the Modern Middle East* (2013), pp. 423–5.

CHAPTER 13

1. Letter from Gray to his mother, 14 March 1918, written in anticipation of his transfer to Yenbo.
2. Letter from Gray to his mother, 24 January 1918.
3. Letter from Gray to his mother, 19 April 1918.
4. Letter from Gray to Mabel Holman, 5 April 1918.
5. Letter from Gray to his mother, 19 April 1918.
6. Letter from Gray to Mabel, 8 May 1918.
7. Mabel was concerned: 'I don't like the sound of having to disguise yourself in order to go out riding in the desert.' Letter from Mabel to Gray, 8 May 1918.
8. Letter from Gray to his mother, 27 April 1918. Fred Karno was a famous Music Hall comedian who introduced circus slapstick comedy to the stage. His name became synonymous with anything chaotic. Gray would have been familiar with British soldiers singing *We Are Fred Karno's Army* to the tune of the hymn *The Church's One Foundation*.
9. Letter from Gray to Mabel, 8 May 1918.
10. TNA, WO 95/4415, Hejaz Operations War Diary, 10 May 1918.
11. Letter from Gray to his sister, Cecil, 22 May 1918.
12. Letter from Gray to Cecil, 2 June 1918.
13. T. E. Lawrence, *Seven Pillars of Wisdom* (1935), p. 508.
14. See Eugene Rogan, *The Fall of the Ottomans: The Great War in the Middle East, 1914–1920* (2015), p. 367.
15. T. E. Lawrence, *Seven Pillars of Wisdom* (1935), p. 527. See Scott Anderson, *Lawrence in Arabia. War, Deceit, Imperial Folly and the Making of the Modern Middle East* (2013), p. 442.
16. Bright's friend in the same battalion, the war poet Charles Sorley, was killed at Loos—Bright wrote 'Unforgettable, unforgotten' in a copy of Sorley's posthumously published *Marlborough and Other Poems* (1916), which he took with him to the desert. This volume is at the National Army Museum, Papers of Captain Leslie Leonard Bright, 9411-118-25.
17. The term 'base commandant' was no longer used at Wejh or Yenbo soon after March 1918, because unlike Aqaba, the ports were no longer used as bases for forward operations. Bright and Goldie were 'at present actually employed on intelligence and demolition work on the Hejaz Railway': TNA, WO 158/615, Wingate to secretary at the War Office, 14 March 1918.
18. AWM 4, 1/8/13, Intelligence Diary, GHQ, EEF, 6 June 1917. Suleiman Rifada was killed in November 1917 when the Arabs ambushed a train north of Al Ula. Bright was to write detailed reports on the allegiances of Suleiman's sons.

19. See Eveline van der Steen, 'Lawrence and the Tribes', in *Journal of the T. E. Lawrence Society*, Vol. XXI, No. 2 (2011/12), p. 25.

20. National Army Museum, Papers of Captain Leslie Leonard Bright, 9411-118-12, 'Tribes of centre' notebook (undated). Bright also had with him *A Tribal Handbook of Syria and Parts of the Sinai Peninsula* (1918, paper wrappers) marked 'Provisional only. Incomplete' (9411-118-11). The book is heavily annotated in Bright's hand, particularly the Jordan Valley section, though unfortunately pages 52–64 are missing. The Arab Bureau prepared what it called this 'compendium'.

21. John Buchan, *Greenmantle* (1916), p. 20. Buchan was referring to his hero, Sandy Arbuthnot, who was based on the adventurous and half-blind Aubrey Herbert of the Arab Bureau.

22. T. E. Lawrence, *Seven Pillars of Wisdom* (1935), p. 142.

23. The *Arab Bulletin* No. 84, 7 April 1918, in R. Bidwell (ed.), *The Arab Bulletin 1916–19*, Vols I–IV (1986), p. 111. Sherif Sharaf had arrived back in Wejh on 21 February and Bright's report had been sent on 21 March.

24. The *Arab Bulletin* No. 94, 25 June 1918, in R. Bidwell (ed.), *The Arab Bulletin 1916–19*, Vols I–IV (1986), pp. 216–17.

25. See Eugene Rogan, *The Fall of the Ottomans: The Great War in the Middle East, 1914–1920* (2015), p. 16.

26. Entry for 4 March 1918 in secret cipher message notebook left at Aqaba for Lieutenant Lionel Gray when he was transferred there in summer 1918. At the time of writing the notebook was still in the ownership of the Gray family.

27. National Army Museum, Papers of Captain Leslie Leonard Bright, 9411-118-12. The two-volume set is in the first edition of 1888. Lawrence was a great admirer of Doughty, one of the most outstanding Arabian travellers, and had corresponded with him before the war. Inscriptions in the books read: 'L. L. Bright/"Blood Brother of the Bedouins"/1921/from T. E. Lawrence'. The handwriting is not that of Bright or Lawrence (who in any case would have written 'Beduins'), and seems to be that of a family member who annotated other books of Bright's after his untimely death in 1923. January 1921 saw the publication of a new edition of *Travels in Arabia Deserta*, with an introduction by Lawrence. It would be entirely in character for Lawrence, who was self-denying and wanted to forget about his traumatic Arabian experiences, to give to his friend, Leo Bright, a first edition that he had once valued so highly. He had used the book to write his introduction and its place in his austere life was now over.

28. Sir Mark Allen, 'Lawrence Among the Arabs', in *Journal of the T. E. Lawrence Society*, Vol. XX, No. 1 (2010/11), p. 17.

29. From Bright's obituary in *The Blue*, the Christ's Hospital School magazine, Vol. L, No. 3, July 1923. At National Army Museum, Papers of Captain Leslie Leonard Bright, 9411-118-1.

CHAPTER 14

1. Letter from Colonel Wilson to Gray, 6 June 1918. In Gray collection.
2. Letter from Major Garland to Gray, 11 June 1918. In Gray collection.

3. Letter from Gray to Mabel Holman, 10 July 1918.

4. Letter from Colonel Bassett to Gray, 24 July 1918. In Gray collection.

5. Letter from Colonel Wilson to Gray, 23 June 1918. In Gray collection.

6. Draft letter from Gray to Colonel Wilson, headed 'Akaba', 2 July 1918. A reply to Wilson's letter of 23 June.

7. Letter from Gray to Mabel, 10 July 1918.

8. Letter from Mabel to Gray, 21 August 1918.

9. Gray's restlessness unnerved Mabel, who was still grieving for her young pilot officer brother Gerald: 'for goodness sake don't get the flying craze—it is too dangerous a stunt'. Letter from Mabel to Gray, 24 July 1918.

10. Letter from Gray to his mother, 15 July 1918.

11. Draft letter from Gray to Colonel Wilson, 2 July 1918.

12. Gray wrote to her: 'Many thanks for the ciphers which you influenced & please thank E.L.B. [Bentley] for letter, paper & ciphers.' Letter from Gray to Mabel, 10 July 1918.

13. The camera, documented as having been used in Arabia, was a No. 3 folding Pocket Kodak and is still with Gilman's family.

14. See Joseph Berton, T. E. Lawrence and the Arab Revolt. An Illustrated Guide (2011), p. 55.

15. T. E. Lawrence, Seven Pillars of Wisdom (1935), p. 458.

16. Gilman's unpublished photograph, at the Huntington Library in California, was shown to John Winterburn, one of the leaders of the archaeological project, by the Arab Revolt expert, Joe Berton.

17. The memoir, which is owned by Gilman's family, is entitled Reminiscences of the Far East and Elsewhere (86 pages survive). The First World War is summarized as 'those agonising years'.

18. The sketch map, like the memoir, is owned by Gilman's family. The Ottoman guns were in fact two Austrian mountain howitzers at 7,000 yards, range: see Neil Faulkner, Lawrence of Arabia's War (2016), p. 414.

19. T. E. Lawrence, Seven Pillars of Wisdom (1935), p. 524.

20. Gilman's mention of 'about August' for his breakdown can be qualified: Lawrence seems not to have been in Cairo that month, though he was there on 6, 9, and 13 July, and perhaps on other days that month too. So it appears that Gilman's breakdown happened in July 1918.

21. David Garnett (ed.), The Letters of T. E. Lawrence (1938), pp. 244, 246.

22. TNA, FO 686/38, Bassett to Hussein, 2 May 1918.

23. LHCMA, Joyce Papers, 1/271, Bassett to Arab Bureau, 8 May 1918.

24. 'MECA, St Antony's College, Oxford, Sir Mark Sykes Collection, GB165-0275, Clayton to Sykes, 28 November 1917. See James Barr, Setting the Desert on Fire (2006), p. 205.

25. Wilson admitted 'It is not an easy subject to talk to the King about as he is most impatient of any criticism.' TNA, FO 686/38, Wilson's notes of conversation with King Hussein, 6 June 1918. Cited in Barr, Setting the Desert on Fire (2007), p. 205.

26. TNA, FO 686/38, Wilson, note on conversation with King Hussein, 27 May 1918.

27. TNA, FO 686/38, Wilson to Wingate, 5 June 1918.

28. TNA, FO 686/9, Wilson's report, 19 July 1918.

29. TNA, FO 686/10, Bassett to Hussein, 3 August 1918. See James Barr, *Setting the Desert on Fire* (2007), pp. 262–4.

CHAPTER 15

1. The commandant, Major Robert Hamilton Scott, wrote in his diary: 'Monkey loose and playing Old Harry all round.' The handwritten contemporary diary covers Scott's entire period at Aqaba, as well as time before and after his service there. It is privately owned by his immediate descendants and is published here for the first time.

2. Lowell Thomas, *With Lawrence in Arabia* (1924), p. 249. Goslett's two salukis became one on 6 July 1918: Scott's diary for 7 July records: 'Goslett's dog shot last night'.

3. A few days earlier M31 had replaced the monitor HMS *Humber*, which had been temporarily withdrawn for refitting: AWM, 4, 1/6/22, War Diary of GHQ, EEF, 2 February 1918.

4. Noted at the back of Scott's diary: '9/2/18. Monthly grant received from Cairo £103,823'.

5. Owned by Scott's family.

6. Scott was away in Egypt and Palestine from 2 May to 22 June.

7. Abah Bedrossian was to praise Scott's and Marshall's 'vibrating heart' and their willingness 'to help the Armenians who were escaping from the terror of the Turks'. Letter from Bedrossian to Scott, 15 October 1918, in possession of the Scott family. A copy is at the Liddell Hart Centre, King's College, London, Joyce Papers/2/9.

8. Letter from Bedrossian to Scott, 28 September 1918. Owned by Scott family.

9. T. E. Lawrence, *Seven Pillars of Wisdom* (1935), p. 528.

10. Lowell Thomas, *With Lawrence in Arabia* (1925), Foreword, p. 6. Thomas's post-war travelogue and book would help create the 'Lawrence legend'.

11. Lowell Thomas, *With Lawrence in Arabia* (1925), p. 249.

12. From Jackson's memoir, transcribed by him from a diary in a notebook-cum-scrapbook which also contains photographs, sketches, and Royal Flying Corps (RFC) documents. This was probably Ronald Jackson, born in 1898, who died in Coventry, where the documents were found, in 1980. A photograph of him in RFC uniform in Egypt shows a man of the right age for this suggested identification. The collection is in private ownership. Diaries of RFC mechanics are exceptionally rare and Jackson's complements that of Flight Sergeant George Hynes, published in *Lawrence of Arabia's Secret Air Force* by James Patrick Hynes (2010). In fact 'X Flight' might sound cloak-and-dagger but there was nothing secret about it beyond the usual military censorship.

13. Lowell Thomas, *With Lawrence in Arabia* (1925), p. 250.

14. The diary entry for 7 December includes: 'Went off on recce for missing bus [RFC term for aircraft]. During lunchtime Major Lawrence and Lt. Morgan walked in from Crossley in which they had set out early in the morning, also in search of the missing bus. Boy came in with news.' Lawrence's car had broken down; it was later discovered that 2nd Lieutenant Buchanan had landed the missing aircraft safely south of Aqaba.

15. Jackson's 1918 diary was lost, he says in some notes, 'as a result of the 1940 upheaval'—perhaps the devastating bombing of Coventry in November that year. Jackson signs off his notes with another broadside at Captain (as he became) Victor Siddons: 'Had we known or been told by the puerile "apprentice parson" of the object or aim of the campaign much more might have impinged on one's memory'. Siddons became commander of X Flight in June 1918 when it was moved to the forward base at Guweira. Jackson stayed in Arabia until at least the end of 1918.

16. Interview with Gray in *The Hornsey Journal*, 24 May 1935.

17. Lawrence was speaking to Gray at least four years before he joined the Royal Air Force (RAF), in 1922, under a pseudonym as 2nd Aircraftman John Hume Ross. His continued desire for anonymity and to escape from the psychic burdens of his time in Arabia led to spells as a private in the Tank Corps (under another pseudonym, T. E. Shaw), and then a return to the RAF. See also Jeremy Wilson, *Lawrence of Arabia* (1990), p. 667. Gray also recalled: 'Arabs used to call our golden sovereigns "King George's cavalry". Lawrence was rather casual about the way he distributed the gold, and on one occasion I remember he offered an Arab chief as much gold as he could take in one hand. Unfortunately for him, the man had a very large hand' (interview with Gray, *The Hornsey Journal*, 24 May 1935). Gray found Lawrence annoying at times (he was not the only one), because he did not always turn up where and when he said he would. Gray called Lawrence 'a free spirit' (personal communication from Gray's daughter to the author).

18. Voyage on SS *Borulos*: TNA, WO 95/4415, Hejaz Operations War Diary, 10 May 1918. Rushie Grey's recollections: personal communication from his daughter in Jamaica.

19. The original messages on 'Pigeon Service' paper, signed by Major Marshall, are privately owned by the family of their recipient, Major Robert Scott. The pigeon loft at Aqaba was in use until the end of the war.

20. The original message, in Scott's distinctive hand and torn from a notebook, is in the Gray collection.

21. Gray's flight alarmed Mabel, still grieving for her pilot brother, and she also had a bone to pick with him over a remark in his last letter, sent from the Grand Continental Hotel in Cairo: 'P. S. What do you mean by looking at a lady doctor's legs?' Letter from Mabel to Gray, 1 October 1918.

22. Letters from Major Marshall to Gray, 27 January 1918 and 9 June 1918. Marshall particularly enjoyed Gray's 'London jokes'. Marshall was one of the four original officers of the Hejaz Military Mission.

CHAPTER 16

1. Henry Brocklehurst's diary, 10 May 1918, Van Haeften collection. The diary is privately owned by his family and extracts are published here for the first time. Brocklehurst, who later had the dubious distinction of being the first Englishman to shoot a giant panda, bravely led a Special Service Detachment of commandos as a Lieutenant-Colonel in Burma during the Second World War; he drowned there while fording a river.

2. Brocklehurst's diary, 13 and 17 May 1918, Van Haeften collection.

3. Brocklehurst's condemnation recalls the attitude taken towards Lawrence's untidy appearance in his early weeks in Arabia (though that had earlier been Lawrence's default position at GHQ in Egypt too).

4. Taken from the memoir of Captain Lewen Weldon of the Eastern Mediterranean Special Intelligence Bureau, pp. 173–4. Weldon captained spy ships and extracts from the typescript document, which is privately owned by his family, are published here for the first time.

5. See H. V. F. Winstone, *The Diaries of Parker Pasha* (1983), p. 105.

6. Captain Lewen Weldon's unpublished memoir, p. 173.

7. See Yigal Sheffy, *British Military Intelligence in the Palestine Campaign, 1914–1918* (1998), pp. 223, 227.

8. Captain Lewen Weldon's unpublished memoir, p. 241. Weldon's memoir reveals that he worked for the Egyptian Survey and had begun a six-year survey of Sinai in 1908–9. The British military were concerned to have up-to-date information on this strategically vital region which bordered the Suez Canal, their lifeline to India (the British had in effect been in control of Egypt since 1882). Weldon was the first to identify and map the wells in Sinai: they were known as 'Weldon's wells'. The Jewish agronomist and British spy, Aaron Aaronsohn, subsequently gained kudos with the British for his knowledge of water sources in Sinai—but his apparently arcane information was already sitting in a file somewhere in Cairo thanks to Weldon's work. A final note on Weldon: the Sinai survey work of Newcombe, Lawrence, and Woolley in early 1914, which was an archaeological fig-leaf to cover a military survey, was not a one-off episode carried out because of rising tensions and the risk of war. In fact Lawrence was helping with the final phase of a well-established project which had had Weldon at its centre.

9. Joshua Teitelbaum, *The Rise and Fall of the Hashemite Kingdom of Arabia* (2001), pp. 78–9.

10. George Wyman Bury, *Pan-Islam* (1919), p. 25.

11. George Wyman Bury, *Pan-Islam* (1919), p. 31.

12. The ships were cruisers *Fox*, *Minerva*; R. I. M. ships *Northbrook*, *Dufferin*, *Hardinge*, *Minto*; armed boarding steamers *Suva*, *Lunka*, *Lama*, *Perth*, *Scotia*, *Enterprise*; armed tug *Slieve Foy*; armed launch *Kameran*. See Gregory P. Gilbert, 'HMS Suva, Captain W. H. D. Boyle and the Red Sea Patrol 1916–1918: The Strategic

Effects of an Auxiliary Cruiser upon the Arab Revolt', in *International Journal of Naval History*, Vol. 8, No. 1 (April 2009); and The Earl of Cork and Orrery, *My Naval Life* (1942), p. 96. Captain Boyle later became the Earl of Cork and Orrery.

13. SAD, Wingate Papers, 139/7/1, Wingate to Wilson, 28 August 1916.

14. See Gregory P. Gilbert, 'HMS Suva, Captain W. H. D. Boyle and the Red Sea Patrol 1916–1918: The Strategic Effects of an Auxiliary Cruiser upon the Arab Revolt', in *International Journal of Naval History*, Vol. 8, No. 1 (April 2009).

15. Lady Wester Wemyss, *The Life and Letters of Lord Wester Wemyss* (1935), p. 317.

16. Lady Wester Wemyss, *The Life and Letters of Lord Wester Wemyss* (1935), p. 345.

17. 'The skill and daring of the commanders of our patrol-ships have now found ways through those reefs, and left us little or nothing to learn about the coastal development of either Hejaz or Asir-Yemen'. D. G. Hogarth, 'War and Discovery in Arabia', *The Geographical Journal*, Vol. LV, No. 5 (May 1920), p. 434.

18. The account is in Gray's hand in his capacity as president of the Mess Committee. The bill was for six shillings per day, with nineteen shillings and ten pence (nearly £1 in today's money) owed for bridge. Privately owned by Gray's family.

19. The note is undated, but must have been written shortly before Gray left for leave in Egypt on 9 May 1917. Dugdale wanted a dreadnought driver, a broad head mashie, a putter 'similar to the Colonel's', and a dozen golf balls. As an afterthought, he asked for a mashie for Lieutenant 'Hoppy' Hopwood.

20. Letter from Gray to his fiancée, Mabel, 5 April 1918.

21. SAD, Wingate Papers, 145/8/87–8, Wingate to secretary of state for war, 25 June 1917.

22. Malcolm Brown (ed.), *Lawrence of Arabia: The Selected Letters* (2005), p. 109.

23. T. E. Lawrence, *Seven Pillars of Wisdom* (1935), pp. 109–10.

24. Lady Wester Wemyss, *The Life and Letters of Lord Wester Wemyss* (1935), p. 359.

CHAPTER 17

1. The Aqaba cipher officer for most of the time covered by the secret message notebooks (and later) was Lieutenant Montagu Pemell Leith. In a letter to Gray dated 16 January 1918, his friend and fellow cipher officer at GHQ Cairo, Lieutenant John Kealy, mentions that Leith ('a great fellow') was then cipher officer at Aqaba. Major Scott also mentions Leith in his diary. Captain Henry Hornby, an explosives expert, took over as cipher officer for about nine days in February, when Leith had to go on urgent leave to England. Hornby had been left partially blind and deaf after part of an explosive blew up in his face, and did the ciphering work after his recovery while awaiting the doctor's go-ahead to return to the desert. Secret message notebook, cables dated 30 January, 2 February, and 8 February 1918. Two separate hands, that of Leith and presumably Hornby, are apparent in the three notebooks, which are privately owned by Gray's family.

2. The text in the messages is given with the original, sometimes erratic, spelling, punctuation, and syntax.

3. AWM, 4, 1/10/11, War Diary, Political Intelligence, GHQ, EEF, 23 January 1918.

4. Ottoman intelligence comprised the Teşkilât-i Mahsusa or Special Organization (the expression also suggests special operations) and military intelligence. The military intelligence department of the 4th Army, and later the Yilderim Army Group, was in charge of counter-intelligence and counter-espionage, including the handling of double agents. If Maurice had indeed become a double agent, he was probably under the joint control of Ottoman military intelligence and German intelligence, though there is no positive evidence of this (personal communication from Professor Yigal Sheffy, who has been on the trail of Maurice for some years).

5. WO 157/700: Cairo Intelligence Summary, 28 January 1916. Cited in Yigal Sheffy, *British Military Intelligence in the Palestine Campaign, 1914–1918* (1998), p. 190. The fuller name used was Mustafa al-Libai, perhaps a misleading ploy to suggest that Maurice was Libyan; he used a number of names (personal communication from Professor Yigal Sheffy). Mustafa/Maurice's intelligence was corroborated by another source, though this does not necessarily imply that he was working solely or at all for the British.

6. WO 157/705: EEF Intelligence Diary, 2 and 5 June 1916. Cited in Yigal Sheffy, *British Military Intelligence in the Palestine Campaign, 1914–1918* (1998), pp. 81, 121, who describes Maurice as 'the highly regarded British-controlled agent'.

7. Clayton did, however, point out that Maurice was now less useful in Syria, because he would not work with the French, who were affronted by Maurice's telling them they were not wanted by the Syrian people. It seems likely, though it cannot be proved, that Maurice was Syrian. HUA, Papers of Sir Mark Sykes, U DDSY2/4/129, letter from Clayton to Sykes, 26 December 1916.

8. Keith Jeffery, *MI6: The History of the Secret Intelligence Service, 1909–1949* (2010), p. 90.

9. TNA, WO 33/935, No. 7477, Macdonogh to Murray, 27 May 1917. Cited in Polly A. Mohs, *Military Intelligence and the Arab Revolt* (2008), p. 145.

10. The British 'representative', however, would not have been Maurice, as the Eastern Mediterranean Special Intelligence Bureau (EMSIB) used this word to describe case officers (to use a modern intelligence term). The officer in this case was Major (later Lieutenant-Colonel) Cuthbert Binns, who was EMSIB's man in Berne. Binns and Aubrey Herbert were busy with Ottoman–British peace overtures during the war (Professor Yigal Sheffy, personal communication).

11. A plausible case could be made for Maurice becoming a double agent for the Ottomans and Germans only after he was released from Berlin following his apparent defection. He could have been working solely for the British until that point, loyally serving his case officers while this suited his own interests. We cannot be sure, moreover, that the German and Ottoman services were convinced that they had managed to turn him against his British employers. It would be

intriguing to study the interrogation reports, if they still exist in German arch-ives. I am grateful to Professor Yigal Sheffy for making these points (personal communication).

12. AWM, 4, 1/10/12, War Diary, Political Intelligence, GHQ, EEF, 21 February 1918.

13. In 'Extracts from Summary of the Hejaz Revolt, War Office, London 1918', in *Journal of the T. E. Lawrence Society*, Vol. III. No. 1 (Summer 1993), p. 24.

14. 'For Lawrence from Col. Deedes. Am very anxious to start without delay. Am short agents east of Jordan to tap country round Damascus & within Syria. If you can organise from your present position I will arrange connection between yourself & us. Service will eventually be run by E.M.S.I.B.' Major Wyndham Henry Deedes (promoted to Lieutenant-Colonel on 21 March 1917) was chief of section 1b in the EEF Intelligence Department. The Arab Bureau was the communication chan-nel through which the cables were transmitted to the Aqaba base. See Yigal Sheffy, *British Military Intelligence in the Palestine Campaign, 1914–1918* (London: Frank Cass & Co. Ltd, 1998), chart 3 after p. 330.

15. Secret cable to Aqaba, 31 December 1917.

16. Secret cable from Aqaba to Arab Bureau, 20 January 1918.

17. Secret cable from Aqaba to Arab Bureau, 6 January 1918.

18. Yigal Sheffy, *British Military Intelligence in the Palestine Campaign, 1914–1918* (1998), pp. 223, 237.

19. AWM 1/12/5, Intelligence Reports, GHQ, EEF, 31 May 1916.

20. AWM 1/12/7, Intelligence Reports, GHQ, EEF, 14 November 1916.

21. The *Arab Bulletin* No. 94, 25 June 1918, in R. Bidwell (ed.), *The Arab Bulletin 1916–19*, Vols I–IV (1986), p. 216. The date of the attack is given in the Hejaz Armoured Car Section War Diary: TNA, WO 95/4415, 12 June 1918.

22. TNA, WO 95/4415, Hejaz Operations War Diary, 23 June 1918. 'Multiple stab wounds' are recorded in Powell's army record. His son told me that the knife wounds went through his father's wrist and into his stomach, and also through his shoulder and into his lung. Powell spoke Arabic well and was able to plead for his life. He risked serious peritonitis but pulled through. His passport records a legacy of the attack: 'left thumb defective'.

23. Message sent on 12 January 1918. Arnold was then only 17 years old and a stu-dent at New College, Oxford. Lawrence replied on 13 January that he would ask Arnold, who did not join the Arab Bureau.

24. AWM, 4, 1/7/10, War Diary, Political Intelligence, GHQ, EEF, Appendix No. 2, July 1917.

25. AWM, 4, 1/7/10, War Diary, Political Intelligence, GHQ, EEF, 26 July 1917.

26. The *Arab Bulletin* No. 90, 24 May 1918, in R. Bidwell (ed.), *The Arab Bulletin 1916–19*, Vols I–IV (1986), p. 171. Soon after, Aqaba learned that: 'Abdullah reports Fakreddin Pasha left Medina for Syria on Feb. 6 ... confirmed by deserters and by French Missionary [almost certainly the spy, Père Jaussen] & prisoners taken Feb 8th Bir Jedid'.

27. Secret cable from Aqaba to Bright, 8 February 1918.

28. CAC, Papers of George Lloyd, GLLD 9/10, Clayton to Captain George Lloyd, 25 October 1917.

29. LHCMA, Joyce Papers 1/M/13, Dawnay to Joyce, 22 February 1918.

30. The *Arab Bulletin*, Vol. IV, 1919, in R. Bidwell (ed.), *The Arab Bulletin 1916–19*, Vols I–IV (1986), p. 50. Bassett obtained the accounts during his lengthy interrogation of Fakhri Pasha, the Commandant at Medina, when he finally surrendered in January 1919.

31. A study of the files of the 2nd Division (Intelligence) of the Ottoman General Staff in the military archives at Ankara (known as ATASE) would be very rewarding and undoubtedly give a more complete picture of the Ottomans and the Arab Revolt. Like all the Turkish records, the files are extensive and include intelligence estimates, missions, and reports. See Edward Erickson, 'The Turkish Official Military Histories of the First World War: a Bibliographic Essay', *Middle Eastern Studies*, Vol. 39, No. 3 (2003), pp. 190–8.

CHAPTER 18

1. T. E. Lawrence, *Seven Pillars of Wisdom* (1935), p. 579.

2. T. E. Lawrence, *Seven Pillars of Wisdom: The Complete 1922 'Oxford' Text* (2004), p. 702, cited by James Barr, *Setting the Desert on Fire* (2007), p. 270.

3. T. E. Lawrence, *Seven Pillars of Wisdom* (1935), p. 578.

4. Major Sir Hubert Young, *The Independent Arab* (1933), p. 206.

5. Major Scott's diary entry.

6. Gray told Mabel that flies 'have come from somewhere in millions. The Camel Corps must have brought them for last stunt. They camped near here'. Letter from Gray to Mabel, 14 September 1918.

7. Letter from Gray to Mabel, 14 September 1918.

8. The leaflet explained that holidaymakers had the choice of the overland route through Sinai ('all the delights of riding on a "ship of the desert"') or—a dig at some of the cramped and noisy steamers taken over by the Royal Navy—the sea passage on 'magnificently appointed saloon steamers' from Suez. Attractions did not stop at bathing, sea fishing, and 'motor trips up the beautiful wadis into the bracing interior': 'There is plenty of shooting at Aqaba' (Gray had experienced both excitable Bedouins celebrating a holiday and attacks by enemy aircraft). Forthcoming publications would include *Wonderful Wejh, Youth-Restoring Yenbo*, and *Jaunts round Jeddah*.

9. The *Arab Bulletin* No. 99, 6 August 1918, in R. Bidwell (ed.), *The Arab Bulletin 1916–19*, Vols I–IV (1986), p. 270.

10. TNA, WO 95/4415, Hejaz Operations War Diary, 21 August 1918.

11. TNA FO 882/17, cable from Bassett to director of Arab Bureau, 10 September 1918.

12. The *Arab Bulletin* No. 105, 8 October 1918, in R. Bidwell (ed.), *The Arab Bulletin 1916–19*, Vols I–IV (1986), p. 339.

13. See Eugene Rogan, *The Fall of the Ottomans: The Great War in the Middle East, 1914–1920* (London: Allen Lane, 2015), p. 373.

14. See Anthony Bruce, *The Last Crusade* (2003), pp. 213 and 228–9.

15. Major Scott's diary confirms that Powell arrived at Aqaba on SS *Imogene* on 7 August. The diary for that day also records: 'Lawrence arrived back at lunchtime by RAF car'. It is possible that Lawrence discussed Powell's new intelligence mission with him.

16. The original 'Pigeon Service' intelligence report, signed by Powell, is with Major Scott's descendants. It records that two copies were sent in case one pigeon went astray. These avian intelligence operatives were extensively used by the British in Palestine, Salonica, and Egypt as well as Arabia. In late 1916 the Arab Bureau had suggested that pigeons should be given to Lawrence for message carrying between Feisal and Yenbo: SAD, Wingate Papers, 144/3/19, Wingate to Wilson, 3 December 1916. One occasion when carrier pigeons were taken to Aqaba was on 1 June 1918, on SS *Spey*: TNA, WO 95/4415, Hejaz Operations War Diary. Scott's diary records that the pigeons left Aqaba on 21 October.

17. LHCMA, King's College, London, Joyce Papers, 1/263, Dawnay to Joyce, not dated but from context 20 September 1918. Cited in James Barr, *Setting the Desert on Fire* (2006), p. 280.

18. In treating Baku as his priority, and recovering Ottoman territory in the Caucasus from Russia to secure his country's eastern frontiers, Enver had in effect invited defeat in Palestine and Syria. He may even have made a political calculation to this effect—if so, it had a disastrous impact on the preservation of the Ottoman Empire. See Sean McMeekin, *The Ottoman Endgame: War, Revolution and the Making of the Modern Middle East, 1908–1923* (2015). pp. 398–401 and Eugene Rogan, *The Fall of the Ottomans: The Great War in the Middle East, 1914–1920* (2015) pp. 372–3.

19. IWM, Wilson Papers (Sir Henry Wilson, Chief of the Imperial General Staff), HHW2/33A/28, Allenby to Wilson, 19 October 1918. Cited by James Barr, *Setting the Desert on Fire* (2006), p. 299. Allenby was obeying orders from politicians, but it is worth saying that by 1917–18 most of the British government thought the Sykes-Picot map was dead as a blueprint. They saw it, as did the French premier Clemenceau, as an essay in pragmatism, a vague expression of spheres of influence, with details to be resolved by the winners when the time was right. The distinction would have been irrelevant to Feisal.

20. See James Barr, *Setting the Desert on Fire* (2007), p. 310.

21. Lawrence did not tell his superiors when Feisal appeared to be negotiating with the Turks in summer 1918. Elie Kedourie, 'Colonel Lawrence', in *The Cambridge Journal*, Vol. VII, No. 9 (June 1954), p. 525.

22. British Library, T. E. Lawrence Papers, Add 45914, f.42. Cited by James Barr, *Setting the Desert on Fire* (2006), p. 297.

23. Letter from Gray to Mabel, 17 October 1918.

24. Letter from Gray to Mabel, 17 October 1918.
25. The base commandant, Major Scott, was well aware of Gray's novel fishing methods. He had sent a surreal order to Gray the previous week: 'O.C. Works reports that bombing close to the North Pier is damaging same. Please give instructions that in future no bombs must be exploded within 500 yards of Pier.' Typed order signed by Scott, 24 October 1918. In the Gray collection.
26. Letter from Gray to his sister, Cecil, 29 October 1918. Mabel, still locked into depression over her brother Gerald's death, would feel no elation. In a letter to Gray dated 19 November 1918, Mabel said she felt 'ill and depressed', like so many others on the Home Front suffering bereavement, at the announcement of the Armistice with Germany on 11 November.
27. The original letter from Joyce to Scott, 2 October 1918, is still with Scott's family.
28. Letter from Gray to his mother, 6 November 1918.
29. The document, in Gray's hand, is in the Gray family collection.
30. Letter from Gray to his sister Cecil, 15 December 1918 (completed on 18 December).

CHAPTER 19

1. Letter from Lawrence to Charlotte Shaw, 18 October 1927, in Malcolm Brown (ed.), *Lawrence of Arabia: The Selected Letters* (2005), p. 371.
2. Gray to Mabel, 22 December 1918.
3. Gray to his mother, 22 December 1918.
4. MECA, Hogarth Papers, Hogarth to Clayton, 1 November 1918, cited in James Barr, *Setting the Desert on Fire* (2007), p. 300.
5. Gray to his sister, Cecil, 3 January 1919.
6. Gray to Mabel, 3 January 1919.
7. AWM 4, 1/6/32, Pt. 1, War Diary, General Staff, GHQ, EEF, 16 January 1919.
8. Cable no. 72 from Sykes in Aleppo to Prodrome (War Office), London, 10 January 1919. In Gray collection. There are crossings-out and edits, so the author seems to have drawn on conflicting accounts: the first version says the Bishop was publicly burned with paraffin, and the truth remains elusive. From the same source comes a 'Sworn declaration by Khafihadow Shirighdgian, Aleppo, Syria, January 1919' regarding the infamous massacres of 1915–16. Three thousand Armenians were deported from Aintab in July 1915 by road and boat to Derzor. After a year Zeki Bey arrived from Constantinople and forced about ten thousand Armenians to walk into the desert: 'Massacres then commenced and I saw 1200 surrounded by Chuchuns and Gendarmes in command of Zeki Bey who fired the first shot amongst these massed Armenians, men, women and children'. There are more assertions in a similar vein: typescript document in Gray family collection. Another curious document, typescript and also in Gray's hand, is headed 'Copy of secret telegram sent by Enver Pasha on 18/2/18'. It purports to be the Sultan's approval of 'the annihilation of the Armenian nation',

and orders that all Armenians apart from children under 5 years old should be 'conducted outside of the towns and massacred'; Armenian soldiers in the Turkish army should be secretly shot; and Armenian officers in the Turkish army should be imprisoned 'until further orders are issued'. Orders would be sent 'to all places by the Commander-in-Chief in 24 hours time to put these three items into effect'. Gray sent the document to Mabel with his letter of 16 April 1919, and the comment 'possibly a fake'. Certainly in the case of the 1915–16 Armenian genocide, orders were given to provincial governors orally and were not written down: see Eugene Rogan, *The Fall of the Ottomans: The Great War in the Middle East, 1914–1920* (2015), pp. 172–3. It seems that Gray's caution was justified and that the original telegram was most likely a fake (personal communication from Eugene Rogan).

9. Gray to Mabel, 10 March 1919. Major Frank Brayne, the political officer who was Gray's immediate superior, would have called Sykes something less complimentary. He grumpily complained that Sykes 'is quite without administrative experience. Thinks by a wave of the hand he can clean the town, organise up-to-date sanitation, collect all the girl prostitutes and rescue them, etc.' British Library, Brayne Papers, Mss Eur F152/20/113, undated but from context January 1919.

10. Letter from Gray to Mabel, 25 March 1919.

11. Letters of Hugh Drummond Pearson, Cambridge University Library, Royal Commonwealth Society, GBR/0115/RCMS 356, Pearson to his mother, 12 January 1919.

12. Letters of Hugh Drummond Pearson, Cambridge University Library, Royal Commonwealth Society, GBR/0115/RCMS 356, Pearson to his mother, 25 April 1919.

13. Letters of Hugh Drummond Pearson, Cambridge University Library, Royal Commonwealth Society, GBR/0115/RCMS 356, Pearson to his sister Ursula, 9 February 1919.

14. Letters of Hugh Drummond Pearson, Cambridge University Library, Royal Commonwealth Society, GBR/0115/RCMS 356, Pearson to his mother, 13 February 1919.

15. 'Urgent need at Aleppo, Aintab, Marash 5000 blankets, winter clothing 1000 men, 3000 women, 6000 children . . . also all kinds of hospital stores, drugs & equipment for 300 beds and 1000 outpatients'. Original transcription in Gray collection.

16. Gray to Mabel, 10 March 1919. Gray also referred to the massacre in a letter to his mother dated 8 March.

17. Gray to Mabel, 14 April 1919. Gray's presumption was correct: mass anti-French demonstrations by Arabs had degenerated into anti-Armenian rioting and then massacre. One of the triggers were reports that Armenians in Cilicia, Turkey had mistreated Arab troops of the Ottoman Army who were surrendering. Armenian-owned buildings and a French-sponsored orphanage were targeted, and in fact nearly two hundred Armenians were killed or injured. See Ali A. Allawi, *Faisal I of Iraq* (2014), p. 218.

18. Gray to Mabel, 9 June 1919.

19. 11 June 1919. The telegram conveying Feisal's message was officially sent from General Macandrew, GOC 5th Cavalry Division, Aleppo to Allenby. In Gray collection.

20. Messages undated but, from context, mid-June 1919. In Gray collection.

21. Gray was in the doghouse because he had said he would have to call on some American Red Cross nurses for tea, and then made things worse by adding: 'I don't think they are beautiful or young either...it will have to be a very beautiful face that will make me look at it twice'. Gray to Mabel, 14 April 1919. Mabel also chided him because his last letter was 'full of the girls you are meeting & beautiful Norah' [Altounyan, the doctor's daughter]: Mabel to Gray, 2 May 1919.

22. AWM 4, 1/6/32 Pt. 1, War Diary, GHQ, EEF, 10 January 1919.

23. *The Arab Bulletin* Vol. 4, 1919, in R. Bidwell (ed.), *The Arab Bulletin 1916–19*, Vols I–IV (1986), pp. 43–9.

24. At the IWM the two photographs described are credited to Ruhi (e.g Q 59999, showing Abdullah and Ali in Medina). But the same images, and others taken in and near Medina, are also in Bright's photograph albums at the National Army Museum. Q 59999 at IWM, for example, is 9411-120-34 at NAM. It seems feasible that Bright took all the photographs and gave some to Ruhi, which ended up at the IWM.

25. AWM 4, 1/6/32 Pt. 1, War Diary, GHQ, EEF, 11 January 1919.

26. *The Arab Bulletin* No. 113, 17 July 1919, in R. Bidwell (ed.), *The Arab Bulletin 1916–19*, Vols I–IV (1986), p. 127.

27. TNA, FO 882/23, Bassett to Arab Bureau, 27 May 1919, forwarding another copy of Yahya's report. Cited in Elie Kedourie, 'The Surrender of Medina in 1919', in *Islam in the Modern World and Other Studies* (1980), p. 288.

28. *The Arab Bulletin* No. 110, 30 April 1919, in R. Bidwell (ed.), *The Arab Bulletin 1916–19*, Vols I–IV (1986), p. 33.

29. AWM 4,1/6/32 Pt. 1, War Diary, GHQ, EEF, 18 January 1919.

30. AWM 4,1/6/32 Pt. 1, War Diary, GHQ, EEF, 8 January 1919.

31. TNA, WO 95/4415, Hejaz Operations War Diary, 5 March 1919.

32. From Bright's obituary in Christ's Hospital School magazine, *The Blue*, Vol. L, No. 3 (July 1923). At National Army Museum, Papers of Captain Leslie Leonard Bright, 9411-118-1.

33. *The Arab Bulletin* No. 111, 24 May 1919, in R. Bidwell (ed.), *The Arab Bulletin 1916–19*, Vols I–IV (1986), pp. 59–60, based on Ruhi's reports.

34. *The Arab Bulletin* No. 112, 24 June 1919, in R. Bidwell (ed.), *The Arab Bulletin 1916–19*, Vols I–IV (1986), p. 85.

35. TNA, FO 882/21, Bassett to Arab Bureau, 27 May 1919.

36. TNA, WO 95/4415, Hejaz Operations War Diary, 19 July 1919.

37. T. E. Lawrence, *Seven Pillars of Wisdom: The Complete 1922 'Oxford' Text* (2004), p. 352. Lawrence toned down these comments considerably in the privately printed edition of 1926 and in the trade edition that appeared after his death in 1935.

38. Jeremy Wilson, Lawrence's official biographer, has consistently made this point in his many indispensable writings; as has Professor Stephen E. Tabachnick. See, for example, the latter's comments at telawrence.blogspot.co.uk (2012).

39. See Brian Holden Reid, 'The Experience of the Arab Revolt as Interpreted in T. E. Lawrence's Seven Pillars of Wisdom', in *Journal of the T. E. Lawrence Society*, Vol. IV, No. 2 (Spring 1995).

40. If Wilson ever confided any of his feelings to his wife or daughter, or to friends in rural Hampshire when he retired, they sank to oblivion, lost fragments of his forgotten story.

EPILOGUE

1. D. G. Hogarth, 'War and Discovery in Arabia', *The Geographical Journal*, Vol. LV, No. 5 (May 1920), p. 438. McMahon's remarks are preceded by: '*(Colonel Lawrence could not be persuaded to speak)*'. This was not the first such occasion. After a stirring talk to the Royal Geographical Society on 15 December 1919 by Captain E. H. Keeling, on his escape as a prisoner of war in Turkey, the president reluctantly had to say: 'Colonel Lawrence of Arabian fame is present, but he has asked to be excused from speaking': *The Geographical Journal*, Vol. LV, No. 4 (April 1920), p. 288. Neither reference has been noted before, to the best of my knowledge, in publications about Lawrence.

2. Lawrence seems to have been both attracted and repelled by this realization.

3. Lowell Thomas, *Publicity*, in A. W. Lawrence (ed.), *T. E. Lawrence by His Friends* (1937), p. 215.

4. David Garnett (ed.), *The Letters of T. E. Lawrence* (1938), p. 379. Letter from Lawrence to Robert Graves, 12 November 1922.

5. LHCMA, Joyce Papers, Akaba II/19, transcript of Joyce's BBC broadcast of 14 July 1941.

6. Robert Graves, *Lawrence and the Arabs* (1927), p. 6.

7. T. E. Lawrence, *Seven Pillars of Wisdom* (1935), Preface.

8. E. M. Forster, *Abinger Harvest* (1936), p. 136.

9. See Neil Dearberg, 'Comments on *Seven Pillars of Wisdom* by Lt-Gen. Sir Henry Chauvel, GCMG, KCB, Commander Desert Mounted Corps', in *Journal of the T. E. Lawrence Society*, Vol. XXIV, No. 1 (2014/15), pp. 9–37.

10. H. V. F. Winstone, *The Diaries of Parker Pasha* (1983), p. 153.

11. Lawrence's accurate account of details of the military campaign, however, has been borne out by the painstaking archaeological fieldwork of the Great Arab Revolt Project, carried out between 2006 and 2014. See Neil Faulkner, *Lawrence of Arabia's War* (2016) and Nicholas J. Saunders, *Desert Insurgency: Archaeology, T. E. Lawrence and the Great Arab Revolt* (2017).

12. See Scott Anderson, *Lawrence in Arabia. War, Deceit, Imperial Folly and the Making of the Modern Middle East* (2013), pp. 385 and 409–10.

13. *Tactics of the Arab Army*, pamphlet (5 pages, restricted use), 13 August 1920, issued by the General Staff of the Mesopotamia Expeditionary Force and 'obtained from the General Staff, EEF. The contents are not all applicable to this country'. The EEF give forthright views on the considerable limitations of Bedouin fighters and the Regular Arab Army alike during the Arab Revolt (the sort of things that Garland, Newcombe, and almost every officer apart from Lawrence tended to say). The date of publication seems significant, given that the armed revolt in Iraq had broken out just two months earlier, in June 1920. So the British Army there must have been anxious to hear from the EEF about weaknesses they could exploit in the tactics of the Iraqi rebels, assuming they would fight like the Hashemites. While the EEF's comments are accurate in general, they do not take into account the Arab rebels' value to Allenby as guerrilla fighters and in pinning down Turkish troops who might otherwise have been moved to confront him in Palestine—though it is arguable that the massive numerical superiority of Allenby's army and his excellent use of deception schemes (and the fact that many of the Medina garrison were debilitated through disease) would have taken him to Damascus in any case. I am grateful to Gregory Pos for drawing this pamphlet to my attention.

14. This has been pointed out, for example, by John E. Mack, *A Prince of Our Disorder: the Life of T. E. Lawrence* (1976) and by Stephen E. Tabachnick. See, for example, the latter's comments at telawrence.blogspot.co.uk (2012).

15. LHCMA, King's College, London, Joyce Papers, 1/M/42, 21/2/36, Wingate to Wilson, 21 February 1936.

16. TNA, London, part of the map series MPK 1/410.

17. Tran, Mark, and Weaver, Matthew, 'ISIS Announces Islamic Caliphate in area Straddling Iraq and Syria', *The Guardian*, 30 June 2014.

18. *LA Daily News*, 7 February 2014.

19. Eretz Zen, 'Is Abu Bakr al-Baghdadi the Man in the Recent ISIL Video?', youtube.com.

20. See Patrick Coburn, *Why Join Islamic State?* in *London Review of Books*, Vol. 37, No. 13 (2 July 2015). At the time of writing (November 2016) another Sunni rebel group in Syria, Ahrar al-Sham, is receiving support from Saudi Arabia and is allied with Jabhat Fatah al-Sham.

21. A perceptive observation made in 2011 is still applicable: 'when one notices the paucity of current information (not just in the media) about tribal structures and composition, whether in Afghanistan, Yemen, Libya, or Syria (and to a lesser degree in Iraq), the absence of present-day Lawrences is keenly felt. Indeed, can anyone hope to understand the conflict in Libya without a thorough appreciation of the tribes that make up Libyan society?' Jacob Rosen, 'The Legacy of Lawrence and the New Arab Awakening', in *Israeli Journal of Foreign Affairs*, Vol. 5, No. 3 (2011).

Bibliography

ARCHIVAL SOURCES

Australian War Memorial (AWM)
War Diaries, Political Intelligence, General Headquarters (GHQ), Egyptian Expeditionary Force (EEF), accessed online, http://www.awm.gov.au/collection/records
Intelligence Diaries, GHQ, EEF, accessed online, http://www.awm.gov.au/collection/
records

British Library, India Office Records (IOR)
Brayne Papers
Arabia: British Agency, Jeddah—Services of Hussein Effendi Ruhi
Arabia: Report on Mecca

Cambridge University Library
The papers of Charles Hardinge, 1st Baron Hardinge of Penshurst
Letters of Hugh Drummond Pearson

Churchill Archives Centre (CAC), Churchill College, Cambridge
Lord Lloyd Papers
Wemyss Papers

Hull University Archives (HUA), Hull History Centre
Papers of Sir Mark Sykes, accessed online, http://www.britishonlinearchives.co.uk/
collection.php?cid=9781851171507
Online catalogue: http://catalogue.hullhistorycentre.org.uk/catalogue/U-DDSY
(Home page for the Sykes Collection)
http://hullhistorycentre.org.uk/ (Home page for the History Centre)

Imperial War Museum (IWM), London
Private Papers of Major-General Sir Arthur Lynden-Bell

Liddell Hart Centre for Military Archives (LHCMA), King's College, London
Joyce Papers

Middle East Centre Archive (MECA), St Antony's College, Oxford
J. W. A. Young collection
Thomas Edward Lawrence collection

National Army Museum
Papers of Captain Leslie Leonard Bright

Pembroke College, University of Cambridge
Storrs Papers

Sudan Archive, University of Durham (SAD)
Wingate Papers
Clayton Papers

The National Archives (TNA)
AIR 30
ADM 53
FO 141
FO 371
FO 686
FO 847
FO 882
WO 33
WO 95
WO 157
WO 158

PRIVATE COLLECTIONS

Adam collection (Rushie Grey)
Bray collection
Cochrane collection
Duce collection (Gilman)
Gilman collection
Gray collection
McCrum collection (Weldon)
Powell collection
Scott collection
Van Haeften collection (Brocklehurst)
Walker collection (Goodchild)
Zuber collection (Jackson)

PUBLISHED SOURCES

[Anon.] *A Brief Record of the Advance of the Egyptian Expeditionary Force* (Cairo: Government Press and Survey of Egypt, 1919).
Aldington, Richard, *Lawrence of Arabia* (London: Collins, 1955).
Allawi, Ali A., *Faisal I of Iraq* (London: Yale University Press, 2014).
Allen, Sir Mark, 'Lawrence Among the Arabs', in *Journal of the T. E. Lawrence Society*, Vol. XX, No. 1, (2010/11), pp. 10–20.

Anderson, Scott, *Lawrence in Arabia. War, Deceit, Imperial Folly and the Making of the Modern Middle East* (New York: Doubleday, 2013).

Antonius, George, *The Arab Awakening* (London: Hamish Hamilton, 1938).

Arab Bureau (ed.), *A Tribal Handbook of Syria and Parts of the Sinai Peninsula* (Cairo: Arab Bureau, 1918).

Asher, Michael, *Lawrence: the Uncrowned King of Arabia* (New York: Viking, 1998).

Atwan, Abdel Bari, *Islamic State: the Digital Caliphate* (London: Saqi Books, 2015).

Badcock, G. E., *A History of the Transport Services of the Egyptian Expeditionary Force, 1916–1917–1918* (London: Hugh Rees, 1925).

Barbor, Patricia, *Desert Treks from Jeddah* (London: Stacey International, 1996).

Barr, James, *Setting the Desert on Fire* (London: Bloomsbury, 2007).

Barr, James, *A Line in the Sand: Britain, France and the Struggle that Shaped the Middle East* (London: Simon & Schuster UK Ltd, 2011).

Batey, Mavis, *Dilly: The Man who Broke Enigmas* (London: Dialogue, 2009).

Berton, Joseph, 'Lawrence and the Imperial Camel Corps', in *Journal of the T. E. Lawrence Society*, Vol. XX, No. 2 (2010/11), pp. 88–110.

Berton, Joseph, *T. E. Lawrence and the Arab Revolt. An Illustrated Guide* (Madrid: Andrea Press, 2011).

Bidwell, R. (ed.), *The Arab Bulletin 1916–19*, Vols I–IV (Cambridge: Cambridge Archive Editions, 1986).

Bidwell, R. (ed.), *Arabian Personalities of the Early Twentieth Century* (Cambridge: Oleander Press, 1986). Reprint of 1917 first edition (Cairo: Arab Bureau).

Blackmore, Charles, *In the Footsteps of Lawrence of Arabia* (London: Harrap, 1986).

Blenkinsop, Sir L. J. and Rainey, J. W., *History of the Great War based on Official Documents. Veterinary Series* (London: HMSO, 1925).

Bray, N. N. E., *Shifting Sands* (London: Unicorn Press, 1934).

Brémond, E., *Le Hedjaz dans la guerre mondiale*, (Paris: Payot, 1931).

Briggs, Martin S., *Through Egypt in War-Time* (London: T. Fisher Unwin, 1918).

Brown, Malcolm (ed.), *Lawrence of Arabia: The Selected Letters* (London: Little Books, 2005).

Brown, Malcolm (ed.), *T. E. Lawrence in War and Peace: An Anthology of the Military Writings of Lawrence of Arabia* (London: Greenhill, 2005).

Brown, Michael and Cave, Julia, *A Touch of Genius: The Life of T. E. Lawrence* (London: J. M. Dent & Sons Ltd, 1988).

Bruce, Anthony, *The Last Crusade* (London: John Murray, 2002).

Buchan, John, *Greenmantle* (London: Hodder & Stoughton, 1916).

Bury, George Wyman, *Pan-Islam* (London: Macmillan & Co., 1919).

Cameliers and camels at war, https://nzhistory.govt.nz/war/camel-corps/camels-and-cameliers (New Zealand Ministry for Culture and Heritage, 2009), accessed online.

Carman, Barry and McPherson, John (eds), *Bimbashi McPherson, A Life in Egypt* (London: BBC, 1983).

Carruthers, Douglas, *Arabian Adventure: to the Great Nafud in Quest of the Oryx* (London, H. F. & G. Witherby, 1935).

Carver, Field Marshall Lord, *The Turkish Front 1914–1918* (London: Sidgwick & Jackson, 2003).

Charmley, John, *Lord Lloyd and the Decline of the British Empire* (London: Weidenfeld & Nicolson, 1987).

Coburn, Patrick, 'Why Join Islamic State?' in *London Review of Books*, Vol. 37, No. 13 (2 July 2015).

Dearberg, Neil, 'Comments on *Seven Pillars of Wisdom* by Lt-Gen. Sir Henry Chauvel, GCMG, KCB, Commander Desert Mounted Corps', in *Journal of the T. E. Lawrence Society*, Vol. XXIV, No. 1 (2014/15), pp. 9–37.

Dingli, Sophia and Kennedy, Caroline, 'Lawrence, Tribes, Insurgents and Lessons', *Journal of the T. E. Lawrence Society*, Vol. XXIII, No. 1 (2013/14), pp. 7–27.

Earl of Cork and Orrery (William Boyle), *My Naval Life* (London: Hutchinson, 1942).

Erickson, Edward, 'The Turkish Official Military Histories of the First World War: a Bibliographic Essay', in *Middle Eastern Studies*, Vol. 39, No. 3 (2003), pp. 190–8.

Faulkner, Neil, *Lawrence of Arabia's War: the Arabs, the British and the Remaking of the Middle East in WW1* (New Haven: Yale University Press, 2016).

Fisher, John, 'The Rabegh Crisis, 1916–17: "A Comparatively Trivial Question" or "A Self-Willed Disaster"', in *Middle Eastern Studies*, Vol. 38, No. 3 (2002), pp. 73–92.

Forster, E. M., *Abinger Harvest* (London: Edward Arnold & Co., 1936).

Fussell, Paul, *The Great War and Modern Memory* (Oxford: Oxford University Press, 1975).

Garnett, David (ed.), *The Letters of T. E. Lawrence* (London: Jonathan Cape, 1938).

Gilbert, Gregory P., 'HMS Suva, Captain W. H. D. Boyle and the Red Sea Patrol 1916–1918: The Strategic Effects of an Auxiliary Cruiser upon the Arab Revolt', in *International Journal of Naval History*, Vol. 8, No. 1 (April 2009).

Glen, Douglas, *In the Steps of Lawrence of Arabia* (London: Rich & Cowan Ltd, no date given, but 1939).

Grainger, John D., *The Battle for Palestine 1917* (Woodbridge: The Boydell Press, 2006).

Graves, P. (ed.), *Memoirs of King Abdullah of Transjordan* (London: Jonathan Cape, 1950).

Graves, Robert, *Lawrence and the Arabs* (London: Jonathan Cape, 1927).

Greaves, Adrian, *Lawrence of Arabia: Mirage of a Desert War* (London: Weidenfeld & Nicolson, 2007).

Guillaume, Renée and Guillaume, André, *An Introduction and Notes: Seven Pillars of Wisdom* (Oxshott: Tabard Press, 1998).

Henty, George, *The Dash for Khartoum: a Tale of the Nile Expedition* (London: Blackie & Son, 1892).

Hogarth, D. G., 'War and Discovery in Arabia', *The Geographical Journal*, Vol. LV, No. 5 (May 1920), pp. 422–39.

Hogarth, D. G., *Hejaz Before World War One: A Handbook* (Cairo: Arab Bureau, 2nd edition, 1917). Reprinted 1978 (Cambridge, UK: Oleander Press).

Hynes, James Patrick, *Lawrence of Arabia's Secret Air Force* (Barnsley: Pen & Sword Aviation, 2010).

Institut du monde arabe, *Photographies d'Arabie: Hedjaz 1907–1917* (Paris: Institut du monde arabe, 1999).

James, Lawrence, *The Golden Warrior* (New York: Skyhorse, 2008). Originally published 1990.

Jarar, Salah (ed.), *Min watha'iq al-thawra al-`arabiyya al-kubra: al-rahla al-rabi`a* (From the Documents of the Great Arab Revolt: The Fourth Journey by Husayn Ruhi), (Amman: The Military Presses, no date given, but 1997).

Jeffery, Keith, *MI6: The History of the Secret Intelligence Service, 1909–1949* (London: Bloomsbury, 2010).

Johnson-Allen, John, *T. E. Lawrence and the Red Sea Patrol* (Barnsley: Pen & Sword Military, 2015).

Karsh, Efraim and Karsh, Inari, 'Myth in the Desert, or Not the Great Arab Revolt', in *Middle Eastern Studies*, Vol. 33, No. 2 (April 1997), pp. 267–312.

Kedourie, Elie, 'Colonel Lawrence', in *The Cambridge Journal*, Vol. VII, No. 9 (June 1954).

Kedourie, Elie (ed.), 'The Surrender of Medina in 1919', in *Islam in the Modern World and Other Studies* (London: Mansell, 1980).

Keeling, Captain E. H., 'In Northern Anatolia, 1917', in *The Geographical Journal*, Vol. LV, No. 4 (April 1920), pp. 270–89.

Kirkbride, Alec Seath, *A Crackle of Thorns* (London: John Murray, 1956).

Knightley, Phillip and Simpson, Colin, *The Secret Lives of Lawrence of Arabia* (London: Nelson, 1969).

Korda, Michael, *Hero: the Life and Legend of Lawrence of Arabia* (New York: Harper, 2010).

Lawrence, A. W. (ed.), *T. E. Lawrence by his Friends* (London: Jonathan Cape, 1937).

Lawrence, A. W. (ed.), *Letters to T. E. Lawrence* (London: Jonathan Cape, 1962).

Lawrence, M. R. (ed.), *The Home Letters of T. E. Lawrence and His Brothers* (Oxford: Blackwell, 1954).

Lawrence, T. E., *Seven Pillars of Wisdom* (London: Jonathan Cape, 1935).

Lawrence, T. E., *Oriental Assembly* (London: Williams and Norgate, 1939).

Lawrence, T. E., *Seven Pillars of Wisdom: the Complete 1922 "Oxford" Text* (Fordingbridge: Castle Hill/J. and N. Wilson, 2nd edition, 2004).

Leclerc, Christophe, 'The French Soldiers in the Arab Revolt: Some Aspects of Their Contribution', in *Journal of the T. E. Lawrence Society*, Vol. IX, No. 1 (Autumn 1999), pp. 7–27.

Leclerc, Christophe, 'French Eye-Witness Accounts of Lawrence and the Arab Revolt, Part 1', in *Journal of the T. E. Lawrence Society*, Vol. XX, No. 1 (2010/11).

Leclerc, Christophe, 'French Eye-Witness Accounts of Lawrence and the Arab Revolt, Part 2', in *Journal of the T. E. Lawrence Society*, Vol. XX, No. 2 (2010/11).

Leclerc, Christophe, 'T. E. Lawrence and Edouard Brémond: Two Views of the Middle East, Two Experiences of the Guerrilla', in *Journal of the T. E. Lawrence Society*, Vol. XXV, No. 1 (2015/16).

Liddell Hart, B. H., *'T. E. Lawrence': In Arabia and After* (London: Jonathan Cape, 1934).

Lockman, J. N., *Scattered Tracks on the Lawrence Trail* (Whitmore Lake, Michigan: Falcon Books, 1996).

Lüdke, Tilman, *Jihad Made in Germany: Ottoman and German Propaganda and Intelligence Operations in the First World War* (Münster: LIT Verlag, 2005).

Lunt, Lieutenant-Colonel J. D., 'An Unsolicited Tribute', in *Blackwood's Magazine*, April 1955, pp. 289–96.

Mack, John E., *A Prince of Our Disorder: The Life of T. E. Lawrence* (London: Weidenfeld and Nicholson, 1976).

Marquess of Anglesey, *A History of the British Cavalry, 1816–1919,* Vol. 5: 1914–1919, Egypt, Palestine and Syria (London: Pen & Sword Books, 1994).

McGuirk, Russell, *The Sanusi's Little War* (London: Arabian Publishing, 2007).

McMeekin, Sean, *The Berlin-Baghdad Express: The Ottoman Empire and Germany's Bid for World Power, 1898–1918* (London: Allen Lane, 2010).

McMeekin, Sean, *The Ottoman Endgame: War, Revolution and the Making of the Modern Middle East, 1908–1923* (London: Allen Lane, 2015).

Melotte, Edward (ed.), *Mons, Anzac and Kut by an M.P. (Lieutenant Colonel the Hon. Aubrey Herbert M.P.)* (Barnsley: Pen & Sword Military, 2009).

Mohs, Polly A., *Military Intelligence and the Arab Revolt. The First Modern Intelligence War* (London: Routledge, 2008).

Mousa, Suleiman, *T. E. Lawrence: An Arab View* (London: Oxford University Press, 1966).

Murphy, David, *The Arab Revolt 1916–18: Lawrence Sets Arabia Ablaze* (Oxford: Osprey, 2008).

Newbolt, Henry, *Collected Poems 1897–1907* (London: Thomas Nelson, no date given, but 1910).

Nutting, Anthony, *Lawrence of Arabia: the Man and the Motive* (London: Hollis & Carter, 1961).

Philby, H. St. John B., *Arabian Days: An Autobiography* (London: Robert Hale, 1948).

Raswan, Carl R., *The Black Tents of Arabia (My Life Amongst the Bedouins)* (London: Paternoster Library, no date given but c. 1935).

Reid, Brian Holden, 'The Experience of the Arab Revolt as Interpreted in T. E. Lawrence's *Seven Pillars of Wisdom*', in *Journal of the T. E. Lawrence Society*, Vol. IV, No. 2 (Spring 1995).

Rogan, Eugene, *The Fall of the Ottomans: The Great War in the Middle East, 1914–1920* (London: Allen Lane, 2015).

Rosen, Jacob, 'The Legacy of Lawrence and the New Arab Awakening', in *Israeli Journal of Foreign Affairs*, Vol. 5, No. 3 (2011).

Satia, Priya, *Spies in Arabia* (Oxford: Oxford University Press, 2008).

Saunders, Nicholas J., *Desert Insurgency: Archaeology, T. E. Lawrence and the Great Arab Revolt* (Oxford: Oxford University Press, 2017).

Schneider, James J., *Guerrilla Leader: T. E. Lawrence and the Arab Revolt* (New York: Bantam, 2011).

Sheffy, Yigal, *British Military Intelligence in the Palestine Campaign, 1914–1918* (London: Frank Cass & Co. Ltd, 1998).

Shepherdson, Andrew, *Journeys of a Light Horseman* (Tasmania: Franklin Press, 2002).

Simpson, Andrew B., *Another Life: Lawrence After Arabia* (Stroud: Spellmount, 2011).

Smith, Clare Sydney, *The Golden Reign* (London: Cassell, 1940).

Stewart, Desmond, *T. E. Lawrence: a New Biography* (New York: Harper & Row, 1977).

Stirling, Colonel W. F., *Safety Last* (London: Hollis and Carter, 1953).

Storrs, Ronald, *Orientations* (London: Nicholson & Watson, Definitive Edition, 1943).

Tamari, Salim, *Year of the Locust: A Soldier's Diary and the Erasure of Palestine's Ottoman Past* (Berkeley: University of California Press, 2011).

Teitelbaum, Joshua, *The Rise and Fall of the Hashemite Kingdom of Arabia* (London: C. Hurst & Co., 2001).

Thomas, Lowell, *With Lawrence in Arabia* (London: Hutchinson & Co., 1924).

Thomas, Lowell, 'Publicity', in Lawrence, A. W. (ed.), *T. E. Lawrence by His Friends* (London: Jonathan Cape, 1937), pp. 205–15.

van der Steen, Eveline, 'Lawrence and the Tribes', in *Journal of the T. E. Lawrence Society*, Vol. XXI, No. 2 (2011/12), pp. 9–29.

Villars, Jean Beraud, *T. E. Lawrence or the Search for the Absolute* (London: Sidgwick and Jackson, 1958).

Walker, Philip, 'The Jeddah Diary of Captain Thomas Goodchild During the Arab Revolt', in *Journal of the T. E. Lawrence Society*, Vol. XXI, No. 2 (2011/12), pp. 31–73.

War Office, 'Extracts from Summary of the Hejaz Revolt, War Office, London 1918', in *Journal of the T. E. Lawrence Society*, Vol. III. No. 1 (Summer 1993).

Weldon, Captain L. B., *Hard Lying* (London: Herbert Jenkins, 1925).

Wemyss, Lady Wester, *The Life and Letters of Lord Wester Wemyss* (London: Eyre & Spottiswood, 1935).

Westrate, Bruce, *The Arab Bureau* (University Park: Pennsylvania State University Press, 1992).

Wilford, Hugh, *America's Great Game: The CIA's Secret Arabists and the Shaping of the Modern Middle East* (New York: Basic Books, 2013).

Wilson, Jeremy, *T. E. Lawrence. Lawrence of Arabia* (London: National Portrait Gallery, 1988).

Wilson, Jeremy, *Lawrence of Arabia: the Authorised Biography of T. E. Lawrence* (London: Heinemann, 1989).

Woodward, David B., *Forgotten Soldiers of the First World War* (Stroud: Tempus, 2006).

Winstone, H. V. F., *Leachman: 'OC Desert': the Life of Lieutenant-Colonel Gerard Leachman DSO* (London: Quartet Books, 1982).

Winstone, H.V. F., *The Diaries of Parker Pasha* (London: Quartet Books, 1983).

Yardley, Michael, *Backing into the Limelight: a Biography of T. E. Lawrence* (London: Harrap Limited, 1985).

Young, Major Sir Hubert, *The Independent Arab* (London: John Murray, 1933).

NEWSPAPERS

(Writer not named), 'Man Who Worked with Lawrence', *The Hornsey Journal*, 24 May 1935.

Tran, Mark and Weaver, Matthew, 'ISIS Announces Islamic Caliphate in Area Straddling Iraq and Syria', *The Guardian*, 30 June 2014.

UNPUBLISHED DOCTORAL THESES

Oppenheim, Jean-Marc Ran, 'Twilight of a Colonial Ethos: The Alexandria Sporting Club, 1890–1956' Ph. D. diss. (Columbia University, 1991).

Picture Acknowledgements

1–2, 4–18, 20–6, 28, 31–2, 34–5: Anthea Gray
19, 33: The Tank Museum, Bovington, Dorset, UK and Valerie Gilman
3: Anthony Cochrane
27, 29: Barbara Duce
30: Mark Scott

Index

Photos are in italics